RAY'S
PRACTICAL
INHERITANCE TAX
PLANNING

RAY'S
PRACTICAL
INHERITANCE TAX
PLANNING

Sixth edition

Joint Authors
Ralph P Ray
Solicitor, FTII, BSc (Econ), TEP, Chartered Tax Adviser,
Consultant with Wilsons, Salisbury
Andrew Hitchmough, **Elizabeth Wilson**, and **Sarah Dunn**
Barristers
Pump Court Tax Chambers, 16 Bedford Row, London

Tolley
A Member of the LexisNexis Group

Members of the LexisNexis Group worldwide

United Kingdom	Butterworths Tolley, a Division of Reed Elsevier (UK) Ltd, Halsbury House, 35 Chancery Lane, LONDON, WC2A 1EL, and 4 Hill Street, EDINBURGH EH2 3JZ
Argentina	Abeledo Perrot, Jurisprudencia Argentina and Depalma, BUENOS AIRES
Australia	Butterworths, a Division of Reed International Books Australia Pty Ltd, CHATSWOOD, New South Wales
Austria	ARD Betriebsdienst and Verlag Orac, VIENNA
Canada	Butterworths Canada Ltd, MARKHAM, Ontario
Chile	Publitecsa and Conosur Ltda, SANTIAGO DE CHILE
Czech Republic	Orac sro, PRAGUE
France	Editions du Juris-Classeur SA, PARIS
Hong Kong	Butterworths Asia (Hong Kong), HONG KONG
Hungary	Hvg Orac, BUDAPEST
India	Butterworths India, NEW DELHI
Ireland	Butterworths (Ireland) Ltd, DUBLIN
Italy	Giuffré, MILAN
Malaysia	Malayan Law Journal Sdn Bhd, KUALA LUMPUR
New Zealand	Butterworths of New Zealand, WELLINGTON
Poland	Wydawnictwa Prawnicze PWN, WARSAW
Singapore	Butterworths Asia, SINGAPORE
South Africa	Butterworths Publishers (Pty) Ltd, DURBAN
Switzerland	Stämpfli Verlag AG, BERNE
USA	LexisNexis, DAYTON, Ohio

© Ralph Ray 2001

A CIP Catalogue record for this book is available from the British Library.

First edition 1989
Second edition 1991
Third edition 1994
Fourth edition 1998
Fifth edition 1999
Sixth edition 2001

ISBN 0 406 942846

Typeset by YHT Ltd, London
Printed and bound in Great Britain by William Clowes Limited, Beccles and London

Visit Butterworths LexisNexis *direct* at www.butterworths.com

Preface to Sixth Edition

Under the last government, IHT reform took a back seat, not surprisingly as only about one in 26 estates currently pays IHT, and the yield is only some £2.3 billion per annum – relatively 'chicken feed' (approximately 1.4% of the total direct tax paid).

Contrast CGT, which, although not a significant overall revenue raiser either, has been subject to some substantial changes, in particular in the area of improvements in business taper relief and anti-avoidance legislation as to offshore trusts and partial closing of loopholes such as the 'flip-flop' schemes, utilising trust losses and sales of trust interests.

It is likely, therefore, that under the newly re-elected Labour Government, we can expect some more substantial changes to IHT and overall to the detriment of the taxpayer.

This new edition does update the reader, however, particularly in the area of case law and Revenue practice and is designed to encourage practitioners and their clients to grasp the nettle and undertake steps now – as inherent in the book's title 'Practical Inheritance Tax Planning': the message is to do this in the current bonanza climate and while the going is good.

As for the fourth and fifth Editions, I have very much welcomed the excellent and expert cooperation and input of the Pump Court Tax Chambers team in producing the current edition. The team consists, as previously, of Andrew Hitchmough and Elizabeth Wilson and now joined by Sarah Dunn.

Various parts of the book have been extensively rewritten by the team, particularly Chapters 7, 9 and 10, – a healthy and helpful trend.
I should like to thank Ian Mereweather of Wilsons for again updating Chapter 8 and Appendix 8 on life assurance.

Our excellent relationship with Butterworths Tolley continues, particularly in the form of Julia Clemett, List Development Manager, and Daniel Meredith, Editor.

The law is stated as at September 2001

Ralph Ray
Wilsons, Steynings House, Fisherton Street,
Salisbury, Wiltshire SP2 7RJ
September 2001

CONTENTS

Abbreviations

A&M	accumulation and maintenance (trust)
AIM	Alternative Investment Market
APR	agricultural property relief
BPR	business property relief
CGT	capital gains tax
CTO	Capital Taxes Office
CTT	capital transfer tax
DLT	development land tax
ED	estate duty
ESC	Extra-Statutory Concession
FA	Finance Act (various years)
WR	gift with reservation
IHT	inheritance tax
IHTA	Inheritance Tax Act 1984 (sections, Schedules and paragraphs shown thus: s 10, Sch 6, para 1)
IR	Inland Revenue
PET	potentially exempt transfer
SCA	House of Commons Official Report of Standing Committee A
SP	Inland Revenue Statement of Practice
TA 1988	Income and Corporation Taxes Act 1988
TLATA 1996	Trusts of Land and Appointment of Trustees Act 1996
UITF	Urgent Issues Task Force
USM	Unlisted Securities Market

Table of Statutes

Page references printed in **bold** type in this Table indicate where the section of the Act is set out in part or in full.

References in the right-hand column are to paragraph number. References in *italic* type are to pages of the Appendices.

Table of Cases

Page numbers in italic type are to references in the Appendices

J

K

L

M

Chapter 1

Introduction and Outline

1.0 INTRODUCTION

The subsequent chapters of this book treat the subject of inheritance tax (IHT) mainly from a practical approach, not being directly or primarily concerned with summarising the law as such.

This chapter introduces the tax and outlines certain basic aspects of IHT, namely:

(1) basis of IHT and property chargeable with particular reference to the concept of PETs and the gift with reservation provisions;

(2) calculation of IHT; scale and rates; the extent of the cumulative principle; and the grossing-up concept;

(3) main anti-avoidance provisions;

(4) exemptions and reliefs and excluded property;

(5) payment by instalments;

(6) main valuation rules;

(7) key administration aspects;

(8) practical approach and future of the tax.

IHT has its origins in the FA 1975 which introduced the CTT regime. The CTT legislation was modified in subsequent Finance Acts and eventually consolidated in what was the CTTA 1984 which took effect on 1 January 1985. In the FA 1986 the CTT regime was replaced by the IHT regime with effect from 18 March 1986. In practice and with later modification this has meant that most lifetime gifts—with the exception broadly of gifts on general discretionary trusts, certain gifts via companies, outright gifts to individuals where the donor dies within seven years (or dies outside that period when he has reserved some sort of interest)—are outside the reach of IHT. The IHT regime, although retaining the basic framework and administrative provisions of CTT, has an affinity in some respects with the old ED. The consolidated legislation in the CTTA 1984, as subsequently amended, is now known as the IHTA 1984.

The inheritance tax threshold for 2001–02 is £242,000.

1.1   BASIS OF IHT AND PROPERTY CHARGEABLE

1.1:1   IHT is a direct tax on transfers of capital (for example, gifts) made on or after 18 March 1986. Subject to a few exceptions, it is a cumulative charge on chargeable transfers made within any seven-year period and on death. It is important at the outset to distinguish between different types of gift and see their effect for IHT:

(a)   outright gifts (transfers of value) between individuals are initially exempt from IHT and are termed 'potentially exempt transfers' (they are referred to as PETs);

(b)   outright gifts by an individual into accumulation and maintenance trusts (s 71) or into disabled trusts (s 89) and into 'interest in possession' trusts are also potentially exempt transfers (PETs). A gift into a discretionary trust is excluded from the PET regime (but this has a countervailing advantage as regards CGT holdover relief—see **1.2:1**);

(c)   PETs which turn out to have been made within seven years of the donor's death become liable to IHT. They are charged at death rates. Taper relief is available, however, where the donor survives at least three years after the gift. For example, if the donor makes his gift $5\frac{1}{2}$ years before his death, the rate of tax charged on the gift is reduced to 16% (40% of 40%);

(d)   lifetime gifts by individuals into some settlements and to companies (only close companies would ever be likely to receive gifts) are chargeable transfers subject to immediate charge at lifetime rates (20%) (with adjustment to the full rate (and a measure of taper relief) if the donor dies within seven years);

(e)   gifts where the donor has reserved some benefit enjoyed within the seven-year period before his death. Here the donor is treated for IHT as still being the beneficial owner at his death (this provision does not apply to gifts before 18 March 1986 even if there is reservation after then);

(f)   there are occasions when the donor is *treated* as making a chargeable transfer. For example if an individual gives away his interest in possession in a settlement he can be treated as making a chargeable transfer (although one which could qualify as a PET). In this context different rules apply if there is no interest in possession in the settled property (eg a discretionary trust).

Apart from lifetime chargeable gifts, tax is charged on the value of the deceased's estate immediately before death. Certain key aspects of IHT may be pointed out:

(1)   the first £242,000 for 2001–02 (and subject to further indexation) is liable at a nil rate of IHT. Thereafter there is a single rate of 40% in the case of transfer on death, and 20% in the case of a lifetime transfer. The nil rate band is an important planning tool.

(2)   the IHT legislation is concerned primarily with individuals, although trusts are covered in ss 43–93 and certain companies in s 94 et seq;

(3)   the all-important charging provisions are contained in ss 1, 2, 3, 3A (for PETs) and 10. Particular note must be taken of s 10(1) in relation to the associated operations provisions of s 268;

(4) the nil rate band and the seven-year cut-off point can be important planning tools, particularly where CGT can be minimised or excluded;

(5) certain reversionary interests are excluded from the scope of IHT and thus give rise to considerable planning possibilities.

The IHT regime gives considerable scope for flexibility. Careful use of the nil rate band, exemptions and PETs (watching the interaction with CGT) can significantly reduce an IHT charge. Moreover, the risk that the present government might bring back a comprehensive lifetime gifts tax regime, and the fact that annual exemptions once lost can never be recouped, add an urgency to IHT planning.

1.1:2 Meaning of 'chargeable transfer' and 'transfer of value'

Section 1 IHTA 1984 provides that inheritance tax shall be charged on the value transferred by a chargeable transfer. A 'chargeable transfer' is a transfer of value which is not an exempt transfer (eg a gift to a spouse). Section 3(1) defines transfer of value as a disposition made by the transferor as a result of which the value of the transferor's estate immediately after the disposition is less than it would be but for the disposition. In other words, the value transferred is represented by the fall in the transferor's estate. This consequential loss formula is one of the most important principles of IHT. It is used to determine the extent of chargeable transfers made inter vivos. The idea of a transfer of value on death is of course rather more artificial. By virtue of s 4(1) IHTA 1984 tax is charged on the deceased's estate as if, immediately before his death, he had made a transfer of value and the value transferred by it had been equal to the value of his estate immediately before his death. The following example shows how the IHT method of valuation works in practice and how it can be used to the advantage of the transferor.

Example

Mr Gold holds 80% of the issued share capital of Private Ltd which, let us assume, is not entitled to business relief (see **5.1:2** and **9.0**). He gives 45% to his son and dies within seven years. The method is not to value a separate 45% parcel but to charge IHT on the difference between 80% held immediately *before* the transfer and the 35% remaining afterwards.

If Mr Gold holds 80% of the issued share capital of Private Ltd and instead of the above single transfer decides to give 15% to each of three children, he can (again assuming no business relief) make the gifts on three separate days and then three separate calculations are required.

(1) First Disposition	Estate before including 80% holding and Estate after including 65% holding
(2) Second Disposition	Estate before including 65% holding and Estate after including 50% holding
(3) Third Disposition	Estate before including 50% holding and Estate after including 35% holding

On the footing that each donee bears his own IHT the order specified can be particularly relevant. In such cases the value transferred depends on the order in which the gifts are made: if gifts are made on the same day they are treated as made in the order which produces the lowest chargeable value: s 266.

As noted above, a disposition only gives rise to IHT if there has been a reduction in the value of the transferor's estate or because, on death, the deceased is treated as having made a transfer of value equal to the value of his estate immediately before death. But what comprises an 'estate'? Essentially, an estate is the aggregate of all the property to which the person is beneficially entitled, after deducting excluded property and other allowable deductions. Tangible property, equitable rights, debts, choses in action, are all included in the term 'property'.

A person who has a 'general power' (or would have if he were sui juris), to dispose of, or to charge money on, any property other than settled property is treated as beneficially entitled to the money or property. 'General power' means a power or authority enabling a person by whom it is exercisable to appoint or dispose of property as he thinks fit (s 5 IHTA 1984). A practical approach was taken by the Special Commissioner in *O'Neill and others v IRC* [1998] STC (SCD) 110 (SpC0154) to the question of whether the deceased had a 'general power' to dispose of property within the meaning of s 5. The deceased had set up a bank account in Jersey in the joint names of himself and his daughter. The existence of the bank accounts was a secret known only to himself – not his daughter, his estranged wife, or the Inland Revenue. The Special Commissioner accepted that on the facts the deceased had a general power and that the daughter had no present beneficial interest in the bank account during her father's lifetime. Notwithstanding that the bank accounts passed to the daughter on the father's death through survivorship.

For a discussion of when interests in, and powers over trust property amount to a beneficial entitlement see chapter 4.

IHT is charged by reference to the transferor and not the recipient. This means that the value to the recipient of the transferred property is irrelevant. The valuation of shareholdings is an important area which illustrates the point.

The transfer of a 2% shareholding by A to B might change B from a minority to majority shareholder, thereby giving the 2% interest a high value. This is irrelevant to A's IHT. What is important is the effect of the loss of 2% shareholding on the value of A's overall shareholding and thus on A's estate (see also **1.6:6** below).

Having regard to the consequential loss formula and the related property provisions of s 161, valuations based on a majority shareholding have become more common, particularly for private limited companies where the value transferred may be calculated as between a controlling interest before and a minority interest thereafter, although the introduction of 100% and 50% business relief as from 10 March 1992 (see **9.0**) has greatly mitigated this problem. There can even be a substantial IHT liability (potential or actual) where the value transferred may be calculated as between one such majority holding (say over 75%) and another majority holding (but less than 75% thereafter) as the former carries the power of winding-up. In all such transfers of shares the precise impact and percentage level of business property relief will also need to be very carefully considered. Practitioners should always bear in mind when negotiating values with the Shares Valuation Division or District Valuer that, apart from contingent CGT or other taxes within the company itself, the overhanging effect of IHT, despite business relief, can itself be a depressing factor in arriving at business or other values.

For future reference the IHT method of valuation could well be followed if ever any government decides to introduce a wealth tax.

The consequential loss formula also applies to the trustees of discretionary trusts (s 65(1)(b)).

When an individual makes a transfer of value, unless it is an exempt transfer or a transfer of excluded property (see **1.4:2**) it is either a lifetime chargeable transfer or a PET. However, not all dispositions by the transferor will amount to a transfer of value. The test under s 10(1) is whether the transferor has intended a gratuitous benefit to pass to the transferee directly or indirectly. A gratuitous intent does not have to be in favour of the transferee. There will be no such gratuitous benefit if the transaction is at arm's length between persons not connected with each other (so that a mere bad bargain does not attract an IHT charge) or, should they be connected, if it was such as might be expected to be made in a transaction at arm's length between persons not connected with each other. Again a bad bargain does not itself entail that the transaction was not at arms length. In *IRC v Spencer-Nairn* [1991] STC 60, which was concerned with the sale of a farm to a connected person, the disparity between the actual sale price and the open market value was held to be no more than a single factor to be taken into account in all the circumstances, and the Crown's appeal was dismissed. Connected persons should arm themselves with evidence of commerciality in order to withstand any attack. Ex gratia benefits to employees may be excluded from IHT provided they are made for business purposes and allowable in computing the employer's profits. In the case of unquoted shares or unquoted debentures, there is the additional requirement that 'a price' must have been 'freely negotiated' at the time of sale. Otherwise, sale must be at a price such as might be expected to have been freely negotiated at the time of sale. It is arguable that an exchange of such securities is not a 'sale' for this purpose. 'Connected persons' are defined in s 270 broadly on the same lines as for CGT to cover transfers between husband and wife and other close relatives, trustees and settlor, and between partners (except bona fide sales or purchases of partnership assets). As regards relatives, however, the definition extends to uncles, aunts, nephews, nieces, or such relatives' spouses. In the case of 'connected persons' the onus is much more heavily placed on the taxpayer to show that a transfer was not gratuitous.

In addition to the provisions concerning 'connected persons', s 272 defines a 'disposition' to include dispositions effected by associated operations. 'Associated operations' are defined in s 268 and cover the case where, for example, A wants to grant the freehold to B and does so by granting a lease and then the reversion. Rather than value the two transactions at their separate and lower values, the Revenue will want to tax the total value of the unencumbered freehold (see also **1.3:1** below).

The possibility of avoiding IHT by means of bets or wagers has been aired from time to time. For example a father might lose considerable sums to his son on a round of golf or in a game of poker, in the knowledge, presumably, that the son is a far more proficient player. This type of arrangement is hardly likely to avoid IHT, because there is still the underlying intention to benefit, and because gaming transactions are not enforceable at law. The real gamble is therefore whether or not the Revenue will be convinced, which is hardly sound tax planning.

However, where a winning football coupon or National Lottery ticket has been submitted in the name of one person and so he receives all the winnings from the promoter, the Revenue have indicated that IHT will not be charged on a division of the winnings among others, provided the moneys are paid out on the basis of a pre-existing enforceable arrangement among the members of a syndicate (Revenue announcement 16 September 1977, now redesignated as SP E 14).

1.1:3 Basis of liability

The liability to IHT is based on domicile (including deemed domicile) as discussed in Chapter 10.

1.2 CALCULATION OF IHT; SCALE, RATES AND TAPER RELIEF; THE CUMULATIVE PRINCIPLE; THE GROSSING UP CONCEPT

1.2:1 Scale, rates and taper relief

For transfers on or after 6 April 2001 there is no IHT payable until the cumulative total reaches £242,000. This first tranche is commonly called the 'nil rate band'. There is then a single rate of 40% thereafter (see **Appendix 1**). Unless Parliament decides otherwise, the nil rate band is increased each year on the basis of the retail price index (s 8(1)). Lifetime chargeable transfers (eg gifts into discretionary trusts) are taxed in first instance at one half the normal rate, so that where the nil rate band has been used up by earlier chargeable transfers brought into cumulation the initial rate will be 20%. If the transferor then dies within seven years the IHT is re-calculated by reference to the full rate but with the benefit of any reduction in the scale between the gift and the death (s 9 and Sch 2, para 2). The recalculation may have to take into account any one or more earlier PETs, now chargeable because made within seven years of the death. Finally, taper relief may be due if the chargeable gift was outside three years of the death (s 7(4)). Under this relief the *value* of the transfer stays the same but the full rate(s) of IHT charged are reduced to a percentage of those rates on the following scale:

Transfer more than three but not more than four years before death: rate reduced to:						80%
Transfer	between	four	and	five	years	60%
Transfer	,,	five	,,	six	,,	40%
Transfer	,,	six	,,	seven	,,	20%

If, however, the tax on a lifetime chargeable transfer is re-calculated on death with the benefit of taper relief and produces a lower tax figure than the tax at half rate initially calculated, then the earlier half rate figure stands (s 7(5)). This means that the chargeable transfer cannot obtain taper relief on death after five years because there is no rebate of the 20% (half of normal 40% in lifetime) tax paid.

Example

Mr A is a widower and makes a gift of £276,000 on discretionary trusts $6\frac{1}{2}$ years before his death. He leaves an estate of £300,000.

IHT gift:	
on first £242,000	nil
on £34,000 at half 40%	£6,800
	£6,800
Recalculation at death (full 40% rate tapers to 20% thereof = 8%)	£2,720

Payment of £6,800 must stand. The estate of £300,000 bears IHT of £120,000.

There can be no taper relief where the gift in question is within the nil rate band. This is a potential disadvantage since a failed PET will use up part of the deceased's available nil rate band.

As regards PETs, if the donor survives the PET by seven years it becomes an exempt transfer; but if he dies within seven years of making the PET, it is converted into a chargeable transfer (s 3A). IHT then becomes payable at the full rate on the death (on the value at the time of the gift) with taper relief if the gift took place between three and seven years of the death.

Example

Mr B makes an outright gift of £276,000 to his nephew and dies $3\frac{1}{2}$ years later with an estate of £180,000.
IHT on gift:

on first £242,000	nil
on £34,000 at full 40% tapered to 80% thereof (=32%)	£10,880

The estate bears 40% tax of £72,000.

It follows that, in the case of lifetime gifts, whether initially PETs or lifetime chargeable transfers, the donees or trustees should make a reserve for the necessary (additional) IHT that would become payable by them should the donor die within seven years. Alternatively, the donees or trustees might consider the question of insuring the donor's life on a term or 'inter vivos' basis, see **8.3:4**. In considering the possible IHT charge on gifts, the donor must also take into account the fact that capital gains tax holdover relief has been restricted to a narrow range of cases comprising gifts of business and agricultural assets and shares in trading companies (see TCGA 1992, s165), gifts of heritage property, gifts to political parties, and gifts constituting immediate lifetime chargeable transfers (most commonly those to discretionary trusts)— see TCGA 1992, s 260. In the last case, note that holdover relief can be obtained even if the gift falls within the nil rate band. The relief is not, however, available to PETs which later become chargeable transfers. Any relief for the (ultimate) payment of both IHT and CGT (see s 165 and TCGA 1992, s 260(7)) is given only by way of reduction of value or gain, and not by set off of one tax against the other, so that two taxes at 40% rates may become payable. Bearing in mind that an individual's assets acquire a new base value for CGT on death, the narrow range of gifts covered by holdover relief means very great care must be taken in making gifts in order to avoid unnecessary pitfalls—see **7.1**. In the case of husband and wife it may be appropriate to leave the bulk of the estate (ie, over the nil rate band) by will to the surviving spouse outright or by way of life interest, thereby obtaining the CGT exemption and market value uplift on death and then relying on the surviving spouse to make PETs. This is particularly suitable where the survivor is younger and/or in good health. It may be necessary to have regard to CGT 'pooling' where, for instance, the surviving spouse also holds shares in the same company (TCGA 1992, s 106A) and if need be for the survivor to make gifts out of other assets from the deceased spouse with a complete CGT uplift. Consider also the impact of any gift on CGT taper relief: gifts into trust restart the taper relief clock (see **1.4:3**).

1.2.2 The cumulative principle and seven-year cut-off

The scheme of IHT is based on the simple principle of the cumulation of successive chargeable transfers to form a ladder in order to determine the rate of tax on the latest. There is a seven-year cut-off period (s 7(1)) so that the last chargeable transfer is aggregated with those chargeable transfers made within the previous seven years, and becomes the highest part of them. There are, however, a number of features to bear in mind which can affect and retrospectively upset this cumulative ladder.

First, PETs (outright gifts to individuals or to favoured trusts) are initially treated as exempt. Where an individual makes a lifetime chargeable transfer (eg, a gift on discretionary trusts) there fall to be cumulated with that chargeable transfer only those transfers in the preceding seven years which are themselves lifetime chargeable transfers and PETs are left out of account.

When the donor dies, the cumulative ladder at that point will comprise all chargeable transfers within the previous seven years. These chargeable transfers will now include not merely the lifetime chargeable transfers on which IHT (or the earlier CTT) was paid at the time but also any PETs within seven years of death which now become chargeable transfers and have to be slotted into the ladder at the right chronological point, causing a need for the lifetime chargeable transfers to be re-cumulated.

Each chargeable transfer (including former PETs within seven years of death) will then have its own cumulative ladder of chargeable transfers within seven years of itself. A former PET now chargeable because made, say, just inside seven years of the donor's death has to cumulate chargeable transfers within the seven years preceding its own date. Because of this 'knock on' effect cumulation can be a 14-year problem even though the cut-off is seven years. PETs made in that earlier seven years, however, because outside seven years of death, will have become permanently, not merely potentially, exempt and can be ignored.

Example

Year 1	Settlement on discretionary trusts	Chargeable transfer
Year 3	Outright gift to X	PET
Year 5	Gift to company	Chargeable transfer
Year 7	Outright gift to Y	PET
Year 9	Further settlement on discretionary trusts	Chargeable transfer
Year 11	Outright gift to Z	PET
Year 13	Donor dies	Chargeable estate

On death of donor the PETs in years 7 and 11 become chargeable, so that the estate is cumulated with the successive gifts in years 7, 9 and 11.

The PET in year 11 becomes chargeable and is cumulated with the gifts in years 5, 7 (PET now chargeable) and 9.

The settlement in year 9 is cumulated on a revised basis with the gift in year 5 and the former PET in year 7—but not with the PET in year 3 which has become permanently exempt as outside seven years of the death.

The former PET in year 7 is now chargeable and is cumulated with the chargeable transfers in years 1 and 5, but the now permanently exempt gift in year 3 is ignored. The additional cumulation for the settlement in year 9 by reason of the PET in year 7 becoming chargeable could affect the exit charge on a capital distribution from the settlement.

1.2:3   Avoidance of double charge: FA 1986, s 104

The structure of IHT means that in certain circumstances the same property can be charged twice and enter twice into the cumulation of chargeable transfers as a result of a transferor's death. The Board of Inland Revenue have made regulations (SI 1987/1130) which provide for relief in these circumstances. FA 1986, s 104 empowered the Board to make provision by regulations for avoiding in certain circumstances double charges to IHT in respect of transfers of value and other events occurring on or after 18 March 1986.

These regulations provide for the avoidance of double charges arising in specified circumstances.

Regulation 1 provides the title and commencement date.

Regulation 2 contains definitions.

Regulation 3 describes the scope of the regulations.

Regulation 4 provides for the avoidance of a double charge where property given by a PET is subsequently returned (otherwise than for full consideration) by the donee to the transferor, and as a result of the transferor's death, both that property and the PET become chargeable to tax. If charging the property as part of the death estate produces a higher amount of tax than would be payable if the charge on the PET was taken instead, the value transferred by the original transfer (the PET) is reduced by reference to the amount of the value of that property which is included in the chargeable transfer on the death. Conversely the PET is charged if that produces the higher amount of tax, with a corresponding reduction in the value of that property which is included in the chargeable transfer on the death. To avoid the value of the same property entering twice into the tax calculations this reduction applies for all purposes of the tax.

Example

A gives B a house; B dies and leaves the house to A; A dies within seven years of his gift to B. The gift of the house from A to B is chargeable, because it is made within seven years of death, and the house is also chargeable as part of A's death estate.

There appears to be scope to use regulation 4 for tax avoidance. This is because to the extent that partial consideration is paid by the transferor in buying back an asset previously gifted to the transferee, the value of his estate is diminished and the Regulation allows the Revenue to bring into charge either the PET or the value of the property comprised in the transferor's estate immediately before his death, which ever produces the greater liability to IHT, *but not both.*

Example

A gives his house worth £100,000 to B in 1992. He does not continue to reside there because the gift with reservation provisions would then apply. Shortly before his death in 1994 he buys the property back from B for partial consideration of £75,000. He then dies. Assuming the value of the property increases to £105,000 by A's death this amount will be brought into charge but the PET will not. A's estate has been reduced by the £75,000 consideration paid less the increase in value of the property of £5,000 giving a net reduction of £70,000.

Regulation 5 provides for the avoidance of a double charge where there is a transfer of value by way of gift of property which is or subsequently becomes a chargeable transfer, and the property is (by virtue of the provisions relating to gifts with reservation) subject to a further transfer which is chargeable as a result of the transferor's death. As under regulation 4, whichever transfer produces the higher amount of tax as a result of the death remains chargeable, and the value of the other transfer is reduced by reference to the value of the transfer which produced that amount. However, this reduction in value does not apply for the purposes of any discretionary trust charges arising before the transferor's death if the transfer by way of gift was chargeable to tax when it was made. Further, provision is made for credit to be given on account of any tax already paid on the transfer by way of gift against so much of the tax payable on the other transfer as relates to the value of the property in question.

Example

C gives D a house, but reserves the right to continue to live in it, and does so until he dies five years later. There is a charge on the gift from C to D because it is within seven years of death, but because this is a gift with reservation the house is also charged as part of C's death estate.

Regulation 6 provides for the avoidance of a double charge where a transfer of value is or subsequently becomes a chargeable transfer, and at the transferor's death his estate owes to the transferee a debt which (under the rules relating to such liabilities see **1.6:9** below) falls to be abated or disallowed in determining the value of the estate chargeable on the death. Two separate calculations of tax payable as a result of the death are made. In the first, the amount of the transfer of value is reduced by the amount of the debt which is disallowed or abated, and in the second, the amount of the transfer of value and of the debt are both taken into account. The higher amount of tax is payable, but relief is given either by reducing the value of the transfer of value or by allowing the debt and charging the transfer of value in full. As under regulation 5, the reduction in value does not apply for the purposes of any charges on discretionary trusts arising before the death if the transfer of value was a chargeable transfer when it was made. Credit is allowed for some or all of the tax already paid on that transfer against the tax payable on the transferor's estate at death.

Example

E gives F £100,000; F lends it back to E; E dies three years later with the debt outstanding. There is a charge on the gift from E to F, and the debt of £100,000 is not allowed against E's death estate (FA 1986, s 103) as the consideration for it was property derived from E.

Regulation 7 provides for the avoidance of a double charge where property given by a transfer of value which is chargeable when made, is returned (otherwise than for full consideration) by the donee to the transferor, and that property is also chargeable as part of the transferor's estate on his death. It provides the same relief as is provided under regulation 4 in the case where the transfer of value was a PET when it was made, but credit is available or tax already paid. The reduction in value does not apply for the purposes discretionary trust charges arising before the death.

Regulation 8 provides a rule to determine which of two equal amounts under regulations 4(4), 5(3), 6(3) or 7(4) is to be treated as the higher amount for the purposes of each of those regulations.

Regulation 9 introduces the Schedule, which contains a number of examples illustrating the operation of the regulations.

1.2:4 The estate rate

As discussed at **1.2:1** above, IHT is calculated on the basis of successive bands. An example of the application of the bands to the calculation of IHT is as follows:

Example

Mr A was a widower who died on 1 September 2001. He had made no previous chargeable transfers but left an estate of £176,000 and had an interest in possession under his father's will trust in £150,000. Total IHT on death is £33,600 (40%) on the excess of £84,000 over the then nil rate band of £242,000. The estate rate would be calculated, for apportioning between the estate and the will trust, and between the beneficiaries, as follows:

$$\frac{33,600 \times 100}{326,000} = 10.30\%$$

1.2:5 The grossing up concept

The position for lifetime chargeable transfers (eg, a settlement upon discretionary trusts, or a gift to a company) is that the transferor is primarily accountable for IHT (ss 199(1) and 204(6)). If the transferor wishes to make a gift to the recipient which is net of IHT, the transferor must also make a further gift of the IHT which is paid to the Revenue. In other words, the difference between a gross transfer and a net transfer is this. In the case of a gross transfer it is the transferee who pays the tax, so he will be left with the after tax amount. In the case of a net transfer, where the transferor himself wishes to pay the IHT so that the transferee receives and keeps the net transfer, grossing up of that net transfer is necessary, in order to ascertain the gross amount on which the tax payable (by the transferor) will reduce that gross amount to the net transfer in the hands of the transferee. This concept of grossing up is a direct corollary of the consequential loss formula, namely, one does not measure the benefit received by the donee, but the loss suffered by the donor and in calculating such loss pursuant to s 5(3) and (4) the IHT liability increases the amount of the loss to the donor. Explaining this concept in more detail:

(a) The value transferred is the amount by which the transferor's estate is reduced.

(b) Therefore one must value his estate *before and after* the transfer.

(c) In valuing the transferor's estate certain (but not all) liabilities may be deducted.

(d) Among such deductible liabilities is his liability to pay IHT.

(e) *If the transferor pays IHT his estate is therefore reduced by the actual gift* and *by the IHT on that gift.*

(f) The transferor accordingly makes a transfer of (gift plus tax) such a sum as after deduction of the IHT leaves the net amount with the donee.

Example

Mr B has already used up his nil rate band and makes a net lifetime gift of £80,000 to his son's company, and wishes to pay the IHT himself. The IHT rate (half the normal 40% rate for a chargeable lifetime transfer) is 20%. The value of the gift is accordingly multiplied by 100/80 to gross it up and make it £100,000; and this latter figure is the amount to be added on to Mr B's cumulative ladder. IHT at 20% on £100,000 reduces the amount to the net sum of £80,000 received by the donee company. If, on the other hand, there had been an arrangement for the company to bear the tax, Mr B could either have given £100,000, so that after paying the tax the company would have retained a net £80,000 (value of gift on Mr B's ladder £100,000); or given the company £80,000 only so that after paying the tax of £16,000 the company would have been left with £64,000 (£80,000 on Mr B's ladder).

Of course, the result of the donor not bearing IHT on a chargeable gift is that the value of the gift on the cumulative ladder is reduced. It is always possible to arrange that the donee is not out of pocket by giving him further unrelated cash gifts which are exempt, eg, the annual £3,000 or normal income gifts.

Compared to the days when there were several ascending rate bands, and special tables had to be employed in order to calculate the grossing up, the process is now comparatively simple, with a single uniform rate of 40% (or half that during lifetime) over the nil rate band. If the nil rate band has been exhausted so that the relevant lifetime chargeable gift is liable at 20% the process of grossing up consists of multiplying the amount of the straight gift by 100/80 or $1\frac{1}{4}$. If the amount of the net gift straddles the top of the nil rate band, then the process is first to deduct from the value of the gift the balance remaining of the nil rate band and then to multiply the excess by 100/80.

Example

Mr C settles £242,000 on discretionary trusts. He wants to pay the IHT himself. He made a chargeable transfer of £82,000 gross and net the previous year. The part of the present gift in the nil rate band (£242,000) is £160,000. The proportion of £82,000 is accordingly multiplied by 100/80 giving a figure of £102,500. The grossed up gift is therefore (£160,000 plus 102,500) £262,500. The taxation of the gross figure of £262,500 thus works out at £160,000 (being £242,000 minus the previous gift of £82,000) taking up the balance of the nil rate band with no tax. The excess of £102,500 (£262,500 minus £160,000) at 20% gives tax of £20,500, reducing the gross gift of £262,500 to a net £242,000. The gross transfer of £262,500 is added to Mr B's cumulative ladder, which is now £82,000 plus £262,500, a total of £344,500.

There is of course no grossing up of exempt gifts, eg the annual £3,000 exemption (s 19) or exempt wedding gifts (s 22) or for business/agricultural property at the 100% discount (see Chapter 9).

The position when the donor dies within seven years, both for PETs which then become chargeable transfers and in respect of additional IHT on lifetime chargeable transfers is that the donee is primarily liable for tax payable as a result of the death: and the liability of the donor's personal representatives remains secondary and relevant in so far as the donee has not paid the tax within 12 months of the death (s 204(8))—see **1.7:2** and **7.5:3** for indemnity position.

In the case of PETs, therefore, where the donor dies within seven years, the donee will normally be liable for IHT on the amount of the gifts as made, with no grossing up. As for any additional IHT on death in respect of lifetime chargeable gifts, this tax is payable on the amount of the lifetime transfer, so that if the amount was then grossed up because the donor paid the lifetime tax, it is the amount of the grossed up gift upon which the additional IHT at death will be charged which the donee is called upon to pay. If the lifetime tax was paid by the donee so that the value of the gift was not originally grossed up, the additional IHT on death is calculated on that same ungrossed up value (see s 204(7)).

1.2:6   Order of gifts, s 266(2), (3), (4)

Where two or more chargeable transfers are made on the same day the tax is calculated as if there had been a single transfer and the IHT apportioned pro rata. For example, David Brown on 1 August 2001 gave £138,000 to his sister's discretionary trust and £138,000 to his brother's company. Both gifts are lifetime chargeable transfers. IHT on a gift of £276,000 would be £6,800 (half of 40% on excess of £34,000 over the nil rate ceiling of £242,000) giving an average rate of 5%. Tax payable by the sister's trustees and the brother's company is therefore 5% of £100,000 or £5,000 each.

If David had made the gifts on consecutive days, then if the first gift had been to the sister's discretionary trust, it would have been free of IHT being within the £242,000 exemption, and IHT of £6,800 would have been payable by the brother's company.

It should be noted that this provision governing chargeable transfers made on the same day does not apply on death. Moreover, if the value transferred depends upon the order in which the transfers are made, for example, because one transfer is a gross amount and the other a net amount, then s 266 provides that the transfers taking place on the same day are deemed to take place in the order which produces the lowest level of IHT.

Where the transferor is proposing to make two gifts, one a PET and the other a lifetime chargeable transfer, the respective values and amounts and likely tax should the transferor not survive seven years should be looked at. On death of the transferor within seven years the chargeable transfer cannot obtain taper relief in years six and seven because it has already suffered 50% (ie half) of the normal IHT rate (s 7(5)), which might suggest the PET should come first. However, this view can be complicated by the possible increase in rate on the ten-year periodic and exit charges if the chargeable transfer is a discretionary trust; by the different rates of business relief on successive share transfers (coming down from 100% to 50% on gifts of shares, one a PET, the other a chargeable transfer); and by no means least, the undoubted usefulness of the nil rate band for chargeable transfers. Comparative arithmetic should be looked at rather than relying on intuition. A general rule that does emerge is if there is a chargeable lifetime transfer into a discretionary trust together with other transfers eg PETs, the gift into the discretionary trust should be made *first* so as to minimise ten-yearly charges and exit charges.

1.3   MAIN ANTI-AVOIDANCE PROVISIONS

The IHT legislation contains some far-reaching anti-avoidance provisions, the main ones being summarised in this section (see also **1.8**). See **chapter 7** for specific discussion of the 'anti-*Ingram*' legislation. The point for emphasis in the context of IHT planning generally is always to give proper regard to these anti-avoidance provisions, particularly associated operations (s 268); and wherever possible to use available exemptions and reliefs in as straightforward a manner as possible, rather than to undertake sophisticated and artificial schemes which will be opposed by the Revenue. The following section discusses the doctrine initiated by the House of Lords in the case of *W T Ramsay*

Ltd v IRC [1981] STC 174, which was developed in the later case of *Furniss v Dawson* [1984] STC 153, then relaxed in *Craven v White, IRC v Bowater Property Developments Ltd* and *Baylis v Gregory* all at [1988] STC 476 and developed further in *Fitzwilliam v IRC* [1993] STC 502, *Hatton v IRC* [1992] STC 140 and *IRC v McGuckian* [1997] STC 908. The most recent formulation of the '*Ramsay* principle' is now found in the House of Lords decision in *Macniven v Westmoreland Investments* [2001] STC 237: see **1.8**.

1.3:1   Associated operations (s 268)

We have already seen that in general terms a transfer of value is any disposition made by a person as a result of which the value of his estate immediately after the disposition is less than it would be but for the disposition; and the amount by which it is less is the value transferred by the transfer (s 3(1)). As mentioned above, 'disposition' is defined by s 272 to include a disposition effected by associated operations. The definition of 'associated operations' in s 268 closely follows the wide ED definition (FA 1940, s 59) and enables transactions to be treated as gifts whether made directly or indirectly and made by way of two or more operations.

There is, however, one IHT addition. Under s 3(3) where a person's estate is diminished by an omission to exercise a right, he may be deemed to have made a gift unless 'the omission was not deliberate'. Under s 268(1) an omission can be one of the associated operations (reversing *Nichols v IRC* [1975] STC 278, CA). Instances of such omissions could include failing to take up a favourable rights issue; forgoing the right to sue or contest a will; or failing to apply for a new statutory tenancy. The Revenue have recently raised the question of IHT in the pensions field when, in extreme circumstances, an individual 'omitted' to retire and take his pension at normal retirement date with the result that a lump sum discretionary benefit became payable on his death—see **5.3:4**.

The Special Commissioners decision *Reynaud v IRC* [1999] STC (SCD) 18 usefully reminds us that it is not enough to show that two operations are associated. It must be shown that there is a 'disposition effected by associated operations'.

The associated operations are frequently brought into estate planning discussions and it is important therefore to try to understand them. Examples can be helpful. A Revenue letter in the *Law Society Gazette* of 1 March 1978 posed two cases. In the first, A sold an asset to B for £20,000. The price was left outstanding on loan, and the loan was released in yearly stages by £2,000 each year (the then annual exemption). The view was expressed that the sale and the subsequent releases of parts of the loan were associated, with the result that the Revenue might have regard to the value of the asset at the date of release of the last part of the debt. The second case involved a controlling shareholder of a company who gave all his shares to his son on the footing that his son would pay the tax by instalments of £2,000 per annum. The father then made gifts of £2,000 a year to his son so that he could pay the instalments. Here the Revenue accepted that s 268 would not apply. The fact that the father made subsequent gifts to his son did not call for the original chargeable transfer of shares to be reviewed. These two cases are difficult to reconcile.

Other helpful examples are those posed by counsel for the taxpayer, together with the comments of counsel for the Crown, in the case stated by the Special Commissioners set out in the report of *IRC v Brandenburg* [1982] STC 555.

Generally the Revenue will regard operations as associated with each other if the prime reason for each of them taking place is that the other will also take place, or indeed has already done so. Channelling operations between spouses are not normally regarded as associated, unless there is clear evidence that the transfer from one spouse to the other was subject to a condition that the donee spouse made particular gifts in an agreed direction. A general conclusion on associated operations would be that a carefully laid down series of steps accompanied by an understanding or expectation that they will all take place is almost bound to run into Revenue opposition; whereas a number of disparate transactions, each entered into separately for its own particular reasons at the time, may escape attack.

In deciding whether two operations might be associated under s 268, proximity in time might be an important factor, in this respect it is helpful to note that s 268(2) states that a lease for full consideration is not treated as associated with any operation effected more than three years later. There is also the five-year charity rule in the related property provisions s 161. Comparison might also be drawn with the anti-avoidance case *Pigott v Staines Investments Co Ltd* [1995] STC 114, which established that there is no mechanistic time period after which transactions cannot be linked and even steps taken ten months apart could be linked. It is also interesting to note the income tax case of *Bambridge v IRC* (1955) 36 TC 313, HL which indicates that death itself is not an 'associated operation' for the purposes of what is now ss 739 and 742 ICTA 1988 (dicta in the Court of Appeal (1954) 36 TC 313) although the execution of a will can be.

In the context of the family company, the Revenue are likely to attack artificial arrangements designed to mitigate the diminution in value formula where there is loss of control. For example, ignoring business relief, A owns 51% of the shares of a company and transfers 2% to his wife who thereupon gifts that 2% interest to her son. This could incur a (manageable) related property charge on 2/51 × 51% of the value of these shares; and thereafter A could proceed to make gifts out of a 49% holding ie valued on a minority basis. The Revenue are likely to attack this arrangement as being an associated operation, and ignore the intermediate gift from A to his wife with the result that A's gift is out of a 51% controlling interest not out of a 49% holding.

The question is sometimes raised whether the IHT code of associated operations is now necessary in view of the principles enunciated by the House of Lords in *W T Ramsay Ltd v IRC* [1981] STC 174; *Furniss v Dawson* [1984] STC 153 and *Craven v White, IRC v Bowater Property Developments Ltd* and *Baylis v Gregory*, all at [1988] STC 476 (see **1.8**). The answer might well be that, had there been a similar code in the CGT legislation, the new principles in those cases (all were CGT appeals except *Bowater* which was DLT) would have been unnecessary. Indeed, s 268 is wider in its effect than the dicta of Lord Brightman in *Furniss* because the operations merely have to affect the same property or property representing that property, or the one operation be effected with reference to the other. The fact that in the CTT cases of *Brandenburg* and *IRC v Trustees of Sir John Aird's Settlement* [1983] STC 700, CA the courts ignored arguments on associated operations, and decided the cases on other grounds, would seem to indicate a reluctance to resort to the s 268 code where there is another basis for proceeding with the problem.

It is instructive therefore to read the speech of Lord Jauncey (with which their other Lordships agreed) in *Macpherson v IRC* [1988] STC 362, HL. This was a case of a discretionary trust fund which included paintings. On 29 March 1977 the trustees entered into an agreement (the 1977 agreement) with DJR whereby his liability for insurance and loss of the paintings was curtailed with the effect that the value of the paintings was reduced. On 30 March 1977 the trustees then appointed a protected life interest in the paintings to DJR's son. Both sides agreed that this appointment constituted a capital distribution for CTT purposes. The question was whether the value for CTT was the reduced value of the paintings or whether, as the Crown claimed, the 29 March agreement was an associated operation so that the full value had to be taken. Lord Jauncey noted that the Crown, rightly in his view, had accepted that, since the associated operations rules in what is now s 268 could cover a multitude of events affecting the same property, some limitation had to be placed on them. Reference was made to *IRC v Herdman* (1967) 45 TC 394 (Northern Ireland CA). This was an income tax case concerned with transfer of assets abroad under what is now TA 1988, s 739, which also contains associated operations provisions. There the court had decided that the only associated operations which were relevant were those by which, in conjunction with the transfer, the income of the assets could be enjoyed, and did not include those associated operations taking place after the taxpayer had obtained the power to enjoy the income. After referring to *IRC v Herdman*, Lord Jauncey then quoted the definition of disposition in what is now s 10(1) expanded to include (s 10(3)) a series of transactions and any associated operations. It was clear in his view that gratuitous benefit qualified both 'transactions' and 'associated operations'. If an associated operation was not intended to confer such a benefit (or did not form part of and contribute to a scheme which did confer such a benefit) it was not relevant. Since it was common ground that the appointment in favour of the son conferred a gratuitous benefit on him, and clear that the appointment would not have been made without the 1977 agreement, it followed that the 1977 agreement was not only effected with reference to the appointment, but was a contributory part of a scheme to confer a benefit on the son. Thus, the 1977 agreement, being the disposition for s 10(1) was made in a transaction consisting of the agreement and the appointment, intended to confer a gratuitous benefit on the son. This House of Lords decision, narrowing the scope of associated operations to clearly relevant transactions, provides a clear working hypothesis in this difficult area, although the application of the hypothesis to particular circumstances may well provoke difficulty.

Thus with a code of associated operations construed in a practical way there does not seem to be any need for the Revenue to pursue a *Ramsay* line. In *Kwok Chi Leung Karl v Comr of Estate Duty* [1988] STC 728, a Privy Council case from Hong Kong discussed in more detail at **1.8**, where Lord Oliver (who had agreed with Lord Jauncey's speech in *Macpherson*) expressed surprise that *Ramsay* arguments had not been put forward, there was no reference to any Hong Kong associated operations rules.

Perhaps the Revenue were unhappy at the way the scope of the associated operations code was narrowed in *Macpherson*, or perhaps they were encouraged, from observations such as Lord Oliver's in *Kwok*, to think that the *Ramsay* principle would furnish a more powerful instrument, because in the successive court appeals (stretching from 1989 to 1993) of the case of *Fitzwilliam v IRC* [1993] STC 502, HL, there was no attempt to use the associated operations argument but, instead, a total reliance on *Ramsay*. Before the Special Commissioners, the Crown referred to the associated operations provisions but then abandoned any intention to rely on the code (see [1990] STC at 83) and based their case wholly on *Ramsay*.

It will be interesting, therefore, to see whether *Fitzwilliam* leads the Revenue to seek to rely once more on the associated operations argument instead of the sole *Ramsay* argument, perhaps running the two arguments in tandem. It will also be interesting to see if the Revenue rely first on the *Ramsay* doctrine to establish the facts of the case to which they can then apply s 268. Of course, if s 268 simply does not apply, the *Ramsay* doctrine will always be of potential use to the Revenue. Similarly the taxpayer could remain at risk from the application of *Ramsay* if the facts are within the exclusion at s 268(2).

Finally, for the view that the effect and 'bite' of s 268 is over exaggerated, see Robert Venables' QC, article 'Gifts by associated operations' (PTPR Vol 5, Issue 1, p 11).

Since the associated operations code may perhaps become more significant it may be appropriate to mention (if only to dismiss it in this context) the rule of interpretation introduced by the House of Lords in *Pepper v Hart* [1992] STC 898. This case decided, inter alia, that where statutory provisions were ambiguous or produced absurdity, regard could be had to 'parliamentary material', eg ministerial statements in Hansard, in order to resolve the ambiguity, provided that the ministerial statements are themselves free from any ambiguity (see further *Melluish v BMI (No 3) Ltd* [1995] STC 964, HL). As regards the associated operations provisions in s 268, it may be thought that, although difficulty can arise in applying the code to a set of facts, the provisions themselves are not ambiguous. If nevertheless ambiguity could be demonstrated, there appears in any event a lack of relevant statements in the parliamentary record (apart from the ministerial comments on the general approach and on channelling gifts via the spouse quoted in **3.3**) which could offer further understanding in the more complicated type of case. As for the *Ramsay* doctrine, since this was introduced and developed by the courts as a principle of statutory interpretation, the *Pepper v Hart* rule can of course have no influence. There is a useful article on Hansard research by Victor Tunkel in *Taxation*, 22 July 1993, p 392, which gives some useful advice and directions.

1.3:2 Restriction on freedom to dispose (s 163)

Provisions in a contract whereby the right to dispose has in some way been excluded or restricted are to be ignored in valuing the transfer to the extent that such exclusion or restriction is not for a consideration in money or money's worth. This anti-avoidance provision is particularly designed to deter artificial arrangements in partnership agreements, for instance, as regards options below market value and transfers of goodwill, and pre-emption provisions in articles of association of a company which aim at artificially reducing the market value of the shares.

1.3:3 Artificial reductions in the value of settled property—depreciatory transactions (ss 52(3), 65(1)(b))

Transactions between the trustees and the beneficiaries (or persons connected with the beneficiaries) will be assessed as a transfer of value in a fixed trust or the occasion of an interim charge in a discretionary trust where the transaction results in a reduction in value of the trust fund, for example, the creation of a lease designed to reduce the freehold value, or value-shifting operations with company shares (see also **4.8:3**).

1.3:4   The 'related property' provisions in s 161

These provisions give rise to particularly sinister valuation problems because of a special rule in respect of property held by husband and wife or transferred by either of them to a charity or public body within the last five years. The period of five years in the case of a transfer to a charity or public body still continues from the date of transfer whether or not the transferee is still holding the property, and thus inhibits planning. The section provides that property in a spouse's estate is related to property comprised in the estate of his spouse, or property which is or has been within the preceding five years the property of a charity or public body. The effect of the section is that when the spouse transfers his property and the value of that property is less than the value of the 'appropriate portion' of that property and the related property, then that appropriate portion of the aggregate value is the value transferred. This rule applies in general to lifetime transfers and dispositions on death and can have particular application to private company shares, freehold and leasehold properties, and to jointly held sets or collections of valuable objects. It is far less likely to have application to quoted securities. The Shares Valuation Division are of course able to (and do) make use of Companies House records for this purpose. For instance, in the example in **1.1:2**, if Mr Gold had owned only 50% and Mrs Gold 30%, the position would still have been as in that example, namely, as if Mr Gold had been disposing of a proportion of an 80% holding.

Of course, with the advent of 100% business relief (alongside 50% relief) for transfers of relevant business property on or after 10 March 1992—see **9.0**—the problems associated with transfers out of related property may no longer be so formidable. Nevertheless, care is still required, not least because business relief is not available to all companies or businesses (see s 105(3)–(7)). The rules on related property have a most unfortunate retrospective effect where a family company has been set up before the CTT/IHT era and the shares issued to husband and wife, and where the shares have now become valuable. Having regard to the related property provisions, any transfer of shares, however small, will involve a valuation of the aggregate shareholding owned by the spouses. Although the aim of the related property provisions is to avoid fragmentation of values, its application is much wider; thus the fact that the spouse in question has acquired an asset independently and for full consideration is irrelevant.

Moreover, the related property provisions extend beyond s 161 because by virtue of s 49(1) a person beneficially entitled to an interest in possession is treated as beneficially entitled to the property in which the interest subsists (see also **4.2:1** and **4.2:4**).

This would indicate that a holding of family company shares in an individual's estate is related always with a holding of similar shares in which the individual has an interest in possession under a settlement. However, following a statement by the Revenue (Press Release, 9 May 1990), this aggregation is no longer considered to apply when an interest in possession comes to an end during the lifetime of the individual entitled to it. Under s 52(1) the value for IHT is 'equal to the value of the property in which his interest subsisted'. The statement went on to say that the settled property 'should be valued *in isolation* without reference to any similar property'. The statement concluded that the practice was without prejudice to the application of the *Ramsay* principle or the associated operations code in any appropriate case. The statement does not apply to excluded property—see **1.4:2**.

The practice applies only to the valuation of settled property on the termination of an interest in possession in lifetime (which is a PET and becomes chargeable only on the death of the former life tenant within seven years), and is based purely on the peculiar wording of s 52(1). It does not apply to an interest in possession terminating on death, where the related property provisions still apply; nor to the valuation of property (aggregation) which is part of an individual's free estate. It follows that it is only settled property in which an interest in possession subsists and which is terminated in lifetime where valuation in isolation from other related property (eg, part of the individual's own estate) is in point.

Thus, despite the possible availability of business relief, great care should be taken in making a gift out of related property such as company shares. Subject to the *Ramsay* principle, it may well be better to give part of a shareholding to the donee outright and part to him by way of settlement on an interest in possession trust. The donee will then in the future have the flexibility to terminate his interest in possession without an aggregate valuation (see also **4.5:1**).

It is doubted whether different interests in land, such as a leasehold interest and a freehold reversion, constitute related property. Similarly, different classes of shares held by say husband and wife with different rights attaching thereto, may not be related property.

Example

Hawker sold 10% of the shares in his family company on 17 November 1998 to his nephew for £20,000 (par) and died 1 October 2000. Hawker previously held 41% of the shares and his wife 39%. It was agreed with the Shares Valuation Division of the Inland Revenue that 80% of the shares were worth £1,000,000, 70% were worth £800,000, and 10% were worth £50,000. Hawker is connected with his nephew within the meaning of s 270 and the sale was not at an arm's length price under s 10. The transfer has to be valued at 41/80ths × £1,000,000 = £512,500 less 31/70ths × £800,000 = £354,285, ie £158,215 under the related assets of s 161. The transfer (ignoring business relief) is £158,215 less paid £20,000, ie £138,215.

In particular where husband and wife together have voting control of a company, and it is proposed to reduce their combined holdings so that control is lost, it is generally preferable for the spouse with the lower holding of shares to make the gift that loses control. If this situation is contrived, as illustrated in **1.3:1** above, the s 268 rules on associated operations are likely to be applied, but if the inequality is a given, long standing state of affairs, s 268 should not be applicable. It is therefore wise to plan the allocation of shareholdings in a new company, when the shares are worth their initial subscription price only, with great care. It is at that stage that plans can be laid for a future transaction whereby control of the company can be relinquished with least impact for IHT. The broad principle (which will vary in individual circumstances) is that shares should be spread around eg 45% to the husband, 15% to the wife and, say, 40% to children (in an accumulation and maintenance settlement). If, later, it is desired to make a gift of a 15% shareholding (bringing the related holdings of husband and wife down to 45%) the IHT charge will reflect a diminution in value from a control aggregate holding to a minority. A gift by the wife of her 15% will involve the loss of a 15% holding (a quarter of the value of the combined 60%); but the diminution in value of the husband's shareholding because control has been lost escapes possible IHT. If the 60% had been in his sole name and he had made the 15% gift, the IHT charge would have been on the whole diminution in value of a 45% as against a 60% holding.

Example

The value *per share* of a 60% holding in X Ltd (1,000 shares issued) is £1,500. The value per share of a minority 45% holding is £500. If the 60% holding is in the husband's sole name, and there is no related property, a gift of 15% (150 out of the 600 shares) will produce a diminution of £675,000 for the husband (£900,000 down to £225,000). If the shares are held 45% by the husband and 15% by the wife, and the wife gives away her 15%, the diminution is of £225,000 only. The accompanying diminution of £450,000 in the husband's estate (from 45% on a control basis to 45% on a minority basis) is not caught. Business relief has been ignored in this illustration.

For private trading companies the problems associated with related property have undoubtedly been eased by the introduction of 100% business relief (together with the 50% relief) for transfers and other events on or after 10 March 1992 (see **9.0**). Nevertheless, difficulties still remain and great care is still necessary in considering both IHT and the attendant CGT results.

A further possibility may be worth noting, particularly where the combined husband and wife holding just spans control, say 51%; that is, to sell a small holding of shares, say 2%, at arm's length without any gratuitous intent (see s 10). The purchaser might well be a trusted employee, who should take separate advice both as regards the consideration as well as the effect on him of the Schedule E employees' benefits legislation.

In the context of disposals between connected persons careful consideration should also be given to the CGT aspects having regard in particular to the CGT rules on disposals of assets in a series of transactions to connected persons (see TCGA 1992, s 19). These rules apply to the fragmentation of an asset eg when an individual splits up a large shareholding in a private company by disposing of parts to two or more relatives etc within a six-year period; and the greater value of the undivided asset can be substituted.

1.3:5 Tax chargeable in respect of certain future payments (s 262)

This anti-avoidance provision acts as a deterrent against the sort of transaction where, for example, there is a sale on which the purchaser pays or the vendor delivers more than one year after the original disposal and where either the purchaser pays more than the market value of the asset (ie a disguised gift of cash) or the vendor receives a lower purchase price than the true value of the asset (ie a disguised partial gift of the asset). Section 262 then assumes that the chargeable transfer is made at the time the payment is made or the asset is transferred at the current value on each occasion. The section is an anti-avoidance measure to prevent a transfer of value in advance of an asset likely to increase in value.

Example

Father sells house to son for £60,000, payable by six annual instalments of £10,000 each (discounted present value of instalments, say £40,000). The market value on sale is £180,000 and the gift element therefore £140,000. When the third instalment is paid the value of the house has increased to £240,000.

The formula to be applied to this instalment for s 262 purposes is as follows:

$$\text{Value of asset transferred} \times \frac{\text{original gift element}}{\text{total value at time of gift}}$$

$$\frac{240,000}{6} \times \frac{140,000}{180,000} = £31,111$$

which is grossed up and taxed as a gift at the date of the third instalment payment. One-sixth share of the house passes with each instalment (and a separate similar calculation is done for each instalment).

It should be emphasised, however, that although s 262 applies to a situation where the father agrees to transfer as an asset in stapes to B, it does not apply where the father simply sells an asset to B with payment by instalments.

Since s 262(1) provides that 'tax (if any) shall be charged as if ... ' it would follow from s 3A(6) that the instalment dispositions cannot be PETs and must therefore be taxed as lifetime chargeable transfers. In these circumstances, it would seem far better to replace the instalment transaction by a simple PET, avoiding the traps of the section.

1.3:6   Free loans etc

An interest-free loan can be virtually as beneficial to the borrower as a gift. Accordingly, at an earlier stage of the legislation, a tax charge was imposed on the notional interest forgone on an interest-free or cheap loan. The same principle applied for use or occupation of land or chattels at a non-commercial rent or hire. These provisions were, however, abolished as from 6 April 1981, presumably because in most cases the interest etc forgone would have been exempt from (the then) CTT as normal expenditure. The general use of loans, etc, is discussed in **7.7**.

The loan principle has been used in what are known as 'inheritance trusts' of single premium policies, mentioned at **8.3:11**.

1.3:7   'Back-to-back' life policies

Sections 21(2) and (3) and 263 operate to disqualify so-called back-to-back arrangements from benefiting from the 'normal expenditure' relief. The offending arrangement is one where an individual purchases one or more annuities to enable him to take out one or more life policies in favour of beneficiary(ies) which under normal circumstances would not have been an accepted risk by an insurance company except at weighted premiums. The Revenue practice, as for ED, is that there will be no disqualification of the normal expenditure exemption if it can be shown that the life policy was issued after full evidence of health had been obtained and that the terms on which it was issued would have been the same even if the annuity had not been bought (ESC, E4). In such circumstances the transactions will not be associated operations. For IHT there is, however, one major drawback which makes these sorts of back-to-back arrangements largely impractical; namely that the capital element of the annuity is not regarded as income for the normal expenditure exemption.

The value chargeable where such back-to-back operations have taken place is not to exceed the lesser of:

(1) the cost of the annuity and the premiums paid to date, and

(2) the value of the greatest benefit capable of being conferred at any time by the policy.

The latter part of the formula is capable of quantification for the non-profit life policies but problems arise in the case of with-profit, and equity and unit linked policies.

The above provisions have acted as a deterrent against the linked use of an annuity and a policy as a deathbed planning scheme. Attempts were made to achieve similar ends on slightly different lines. This was the PETA plan whereby the individual effected a single premium pure endowment policy on the one hand (giving regular annual withdrawals of capital to the individual) and also, on the other hand, a term assurance for the specified beneficiary who (because maturity of the endowment was set at age 105) could be expected to take the remaining capital on the individual's death. Use of this plan together with the old style 'inheritance trust' arrangements was terminated by FA 1986, Sch 19, para 7, which brought them within the gifts with reservation regime (a simpler new style inheritance trust, avoiding the reservation problems, has now been brought forward—see **8.3:11**.)

It should be noted that the back-to-back arrangement contemplates a purchased life annuity—bought out of the individual's own resources. The anti-avoidance provisions do not apply where the individual becomes entitled to a pension annuity under an approved occupational pension scheme, personal pension scheme or self-employed retirement annuity arrangement. Here the whole of the pension instalments are subject to income tax (there is no untaxed 'capital content' proportion as with a purchased annuity). The result is that the individual is free to regard the whole of his pension income as available (over and above his living expenses) for normal income exempted gifts (see **7.10**) providing him with a useful opportunity to effect an IHT-free policy in trust for his beneficiaries (see **8.3**).

1.3:8   Close companies (ss 94–102 and 202)

Where a close company as defined for corporation tax (covering the normal family type of company), and whether or not UK resident (s 102(1)), makes a transfer of value, the amount transferred is apportioned among the participators (meaning broadly the shareholders). They are then charged on the grossed up equivalent of such amount according to their rights and interests in the company; but reduced by any amount by which the value of such participators' estate is *increased* by the company's transfer (excluding any rights or interests in the company, for example, allotment of shares in the company). Having regard to this permitted reduction the section operates rarely and is largely restricted to the extended meaning of 'transfer' in s 98 as including any alteration or extinguishment of unquoted company shares or loan capital, for example the variation of rights attaching to shares so that the estate owner's equity is watered down; or the redemption of debentures thereby increasing the equity capital. It also appears that a mere issue of new shares, eg to an outsider, is caught, especially if at a favourable price. Depending on the circumstances, however, it might be possible to argue on the basis of s 10 that the transfer was not intended to confer gratuitous benefit, but was part of the commercial arrangements to secure the transferee's services.

Moreover there will be no liability to the extent that the transferee suffers income tax or corporation tax (see for example TA 1988, ss 209 and 418); or where a participator is domiciled abroad in respect of foreign assets. Transfers of value can be traced through another close company but there is relief against a double charge where a participator holds shares in both companies. A s 94 liability is primarily on the company and therefore the purchasers of shares of such company should obtain an appropriate warranty from the vendors. Secondarily liable are the participators themselves, the value becoming part of their cumulative total grossed up, an exception applying in the case of a person to whom not more than 5% of the value transferred is apportioned. In that case the company remains solely liable and the value is not part of such person's cumulative total. The charge is also adapted in respect of trustee partici-pators.

No part of the transfer of value is apportioned to preference shares if the transfer of value 'has only a small effect on the value' of those shares compared with its effect on the value of other parts of the company's share capital, so that normally they are left out of account (s 96). Where a close company surrenders profits by way of group relief under TA 1988, s 402 or sets surplus Advance Corporation Tax against a subsidiary's liability under TCGA, s 171, such transactions do not give rise to any charge to IHT (s 94(3)). Certain transfers within a group of companies under TCGA s 171 are ignored for purpose of apportionment amongst certain minority participators (s 97). Charges under s 94 benefit by virtue of s 94(5) from the £3,000 per annum exemption referred to in **7.8**. A decrease in value resulting from an alteration of share etc rights under s 98(1) is ignored for the purpose of assessing a person's estate on death in view of s 171(2). It is made clear that bearing in mind the consequential loss formula of s 3(1), alteration of share etc rights only reduces the value *after* the disposition, not before. If it applied both before and after there would be no chargeable fall in value. In the case of a wholly owned subsidiary of a close company which makes a transfer of an asset at an undervalue to its parent or to a wholly owned sister subsidiary or in the case of a dividend paid by such subsidiary to its parent company, the Revenue do not regard it as a transfer of value, so that s 94 does not operate. This is less clear where the parent-subsidiary relationship is not a 100% ownership.

When a close company makes a transfer of value, IHT is charged *as if* each participator has made a transfer (s 94(1)). The transfers attributed to the participators cannot, therefore, be treated as PETs (s 3A(6)). They constitute immediate lifetime chargeable transfers of the grossed up amounts appor-tioned to the respective participators.

Example

X Ltd sells a house worth £400,000 to A for £50,000 thereby making a transfer of value of £350,000. There are two shareholders in X Ltd, A himself with 20% and B with 80%. Of the company's transfer, £70,000 is therefore apportioned to A, but since A's estate is already *increased* by £350,000, his apportioned amount is totally excluded and no IHT is chargeable on it. As regards B, however, to whom £280,000 is apportioned, the calculation of IHT is as follows:

First £242,000 of £280,000 (the nil rate band) gross and net   £242,000

Excess £38,000 $\times \dfrac{100}{80}$ (representing grossing up fraction for half of

40% = 20% rate)   £47,500

Gross transfer   £289,500

IHT on that gross transfer (being 20% on excess of £47,500 over
the nil rate band of £242,000   £ 9,500

Net transfer by B   £280,000

If it seems odd that B who has received no benefit is treated as making a chargeable transfer, then that is a reflection, via the see-through provisions of s 94(1), of the consequential loss principle on which IHT is based (s 3(1)). B has suffered a loss, but A has not.

1.4   EXEMPTIONS AND RELIEFS AND EXCLUDED PROPERTY

1.4:1

The table below outlines in two parts the main current exemptions and reliefs available for IHT. The first part covers the main *exemptions*, namely a *full* release from IHT (or as otherwise stated); and the second part deals with the main *reliefs*, namely where there is a *partial* release or allowance. Only brief details of the exemptions and reliefs are given in the third column of the table either by way of cross references to other parts of this book or a short summary of the provisions. The reader's attention is drawn to the statutory references in the second column as later amended in some instances and to the available textbooks. The material is listed in alphabetical order so as to act as a check list.

PART I: EXEMPTIONS

Type/Transaction	Statutory reference	Application: Lifetime only = L or death only = D both = L+D	Brief summary or cross reference
(1) Active service, killed on	s 154	D	Applies to death from wounds, accident or disease resulting from active service—not restricted to battlefield. A wound etc need only be a contributory factor in the death: *Barty-King v Ministry of Defence* [1979] STC 218. Covered Falkland hostilities and would

Type/Transaction		Statutory reference	Application: Lifetime only = L or death only = D both = L+D	Brief summary or cross reference
				also apply to Gulf War. Also by concession F5 covers deaths of the RUC resulting from terrorist activities
(2)	Cash options under approved personal pension and annuity schemes	s 152	D	**6.3:5** Exercise of cash option under personal pension or retirement annuity scheme, not a chargeable transfer
(3)	Charities, gifts to (including charitable deeds of covenant or more commonly gift aid payment)	s 23	L+D	**7.16**.
(4)	Covenants, deeds of	ss 5(5), 21	L	**7.10:2**. The covenanted payments would generally qualify as exempt normal income expenditure (see para (14) below) (Note that income tax relief for non-charitable deeds of covenant executed on or after 15 March 1988 has been abolished)
(5)	Domicile abroad of transferor, settlor or deceased—as to foreign assets	s 48(3) s 267		**10.2, 10.3**. Excluded property but note restrictive definitions of s 267
(6)	Failure of interest in settled property before possession	ss 47, 48 and effect of s 49	L+D	Where person has a future life interest subject to a previous *subsisting* life interest and that person surrenders or assigns— no charge
(7)	Family maintenance, dispositions for	s 11	L? = Revenue's Interpretation	**7.12**
(8)	First slice—the 'nil rate band'	s 7	L or D but cumulatively (seven years)	**1.2:1**. Charged at nil rate (not strictly an exemption) but very useful in planning. NB possible indexation of rate bands under s 8

Type/Transaction	Statutory reference	Application: Lifetime only = L or death only = D both = L+D	Brief summary or cross reference
(9) Funeral expenses	s 172	D	Reasonable funeral expenses allowed (including cost of tombstone or gravestone—SP 7/87). Also mourning expenses (F1)
(10) Government exempted securities, National Savings etc for Channel Island and Isle of Man individuals and other non-domiciled individuals	s 6(2), (3) s 48(4) s 267(2)	L + D	Certain government securities are exempted from IHT as for ED if the transferor or deceased beneficial owner was both domiciled (general definition, ie not restricted by s 267(1)) and ordinarily resident abroad (see **10.6:1**)
(11) Housing associations	FA 1989, s 161, s 24A	L + D	Covers land in UK given to registered housing association **7.16:5**
(12) Marriage gifts and settlements	s 22, s 57	L	**4.7:2**. Variations £5,000, £2,500, £1,000; also available on termination of interests in possession in settled property
(13) National purposes, gifts for, eg, museums, local authorities, government departments, universities, etc.	s 25(1), Sch 3	L + D	**7.17**
(14) Normal income expenditure not reducing standard of living	s 21	L	**7.10:2**. See *Bennett v IRC* [1995] STC 54 *Nadin v IRC* [1997] STC (SCD) 107

Type/Transaction	Statutory reference	Application: Lifetime only = L or death only = D both = L+D	Brief summary or cross reference
(15) Pensions, generally	ss 151, 152	L + D	Most pensions to dependants whether capitalised or not, and most lump sums on death, should give rise to no IHT charge. Extended to term cover etc under TA 1988 s 621 **5.3:3**
(16) Pensions overseas	s 153	L + D	Most pensions payable by governments of former colonies or protectorates
(17) PETs outside seven years of death of transferor	s 3A(4)	L + D	**1.1:1**
(18) Political parties, gifts to	s 24	L + D	Without any limit on size since 15 March 1988 (FA 1988, s 137)
(19) Public benefit, gifts for	ss 26, 26A	L + D	**7.18**. Covers land, buildings, contents, works of art, maintenance funds, on direction of Treasury. NB s 26 repealed for transfers after 16 March 1998
(20) Reversionary interest (= excluded property)	s 3(2) s 48(1), (3) s 55(1)	L + D	**1.4:2** and **4.7:12**
(21) Reverter to settlor or spouse	s 54	L + D	**4.7:4**. NB must revert during settlor's lifetime and not acquired for consideration. Interest in possession trusts only
(22) Sales, not gifts	s 10	L + D	**7.6**, ie where no gratuitous intent—arm's length

Type/Transaction	Statutory reference	Application: Lifetime only = L or death only = D both = L+D	Brief summary or cross reference
(23) Settlements—certain exempt situations including:			
(a) interest in possession— beneficiary becomes entitled absolutely or to another interest in possession	s 53(2)	L	**4.5:1**
(b) interest in possession disposal to extent consideration in money or money's worth	s 52(2)	L	**4.5:1**
(c) inter-spouse trusts	s 18	L+	**4.7:1**
(d) accumulation and maintenance	s 71	L+D	**4.4**
(e) superannuation schemes	ss 151–153	L+D	**4.7:5**
(f) for benefit of employees	s 86	L+D	**4.7:6**
(g) protective trusts	s 88	L+D	Mainly exempt but exemption does not extend to *all* circumstances **4.7:7**
(h) trusts for the disabled	s 89	L+D	**4.7:8**
(i) charitable trusts	ss 76, 84	L+D	**4.7:9**
(j) compensation funds		L+D	**4.7:10**
(24) Small gifts:			
(a) £3,000 pa=tax year	s 19 s 57(1) s 94(5)		**7.8.** Cumulative for one year only; to the extent that full value of exemption not used up the shortfall can be carried over to the next year only; available on termination of an interest in possession in a settlement
(b) £250 pa outright per donee per tax year	s 20	L	**7.9.** Outright, ie not *into* settlement, and not the first £250 of a larger gift (whether exempt or not); not on termination of an interest in a settlement

Type/Transaction	Statutory reference	Application: Lifetime only = L or death only = D both = L+D	Brief summary or cross reference
(25) Spouses, transfers between	s 18	L + D	**3.1**. If transferor spouse UK domiciled and transferee spouse non domiciled exemption limit £55,000 cumulative (**3.1:3** in particular)
(26) Surviving spouse exemption—IHT relief for settled property where first spouse died pre-13 November 1974 and ED paid on his/her death	s 18; and Sch 6 para 2	L + D	**4.5:1**
(27) Trading expense transfers	s 12(1)	L + D	Exempt if allowed for income tax, etc purposes, eg, provision of some pensions by employers for employees
(28) Trustee and personal representative, property held by transferor or deceased as	s 204	L + D	ie exemption applies if the property held purely in a *fiduciary* capacity
(29) Trustees' remuneration	s 90	L	Reasonable remuneration to a trustee not assessable to IHT
(30) Visiting forces (=excluded property)	s 6(4) s 155	L + D	Gives limited exemption, eg US forces and civilian auxiliaries
(31) Voidable transfers	s 150	L + D	**7.19**. IHT cancelled where a transfer set aside by a rule of law or enactment, eg, bankruptcy or a gift made under undue influence

Type/Transaction	Statutory reference	Application: Lifetime only = L or death only = D both = L+D	Brief summary or cross reference
(32) Waivers of remuneration and dividends	ss 14, 15	L + D	**5.1:7, 5.1:8** NB such waivers must be by *deed*, as there is no consideration.

PART II: RELIEFS

Type/Transaction	Statutory reference	Application: Lifetime only = L or death only = D both = L+D	Brief summary or cross reference
(1) Alteration of dispositions taking effect on death	s 142	D	**2.6, 2.7**.
(2) Art etc, works of	s 230	L + D	Certain transfers to eg the Revenue in satisfaction of tax due are exempt transfers (SP 6/87)
	ss 30–35	L + D	**9.14**. Conditional exemption. Treasury approval necessary
(3) Agricultural property	ss 115–124B		**9.10**. Value of agricultural property reduced by 100% (primarily if owner occupied or let on a tenancy after 1 Sep 1995 and 50% for other cases)
(4) Business relief	ss 103–114	L + D	**9.8**. Reduction of value for interest in a business 100%; unquoted securities which by themselves or together with other such shares or securities gave control—100%; unquoted shares—100%; quoted shares or securities which by themselves or together with other such shares or securities gave control—50%; property used by company controlled by transferor or by his partnership—50%; and settled property used in business by beneficiary of settlement with interest in possession—50%

Type/Transaction		Statutory reference	Application: Lifetime only = L or death only = D both = L+D	Brief summary or cross reference
(5)	*Commorientes*, rule as to (survivorship)	s 92	D	**2.5:1**. Need for survivorship clauses in defined circumstances
(6)	Double taxation relief	ss 158, 159	L + D	Application of relevant double taxation agreement or available unilateral relief
(7)	Instalment payments	s 227	L+D	**1.5**
(8)	Quick successions reliefs:	s 141		
(a)	interest in possession		L+D	Occurrence of chargeable events in a 5-year period with decreasing relief
(b)	cash or identifiable asset		D	
(9)	Quoted securities etc. Sale within 12 months of death	ss 178–189	D	**1.6:3**. Adjustment of value
(10)	Taper relief	s 7(4)	D	**1.2:1**
(11)	Valuation reliefs— others:			
(a)	transfers of any property within 7 years *before* death	ss 131–40	D	**1.6:2**
(b)	falls in value of land 3 years after death (sometimes 4 years: see **1.6:4**)	ss 190–198	D	**1.6:4** (See *Jones v IRC* [1997] STC 358)
(c)	Sales of related property within 3 years after a death	s 176	D	**1.6:5**
(12)	Woodlands	ss 125–130	D	**9.12**
(13)	Reinvestment relief in relation to IHT	ss 164A–N TCGA 1992	L	**1.4:3**. Now repealed and replaced in part by CGT taper relief and in part by EIS relief

1.4:2 Excluded property

Various categories of property are taken outside the ambit of the IHT charge as 'excluded property'. No account is to be taken of a disposal of excluded property in measuring the diminution in the value of a person's estate (s 3(2)) and it is left out of an estate for the purpose of a charge on death (ss 4(1) and 5(1)). The main category of excluded property is property situate abroad belonging to a person not domiciled or treated as domiciled in the United Kingdom (see **10.3**), or settled by such non-domiciled person (see **4.7:11**); and reversionary interests not acquired for a consideration in money or money's worth or to which the settlor or his spouse is not or has not been entitled (s 48) (**4.7:12**). The separate treatment of excluded property from exemptions appears in practice mainly a difference without a distinction in respect of a *death* situation. In the case of *lifetime* dispositions, however, where the estate includes assets required to be valued in conjunction with the excluded property, the consequential loss in value of those other assets could be considerably higher than if no excluded property existed. For example, A owns absolutely 30% of the shares of an overseas company, and also has a life interest in a further 25% of such shares as settled by a non-domiciled individual. Although the 25% holding by way of interest in possession is excluded property, if A gives away 6% of his absolute holding he is losing control because he is treated as holding 55% of the shares in that company. Depending on the circumstances, it may be that A should first terminate his interest in possession in say 6% of the excluded settled holding (no IHT consequences) so that the aggregate of the shares falls below 50% before he comes to make a gift out of his own holding. Note that because this interest in possession is excluded property, the May 1990 Revenue statement (see **1.3:4**) is not applicable.

1.4:3 CGT reliefs and inheritance tax

The art of estate planning is to combine capital gains tax and inheritance tax reliefs and exemptions. To deal with these taxes in isolation can be of little avail. A good example of this art lies in the interaction of the old reinvestment relief under ss 164A–N TCGA 1992 and the inheritance tax business property relief providing a 50% or 100% discount. Reinvestment relief was repealed by FA 1998 with effect in relation to acquisitions made on or after 6 April 1998.

Reinvestment relief and indexation relief are replaced by a different regime called taper relief with effect for the year 1998/9 onwards. Under the new regime, CGT relief on disposals of assets increases in proportion to the length of time of the asset has been owned by the donor. The donee (whether an individual or a trustee) starts his period of ownership from the date of the gift. This is a significant disadvantage which may make PETs less attractive. Although special provision is made for transfers between spouses which fall within s 58 TCGA 1992 (para 15, sch A1, TCGA 1992).

1.5 PAYMENT BY INSTALMENTS (ss 227, 228)

In these days when cash flow is an increasingly important factor, the right to pay IHT by instalments can be of great value, especially in the case of farmers and shareholders of family companies, subject to the availability of business/agricultural property relief. This right is, however, subject to stringent conditions which vary depending on whether IHT liability arises on death or by way of lifetime transfers. Personal representatives remain personally liable for any unpaid tax instalments even after the relevant assets have been transferred to the beneficiary (*Howarth's Executors v IRC* [1997] STC (SCD) 162).

1.5:1 The position on death

Six types of property are eligible:

(1) land (including buildings of any description, wherever situated);
(2) shares or securities of a company which gave the deceased control of the company immediately before his death;
(3) shares or securities of a company which did *not* give such control but which are unquoted, if either the '20% rule' (see below) applies or the Board of Inland Revenue are satisfied that payment otherwise than by instalments would cause undue hardship;
(4) shares of a company (not securities) which did not give such control and which are unquoted where the '£20,000/10% rule' (see below) applies;
(5) the net value of business interests provided they are carried on for gain and not as a hobby;
(6) trees or underwood (s 229).

Under s 269, a person has 'control' of a company for the above purpose at any time if he then has the control of powers of voting on all questions (but class rights giving voting powers in certain cases, for example, on liquidation or on matters affecting shares of that class are ignored).

The definition of 'unquoted' comprises shares which are not listed on a recognised stock exchange. Accordingly, shares quoted on the Alternative Investment Market are unquoted for s 227. (Contrast s 272).

As regards the '20% rule', the condition requires that the party accountable for the IHT is liable for at least 20% of the total tax for which he is accountable (in the same capacity) for the *defined assets*, namely assets numbered 1 to 5 inclusive above.

The '£20,000/10% rule' requires that the value of the shares transferred exceeds £20,000 and that either the nominal value of the shares is not less than 10% of the nominal value of all shares of the company at the time of death (it is assumed that this refers to issued shares) or the shares are ordinary shares (ie the equity) and that their nominal value is not less than 10% of the nominal value of all ordinary shares of the company at the time of death.

As regards business interests, including professions or vocations, this term covers the net value of the business interests, net value being the principal value of the assets used in the business (including any goodwill) reduced by the aggregate liabilities of the business.

If the relevant conditions are met, the taxpayer can elect to pay the IHT by ten equal yearly instalments, the first instalment becoming payable six months following the end of the month in which the death occurs (s 227(3)(a)). Provided the asset is a business asset, either directly or through shares of a trading company, or is property subject to agricultural relief (which includes *tenanted* land subject to the relief) or constitutes woodlands, interest (which is non-deductible for income tax purposes) is payable (see FA 1989, s 178 and SI 1989/1297) but only from the date when the instalment is in arrears. In the case of shares or securities of an investment or land-owning company (ie where the land and buildings are not used for the purposes of a trade and do not qualify for agricultural relief), interest runs on the *whole* of the outstanding tax, see s 234(2). This makes the instalment relief for these investment-type assets indeed a mixed blessing, not to be claimed lightly.

Under s 227(1A) and (1C) the instalment provisions apply to PETs which became chargeable transfers by reason of the transferor's death within seven years of the transfer and to additional IHT on a lifetime chargeable transfer because the transferor dies within seven years on condition that:

(a) *either* the relevant property is owned throughout by the transferee from the date of the transfer to the death of the transferor (or if earlier the death of the transferee);
or the property qualifies as 'replacement property' for business or agricultural relief purposes (ss 113 B or 124 B, as amended in each case by FA 1994, s 247; **9.1:1** and **9.6:5**);
and

(b) in the case of shares or securities, they remain unquoted from the transfer to the transferor's death (or that of the transferee if earlier).

1.5:2   Payment by instalments—lifetime chargeable transfer

The above rules are adapted for lifetime chargeable transfers in various respects. First and foremost in the case of a lifetime gift, the right is only available if the *donee* pays or bears the tax (s 227(1)(b)). Secondly, where the property is settled, the right is only available so long as the asset is retained as settled property by the trustees (s 227(1)(c)). Thirdly, the date of the lifetime chargeable transfer of value is substituted for the date of death; and fourthly the '20% rule' does not apply (effect of s 228(1)(b) and (2)). The rate of interest is non-deductible for tax purposes. (The rates of interest on overdue lifetime tax and tax on death are, unlike as in the past, the one same rate.)

Example

Payments by instalments
Chris made a gift of shares on discretionary trusts (an immediate chargeable transfer) on 17 May 1999. The shares were valued (after business relief) at £342,000 and represented 15% of the ordinary share capital in an unquoted company. The gift was on condition that the donee/trustees paid the IHT. Chris made a PET of £100,000 on 20 December 1998 which can at present be ignored but had made no previous chargeable transfers. He had used his exemptions.

The IHT payable on the gift of shares is accordingly (£242,000 at nil rate and the balance at one half of 40%) £20,000, which may be paid by instalments. Under s 227(3) £2,000 is due on 1 December 1999 (s 226(1)) followed by nine similar payments at yearly intervals. Interest is not charged on the outstanding balance if payment is made on the due dates. If the trustees were at any point to sell the shares, the tax then outstanding plus any accrued interest would be payable forthwith (s 227(4)).

1.6   MAIN VALUATION RULES

1.6:1   The open market price (s 160)

As for CGT, the general rule, in the absence of special valuation rules, is that the value at any time of any property shall be the price which the property might reasonably be expected to fetch if sold in the open market at that time. No allowance is made on the ground that the whole property is to be placed on the market at one and the same time, namely that the market is being 'flooded'. On the other hand one might argue that the mere existence of overhanging IHT makes an asset less valuable.

In order to reach the hypothetical value of the hypothetical property a fiction is created of a sale between hypothetical partners of the hypothetical property. This does not mean, however, that evidence of actual transactions is inadmissible, although it is a question of fact, how much, if any, weight is given to the evidence (*IRC v Stenhouse's Trustees* [1992] STC 103, Ct of Session).

This 'statutory hypothesis' is helpfully summarised by Hoffman LJ in *IRC v Gray* [1994] STC 360, CA, at pp 371–2. This case is also relevant to the valuation of agricultural property (see **9.10** and *Walton v IRC* [1996] STC 68, CA).

1.6:2   Transfers within seven years before death (ss 131–140)

The additional tax payable on transfers of any property (former PETs or lifetime chargeable transfers) made within seven years before death may be relieved where the value of the gift has fallen between the time the gift was made and death. (Note that the original period of three years in s 131 was amended to seven by FA 1986, s 101(1)(a), (3) and Sch 19, para 23.) If the market value of the transferred property at the time of the chargeable transfer (ie date of gift) exceeds its market value at 'the relevant date' (normally the date of death), the additional tax is to be calculated as if the value transferred were *reduced* by the amount of that excess (ie in effect the lower value is substituted). 'Relevant date' means the date of death where the transferee or his spouse still holds that property, or if that property is sold before the transferor's death, the relevant date is the date of a qualifying sale, namely an open market, arm's length arrangement. For example, Albert gives Whiteacre to his son in 1995; it is then worth £300,000. This crystallises the initial potential IHT value and if Albert dies in 1999 when the value has fallen to, say, £200,000, this value can be substituted, although if the son had sold the property in 1996 for £250,000 that would represent the substituted value. Common sense rules apply to changes in the property. Thus capital receipts on shares are added to the market value of the transferred property, whereas calls on shares reduce it. Adjustments also have to be made for reorganisation and alterations of share capital and demergers as well as changes in interest in land and leases not exceeding 50 years.

The relief does not apply to tangible property that is a wasting asset, ie plant and machinery and other assets of a predictable useful life not exceeding 50 years.

As to PETs which become chargeable on the death of the transferor within seven years and the application of taper relief, see **1.2:1**.

1.6:3   Valuation of certain securities sold within 12 months of death (ss 178–189)

Where quoted or USM (NB the USM closed on 31 December 1996, see **1.5:1**) shares and securities or authorised unit trust holdings are sold within 12 months of a death at a genuinely lower level, the persons accountable for IHT, normally the personal representatives, may in effect claim that the total of the sale prices be substituted for the date of death values. This relief is restricted if at any time during the period beginning on the date of the death in question and ending two months after the date of the last sale (ie a maximum of 14 months from the date of death), the person making the claim purchases any of the qualified investments in the same capacity as that in which he made the claim. The loss on sale is then reduced on a pro rata basis as set out in s 180(1). Where the 'appropriate persons', ie the claimants, are personal representatives or trustees the purchase in such capacity of *any* qualifying investments would restrict the relief. For other accountable persons, for example, donees, the relief is only restricted if an investment of the same description is made (a share separately quoted from another share is not of the same description for this purpose). Note also that where personal representatives make payments by way of legacies or other distributions under the will to the beneficiaries and the beneficiaries themselves acquire qualifying investments (whether of the same description or not), there will be no restriction of the loss relief because the purchase by such beneficiaries will not have been in the same capacity as the holdings of the personal representatives.

The above treatment for investment holdings sold within 12 months of death at a loss has been adapted to investments cancelled during that period or whose listing on a recognised stock exchange or where dealing on the USM is suspended by the end of the 12 months (see ss 186A, 186B). Although introduced by FA 1993, s 198, the adaptation applies to deaths on or after 16 March 1992.

These rules deal with losses incurred on investments within 12 months of death. Should an investment become worthless in the second year after the death, consideration might be given to a variation of the will within two years of death under s 142 (see **2.6**). The now worthless shares could be given to an exempt beneficiary such as the spouse or a charity so as to save the IHT on the value of the shares at death.

The valuation of quoted shares and securities on the '$\frac{1}{4}$ up' rule as provided for CGT (TCGA 1992, s 272) will in practice apply for IHT, although there is no corresponding statutory provision.

1.6:4 Falls in value of land four years after death (ss 190–198)

These provisions apply similar relief to that set out in **1.6:3** to land. The relief applies where an interest in land (including buildings) in a person's estate immediately before death is sold by 'the appropriate person', ie the person liable for the IHT thereon (normally the personal representatives), within three years of the death at a genuinely lower value. That value is then to be the taxable value subject to certain conditions. These conditions include a de minimis rule if the difference is only £1,000 or 5% of death value, whichever is the lower; and various anti-avoidance provisions are introduced where the purchaser is 'associated'. The meaning of the word 'sold' was considered in *Jones v IRC* [1997] STC 358 where Lightman J held that in the context of ss 190–198 it is 'clear beyond question that "sold" means "conveyed or transferred on completion of a sale" '.

Where the appropriate person has received other land from the estate and sells it, the claim must be for all or none of the land (this perhaps affords a loophole in so far as the sale of the profitable land can be left until later after the four-year period). There are similar adjustments for changes as described in **1.6:3** as well as adjustments for further purchases up to four months from the last sale. Where the claimant purchases any interest in land in the *same capacity* the claim is reduced, ie the sale price is increased by the following addition:

$$\text{Date of death value minus sale price} \times \frac{\text{The aggregate purchase prices}}{\text{The aggregate sale prices}}$$

The aim is that the relief is to apply only to the *net* loss. Note the importance of the relief only being restricted where the sales and purchases are in the same capacity.

The earlier relief period was three years. In recognition of difficulties in selling land a new s 197A was introduced by FA 1993, s 199, applying to deaths on or after 16 March 1990, whereby a sale (not by compulsory purchase) of land at a loss in the fourth year after death is treated as a sale within the first three years. Putting such a fourth year loss back into the initial three years rather than merely extending the period from three to four years excludes any problems with other fourth-year sales either at a profit or to associated persons which could otherwise limit the relief on the loss.

1.6:5 Sales of related property within three years after death (s 176)

This relief applies where within three years after a person's death there is a sale of any property comprised in his estate immediately before his death and valued for IHT purposes under s 161 with related property or in conjunction with property which was also comprised in the estate but has not at any time since death been vested in the vendors (for example the deceased's interest in possession). A claim can then be made that the property at the death be valued freed from the related etc property provisions. There are various conditions including that the vendors must be the persons in whom the property is vested or the deceased's personal representatives; that the sale must be at arm's length and not in conjunction with other related property sales; that the vendor and the purchaser are not associated or connected; that the vendor has no right to have the property sold back to him; and that the relief is not available if there has been an alteration of shares or rights under s 94 between the death and the sale.

Example

Mr Wright died on 3 August 1997. His estate included 2,000 shares (20%) in Leatherhead Ltd, an unquoted company. His wife held 40% of the shares. His shares were valued, under the related property rules of s 161 at £100 per share, ie £200,000. On 15 September 1998 the shares were sold by his executors to a venture capital company for £25 per share on an arm's length sale, thus realising £50,000. The executors claimed to have the original probate value amended to value the shares as unrelated property at death when it was agreed that at that time the value was £20 per share, ie a total of £40,000, on the basis of a 20% shareholding. £40,000 is therefore substituted for the related property value of £200,000.

Business relief has been ignored in the above example. Where shares which have obtained business or agricultural relief on the footing that the deceased had control of the company are then revalued under these provisions, the relief will be available only if the shares subject to the revaluation would themselves have given the deceased control without taking into account any other shares with which they were valued (s 105(2) and s 122(2)).

1.6:6   Undivided or joint shares

The discount for the lower marketability of assets such as land and buildings held in joint shares continues to be reflected in IHT valuations (a 10% reduction is fairly normal). This position may not, however, exist in strictness (although it may do in practice) where the related property provisions apply, ie between husband and wife or where held by a charity within five years of a transfer from either of them (see **1.3:4**). Moreover the loss on the *creation* of such an interest would be *greater* and taxed at that time. For example, father A transfers his house into joint names of himself and son. Before the transfer the house was worth, say, £200,000; afterwards A's half share is worth, say, £90,000. On the consequential loss formula A's transfer of value is £110,000.

For a detailed discussion of the valuation of the value of an interest in an agricultural tenancy see **9.11:9** (*IRC v Gray, Walton v IRC*)

1.6:7   Unquoted shares and unquoted securities

Here the open market value position applies. However, in many cases, partic-ularly where loss of control is involved, the consequential loss formula may produce a different valuation than applies for CGT. Subject to this, s 168 provides that it shall be assumed that there is available to any prospective purchaser of the shares or securities all the information which a prudent prospective purchaser of the shares or securities might reasonably require if he were proposing to purchase them from a willing vendor by private treaty and at arm's length. The concept of consequential loss is so fundamental to IHT, it is worth illustrating again.

Example

Armstrong, on 3 September 1999, gave to No 1 discretionary trust 10% of the shares in Altitude Ltd (a land dealing company without business relief), reducing his holding from 55% to 45%, and to No 2 discretionary trust a Ming vase, one of a pair, valued at £8,000, both sets of trustees to pay the tax. The Shares Valuation Division of the Inland Revenue agreed the following values of the shares (the remaining 45% were held by non-related parties).

55%	£240,000
45%	£160,000
10%	£10,000

The pair of Ming vases was valued at £23,000.

There was one previous chargeable transfer and he had used up his annual exemptions so that the present transfers were in the taxable band.

Chargeable transfers	
Shares £240,000 less £160,000	£80,000
Vase £23,000 less £8,000	£15,000
	£95,000
Tax payable thereon at half of 40%	£19,000

However, if Armstrong had given cash of, say, £10,000 to the No 1 discretionary trust and £8,000 to the No 2 trust it would appear that the respective trustees could have used the money at a later date to buy the shares and vase. The transfer of assets should not be transfers of value in view of s 10 and therefore not chargeable transfers under s 3. It would be necessary to show that the sales were not intended to confer any gratuitous benefit and that the operations were not associated transactions under s 268.

1.6:8   Debts due to the transferor/estate owner

The assumption is made in s 166 that any debt will be discharged in full, the onus being on the taxpayer to show that recovery is impossible or not reasonably practicable. It will therefore need to be brought into account at its face value unless the taxpayer can produce evidence to the contrary. This concept is important in the context of interest-free loans (see **7.7**). Provided such loans are repayable on demand no IHT liability on the consequential loss formula should arise when they are made. However, if a debt forming part of a deceased person's estate is not *currently* due, it should still be possible to argue that its value for IHT on the death must be discounted. If after death an irrecoverable debt is in fact paid, the deceased's estate will be increased by that amount.

1.6:9   Deductible liabilities and restrictions on deduction

The basic provisions in relation to deductibility on death are contained in s 5(5). Except for liabilities imposed by law, a liability incurred by a transferor shall be taken into account only to the extent that it was incurred for a consideration in money or money's worth, eg, a voluntary covenant to X is not a deductible debt and is ignored. The provisions have been tightened to counter the ease of making PETs and as an adjunct to the reservation of benefit rules—see FA 1986, s 103. This gives rise to an abatement of the deductible liabilities in certain circumstances.

Abatement (ie, full or partial disallowance of deductibility against the deceased's estate) applies:

(a) Where, and to the extent that, consideration received by the deceased (ie, the money or other property advanced to him giving rise to the debt or incumbrance) consists of 'property derived from the deceased'. Examples would include annual or periodical payments made by the deceased which are lent back to him; or the case where a donor transfers an asset to the donee and the donee sells it back to the donor leaving the purchase price outstanding on loan (or where the donee sells the original asset, buys another, and sells that one to the donor on a loan arrangement); and

(b) Where, and to the extent that, the consideration is given by anyone who was at any time 'entitled' to, or whose resources at any time included, property derived from the deceased. An example would be where A gives Blackacre to B; B sells Blackacre to C; C sells it to D; C sells Whiteacre to A leaving the sale price on loan. It appears that the loan would not be deductible in A's estate.

For the meaning of 'property derived from the deceased' see FA 1986, s 103(4), which covers circumstances where the arrangements are in concert, or are direct/indirect/intermediate dispositions.

The following points should be borne in mind:

(1) *McDougal's Trustees v IRC* 1952 SLT 337. In this case M bought park land

and donated it to Edinburgh City Council, from which he borrowed the purchase price. On M's death the loan due to the Council was not deductible because the consideration for the loan by the Council was in respect of property derived from the deceased.

(2) These provisions undermine most old style inheritance trust schemes. New style inheritance trust arrangements seek to avoid the trap: see **8.3:11**.

(3) The abatement provisions are avoided if the person receiving the property derived from the deceased received it in a different capacity to that in which the consideration for the debt is given; or the disposition was not made with reference to or with a view to enabling or facilitating the giving of the consideration.

(4) Abatement will not be applied to the extent that consideration exceeds the value of the property derived from the deceased.

(5) If and to the extent that the estate owner discharges non-deductible liabilities he is treated as having made a PET (FA 1986, s 103(5)).

There are specific provisions on life policies under FA 1986, s 103(7), which deny relief for a deduction claimed against a deceased's estate relating to a life policy issued on or after 1 July 1986 unless the whole proceeds form part of the deceased's estate. These provisions counter:

(1) The decision in *Re Whitfield's Estate, IRC v Whitfield* [1976] STC 89, CA. In that case a death bed life assurance arrangement was allowed as an ED deduction as the debt was incurred for 'full consideration in money or money's worth wholly for the deceased's own use and benefit' as between the lender and the deceased even though applied by way of gift.

(2) Schemes whereby an individual took out life assurance in trust for beneficiaries and paid a small initial premium, the substantial part of the premium being payable after death and claimed to be a deduction from the estate.

Where these restrictions on deductibility give rise to a double charge of IHT (eg, where property given by a PET is lent back by the donee and both the property and the PET become chargeable to IHT because the transferor of the PET dies within seven years) relief may be obtainable under the regulations (SI 1987/1130) issued under FA 1986, s 104, for the avoidance of double charges: see **1.2:3**.

The question came up in *Alexander v IRC* [1991] STC 112 in the case of a council flat sold to the tenant under the 'right to buy' rules with an obligation on the tenant to repay a percentage of the discount on the price if a disposal occurred within five years. The tenant died within that period. The Court of Appeal directed that the Lands Tribunal should determine the value for CTT on the owner's death taking into account the liability to repay, being the amount a hypothetical purchaser would pay to stand in the shoes of the deceased subject to the obligation (following *IRC v Crossman* [1937] AC 26, HL dealing with restrictions on transfer of shares in a private company).

1.6:10   Demutualisation: IHT consequences

The Special Commissioners held in *Ward v IRC* [1999] STC (SCD) that rights to windfall payments which arise on the conversion of a building society into a public limited company should be included as part of the deceased's death estate. In this case, although the deceased had died shortly before the society's flotation was confirmed, under the terms of the Transfer Document the first named executor under her will was entitled to the shares on behalf of her estate. The CTO has published guidance on how to value the rights to the shares. The guidance includes a valuation table to help calculate the open market value of deceased members' shares and lists the various building societies which have converted in the last few years. See Tax Bulletin issue 34 April 1998.

1.7 KEY ADMINISTRATION ASPECTS

1.7:1 The burden of IHT

The relevant rules as found in ss 199–214 are somewhat detailed. Generally, the persons liable for tax due on a chargeable transfer are the transferor, the transferee, any person in whom the property is vested at any time after the transfer or who is beneficially entitled to an interest in possession in the property and where the chargeable transfer results in property being comprised in a settlement, any person for whose benefit the property or its income is applied. Certain key aspects in relation to personal representatives are summarised as follows.

1.7:2 Administration and liability for IHT

The tax due on a PET or the extra tax due as a result of the transferor's death within seven years of a chargeable transfer is due primarily from the donee and secondly from the personal representatives of the transferor.

The position of the personal representatives in more detail is as follows:

(1) If the donee of a PET which becomes chargeable fails to pay the IHT within 12 months from the end of the month of death, the personal representatives become liable for the IHT (ss 199(2), 204(8)) plus interest due after six months. The personal representatives have no indemnity against the donee.

(2) Likewise the additional rate charge on the donee of a chargeable lifetime transfer.

(3) Contrast the position where there is a gift with reservation (FA 1986, s 102(3)) and the donee fails to pay the IHT. Here the personal representatives do have an indemnity against the donee under s 211(3)).

(4) Practical problems arise where the personal representatives have completed the administration of the estate and/or hold a certificate of discharge (see s 239). It seems that a certificate may not wholly protect the personal representatives from increased liability to IHT as a result, say, of the discovery of a hitherto unknown PET, because s 239(4) nullifies a certificate in case of fraud or 'failure to disclose material facts'. An innocent failure to disclose is still a failure and ostensibly could take away the protection of the certificate.

(5) Prudent action by the donor and/or personal representatives could avoid the problems of (4) above:

(a) The personal representatives should retain sufficient funds for the tax.

(b) The donor should always obtain a specific indemnity on making PETs or chargeable lifetime transfers (see the precedent at **7.5:3**).

(c) The personal representatives could insure against the liability (maximum to be the liability in the estate).

(d) If the donee of a PET also benefits under the deceased's will or intestacy, the personal representatives could set off their IHT liability against the donee's share of the estate.

(6) Further practical problems arise because the account must be delivered, and tax due paid, before grant of representation can be obtained. This means that money must be raised to pay IHT before the personal representative is in a position to obtain and deal with the deceased's property. Solutions include:

(a) **The Building Society method**: One potential way around the funding problem is for appropriate funds to be taken out of a bank account and transferred to a building society account. This helps because as a general rule most building societies will transfer funds out of an account without probate or letters of administration. For example, the production of a death certificate and will may suffice. Banks are not generally so amenable. In any case a building society may well pay a better rate of interest. Alternatively it may be possible to negotiate a similar facility with the bank (especially when they realise that a transfer out of the funds is the alternative). However, the arrangements, ie the transfer of funds to the building society or negotiation with the bank, must be done prior to the death of the estate owner. Written assurance should be obtained during the estate owner's lifetime that the arrangements referred to will have the required effect. If the individual has entered into an (enduring) power of attorney, the attorneys will be in a position to arrange matters.

(b) **Lifetime arrangements**: Alternatively, appropriate bank accounts could be set up during the lifetime of the estate owner. For example, a husband and wife or the proposed beneficiary could hold separate bank accounts containing the required amounts. As between spouses, the account could be a joint account, with each party having full signing power and/or a mandate. This latter proposal is not to be recommended as between non-spouses because the Capital Taxes Office are likely to assess the entire balance in the joint account on the first death. In view of the inter-spouse exemption this is not relevant as between husband and wife.

(c) **Insurance solution**: Another option is to take out appropriate whole life, endowment or term insurance cover. For example, this could be done under the Married Women's Property Acts, other trust policies, or joint survivor trust policies. It is of primary importance that the policies are written in trust in favour of the intended beneficiary(ies) so as not to swell the estate of the individual whose life is being assured.

(7) However, although personal representatives still need to exercise pru-

dence, it would appear that the Revenue will act reasonably in genuine cases. In a letter to the Law Society (published in the *Law Society Gazette*, 13 March 1991) they indicated their practice in the following terms:

'The capital taxes offices will not usually pursue for inheritance tax personal representatives who—

– after making the fullest enquiries that are reasonably practicable in the circumstances to discover lifetime transfers, and so
– having done all in their power to make full disclosure of them to the Board of Inland Revenue

have obtained a certificate of discharge and distributed the estate before a chargeable lifetime transfer comes to light.

This statement of the Board's position is made without prejudice to the application in an appropriate case of IHTA 1984, s 199(2).'

On this footing personal representatives may feel a little more comforted. The case of *Howarth's Executors v IRC* [1997] STC (SCD) 162 deals with the personal liability of executors — a lesson to be learnt! The executors distributed the estate, the beneficiary agreeing to settle the outstanding IHT instalments. When he went bankrupt, the remaining executor became personally liable for the IHT.

1.7:3 Certificate of discharge

Pursuant to s 214, the Revenue on application must issue a certificate of the amount of IHT recoverable where a person has paid or borne tax attributable to the value of any property but for which he is not ultimately liable, eg trustees. Under s 239, there are provisions for the issue of a certificate of discharge to a person liable for any IHT. The Revenue must issue a certificate if the person liable applies in circumstances where the transfer is on death or the transferor has died, but issue of a certificate is discretionary in other circumstances. It seems that strictly a certificate may not protect personal representatives, although the Revenue have adopted a reasonable stance: see **1.7:2**.

1.7:4 The Revenue charge

Under ss 237 and 238, the Revenue have an enforceable charge, subject to certain limits, in respect of unpaid IHT and interest, the charge being imposed on the property itself. The charge does not affect purchasers without notice, nor does the charge arise in respect of any personal or moveable property, if the property was beneficially owned by the deceased immediately before his death and the transfer was made on death. Personal property does not include leaseholds which may be charged by the Revenue in relation to deaths occurring on or after 9 March 1999 (FA 1999).

1.7:5 Recovery from spouse

Under s 203, when a transferor has made a transfer of value to his spouse, IHT otherwise payable by the transferor, for example on chargeable transfers to a third party, may be recovered from such transferor's spouse up to the market value of the assets transferred to that spouse at the date of that spouse transfer. (This may cause some matrimonial consternation: for example, a wife could be liable for the IHT in respect of a discretionary settlement set up by her husband for his mistress.) The section enables the transferee spouse to apply a lower valuation to the gifted property received, particularly if the market value of the gift to that spouse has fallen by the time that the chargeable transfer to the third party is made.

1.7:6 Delivery of accounts and payment of interest

The transferor or trustee of a settlement must give an account of all chargeable transfers unless some other person liable for tax (eg the transferee) has done so. The account should include transfers which are exempt or within the nil rate band. Delivery to the Capital Taxes Office must be made within 12 months or, if later, three months from the date liability to tax arises.

Personal representatives must deliver an account within 12 months of the death or if later, within three months of beginning to act as such. In cases where no grant of representation has been obtained within 12 months of death those in whom the property invested (at the time of death or at any time after) or those beneficially entitled to an interest in possession are under a duty to account under s 216(2).

A contradictory position exists in that, whereas an account of chargeable transfers has only to be rendered 12 months from the end of the month in which the death occurs or the chargeable transfer is made (s 216), tax is due and interest accrues at the current rate six months after the end of the month in which death occurs or the transfer is made (subject to the right to pay by instalments; see **1.5** above). This applies in respect of transfers other than on death between 1 October and the following 5 April. For transfers after 5 April but before 1 October in any year, the IHT is due on 30 April of the next year. This can be usefully used as a cash flow exercise. Thus a chargeable gift made on 5 April 1992 is due for payment on 1 November 1992, whereas tax on a gift on 6 April 1992 is not due until 30 April 1993. The rules as to lifetime chargeable transfers apply to trustees.

The interest on the IHT is non-deductible for income tax purposes. Thus, for example, for lifetime transfers the true rate of interest of 4% for a taxpayer who pays income tax at the top rate of 40% is 6.66%: the rate for 2000 is 5%.

Penalties may be incurred for failing to deliver an account, make a return or comply with a notice seeking information. Fraud or negligence in the provision of information or accounts and returns may also be penalised (ss 245–248). Any penalty is in addition to tax and interest. Penalties were increased considerably by FA 1999. However, the new ss 245 and 245A retain the 'reasonable excuse' clause. Considerable guidance on the scope and meaning of this expression can be found in cases brought under the Value Added Tax Act 1994 and the Taxes Management Act 1970.

It is clearly of vital importance that practitioners should maintain diary reminders of these due dates. In many cases, for example, where private company shares are involved (and subject to business relief), an IHT assessment will not have been made within the six-month period, and clients should be advised as to the desirability of making a payment on account. By virtue of s 235 the Inland Revenue must pay interest at the same rate on an overpayment of IHT from the date when the overpayment was made. As this interest will likewise be non-taxable, no doubt a generous overpayment can be a sound investment.

Where private company shares need to be valued, it is unlikely that the IHT valuation will be finalised within the six-month period.

In relation to their overall taxation, holdover relief for CGT, despite the substantial withdrawal for disposals on or after 14 March 1989 by FA 1989, s 124 and Sch 14, still remains available (see now TCGA 1992, s 165) for shares in trading companies and holding companies of trading groups where either:

(a) the shares are neither listed nor dealt in on the former USM; or

(b) the company concerned (including a quoted or a USM company) is the transferor's personal company (ie, at least 5% of the voting rights are exercisable by him).

The company definitions are linked to CGT retirement relief in TCGA 1992, Sch 6.

Holdover relief for CGT also remains available (under TCGA 1992, s 260) in cases of IHT lifetime chargeable transfers (usually gifts on discretionary trusts) even those within the IHT nil rate band or covered by the annual exemption under s 19. Under SP 8/92 dated 26 October 1992, a taxpayer can elect not to compute when holding over the gain. This means that valuations for purposes other than IHT are unlikely. If it is wished to finalise the valuation as quickly as possible the appropriate IHT return should be accompanied by a professional valuation.

1.7:7 'Snoopers charter'

Under s 218, *any* professional person (other than a barrister) must report a post-26 March 1974 settlement in which he is concerned 'with the making' where the settlor is domiciled in the UK but the trustees are or will be non-resident. A person is absolved from reporting the settlement where the settlement is one made by will, or where someone else has already delivered an account or return. Section 219 gives the Revenue very wide powers of obtaining information from any person, although in the case of a barrister or solicitor privileged information is excluded without the consent of his client. A solicitor may nevertheless be required to give the name and address of the client and, if non-resident, his UK associates. (See also TCGA 1992, Sch 5, para 10, and Sch 5A in relation to settlements with a foreign element for CGT).

The FA 1999 introduced a new statutory power for the Revenue to call for such documents as are in the executor's possession or power as the officer may reasonably require for the purpose of determining or enquiring into an account or determining tax due. Further or alternatively, to furnish the officer with such accounts or particulars as he may reasonably require for any of the above-mentioned purposes. The officer must make his request by notice in writing and give the executor at least 30 days within which to comply. Legal privilege for appeals pending is expressly preserved (s 219A).

An appeal may be brought against any requirement imposed by notice under s 219A. The appeal must be brought within 30 days of the date on which the s 219A notice is given. The decision of the Special Commissioners will be final. Any further appeal will be limited to the judicial review procedure the jurisdiction of which is very different to a normal appeal to the High Court on a point of law against a decision of the Commissioners.

The exchange of information with other countries is also facilitated by FA

2000 which introduced s 220A into the IHTA 1984 with effect from 28 July 2000.

1.7:8   IHT returns

Two main lifetime forms are used. The general return (replacing the old Cap C5, still in use for transfers before 18 March 1986) is form IHT 100 which covers all lifetime transfers of value including PETs becoming chargeable on the death of the transferor within seven years; gifts with reservation; termination of interests in possession in settled property; and other chargeable lifetime transfers; but not charges arising out of discretionary trusts. Chargeable events in discretionary trusts are reported on the other main form, which is form IHT 101 (which replaces Cap C 7, still in use for events before 25 July 1986). It appears that if an exemption or relief entirely covers the transfer of value in question there is no need to make a return of the gift; it is only if the exemption or relief only *partially* franks the transfer or value that the return has to be made; and if there is any doubt, eg, as regards normal income expenditure exemption, then a return should be made, to avoid any difficulty. There is no requirement to report PETs when made: they need to be returned only on the death of the transferor within seven years (s 216(1)(bb) and(6)(aa)). By SI 1981/1440 (still operative) the Commissioners of Inland Revenue have dispensed with the need to deliver an account of *lifetime* chargeable transfers where the total value of an individual's chargeable transfers in any one year (6 April–5 April) does not exceed £10,000 and where his cumulative total in the last ten years does not exceed £40,000. (Note it is still ten years even though the cumulation period is now seven years only.) The regulations also dispense with the need for trustees to deliver an account where the termination of an interest in possession in settled property is wholly covered by an annual (£3,000) exemption or marriage gift exemption available to the trustees. It is nevertheless advisable in all these cases to keep records of all transfers not so notified, so that the information is to hand if required at a later date.

As for IHT on estates at death, the relevant forms are:

(a) form IHT 200/200N for use where the deceased dies domiciled within the UK;

(b) form IHT 201/201N for use in most cases where the deceased dies domiciled outside the UK; and

(c) form IHT 202/202N for what are regarded as 'small estates'. These are cases where the gross value of the estate (before deducting exemptions and reliefs) does not exceed twice the IHT nil rate band on death.

IHT forms, leaflets and guidance can all be found on the Inland Revenue website (www.inlandrevenue.gov.uk)

Personal representatives are excused from the need to deliver an account for IHT for deaths on or after 4 April 2000 (Inheritance Tax (Delivery of Accounts) Regs. 2000 SI No 967 – separate SI's for Scotland and Northern Ireland – but to the same effect). This applies where:

(a) the *gross* value of the estate does not exceed £210,000;

(b) the estate comprises only property passing under the deceased's will or intestacy or by nomination or by survivorship (here it is the value of the deceased's beneficial interest in the joint property which is relevant);

(c) not more than £50,000 consists of property situate outside the UK;

(d) the deceased died domiciled within the UK; and

(e) had not made any chargeable lifetime gifts (including gifts with reservation and former PETs) liable to IHT (except gifts of cash quoted shares/ securities not exceeding £75,000 in total).

(f) had not enjoyed an interest in settled property.

Qualifying cases are termed 'excepted estates'. The Revenue reserve the right to call for a proper account within 35 days of the grant of representation (60 days from confirmation in Scotland). Personal representatives who later discover the estate is outside the limits must also deliver an account.

1.8 PRACTICAL APPROACH AND FUTURE OF THE TAX

As a first step the client must be interviewed, preferably with his solicitor and accountant present, and detailed facts as to his individual circumstances, for example, his assets, age, health, family, business, previous transfers of value etc and his planning proposals. To assist the practitioner an outline agenda of such preliminary discussion is set out in **Appendix 4.** This agenda can, after the interview, be enlarged into a detailed memorandum of recommendation and submitted to the client and other interested parties, for example, solicitor, accountant, counsel, insurance broker and bank manager, for perusal, comment and approval.

Despite the (limited) cumulative aspect of lifetime and death disposals, there is still considerable scope for minimising IHT, particularly by using the relatively generous exemptions and reliefs, and taking advantage of the seven-year cut-off of cumulation. There is always a political risk of changes in the law when undertaking future planning, and opportunities which are available now may disappear in the future. The last decade has seen CTT turned into IHT in 1986 bringing seven year cumulation only and an overall flat single rate of 40% above the nil rate band as from 1988. In 1988, too, the CGT charge went up to a top rate of 40% from 30%; and in 1989 CGT holdover relief was severely restricted. These are major tax changes, and who can say what other significant changes for better or worse may not occur over the next few years. The instability produced by annual budget changes add an impetus to current planning. Even at a minor level, the failure to use one annual IHT exemption of £3,000 incurs (at 40%) a penalty of £1,200. At higher levels, failure to plan incurs much larger costs.

Tax planning which relies on artificial technical loopholes is questionable. In the case of *W T Ramsay Ltd v IRC* [1981] STC 174 Lord Wilberforce stated:

> 'It is the task of the court to ascertain the legal nature of any transaction to which it is sought to attach a tax or a tax consequence and if that emerges from a series or combination of transactions, intended to operate as such, it is that series or combination which may be regarded.'

The House of Lords decision in *IRC v Burmah Oil Co Ltd* [1982] STC 30 took this stance a stage further. Lord Diplock acknowledged that the *Ramsay* case marked a significant change in the approach adopted by the House of Lords in relation to 'a pre-ordained series of transactions (whether or not they include the achievement of a legitimate commercial end) into which there are inserted steps that have no commercial purpose apart from the avoidance of a liability to tax which in the absence of these particular steps would have been payable'. The House of Lords in *Furniss v Dawson* [1984] STC 153 confirmed this new approach, adding that 'no commercial purpose' meant 'no commercial (business) purpose', *not* 'no commercial (business) *effect*'. The lower courts had sought to distinguish *Ramsay* and *Burmah Oil* because, unlike those cases, the steps here had 'enduring legal consequences'. Their Lordships roundly rejected this attempt to distinguish the case, and confirmed the new principle. In the words of Lord Brightman:

> 'The formulation, therefore, involves two findings of fact, first whether there was a preordained series of transactions, ie a single composite transaction. Secondly, whether that transaction contained steps which were inserted without any commercial or business purpose apart from a tax advantage'.

A swing of the pendulum back towards the taxpayer emerged from the House of Lords in three appeals taken for convenience together, *Craven v White, IRC v Bowater Property Developments Ltd* and *Baylis v Gregory* [1988] STC 476. The first and third cases involved disposals for CGT, the second with DLT, but the facts in all three included a series of steps taken to avoid tax on a final sale. The steps in *Craven v White* were similar to the *Dawson* case except that there were two possible purchasers in view when the earlier steps were taken. In *Baylis v Gregory* the original purchaser dropped out and the sale was to someone else. In *Bowater* land was divided up and transferred into five group companies in order to take advantage of the £50,000 DLT exemption in each; but the expected purchaser dropped out. He came back six months later and the sale was agreed at a higher price and on fresh terms. The question in all three was whether the changes with the purchaser at the final stage were disassociated and hence not part of the preordained series. The Revenue argued for a subjective test, that regard must be had to the purpose of the taxpayer at outset. He intended to sell in all three cases and took a series of steps to avoid the tax on the ultimate sale. The House of Lords, however, decided in favour of an objective test: was there at outset an already arranged series of actual transactions which included the specific sale which took place? The answer in all three cases was no, and the Crown's appeals were dismissed (unanimously in *Bowater* and *Gregory*; by a three to two majority in *Craven* which was nearer the line). It was recognised that problems still remained, eg, on auction sales, which must be dealt with in future cases.

In *Fitzwilliam v IRC* [1993] STC 502, HL, Lord Keith further clarifed the *Ramsay* test. The question for decision was whether certain steps taken by the trustees of the will of the 10th Earl after his death together with transactions between the Earl's widow and her daughter taken with advice with the aim of CTT mitigation, and based on the then mutual gifts exemption (see **7.14**) combined with the reverter to settlor exemption (see **4.7:4**) achieved their objective of saving CTT. Alternatively, the court had to consider whether the steps taken (or part of them) constituted one single composite transaction which, because of the *Ramsay* doctrine, failed to achieve any CTT saving. The High Court rejected the *Ramsay* argument and found for the taxpayer ([1990] STC 65). The Court of Appeal approved the High Court in also rejecting *Ramsay* on the grounds that a single composite transaction could not be supported by the facts ([1992] STC 185). The House of Lords, by a majority of four to one, also decided for the taxpayer ([1993] STC 502). As Lord Keith pointed out in the leading speech, steps 2–5 were pre-ordained, but the pre-ordained nature of the steps could not negative the application of the exempting provisions. The correct approach was to ask whether steps 2–5 realistically constituted a simple and indivisible whole in which one or more of them was simply an element without independent effect, and to ask whether it was intellectually possible to so treat them. He concluded it was not so possible in the case of *Fitzwilliam*.

In the meantime, *Hatton v IRC* [1992] STC 140, another mutual gifts/reverter to settlor scheme, was decided by the High Court in favour of the Crown on *Ramsay* grounds, again the sole argument taken. Unlike *Fitzwilliam*, *Hatton* involved a marketed scheme.

All of the above must now be reviewed in light of the House of Lords decision in *Macniven v Westmoreland Investments* [2001] STC 237. Their Lordships held that *Ramsay* is relevant only where the statutory words refer to commercial concepts such as 'loss,' 'gain' and 'disposal'. In *Ramsay,* where these concepts were in issue, this approach meant that the legislation could be applied to a pre-planned series of transactions by reference to the overall effect rather than the various distinct parts of that series. However, not all statutory words refer to commercial concepts. If the statutory word is a legal (or juristic) concept such as 'conveyance or transfer on sale' then *Ramsay* will not apply to determine whether, commercially, a sale was effected.

Its application to the facts in *Westmoreland* was reasonably straightforward. Under TA 1988 s 338, payments of interest could be set against profits and any excess carried forward under section 75. Westmoreland owed a group pension scheme a substantial amount of accrued interest under loans; if it paid that interest, that amount would be available for relief (and Westmoreland could be sold to a purchaser with income profits that needed sheltering). In order to fund repayment of the interest, the pension scheme made a further loan. The Revenue contended that a circular payment such as this should be ignored for tax purposes. Their Lordships, however, held that Westmoreland had made a 'payment' of interest within the normal (legal or juristic) meaning of that word and that there was nothing in the legislation to justify a different meaning.

Lord Hoffmann also commented on the relevance of the distinction between 'tax avoidance' and 'tax mitigation'. These concepts put 'the cart before the horse'. Essentially, one only knows whether one has achieved acceptable tax mitigation after the statutory language has been applied to the transaction. How should this be applied to inheritance tax? The crucial question when construing IHTA 1984 or FA 1986 is whether a given word has, in context, a 'commercial' or a 'juristic' meaning. Certainly some words will have no recognised legal meaning and in such cases, a commercial or 'ordinary business' approach will have to be adopted. In other cases the statutory language clearly refers to juristic language: 'conveyance on sale' was an example of a term that lawyers, rather than businessmen, would recognise. The term 'property' in relation to reservation of benefit is also likely to be a juristic term given the decision of the House of Lords in *Ingram.* Other cases will be more difficult—what about 'interest in land' in s 102A; does that include a debt which is practically certain to be charged on land one week after the date of the gift?

Consider the case of *Kwok Chi Leung Karl v Comr of Estate Duty* [1988] STC 728 which was an appeal to the Privy Council from Hong Kong. A Hong Kong individual was terminally ill. Under Hong Kong law only assets situate within Hong Kong are liable to ED. Two months before his death a Liberian company was formed. The individual sold certain shareholdings to the company in return for a promissory note. There was no element of an associated operations code in the case. Lord Oliver in giving the decision expressed surprise that the transactions had not been attacked on the principles in *Ramsay*, but since they had not their Lordships had to deal on first principles. The chose in action represented by the promissory note, it was decided, was situate in Liberia where the obligation was to be performed, and outside Hong Kong.

Lord Oliver's attitude undoubtedly caused a certain amount of rethinking on *Ramsay* and IHT. Nevertheless, would a *Ramsay* argument have succeeded in *Kwok*? Applying *Westmoreland*, the answer will depend upon whether the concept in question (here the 'situation' of an asset) is juristic or a commercial concept. Only if it is a commercial concept can *Ramsay* apply. The difficulty in the *Kwok* case is as Lord Oliver said, none of the background facts had been investigated in *Kwok*. The sale of shareholdings took place by attorney one day before the death. It is perhaps more usual with offshore companies to transfer assets to the company in return for shares in it, but that might take time. If, for instance, the sale for the promissory note was a hastily thought up alternative, it would ruin any preordained plan. This, however, is conjecture. The *Westmoreland* decision has drawn a relatively clear line between the *Ramsay* doctrine and associated operations. The former is a principle of construction and it applies only where the statutory term is a commercial or business term. The latter is a deeming provision which is not concerned with the distinction between legal and commercial terms. Where it applies it rewrites the facts and determines when and to what extent a transfer of value occurred.

In conclusion, it is suggested that an estate owner intent on planning should first make maximum use of his annual and other exemptions. Then he should, on the one hand, make PETs preferably of assets with no or a low liability for CGT, and on the other, make use of the nil rate band for chargeable transfers (say on discretionary trusts if not yet sure of ultimate destination) which is one of the circumstances where CGT holdover can still at present be obtained. Some comfort can be obtained where CGT has to be paid on an outright gift that, unlike holdover, the donee does get a market value uplift. It may, however, be appropriate to use the inter-spouse exemption to pass assets by will to the surviving spouse with CGT uplift on death, so that the survivor can then consider making PETs. The main advantages to be gained, however, would be the availability of the new cumulative clock after seven years (including a new nil rate band) and the ability to transfer appreciating assets to the transferee. On the downside is the fact that whether CGT is paid or deferred, one will not get the market value uplift and exemption that would apply on death of the surviving spouse in respect of the assets in question. The new government could revoke the seven-year cumulation period but, all being well, if that period has started, the legislation will not be retrospective.

1.9 TAX PRACTITIONERS AND ADVISERS

A note on two recent cases, *Cancer Research Campaign v Brown* [1997] STC 1425 and *Hurlingham Estate Limited v Wilde & Partners* [1997] STC 627. In *Hurlingham* the judge held that a reasonably competent conveyancer and commercial lawyer owed a duty to his client to advise on the tax implications of the transaction unless his retainer was limited or it was apparent that advice was not needed by the client.

The facts in *Cancer Research Campaign* were as follows:

N died on 11 December 1986 leaving a will dated 21 October 1985 giving his residuary estate to his sister, the testatrix, who died on 28 May 1988. The plaintiffs, seven charities named as residuary beneficiaries under the testatrix's will dated 14 September 1987, brought an action for damages for negligence against the defendant firm of solicitors, who had acted for the testatrix in connection with the preparation of the will, and P, a legal executive employed by them and principal executor of both wills. The plaintiffs claimed that by reason of the defendants' negligence they were unable to take advantage of a deed of arrangement under s 142 of the Inheritance Tax Act 1984 at a cost to them of some £200,000 of unnecessarily paid inheritance tax on N's estate, since the statutory period of two years within which such a deed should have been executed had expired on 10 December 1988. The plaintiffs contended that the defendants were in breach of their duty of care during the testatrix's lifetime in failing to advise her of the possibility of executing a deed of variation of N's bequests and in breach of their duty of care, following her death, in the administration of the estate in failing to notify them of their prospective legacies.

Harman J held (dismissing the action) that although it was established that a solicitor was under a duty to take care to ensure that an intended beneficiary received the benefit intended, there was no duty to advise an intended testator about the tax avoidance schemes of another estate. In the instant case the defendants' retainer was to draw the testatrix's will, therefore their duty was limited to drawing that will and to ensuring that it was properly executed, both of which they had done. No duty to the residuary beneficiaries to consider and advise the testatrix about possible ways of rearranging the dispositions under N's will could have arisen. Moreover, no tortious duty of care would arise in favour of an intended beneficiary unless and until the client had (a) decided to confer on the intended beneficiary a particular intended testamentary benefit (being the benefit for the loss of which the intended beneficiary sought to hold the solicitor liable), and (b) retained the solicitor for that purpose. There being, in the instant case, no particular testamentary benefit intended by the testatrix for the plaintiffs out of the net assets of N's estate which would come to her, that loss could not be recovered by the plaintiffs against the solicitors. Accordingly, the defendants owed no duty to the plaintiffs during the testatrix's life to advise her that she could or might execute a deed of variation pursuant to s 142 as to confer the benefits which she would get out of N's estate on the plaintiffs. In any event, even if there had been such a duty, the plaintiffs had to satisfy the court that, on a balance of probabilities, they would have received benefits under the putative deed of variation. However, there was no basis for reaching such a conclusion. Indeed on the exiguous material before the court, the most likely result of a thorough discussion between the testatrix and her solicitors would have been a decision that she could not know what the future held and that she should retain N's estate in her own hands. Accordingly, the plaintiffs had not discharged the burden of proving that they had suffered any damage. *White v Jones* [1995] 2 AC 207 and *Trusted v Clifford Chance (a firm)* (17 May 1996, unreported), Ch D, applied.

Furthermore there was no duty either on the solicitors or on the executor after the testatrix's death to communicate with the residuary beneficiaries and thereby enable them to arrange and execute a deed of variation themselves. The firm of solicitors did not come under any direct duty of their own to the plaintiffs since there was no separate duty upon solicitors acting for executors after the death of a testator to legatees under the will. Moreover, an executor's duty was to collect the assets and he was under no obligation to inform a legatee that there was a prospective legacy. *Re Lewis* [1904] 2 Ch 656, *Chauncy v Graydon* (1843) 2 Atk 616 and *Re Mackay* [1906] 1 Ch 25 followed.

More detailed discussion of the principles involved can be obtained from a specialist text book on professional negligence.

Chapter 2

Wills

2.0 INTRODUCTION

As a will operates from the date of death, it might seem more appropriate to make this chapter the concluding one. The reason for dealing with this subject early in this book is that it is often only when an individual is thinking of making his will that the idea of estate planning occurs to him and it is at that stage that the wider IHT issues can be explored. Although the will is a key vehicle in planning, it is also a very personal document. Sometimes the tax advantages have to compete with the personal aims and feelings of the individual which may have to receive priority. Great care should be taken when receiving and taking instructions for a will and a suggested 'Instruction Sheet' is set out at **Appendix 5**.

Choosing the correct type of will can result in substantial IHT mitigation, particularly if advantage is taken of the nil rate band, business and agricultural property reliefs and the exemption between spouses. However, the law does change. A new case may alter the way we understand the law (for better or worse – see *Re Benham* as an example later clarified by *Re Ratcliffe*). Alternatively, a change of administration may remove, amend or introduce reliefs, exemptions and charges. This means that the will must be kept under regular review.

When advising on a will seven key aspects should be borne in mind. First, the importance of reciprocity, namely that husband and wife should each make appropriate wills. It may well be appropriate to leave business or agricultural assets specifically to chargeable parties including a discretionary trust. Second, wills are ambulatory, ie they operate as from death and in respect of the assets **then owned** by the testator or testatrix. Third, the need to draft wills with the maximum flexibility. Fourth, the liquidity of the estate: debts and liabilities will need to be paid as will the IHT. The estate will often be tied-up in the matrimonial home, in unquoted shares or in other business assets. Fifth, in preparing a will, the tax aspect is only one factor to be taken into consideration and must be subject to particular family and other circumstances. Sixth, a subsequent marriage revokes a will (unless the will was expressly made in contemplation of that marriage) and the matter of the revocation of gifts made in a will to a spouse will arise on the termination of the marriage (see **Appendix 5, Part V, para (2)**). The seventh aspect which is not limited to the question of wills is that detailed records should be maintained of lifetime gifts, whether PETs or immediately chargeable transfers.

Why make a will? There are six main advantages of leaving a will rather than dying without one—ie intestate:

(1) Choosing one's own executors and trustees (persons entitled to the equivalent office on an intestacy, ie 'administrators' may be inappropriate).

Executors

An executor's functions include collecting in the deceased's property, paying off any debts, and distributing to those persons entitled under the will. When the executors have collected in the deceased's estate and paid the liabilities, it is common for the will to provide that they will then become trustees. The change in capacity is necessary if the will is to contain gifts to minors conditional on attaining a defined age; or where certain assets may be held in their present state pending sale—'a trust for sale.' Assets are transferred from the executors to trustees (even if these are the same individuals) by means of an assent. An assent can be informal, except in the case of land where a written document is necessary *Re King's Will Trusts* [1964] 1 All ER 833. The assets retained in the administration could be those assets pregnant with a high capital gain, which could then in due course be transferred to the legatees free of CGT.

The trustees' responsibilities include:

– ensuring that the property subject to the trust is transferred to the beneficiaries at the appropriate time or occasion
– exercising various powers given them by statute or in the will
– managing assets of the estate (eg land) subject to the trust
– distributing income or capital from the trust fund
– exercising appropriate discretions.

It is possible to appoint individuals or institutions as executors and trustees. In practice at least two individuals will be appointed with, possibly, a provision that if one dies before the testator or does not accept the office, a third person should be appointed in his stead.

Administrators

These are persons appointed pursuant to statute to deal with the affairs of a deceased person, in circumstances where:

– the deceased has died intestate (ie leaving no will); or
– he has left a will which fails to appoint (or effectively appoint) any executors; or
– he has left a will appointing executors none of whom take a grant of probate, for whatever reason. An administrator's functions are similar to those of an executor.

Administrators are persons having an interest in the estate of a deceased person who wish to become involved in dealing with the deceased's affairs. They obtain grant of letters of administration (contrast grant of probate) which is appropriate in the circumstances referred to above.

(2) Executors can, to a considerable extent, act before grant of probate. An executor derives his power and appointment under the will and can act in that capacity from the moment the testator dies. The executor can do many other things, eg arrange the funeral and generally take over the deceased's affairs including the running of his business and terminating any continuing liability, such as tenancy and disposing of chattels, eg furniture and effects, jewellery or cars. He should also take immediate possession of any valuables and secure their safety and arrange insurances where necessary since as stated, his responsibility begins from the moment the deceased dies.

By contrast, an administrator has no such power although the next of kin or proposed administrator should prudently take some of the steps mentioned such as arranging the funeral, preserving the assets, etc.

(3) Under the terms of a will, guardians of infant children can be appointed: clearly a most important provision. Normally the need to appoint guardians arises only when both parents are dead but either parent of a legitimate minor can appoint a guardian to act jointly with the surviving parent.

(4) The trustees' implied powers under the Trustee Act 1925 can be appropriately extended: for example, the power of applying the whole of a beneficiary's potential entitlement to capital instead of only one half as permitted under s 32 of the Act.

(5) Special requirements can be embodied in a will, for example, powers of appointment (ie distributing capital funds); options, eg on shares of a family company; avoiding complex apportionments; directions as to burial or cremation etc.

(6) The predetermined entitlement of next of kin under an intestacy may be entirely inappropriate. This is because the entitlements are based on statutory provisions designed to meet the likely wishes of the average family man. As everyone has special likes and dislikes and no family is typical, this average is bound to be unsatisfactory to a degree.

Since 1 December 1993, under the Family Provision (Intestate Succession) Order 1993, the statutory legacy for the surviving spouse is increased from £75,000 to £125,000 where issue also survive, and from £125,000 to £200,000 where no issue survive, but there is a surviving parent, brother or sister.

Example

Adam did not bother to make a will. 'Everything will go to my wife Eve in any case' he asserted. WRONG! He left an estate of £300,000. Eve and two nasty brothers survived him.

Eve got the 'personal chattels', ie furniture, etc, £200,000 and half of the balance, ie £50,000. The nasty brothers take £25,000 each.

When an individual considers the terms of his will it may be appropriate at that stage to consider suitable lifetime tax planning measures. For example; making potentially exempt transfers ('PETs'); using the nil and lower lifetime rate of inheritance tax ('IHT'); setting up appropriate family trusts; and undertaking suitable insurance and pension arrangements. See further **Chapter 7**.

Claims under the Inheritance (Provision for Family and Dependants) Act 1975

Under English law (in contrast to certain continental systems) there is no community of goods between husband and wife. However the Inheritance (Provision for Family and Dependants) Act 1975 restricts the free disposal of property by will so that the deceased dependants are provided for. It does so by giving certain dependants of the deceased (including spouses; ex-spouses who have not remarried; common law wives; children, etc) the right to make a claim to the court if they consider that the deceased has not made reasonable provision in his/her will or in accordance with the intestacy rules. The court is given a very wide discretion to direct income and/or capital of the deceased's estate to the claimant, but a claim must be made within six months of the grant of probate.

This chapter treats the subject-matter of wills under the following headings:

(1) Making the correct type of will with particular emphasis on the flexibility gained by wills with life interests.

(2) The appropriate will to the relevant IHT circumstances.

(3) Incidence of IHT and treatment of specific gifts including legacies (s 38).

(4) Will drafting: legacies and bequests (ss 36–42).

(5) Ancillary aspects of wills.

(6) Variations and disclaimers—post death planning (s 142).

The Trusts of Land and Appointment of Trustees Act 1996

All wills of persons dying after the commencement of the 1996 Act, namely 1 January 1997 are subject to the new regime governing trusts relating to land. This means that Settled Land Act precedents will need amendment, and some trust for sale precedents may need altering. It should be noted that trusts involving land will be called 'trusts of land' and the distinction between Settled Land Act Settlements and Trusts for Sale will disappear. Every such trust of land will have an implied power to postpone sale which cannot be excluded by the trust instrument and the doctrine of conversion will no longer apply. Part II of the Act contains administrative provisions. Section 18 of the Act includes within the provisions personal representatives of estates in the course of administration in respect of deaths after commencement of the Act. Part II of the Act applies to trusts of land and personalty, Part I only to trusts of land.

2.1 MAKING THE CORRECT TYPE OF WILL

2.1:1 There are three basic types of will

(1) A will disposing of the estate by one or more outright absolute interests. In that case the recipients will have unfettered control of the assets on which no conditions can be attached.

(2) A will giving a life interest from one spouse to another in the whole or part of the estate, followed by or containing one or more outright, absolute interests.

(3) A will whereby the surviving spouse receives a life interest and full and unrestricted powers are vested in the trustees to enable them to advance capital and to make loans to that spouse and/or to appoint the capital or income onto new trusts thus terminating the spouse's life interest in whole or part.

Such a will might also include an appropriate discretionary trust fund as described below.

Accordingly such a will could contain three main clauses:

– Income to widow(er) for life.
– If no widow(er), then discretionary trust of income and capital.
– Notwithstanding the two previous provisions, a wide overriding power of appointment.

Relevant aspects of life interest wills

Such a life interest will should be drawn flexibly. In particular the executors/ trustees ('the trustees') should be given wide, overriding powers of appointment, so that they can either appoint the capital in whole or part to the surviving spouse absolutely and, or terminate the life interest in whole or part and appoint the capital to one or more of the other beneficiaries named or referred to in the will, eg children or grandchildren.

When drafting the will trust ensure that it is clear whether or not the surviving spouse has an interest in possession in the deceased's share of the home. In *IRC v Lloyds Private Banking* [1998] STC 559 the Special Commissioner decided that the provisions in the deceased's will in relation to the deceased's share of the matrimonial home were not dispositive (i.e. they did not make a disposition of an interest in the deceased's half share to the survivor), they were merely administrative. Lightman J reversed the decision on appeal to the High Court. The key provision which Lightman J held to be dispositive was that no objection restriction or disturbance was to be made to the survivor's continued residence so long as he desired to remain there. Such dispositive provision clearly gives the surviving spouse security as to occupation of the home, but at the cost of IHT on the entirety, as contrasted with say only a half share. See also *Faulkner (trustee of Adams, deceased) v Inland Revenue Commissioners* [2001] STC (SCD) 112 where directions in a will to the trustees to permit two persons to occupy a house constituted a present right of present enjoyment, and gave those persons a chargeable interest in possession, not a mere licence. Of course if the beneficiaries under the will are the persons entitled to the property they are likely to have interests in possession in any event: see *Woodhall v IRC* [2000] STC (SCD) 558. This was a case where the testator gave his children the right to occupy the house and gave the trustees administrative powers to permit the children, or any of them, to occupy. The result was that each child had an interest in possession in the property (the value divided between them).

2.1:2 Advantages of life interest wills

A will which confers a life interest on the surviving spouse has the following advantages:

(1) IHT—gifts with reservation provisions FA 1986, s 102

If a surviving spouse inherits assets absolutely which she then settles so as to reserve a benefit to herself, eg as a discretionary beneficiary, the assets remain in her estate for IHT (FA 1986, s 102 and Sch 20). She will also be a 'settlor' for CGT purposes (TCGA 1992, ss 77–79) (see **2.6:4**) and income tax purposes (TA 1988, s 660A–G). A life interest gift in a will can be used to overcome this. For example a testator could leave a life interest to his widow coupled with wide powers in the trustees to terminate that interest and inter alia settle the funds onto a discretionary trust. If the trustees did terminate the life interest in favour of a discretionary trust, the asset would thereupon fall into a discretionary trust in which the surviving spouse could be one of the discretionary beneficiaries. In those circumstances the surviving spouse would not have reserved a benefit as above because she has made no gift, so that the reservation of benefit rules should not apply. (As to use for the matrimonial home—see **2.5:5** below.)

The transfer into the discretionary trust would not however be a PET and therefore is only effective as far as unused nil rate band is concerned. Consider routing life interest via the surviving spouse's children using their respective nil rate bands.

(2) IHT flexibility 'in lieu' of variations

Instruments of variation under s 142 remain a useful fallback for cases where proper IHT planning has failed (usually because circumstances have changed by the date of death). However, there are restrictions on the s 142 variation (and it is always possible that the relief will be curtailed). Therefore, a will which includes a flexible life interest with wide powers of appointment has the best of both worlds: the will itself is flexible and can be adapted to changed circumstances but a s 142 variation remains an option where necessary and available.

Inclusion of a flexible life interest together with wide powers of appointment written into the will itself means that s 142 powers of variation can be avoided.

(3) CGT: TCGA 1992, ss 4 and 5

Trustees of a life interest trust are liable to CGT at 34% (subject to taper and other reliefs) compared with a maximum of 40% for an individual (eg where a spouse is left an absolute interest and she disposes of assets). As the spouse's interest is as widow(er), the anti-avoidance provisions in TCGA 1992, ss 77–79 do not apply. The trustees will, however, only have the £3,750 small gain exemption rather than the £7,500 for an individual for the year of assessment 2001–02 (s 3, Sch 1).

(4) Reversionary interests and their re-settlement

The creation of the life interest will also create the subsequent interest in reversion, enabling the substantial IHT and CGT savings to be made by the reversioner as described in **2.5:7** below.

(5) Practical use of life interests

Life interest trusts have an important practical use in retaining the capital assets in the estate for the eventual benefit of the testator's children in circumstances where it cannot be guaranteed that the surviving spouse will retain or use the assets for the benefit of the testator's children, for example in circumstances where he/she remarries, and there is a danger that the assets will be diverted to the new husband or wife or their side of the family. Similarly with second or subsequent marriages, the testator spouse can provide for the surviving spouse by way of a life interest trust and ensure that the capital is left to his own children as appropriate.

Moreover with a life interest, as trustees will be involved (of whom the widow(er) may well be one), opportunity can be taken of ensuring that he/she will receive proper financial and investment advice.

2.1:3 Ancillary aspects of life interests

If the surviving spouse's life interest is terminated (in whole or part), eg in the circumstances envisaged in **2.1:2** (1), or where the trustees appoint in favour of issue, the surviving spouse will be treated as having made a potentially exempt transfer ('PET') which will normally give rise to no IHT if she survives seven years (taper relief at the rate of 20% per annum after surviving three years—s 3A(7)).

Avoid automatic termination of the life interest on re-marriage, because such termination can give rise to (i) a CGT liability (subject to the possible, restricted, holdover relief under TCGA 1992, ss 165 and 260); and (ii) a possible IHT liability, ie a failed PET if the spouse does not survive seven years from the re-marriage.

The creation of the life interest in favour of the surviving spouse, as for an absolute interest will normally obtain the benefit of the IHT inter-spouse exemption under s 18. On the survivor's death if still then owning the life interest, it is the capital supporting the same that will be assessed and added to that surviving spouse's own estate to arrive at the amount and rate of IHT.

2.2 THE APPROPRIATE WILL TO THE RELEVANT IHT CIRCUMSTANCES

2.2:1

Six suggestions are made below for six different circumstances. Remember to bear in mind that all families have their own peculiarities and keep s 18 IHTA 1984 in mind (to the effect that husband and wife are treated as separate individuals).

(1) Married—no issue

Here the usual suggestion would be an absolute interest (or possibly a life interest) will to the surviving spouse with only minor exceptions eg legacies and bequests to relatives, charities, etc. Provisions should be included as to alternative gifts over to others if one spouse does not survive the other by, say, one month.

(2) Married—with issue—small/medium estate

Small or medium estate (say under £350,000). An absolute interest (or possibly life interest) will in favour of the surviving spouse but the will should ensure that up to the full amount of the available nil rate band for IHT goes to the children or other issue directly or by way of a mini discretionary trust (see below). Currently the first £242,000 of chargeable transfers (which include chargeable lifetime gifts in the previous seven years) is in effect exempt from IHT. The nil rate band is likely to be increased annually at least in line with inflation. It is possible to word your will so that you gift whatever the nil rate band (or unused balance) will be at your death. A maximum could be imposed, to ensure a particular beneficiary does not obtain more than the testator contemplated. Consider also gifting business/agricultural assets subject to the 100% or 50% relief, to someone other than the surviving spouse eg children, grandchildren or a discretionary trust where the surviving spouse can be a beneficiary—see also **9.0, 2.2:2** (2) and **4.6:2** (3) below.

If the matrimonial home is jointly owned (as tenants in common) the deceased might leave his share to the children (using the nil rate band). The surviving spouse may continue to occupy by reason of his/her own beneficial share in the home. Substantial protection of his/her occupation is given by the Trusts of Land and Appointment of Trustees Act 1996. In particular ss 12 and 13. See **2.5:6** below and the reference to the *Lloyds Private Banking* and other cases mentioned in **2.1:1** above.

(3) Married—with issue—larger estate

Larger estate (say more than £350,000). Where the estates are larger the proposals in (2), namely to take advantage of the nil rate band, become more relevant and practical insofar as the surviving spouse will not normally require the whole estate for her/his personal needs. There will be greater emphasis on the advantages of a life interest will (see **2.1:2** above).

However, for IHT, the incentive to equalise estates, beyond gifting the nil rate band amount as at the date of death to chargeable parties, has largely gone. This is because for deaths since 15 March 1988 there is only one rate, currently 40%, that applies on death; and therefore IHT is no longer a progressive tax beyond the nil rate band, ie there is only one rate thereafter. This is subject to considering the availability of exemptions eg to charities, or reliefs eg for business or agricultural property.

Example 1

Husband has an estate of £718,000, wife of £200,000. Husband dies first and leaves the nil rate band to his children and the balance of £476,000 to his wife (by way of life interest or absolute interest) and she dies three years later. IHT, assuming no change in rates or assets in respect of the two deaths:

on husband's death = NIL
on wife's death:

$$\text{total estate of wife} = £676,000$$
$$\text{IHT} = \begin{array}{r} 676,000 \\ -\ 242,000 \\ \hline 434,000 \end{array} \times 40\% = £173,600\text{: IHT}$$

Example 2

Another husband and wife with the same aggregate assets based on archaic advice, equalise their estates during lifetime, ie each have an estate of £459,000. Husband leaves his estate direct to children:

$$\text{IHT:} = \begin{array}{r} 459,000 \\ -\ 242,000 \\ \hline £217,000 \end{array} \times 40\% = £86,800.$$

Note that in this example, on wife's death the IHT on her estate of £459,000 is also £86,800. IHT on the two deaths is therefore also £173,600—the same aggregate IHT as in **Example 1**. Note also that in **Example 1** the surviving spouse has greater opportunity to make PETs or enjoy a greater income, or make exempt gifts by normal expenditure out of income.

Some steps towards lifetime equalisation between husband and wife may be necessary to ensure that *each* spouse can use his/her nil rate band, whoever dies first.

Therefore the main IHT purpose of giving assets to chargeable parties beyond the nil rate band since 15 March 1988 is because those assets are expected to appreciate substantially; putting such appreciating assets in the hands of the younger generation should defer IHT for a longer period than if given to the surviving spouse. Even that advantage may well be countered by the ability of the surviving spouse (or the will trustees) to make/arrange PETs. But beware: differential or progressive rates of IHT may well be re-introduced so that during the testator's lifetime the will should be subject to regular review; and see also **2.2:2** below. Different motives also apply to business and agricultural property, see **Chapter 9** below.

For income tax purposes, from 6 April 1990 husband and wife are taxed independently on all income—earned and unearned. Married women are now fully responsible for the tax on their income and have their own personal allowance. Therefore equalisation of estates (and the resultant investment income) has become relevant for income tax and capital gains tax rather than IHT. Note the anti-avoidance provisions of TA 1988, of s 660A–G. In the common form trust whereby a husband gives his wife a life interest right to the income, followed by a gift of capital in remainder to the children, the income will not be treated as the wife's, but will be treated as the husband's on the basis that the husband retains an interest in the settlement (s 660A (1) (2)).

At this level (ie for larger estates and subject to business/agricultural property gifts) four motivating factors favour the bulk of the testator's estate (ie beyond the nil rate band—and probably by way of flexible life interest, see **2.1:2** above) going to the surviving spouse, particularly where he/she has reasonable prospects of surviving the vulnerable seven-year period:

(a) the advantage of being able to defer the IHT until the death of the surviving spouse, a clear cash flow advantage;

(b) the ability of the surviving spouse to make IHT effective gifts—especially PETs (ie by way of the trustees' termination of the life interest trust; or by way of absolute gifts by surviving spouse);

(c) because as stated, IHT has ceased to be a progressive tax beyond the nil rate band, there is no present incentive to use up lower rates for chargeable parties;

(d) the greater opportunity to make gifts by normal expenditure out of income particularly on premium of life policies.

For CGT purposes there are circumstances where it can be very beneficial to transfer assets, initially during lifetime, between spouses. For example:

(a) spouse A owns substantial assets showing a large capital gain;

(b) spouse A transfers these assets to spouse B (who is likely to die first) free of CGT and IHT:

(c) spouse B (dutifully) dies:

(d) spouse A receives the assets free of CGT on B's death and uplifted to the then market value. Note, however, that there is no market value uplift if spouse B receives a life interest under a trust of the assets (TCGA, s 73(1)(b)) unless the trust continues after B's death, giving A a life interest and subject thereto life interests for A's children (TCGA 1992, s 72).

The arrangements should be carried out subtly and with *Ramsay* and associated operations in mind. Therefore consider an adaptation of the above whereby spouse B leaves the assets to someone other than spouse A, eg children, grandchildren, family trusts such as a s 144 discretionary trust (see **2.5:3** below). This gift will also be exempt for CGT, but IHT will be payable on the death unless within the nil rate band or if the gift attracts business or agricultural property relief. This alternative also has a CGT taper relief disadvantage. A gift to a spouse within TCGA s 58(1) does not stop and restart the taper clock. By contrast, a gift to one's child does restart the taper clock for CGT: see TCGA 1992, Sch A1.

(4) Single (unmarried) persons

Largely non-tax considerations are applicable here, but exempt transfers may be appropriate, eg nil rate band to relatives, gifts to charities, etc.

(5) Widow(er) or divorced persons

Consider, in this situation using a trust, such as an accumulation and maintenance trust. Such a trust can be very flexible, and only requires that there be an entitlement to income by age 25, the capital entitlement can be left in the trustee's discretion.

(6) The undecided testator

Consider the various uses of discretionary will trusts under **2.5:3** below.

2.2:2 Sharing an estate between spouses and issue—assets qualifying for relief

(1) It is always relevant in sharing an estate between a spouse and issue to consider whether any of the assets qualify for reliefs, and whether any reliefs are being wasted. This is particularly significant where the 100% business and agricultural property relief applies. If, for instance, a testator has an estate comprising a business asset worth £200,000, eligible for 100% relief, which he leaves to the widow (by way of life interest or outright), and general investments worth £200,000 left to children, the widow will receive something worth £200,000 (or a life interest therein) which will be exempt in any case (ie the business relief is wasted); and IHT will be payable on the £200,000 given to the children. If, on the other hand, the bequests are switched round, so that the children get the business and the widow the investments (or a life interest therein), no IHT will be payable at all having regard to the operation of the 100% business and inter-spouse exemption. Alternatively, if the widow needs to benefit from such business assets, they could be bequeathed in the will by way of a discretionary trust in respect of which the widow would be one of the beneficiaries with the particular intention, perhaps, of benefiting her by income distribution. If the business assets are only eligible for the 50% relief, a similar formula

should be considered, with the result that IHT would only be payable on the reduced value of the business assets passing to the children of £100,000, which will probably be eligible for the nil rate band treatment. Consider, however, the complications of s 39A—see **2.3:3** below.

(2) If the business of the deceased required specific qualifications, eg doctor, lawyer, accountant, Lloyds member, and valuable assets were owned in the business, eg office premises, Lloyds assets, business relief would be lost if assets were left to an individual, who will not obtain the relief on their death eg spouse who had to rent out the business premises. It may be a better alternative for the qualified testator to leave assets to a discretionary trust so the transfer is free from IHT and the asset is not part of the surviving spouse's estate on death.

(3) Making arrangements for the surviving spouse to receive wasting assets thereby avoiding or at least reducing the bunching effect on the survivor's death.

(4) Use of nominations

For example the death in service amount of a pension or insurance policy could be nominated at the discretion of the trustees to the deceased's children free of tax, and that sum could be used in purchasing from the deceased's surviving spouse illiquid assets left to her in the will, eg family company shares. (Under current CTO practice, there may be an assessment to IHT on the basis of an omission to exercise a right in circumstances where the deceased failed to retire at the earliest time— s 3(3)). Nominations could be directed into a discretionary trust with the widow/er as a principal beneficiary in respect of income and loan distributions as necessary.

For members of new schemes set up after 13 March 1989 and the new members joining existing schemes on or after 1 June 1989, the death in service benefit is limited to 4 × capped remuneration. The earnings cap for the year of assessment 2001–02 is £95,400.

In deciding whether the cash is to fall into the estate or be nominated in favour of other dependants, the cash could be retained in the pension fund for up to two years from the death.

2.3 INCIDENCE OF IHT AND TREATMENT OF SPECIFIC GIFTS INCLUDING LEGACIES (S 38)

2.3:1 Incidence of IHT: *Re Dougal* [1981] STC 514 and s 211

The incidence of IHT (ie who bears the tax) varies according to whether the gifts are made subject to IHT (so that the recipient bears the tax) or free of IHT (so that the residuary estate bears the IHT). It is most important that the will should state whether any particular gift in a will is to be subject to or free of IHT. If the will is silent on the point IHT will normally be payable out of the residue so that specific gifts are free of IHT whether or not the asset in question is land.

Section 211 expressly provides that in the absence of contrary intention shown by the deceased in his will, the IHT will be payable out of the general testamentary and administrative expenses of the estate. Section 211 applies for deaths on or after 26 July 1983, where the PRs:

(1) are liable for IHT on a death;

(2) in respect of any UK property (ie real or personal) which vests in the PRs; and

(3) where property was not immediately before the death settled property; and

(4) subject to any contrary intention in the will, the IHT plus any interest thereon is treated 'as part of the general testamentary and administrative expenses of the estate' ie the gift is free of IHT payable out of residue. In other cases (eg settled property; property abroad; and property held as joint tenants, where the survivor takes automatically under the jus accrescendi), IHT is to be borne 'where occasion requires' by the person in whom the property vests, eg trustees of settled property, beneficial owner of overseas property, or surviving co-owner.

Re Dougal was a Scottish case where it was held that in Scotland in the absence of express provisions in the will, CTT on realty (as well as CTT on personalty) was payable out of residue. It is considered that *Re Dougal* also applies in England and Wales and for IHT purposes.

The golden rule: ensure that all gifts in wills indicate expressly whether they are free or subject to IHT.

2.3:2 Treatment of specific gifts including legacies (s 38)

Where a transfer (normally the transfer of the whole of the individual's property on death by will) is only partially exempt (because, for instance, he is leaving part of his estate to his spouse or to charity) it is necessary to have provisions which determine the extent and the impact of IHT liabilities on that part or proportion which is not exempt. The rules governing the allocation of exemptions in such circumstances are set out in ss 36–42 (see **2.4**).

Planning aspects of ss 36–42

Where residue goes in whole or part to an exempt party such as the surviving spouse or charity, then legacies which are expressed to be free of IHT must be grossed up either among themselves (if the entire residue goes to the exempt parties) or additionally regrossed at the estate rate of the whole chargeable estate (eg if part of the residue goes to a non-exempt party). Consider the alternatives, for example making legacies which are expressed to be subject to IHT; or converting legacies into a share of residue. The problem need not arise where the 100% business/agricultural property relief applies (see **2.3:3**).

2.3:3

Section s 39A provides that relief relating to business or agricultural property which is not specifically given is apportioned rateably between the exempt and non-exempt parts of the gross estate. Therefore nowadays it is normally good estate planning to make specific gifts of business and agricultural assets which attract 100% relief to chargeable parties, eg children, in addition to the nil rate band, free of IHT.

Section 39A and the nil rate band complication

Section 39A also applies where there are specific gifts of *non*-business or *non*-agricultural assets (eg cash gifts to chargeable parties) and residuary gifts (eg to a surviving spouse) which includes business or agricultural assets. In that case the specific gifts of *non*-BPR/APR assets will be entitled to a due proportion of the BPR/APR. This is particularly relevant where the nil rate band is given to chargeable parties, eg to children or into a mini-discretionary trust.

Example

Albert intends to leave the nil rate band to his children and the residue to his widow Victoria. His will gives the children 'the largest sum at the date of my death as shall not incur any liability for the payment of tax by reason of my death ...'. Albert has an estate of £1.5m, including a 30% shareholding in the family trading company, Albert Widgets Ltd, valued at £1.2m. He dies on 1 August 2001. The children will in fact receive much more than the then nil rate band of £242,000 — in fact £1,210,000 and Victoria gets £290,000.
This is calculated as follows:

Proportion of estate which constists of taxable property is;

$$\frac{£300,000}{£1,500,000} = \frac{1}{5}$$

Proportion of the estate which consists of 100% relief property is

$$\frac{£1.2m}{£1.5m} = \frac{4}{5}$$

The value of the property which therefore passes under the pecuniary gift of the nil band free of IHT (inclusive of the 100% relieved BPR/APR) is therefore:

£242,000 × 5 = £1,210,000

(The multiplier of 5 applies because the 100% relief is spread over the value of the dispositions of property comprised in the estate under section 39A, so that for every £1 of property which is taxable (at a nil rate) passing under the nil band, a further £4 of property which is 100% relieved also passes).

2.4 WILL DRAFTING: LEGACIES AND BEQUESTS (ss 36–42)

Remember: when drafting a will for deaths after 1 January 1997, the new 1996 TLATA will apply.

2.4:1 Background

Where a transfer is only partially exempt (because, for instance, the testator leaves part of his estate to his spouse or to charity) it is necessary to have provisions which determine the extent and the impact of IHT liabilities on that part or proportion which is not exempt. The rules governing the allocation of exemptions in such circumstances are set out in ss 36–42. This area has been the subject of judicial consideration in *Re Benham's Will Trusts* [1995] STC 210 and *Re Ratcliffe* [1999] STC 262. (see **2.4:3**)

2.4:2 The present IHT rules and formula

Apart from exempt gifts which can be specific *or* of residue, chargeable gifts would be:

Type (1) *Specific and bearing own tax* (ie subject to IHT). This would cover gifts expressed to bear their own tax (see **2.3** above); for example:

> 'I give [to my son ... a] [legacy of £x] and direct that [the said legacy] shall be subject to the payment of any IHT attributable thereto'.

Note also that a testator cannot place the burden of IHT on to gifts which are exempt transfers to a spouse, a charity, a political party, or for national purposes or public benefit (s 41 applies 'notwithstanding the terms of any disposition').

Type (2) *Specific gift with tax falling on residue* (ie free of IHT). This could be realty and personalty where there is no direction that the asset in question is to bear its own tax.

Type (3) *Residue or a share or fraction thereof.*

For gifts within Type (1) above the value of the gifts is *not* regrossed. The value taken is the *actual* value. This type of gift is therefore generally the simplest method. For gifts within Type (2) these are regrossed. All such gifts are added together and the *total* then regrossed (s 38(3)).

If *only* gifts within Type (2) (free of IHT) are comprised in the estate apart from exempt gifts, then s 38(3) alone applies and these gifts are only grossed up inter se with no further regrossing. However, if there are any chargeable gifts within Type (1) (subject to IHT) and/or Type (3) (residue), then s 38(4) and (5) operate. The formula and the stages are as follows:

(a) Aggregate all gifts within Type (2) as if a separate transfer and gross up for IHT thereon. In examples below £251,000 + IHT £6,000 = £257,000.

(b) Deduct the above, ie £257,000, from total estate £600,000, leaving £343,000. The *balance* is divided between:

  (i) Exempt specific gifts;

  (ii) Exempt residuary gifts;

  (iii) Gifts within Type (1) and Type (3) above.

(c) Add to grossed-up figure under (*a*), ie, the £257,000, the *actual value* of gifts under Type (1) and Type (3) above. This gives a new total of taxable gifts.

(d) Calculate the IHT on new total. This is the *amount* of IHT calculated to this stage. It is notional only.

(e) Make a fraction:

Numerator is the notional amount of IHT

Denominator is the notional new total of taxable gifts

(f) Express above fraction as a %. Gives new *assumed* or estate rate.

(g) Go back to actual value of gifts within Type (2) (free of IHT) and make *second* regross and calculate by new assumed rate. *Second* regrossed figure: note it.

(h) Deduct the *second* figure from *true* total estate and split balance between exempt and the taxable estate.

(i) Now calculate *final estate rate* on taxable estate, gives true IHT payable.

Example

Estate of £600,000 on death in 2001–02.
Specific legacies of:

(a) £201,000 to son;

(b) £20,000 to each of 2 nephews; and

(c) £10,000 to a friend.

None of the specific legacies is to bear its own tax.

Residue to be shared equally between widow (exempt) and daughter (non-exempt).
No chargeable transfers in the previous seven years.

Values must be attributed to the specific legacies in accordance with section 38, and to residue in accordance with section 39. The specific gifts are not the only gifts which are or might be chargeable: the daughter's share of residue is chargeable. This means that the assumptions described in section 38(5) must be used to work out the 'assumed rate' of tax.

(1) Attribute a hypothetical value to the specific gifts as if they were the only chargeable transfers. This means grossing up the legacies of £251,000. After the nil rate band of £242,000, the grossed-up amount would be £257,000.

The hypothetical value attributable to residue is determined accordingly, ie £600,000 – £257,000 = £343,000.

(2) The assumed amount of tax based on the hypothesis in (1) must now be calculated. This is calculated by aggregating the chargeable transfers: £257,000 (the value currently attributed to the chargeable legacies) + £171,500 (the chargeable half of the value currently attributed to residue) – £428,500.

The tax on £428,500 would be (0% × £242,000) + (40% × £186,500) = £74,600. That is the 'assumed amount of tax'. Accordingly, the 'assumed rate' is:

$$\frac{£\ 74,600}{£428,500} = £17.4\%$$

(3) A value is now attributed to the legacies in accordance with section 38(4), by grossing them up at the assumed rate.

$$£251,000 \times \frac{100}{(100 - 17.4)} = \textbf{£303,874}$$

(4) Having attributed a value to the specific gifts, the value of residue can be worked out, ie £600,000 – £303,874 = £296,126. Half of the residue (ie £148,063) is exempt.

(5)   The total chargeable estate is therefore made up of £148,063 (the other, chargeable half of the residue) + £303,874 (the value attributed to specific gifts) = £451,937.

(6)   The tax on the chargeable part of the estate is (0% × £242,000) + (40% × £209,937) = £83,975. This is an effective rate of 18.58%.

Assuming a *Ratcliffe* rather than *Benham* distribution of residue (as to which, see below), and ignoring other administration expenses, the estate would be paid out in the following way:

Son:	£201,000
Other legacies:	£50,000
Widow:	£148,063
Daughter:	£116,962
IHT:	£83,975
	£600,000

2.4:3   Exempt and non-exempt gifts of residue: *Re Benham's Will Trusts* [1995] STC 210 and *Re Ratcliffe* [1999] STC 262

The debate on the position of exempt and non-exempt gifts of residue under a will trust originated from *Re Benham's Will Trust*. The debate concerns the proper construction of the following commonplace type of clause:

'*I give devise and bequeath all my real and personal estate whatsoever and wheresoever not hereby otherwise disposed of unto my Trustees upon trust to sell and convert the same into money with power at their absolute discretion to postpone any such sale and conversion for so long as they shall think fit without being answerable for any loss and after payment thereout of my debts and funeral and testamentary expenses to stand possessed of the residue as to one half part thereof for my children in equal shares absolutely and as to the remainder of my estate upon trust for the following charities . . .*'

Prior to *Re Benham* it was widely assumed that the proper construction of this type of clause was simply that the children receive their share subject to IHT. Thus receiving less than the charities. The alternative construction, that the Testator intended the IHT to be paid and then the residue split was disregarded. This was because it was prohibited by s 41(b) and so even if it was intended it could not be effected.

Re Benham held that there was a third construction which was not prohibited by s 41(b). This third possibility was that the non-exempt beneficiary's share should be grossed up so that after his share bore the IHT, he would receive an equal sum to the exempt beneficiary. This construction results in more IHT being payable.

Despite the fact that *Re Benham* was widely considered to have been wrongly decided, it creates uncertainty for executors required to divide the estate in accordance with the Will, and to pay the correct amount of IHT. This is so even though the CTO made clear that their view was that *Re Benham* was distinguishable on the wording of the Will (see Private Client Business 1996 No 5 p 29). Not least because the view of the CTO was not necessarily the view of the exempt or non-exempt beneficiary.

The decision of the High Court in *Re Ratcliffe* [1999] STC 262 is therefore welcome. Blackburn J held in *Re Ratcliffe* that the proper construction of the commonplace clause is that the non-exempt beneficiaries receive their share subject to IHT and without grossing up. The learned Judge did not follow *Re Benham* holding that it established no principle of law. The result is that although *Re Benham* has not been overruled in the authors' view it has been effectively sidelined.

The moral is to clarify the position in the will or by way of a variation. The *Benham* decision is defeated if wording such as the following is used:

> 'I give the capital and income of my residuary estate to my [wife] and my [son] in [equal] shares and the division into shares shall be treated as made before deduction of IHT payable on my death in respect of my residuary estate.'

The *Benham* decision can apply where the wording is to the following effect:

> ' . . . to my [wife] and my [son] in such shares that after deducting IHT payable on my death in respect of my residuary estate the two shares are equal.'

See also Butterworth's *Wills, Probate and Administration Service* A22.

2.4:4   Planning aspects of ss 36–42

As already indicated in **2.3:2** (last sub para) there can be complicated grossing and also re-grossing results for legacies given free of IHT when the whole or part of residue goes to an exempt beneficiary (say the surviving spouse or charity). It is again emphasised: look at the alternatives to legacies given free of IHT and consider switching to either legacies which are subject to IHT or a share of residue instead. Again, the problem need not exist where there is 100% business/agricultural relief (see **2.3:3**).

The aim of s 38 is that the net effect of 'free of tax' and 'subject to tax' legacies are neutral as to the total amount charged to IHT.

2.5   ANCILLARY ASPECTS OF WILLS

2.5:1   Survivorship and the rule as to commorientes

Definition of the rule

The rule as to commorientes as set out in Law of Property Act 1925, s 184 provides that:

> 'Where . . . two or more persons have died in circumstances rendering it uncertain which of them survived the other or others, such deaths, shall . . . for all purposes affecting the title to property, be presumed to have occurred in order of seniority, and accordingly the younger shall be deemed to have survived the elder'.

Statutory relief

The operation of the rule could give rise to a double or multiple charge for IHT on such deaths (albeit subject to quick succession relief where there was a chargeable transfer—see s 141). The operation of the commorientes rule can, however, be avoided for IHT. Thus s4(2) provides that where it cannot be known which of two or more persons who have died survived the other or others they shall be presumed to have died at the same instant and therefore the estate of the younger is not swollen.

Section 92 covers the different problem of a possible double or multiple charge to IHT on successive deaths (namely deaths which are not or are not treated as being simultaneous but follow within a short period of time and where it is ascertainable which person survived the other even though only for a relatively short time).

Section 92 provides that where under the terms of the will or otherwise property is held for any person on condition that he survives another for a specified period of not more than six months, and another beneficiary becomes entitled to property by reason of the survivorship condition (ie the original beneficiary not having complied with that condition), the IHT payable is the same as if that other beneficiary had taken the property direct, without the intervention of the survivorship condition. That beneficiary is deemed to have become entitled from the beginning of the survivorship period. Therefore, no problems remain as to the treatment of the intermediate income, under s 65 in particular. Section 92 also prevents the question of whether a 'settlement' has been created by the survivorship condition from arising in relation to the disposition (see s 43).

Recommended action

It is for this reason that the survivorship clauses are to be considered (although not necessarily adopted between spouses) in all cases of the grant of an absolute interest as well as of a life interest or an annuity. Such clauses provide that the gift in question only takes effect if the donee survives the testator by a specified period, say, 30 days or three months (ie contingent gift). If the donee does not survive this period, the gift lapses and no further IHT is payable thereon. The suggested period of three months is usually preferable because it represents an average period in practice for obtaining probate.

The important effects of s 92 (subject to complying with the necessary conditions, for example, the six-month period) can be summarised as follows.

(1) The introduction of the survivorship clause in a will should avoid any double charge.

(2) It will be possible to prevent assets coming into a beneficiary's estate (ie the beneficiary who dies shortly after the testator) in circumstances where it is preferred to make the gift to another party and treat the initial gift as a nullity (this will become particularly relevant if various rates of IHT are re-introduced, ie to prevent the bunching effect).

(3) It is now generally immaterial whether the gift during the survivorship period carries the intermediate income or not or whether the intended beneficiary is to benefit absolutely, by way of interest in possession or accumulation and maintenance trust.

As between husband and wife a survivorship condition can prevent use of nil and any lower rates of IHT, and may be inappropriate for inclusion.

> **Example** (against survivorship condition—poorer surviving spouse without the nil rate band)
>
> H and W are married. H made lifetime gifts having used up his nil rate band available on death and leaves an estate of £125,000 to W conditionally on her surviving him by three months. W made no lifetime gifts and has a nil estate. W dies

within two months of H's death and under the terms of H's will the estate devolves to his three children equally. IHT of £50,000 is payable on the £125,000.

Had H not included a survivorship condition (or had the survivorship condition exceeded six months) the estate would have passed to W and from her estate to the children at a nil rate of IHT, ie by arranging for his estate to pass to W and the children inheriting from W not H, the IHT is washed out because of the application of W's nil rate band.

Example (pro survivorship condition using nil rate bands on *both* deaths)

Romeo and Juliet are married and have a joint estate of £300,000 owned in equal shares. Romeo dies on 1 July 2001 and Juliet on 1 August 2001. If Romeo included no survivorship condition in his will the children who inherit on Juliet's death will bear IHT of £27,600, ie on the aggregated, bunched estate of £300,000.

Had Romeo included an appropriate survivorship condition, and his estate of £150,000 had passed direct to the children and likewise on Juliet's death, no IHT would have been payable, a saving of £27,600.

Note, however, the possibilities available in these types of circumstances by entering into deeds of variation—see **2.6** below.

Statutory anomaly

The interaction of The Law of Property Act 1925, s 184 and the Inheritance Tax Act 1984, s 4(2) appears to have the result that, if spouses die simultaneously (eg in an air crash) or in commorientes circumstances where it is not known which spouse survived the other and no survivorship condition applies in those circumstances, no IHT is payable in the estate of the elder on either deaths: see *Taxation* 24 September 1992, p 649. Therefore if, as between spouses, a survivorship condition is otherwise desirable, exclude its operation for simultaneous deaths in the will of the elder. Alternatively, if the commorientes circumstances in fact arise, exclude the survivorship condition by deed of variation. See the excellent article by Mary McCarthey in July/Aug 2000 *Trusts and Estates Tax Journal*.

2.5:2 Annuities

As a general rule a will should not provide for an annuity because:

(a) this can give rise to additional tax liabilities (especially IHT), because of the creation of a 'settlement' thereby;

(b) the important income tax relief on the 'capital element' of a purchase life annuity (ie from an insurance company) will not be available under TA 1988, s 656 (s 657(2)(b)); s 657(2)(a) may also mean that when trustees exercise a discretion to resort to capital to make up income payment, s 656 relief will not apply; and

(c) payments out of capital can become taxable as income by reason of the regularity of the payments—see *Brodie's Will Trustees v IRC* (1933) 17 TC 432 and *Cunard's Trustees v IRC* [1946] 1 All ER 159, 27 TC 122 although this doctrine has become less applicable since the decision of *Stevenson v Wishart* [1987] STC 266. The Court of Appeal held that if the trustees in exercise of their power over capital chose to make regular payments out of capital to a capital beneficiary rather than release a single sum of a large amount, that did not create an income interest. Apart from their recurrence there was on the facts nothing to indicate that the payments were of an income nature (*Stevenson v Wishart*). The annuity problems could also be avoided by advancing funds to a beneficiary under the Trustee Act 1925, s 32 even though instead of a single advance, payments are made by instalments.

As an alternative it is better to give a lump sum to the individual or even a third party upon terms than an annuity be purchased out of that lump sum.

An annuity left to a widow may be advantageous, see **2.2:2**(3) above.

2.5:3 Discretionary trusts in wills I: 2 years s 144 trusts

Where an individual demonstrates a lack of decision over the ultimate destination of his estate (perhaps because the relative needs of possible beneficiaries are in the process of rapid change), so that it is desired to postpone a choice until the very last moment, advantage can be taken of s 144. These provisions allow distributions to be made within two years of the death without any charge to IHT out of assets settled on discretionary trusts by the will. In the appropriate circumstances, therefore, the individual could make a will settling his estate (or part of it) on discretionary trusts, specifying in the definition of beneficiaries the whole range of persons who might remotely be considered as candidates for his bounty. The trustees could then, within two years of the death, either act on any informal letter or memorandum of wishes left behind by the testator in the choice of beneficiaries and the amount to be appropriated to the chosen beneficiaries; or alternatively, make the decision themselves in the light of the circumstances. The main *advantages* of a s 144 discretionary will trust are:

(a) Flexibility: the allocation of assets is left to the wide discretion of the trustees, eg appointment to spouse who then makes PETs. Contrast the situation of a variation or disclaimer under s 142 where the re-allocation of assets is left to the whim of the person benefiting under the will or intestacy. In any case the future viability of s 142 is in doubt (see **2.1:2**(2))—although this is also the case for s 144.

(b) A s 142 variation is often hampered by the fact that a minor beneficiary's interest cannot, in any way be reduced without the court's consent. Under a s 144 discretionary trust, as all beneficiaries merely have a hope of benefiting, no such obstacle exists.

(c) Under s 92 a survivorship condition has to be limited to six months (see **2.5:1** above). A s 144 discretionary trust in effect gives a longer period, ie two years, for achieving a similar result.

(d) Income tax: if a parent effects a s 142 variation in favour of his minor, unmarried children, he will be regarded as the settlor for income tax purposes under TA 1988, s 660B. To avoid s 660B(2) the trustees should not make any payment to the child until he is no longer a minor (ie 18 years) or no longer unmarried, if earlier. This problem does not exist for a s 144 discretionary trust.

(e) Some testators object to the fact that their bequests can be varied after death under s 142. Under a s 144 discretionary trust as the beneficiaries merely have a hope of benefiting, a s 142 variation is not possible.

(f) Stamp duty: distributions out of a s 144 discretionary trust are exempt from stamp duty and no adjudication requirement, provided the appropriate certificate is given—see Stamp Duty (Exempt Instruments) Regulations 1987 SI 1987/516.

There are, however, some *disadvantages* to a s 144 discretionary trust, namely:

(a) Cash flow: IHT is payable in respect of the creation of the trust fund (ie on the estate at death) and would usually have to be reclaimed if appropriated to an exempt party, eg surviving spouse.

(b) Under s 142 a variation can be made in favour of any person. Under s 144 the beneficiaries are restricted even though the class may be widely defined, including a power to add beneficiaries.

(c) Discretionary trusts are charged to income tax at the rate applicable to trusts under s 686 (currently 34%).

(d) Property transferred within three months of the deceased's death to an interest in possession trust for the benefit of the deceased's spouse is outside the ambit of s 144. In *Frankland v IRC* [1996] STC 735 it was held that for an event to be relevant within s 144(1)(a) it had to be an event on which, apart from s 144, tax would have been chargeable. In the light of s 65(4), the relevant event could not happen within three months of the deceased's death. Thus s 144(2) will not operate to treat the deceased's will as having provided that his property be held on an interest in possession will trust. See also *Loveday dec'd v IRC* [1997] STC (SCD) 321.

(e) Distributions/disposals within the two-year period to any beneficiary will not be eligible to the CGT holdover relief under TCGA 1992, s 260 because such distributions are exempt from IHT. Contrast: distributions by personal representatives to legatees which are exempt from CGT.

In the case of (d) and (e) careful consideration must be given to allowing the respective periods of three months and two years to elapse. In respect of (e) beware of those wills which have been drafted to the effect that there is an automatic termination shortly prior to the two-year period. Such wills need to be reviewed and the automatic termination abandoned to allow for the necessary flexibility.

2.5:4 Discretionary trusts in wills II: using the nil rate band

Under this method the will establishes a nil rate band discretionary trust from which distributions can be made to the surviving spouse in case of need. Assume that a husband and wife each have an estate of £500,000; and that the husband dies first wishing his widow to be the primary beneficiary. Under a commonly used method the husband could give his widow his £500,000 estate (absolutely or by way of life interest) ensuring that no IHT was payable on his death. On her death, however, having regard to the bunching effect IHT would be payable on an estate of £1,000,000 (currently £303,200 of IHT). A more sophisticated alternative advocated here is for the husband to give his widow only £258,000 and settle the remaining £242,000 (constituting the nil rate band) on discretionary trusts, with informal directions to the trustees to treat the widow as the principal beneficiary. So, if she was in need, she could have a capital distribution or, usually, more appropriately, a loan, which should be a deduction from her estate on her death (but watch FA 1986 s 103 especially if there had been lifetime gifts from her to her husband); or she could receive income distributions. In this latter case the IHT at current rates is reduced to £206,400 (ie on the widow's estate of £758,000) and with the discretionary trust fund constituting a nil rate band. Thus there is an IHT saving under this alternative of £96,800 (£303,200 – £206,400).

This is regarded as one of the most effective—yet simple—IHT savings that can be introduced in a will. Moreover, if the use of variations became more restricted that saving of £96,800 by use of the mini-discretionary trust would no longer be a mere alternative to a variation.

An additional advantage is that, especially after the death of the surviving spouse, further tax benefits can be obtained by skipping a generation, eg by making distributions or appointments in favour of grandchildren out of the discretionary trust.

Ensure that in lifetime (nor merely under the Will), the husband and wife each have sufficient assets to take advantage of their respective nil rate bands (one never knows who will die first!). This may require lifetime severance of a joint tenancy so that property is held as tenants-in-common.

An important question is whether an upper limit should be placed on such discretionary trusts in case the nil rate band is increased substantially; and/or because business/agricultural relief applies at 100%/50%. The answer is probably not, if the surviving spouse is a discretionary beneficiary. The reason is that she/he can benefit from income or capital distributions within two years of death where s 144 applies. If the trust fund is a nil rate band then (not taking into account BPR/APR relief at 100%/50% rate because it is not available for calculating the effective rate until first 10-year anniversary: s 68(5)), there is no IHT liability for any distributions before the first 10-year anniversary. However obtain specific instructions when making the Will and do not make distributions to the widow(er) within 3 months of the death, see **2.5:3** above.

NB ensure that there will be some assets in the residuary estate to avoid abatement of the nil rate band.

The surviving spouse can be included in the class of beneficiaries even though he/she is not intended to benefit absolutely. Either include virtually the entire estate in the discretionary trust and distribute to the surviving spouse before the end of the 2-year period relying upon s 144, or before the 10-year period if the trust is a nil rate band discretionary trust. Alternatively let the discretionary trust consist of business/agricultural assets only and transfer the residue to the surviving spouse. (The s 39A rateable apportionment will not then apply because specific gifts of such assets are involved). But do not distribute to a surviving spouse in the first three months following the other spouse's death (see s 65(4) referred to above) unless a nil rate band discretionary trust exists and you are not relying on surviving spouse exemption applying.

There are, however, seven danger areas to consider.

(i) Related settlements (s 62—trusts having same commencement dates and same settlor). The value of the other property settled by the will (ie the related settlement(s)) could form part of the cumulative total of transfers to which the 10-yearly charges on the discretionary testamentary trust will apply.

(ii) If the discretionary trust continues for more than 10 years, IHT 10-year anniversary and interim charges may arise ss 64–69.

(iii) CGT transfers from a trust do not obtain the s 62(4) TCGA relief for testamentary dispositions.

(iv) IHT distributions to a widow(er) within 3 months do not give rise to an exit charge (see s 65(4) IHTA and **2.5:3**.

(v) No CGT holdover relief in the 2-year period from death (if s 144 applies).

(vi) Where assets are left to a beneficiary absolutely or by way of a life interest, CGT exemption and market value uplift apply (subject to the restriction in TCGA, s 74 in respect of a life interest where holdover relief has been claimed on creating the trust).

(vii) From 6 April 1999 discretionary trusts will pay income tax usually at 43% (or more) on dividends, eg on quoted shares. This results from the abolition of the tax credit when trustees distribute to beneficiaries with this additional tax based on their rates: ie trustees will no longer be permitted to include the tax credit on the dividend when calculating the tax they must pay; they cannot frank distributions to beneficiaries, therefore additional liability accrues to the trustees and the beneficiaries will receive less from the dividend distributions. Trustees may need to consider reorganising their investment policies. See the excellent article on this subject by Rupert Baldry in *Trusts and Estates Tax Journal* No 15 (April 2001 p 13).

2.5:5 Implied or precatory trusts (s 143)

It has long proved convenient for testators to give assets such as chattels to the personal representatives or other individuals 'in full confidence, but without imposing a binding legal trust or obligation, that they will distribute the same amongst such members of my family living at my death as they shall think fit'. If this informal trust/request is carried out within two years of the testator's death, no additional IHT is payable beyond what was due in respect of the testator's estate.

Section 143 is particularly useful for items of personal use and ornament (for example jewellery), paintings, antiques, etc, thereby avoiding specific mention in the will itself, and also gifts of money (see **2.5:8**).

This benevolent provision came under threat in the 1989 Finance Bill but the proposals were withdrawn: see **2.1:2**(2). These arrangements were upheld in the case of *Re Beatty* [1990] 1 WLR 1503 against a claim by the residuary beneficiaries that the gift was void for uncertainty, notwithstanding the very wide nature of the class of intended beneficiaries and the wide power of delegation. The case also emphasises the importance of the gift to the 'trustees' being a beneficial one thereby coming within the requirements of s 143. In this context it may become useful to distinguish these precatory arrangements, which are non-binding, from secret trusts which are indeed binding and which therefore can operate without any need for s 143. Under a secret trust the donee named in the will is bound in equity to transfer to the true beneficiary on whose behalf he acts as trustee only; so that the IHT transfer is direct from the testator to the true beneficiary. There is no transfer for IHT when the trustee discharges the trust by delivering the property to the beneficiary.

A further distinction should be noted within secret trusts themselves. On the one hand there is the *fully secret trust* where the testator in his will gives property to X absolutely, with no indication in the will that X does anything but take the property beneficially; but where either before or after making the will the testator tells X that he is to hold the property so given for Y. X can be compelled in equity to carry out the trust because, either expressly or by silence, he has induced the testator to make the gift or, if already made, not to revoke it. However, if X hears about the trust only after the death, he cannot be compelled, and is entitled to keep the property for himself. Fully secret trusts are normally used where complete confidentiality is required; as when the testator leaves a legacy to his brother, which excites no interest, but where the brother is obliged to pay it over to the testator's natural son, of whom few people know.

There is then the *half secret trust*, where the testator gives property in his will to X with an express direction in the will itself that X is to hold the property on trust, but without disclosing the terms of the trust. Thus the testator might leave a sum of money to X 'on the trusts I have already communicated to him'. The testator might, for instance, want to leave the sum between nephews and nieces but in unequal shares, or cutting one out, and not want the world to know. If the trust is notified to X before or at the time the will is made, and the will indicates the trust nature of the gift, X must carry it out; but it is doubtful whether a half secret trust can be notified after the execution of the will, because the testator would be reserving to himself a power to make testamentary dispositions without due formalities.

In some circumstances it may be preferable, even with chattels, to utilise a secret trust rather than a mere non-binding request.

2.5:6   The matrimonial home

Proposal 1: The matrimonial home may be an appropriate asset to use when considering use of the nil rate band by both spouses, either by placing it into the sole name of one spouse or into joint names depending upon circumstances. As regards the holding of land and building in joint names, there are two alternatives, namely a holding as 'joint tenants' and as 'tenants in common'. For the former method, the survivor takes absolutely and by operation of law. Hence it is impossible to make testamentary or lifetime dispositions to third parties. By contrast in the case of a tenancy in common, disposals of one spouse's shares during lifetime or by will are possible, and hence this method of holding is generally to be recommended as affording greater flexibility. In particular as a tenant in common of part, a widow, as co-owner, would be entitled to occupy the whole. On her death, moreover, her share would be eligible for a discount of between 5% to 15%. Such a discount is not available (whether as a joint tenancy or tenancy in common) while husband and wife are both alive having regard to the related property provisions (s 161). The discount does apply, however, for the survivor's interest. See also the Land Tribunal decision in *Wight v IRC* (1982) 264 Estates Gazette 935.

There is, however, a possible danger area, namely for deaths before 1 January 1997 that the other co-owner(s) may be able to force a sale as the house would be held on a trust for sale. For deaths after 1 January 1997 a new regime applies under the TLATA 1996 which means there is no longer a duty to sell, and the trustees have a statutory power to postpone the sale (see **2.0** and **Chapter 3**)

In cases where the property is in fact held as joint tenants, but in which it would be preferable for it to be held as tenants in common, it is a relatively simple matter to 'sever' the joint tenancy to make it into a tenancy in common.

If the testator owns the entire home and wishes to leave the bulk to a chargeable party, eg his son, yet enable his widow to occupy without retaining a life interest in the whole chargeable on her death, consider giving the widow, say, a 25% tenant in common share, with 75% to her son. The widow would then be able to occupy the whole by virtue of her 25% tenancy in common. There must not be a bar against son occupying as co-owner, as such bar would give the widow an interest in possession in whole.

A recommended route:

This situation can satisfactorily be achieved by use of a life interest in favour of the surviving spouse (assume husband/testator owns the home leaving a widow).

The relevant steps would include the following:

– the testator's will establishes a life interest of the whole home in favour of the widow (see also **2.1:2** and **2.1:3** above);
– after the testator's death the trustees (of whom the widow could possibly be one—but see below) appoint, say, 75% of the life interest (ie income entitlement) in favour of the children, the trust remaining subject to the wide overriding powers of appointment;
– the widow remains in occupation, although not exclusively, ie the children must not be barred from occupying the home as well if they wish. (A professional trustee may wish to be armed with an indemnity from the children.)

The advantages of this approach include:

– inter-spouse exemption on husband's death—s 18;
– the termination of the widow's full life interest in whole or part, eg 75%, is a PET (ie she must survive seven years to avoid IHT);
– there is no GWR by the widow because as a co-owner the widow is by law entitled to occupy the whole and because the termination is not 'a disposal by way of gift' under FA 1986, s 102 (for this reason it is somewhat safer if the widow is not a trustee).
– if the part (75% in this example) is owned by a *discretionary trust* there is an argument that the widow should not be treated as having an interest in possession in it. Although, if on the facts she is given exclusive rights of occupation she probably will have an interest in possession (see SP10/79 and *Lloyd's Private Banking* etc, see **2.1:1**).
– CGT. If the property is sold at any time during the widow's lifetime, full CGT private residence exemption should be available by virtue of TCGA 1992, s 225—as the widow is 'entitled to occupy it under the terms of the settlement'.

If an individual, eg a widow, is given any right to occupy the matrimonial home in its entirety, this will normally constitute an 'interest in possession' so that the same IHT will be payable as if the house had been given outright unless the interest terminates more than seven years before such individual's death (ie a PET). To avoid this any such occupation must be informal eg by way of a non-enforceable licence or permission (there should be no gift with reservation problem, because the donor is the deceased who cannot by definition have reserved a benefit). See *Sansom v Peay* [1976] 3 All ER 375 and IR Press Release 15/8/1979—SP 10/1979.

Sufficient security of tenure is likely to exist in practice if the surviving spouse is an executor or executrix of the will.

Proposal 2: Grant of life interest by beneficiary under will to widow(er).

Consider the following possibilities:

Testator leaves home (or share of it) and possibly other assets, eg shares of residue to X, eg his son ...

Son decides to grant his widowed mother a life interest within, say, three months after testator's death.

On widow's death, assuming X survives, no IHT because of the reverter to settlor exemption—s 54(1), (2) and (3). There should be no CGT because on the widow's death the main residence exemption applies—TCGA 1992, s 225.

Proposal 3: If the home is the main asset in the estate of the first spouse to die— say the husband, he could gift the nil rate band in his will to chargeable parties by use of a mini-discretionary trust (see **2.5.4**). The residue (ie in particular the home) is left to the widow. The nil rate band gift would be satisfied by a charge on the property in favour of the trustees of the mini-discretionary trust. That charge could be on favourable terms (under the will itself) for the widow, eg free of interest and deferred as to payment of the capital, albeit preferably, payable on demand by the trustees, and notwithstanding that one of the trustees is the beneficiary of the home. The charge should then be a deduction from the widow's estate on her death and she would have had use and occupation meanwhile.

To this there could be an exception, namely if the widow, as above, had during her husband's lifetime made substantial gifts to him, the loan will not be deductible from the widow's estate to the extent that the loan was property derived from the deceased—the widow (FA 1986, s 103).

Proposal 4: The trustees do not have power to entitle the surviving spouse to occupy because this creates an interest in possession. They do, however, have power and do grant a monthly tenancy at nominal rent. Even though this does create an interest in possession, it will have a low value on the surviving spouse's death.

Note: If a share in a home is left to a discretionary trust, it is inadvisable to make the widow(er) a beneficiary, since the Revenue may regard it as an interest in possession entitlement or even permit her to occupy without being a specific beneficiary.

Proposal 5: The husband leaves his half share in the house to his children under his will. On his death the surviving spouse purchases at full market value her husband's half from the children. The husband could give his spouse a market-value option in the will to ensure the spouse can purchase the share. Alternatively, the half share could be given to the trustees of a will trust (if it is thought that the children will not consent). This arrangement will have a stamp duty cost.

Disclaimer by surviving spouse

To enable a surviving spouse to be in a position to disclaim his/her interest in the home effectively for IHT (ie not having received any benefit—see **2.6:6** below), consider making a gift of the home conditional on surviving the testator for the maximum period ie six months from the testator's death— s 92.

Finally, a proposal that does *not* work. The deceased leaves assets to his son who by a variation grants a life interest for 6 months to the deceased's widow, remainder to the son's children absolutely. The intention is that on the deceased's death the surviving spouse exemption applies and the termination of the widow's life interest would constitute a PET. The trap is that the variation is ineffective if the life interest terminates within 2 years of the deceased's death (s 142(4)). Avoid the trap by ensuring the life interest does not terminate within 2 years of the deceased's death.

2.5:7 Reversionary interests and their re-settlement

A testator may have given a life interest to his widow with remainder to his children. Where any of the children wish to assign their interests in remainder (reversion) to their own children, this can be done without CGT (providing the disposal is to a UK resident) because a disposal of an interest in settled property is exempt where the trust continues—TCGA 1992, s 76 (s 76(1A) and (1B) should not apply here if the trust has always been UK-resident). For IHT the gift of the reversion is exempt as 'excluded property.' Once the life tenant has died it will, of course, be too late to effect this useful estate planning (although there *may* be limited possibilities of disclaiming the interest, and see **2.6:6**(3)). If the assignor of the reversion retained an interest eg as a discretionary beneficiary, once the reversion vests in possession, the value of the trust fund will become part of his estate again because he has reserved a benefit.

As CGT holdover relief is now severly restricted this suggestion is all the more important, see TCGA 1992, ss 165 and 260.

2.5:8 Avoiding the income tax surcharge under TA 1988, s 686 for pecuniary legatees and residuary beneficiaries; and obtaining tax credits

A problem arises where there is a minor beneficiary entitled to a gift contingently on attaining 18 or a later age. As the beneficiary only has a contingent interest in the income before the age of 18 two main disadvantages result. First, up to the age of 18 the trustees must pay the rate applicable to trusts; and secondly there would be no possibility of tax credits for the beneficiary, except insofar as the income is Case III Schedule D income and otherwise within s 687. The solution is to give the beneficiary a vested interest in the income as soon as it arises, with the result that although he has only a contingent interest in the capital, the income will be regarded as his and the income will be taxable in his hands whether or not actually paid to him. However, the sums received by the beneficiary will be grossed up to reflect the basic rate tax paid by the trustees. But consider the IHT danger if beneficiary dies before obtaining a vested interest in capital; this involves termination of an interest in possession and consequent IHT liability (which can presumably be cheaply insured against).

2.5:9   Charity, the will and gift aid

Background and information

Under s 143 a gift by a legatee within two years of the death in compliance with a request by the testator is treated as if the gift had been bequeathed by the testator's will. However in *Harding and Leigh v CIR* [1997] STC (SCD) 321 SpC0140 the trustees who complied with the testator's request could not be treated as legatees because the trustees had exercised fiduciary powers and were not beneficially entitled. Furthermore, under the gift aid provisions of FA 1990, s 25 an individual or a close company is entitled to income tax relief for a donation to charity. Since 1 October 1990, gifts can be made net of basic rate tax and the tax will be reclaimed from the Inland Revenue by the charity. The donor will also be eligible for relief at the higher rate of tax where this applies. The relief cannot apply to gifts by the donor on death.

(1)   Testator gifts £x to beneficiary plus precatory wish for beneficiary to gift to charity (FA 1990, s 25, and s 143)

(2)   After death and within two years, the beneficiary gifts to charity and claims Gift Aid

(3)   Result/Example:
Legacy of £6,000 from say father to son in former's will:
Tax saving
– Testator's charitable gift 40% (s 143) =   £2,400
– Beneficiary's higher rate gift aid relief
   (grossed up at appropriate basic rate = £7,792) =   £1,325
– Charity recovers basic rate on grossed up amount of £7,792 =   £1,792
                                                                            _____
                                                                            £5,517

$$\frac{£5,517}{£6,000} = 91.95\%$$

And charity receives some 30% more (£7,792 – 6,000)

See generally the Revenue leaflet *Gift Aid: A Guide for Donors and Charities*, IR 113.

Notes:

(1)   It may be possible to extend the above suggestion to inter vivos gifts and Gift Aid payment, see *Taxation* 4 June 1992.

(2)   The Revenue may try to use FA 1990, s 25(2)(e) to argue that the requisite condition is not satisfied, namely, that 'either the donor or any person connected with him receives a benefit in consequence of making it [the gift]'. It is considered that this is an incorrect interpretation as the benefit must surely relate to a benefit provided by the charity. Contrast the above proposal where the individuals are merely using recognised exemptions and reliefs. Unfortunately the Special Commissioners upheld the Revenue's view in *St Dunstan's v Major* [1997] STC (SCD) 212. It was held that s 25(2)(e) was not confined to benefits provided by the charity itself.

Moreover when a benefit was received and the permitted limit was exceeded, the gift was disqualified as a qualifying donation, although the donor's assets would still be diminished by the excess of the donation over the benefit. On the facts the residue of the estate was £8,000 more than it would have been had the gift to the charity been made interest taking advantage of s 142. Since the donor was the sole residuary beneficiary of the estate, he had ultimately benefited from the IHT saving. Although the residue had been reduced by the amount of the legacy to the charity less the saving of IHT, the Tribunal held that the benefit of the IHT saving had greatly exceeded the amount of benefit permitted by s 25(2)(e). That benefit had arisen 'in consequence of making [the gift] to the charity by means of the deed of variation'. No such 'benefit' should exist if the beneficiary does not benefit from residue, eg a free of tax legacy; or if the IHT saving is specifically added to the charity's gift.

(3) Instead of using the s 143 precatory trust route, the legatee could achieve the same result by deed of variation under s 142, namely varying the legacy to himself to a legacy to a charity. This was the route taken in *St Dunstan's*. As the variation operates for IHT, but not for income tax, the gift aid advantage should apply. This is because for purposes other than IHT the deed of variation does not alter the deceased's will. This means that the payment to the charity is not made under the will but is a payment of a sum of money under s 25(2)(a) by the legatee who has bound himself to make such payment to the charity. The CTO are, however, likely to resist the variation if there had been an arrangement/agreement between the testator and the beneficiary (contrast the precatory trust route).

2.5:10 Personal representatives

Residence

The residence of personal representatives follows that of the deceased for CGT. Therefore if the deceased was non-resident, and assets of the estate increase sharply after death, the executors should sell the assets, ie free of CGT (TCGA 1992, s 2) and distribute the proceeds of sale to the beneficiaries. By contrast if the assets have fallen in value following the death, the executors should appropriate the assets in specie to the beneficiaries, so that on a sale, the beneficiaries can incur a CGT loss.

Disposal of an interest in an estate before completion of the administration

During this period (ie during the administration), the residuary legatee merely has the right to require the personal representatives to administer the estate in accordance with the terms of the will. That right is a mere chose in action which, it appears, has no base value for CGT. A residuary legatee should therefore wait for the personal representatives to complete the administration or until they assent the asset to him. That assent is exempt from CGT, but with the advantage of the testator's date of death market value uplift. If the legatee disposes of the asset as a chose in action, he is likely to incur a substantial CGT liability unnecessarily, namely when he subsequently disposes of it.

2.6 VARIATIONS AND DISCLAIMERS—POST-DEATH PLANNING (s 142)

2.6:1 Variations and disclaimers—General:

From the taxpayer's point of view s 142 has been (and will continue for some time at least to be) one of the most useful and popular sections in the IHT legislation, because it allows a two-year breathing space in which to re-write the provisions of the deceased's will or the passing of property on intestacy. It is indeed useful, but it needs approaching with care. There are hidden snags and anti-avoidance legislation may be introduced in future finance bills.

This section operates where:

(a) within a period of two years after the individual's death

(b) the destination of any of the assets of his estate including excluded property but not including assets charged under the reservation of benefit rules or settled property in which he had an interest in possession

(c) passing by will, intestacy or 'otherwise'

(d) is varied/altered or the benefits disclaimed by an instrument in writing made by one or more of the original beneficiary(ies); and

(e) (except in the case of disclaimer) an election is made within six months of the variation.

(The Revenue have no discretion to extend the two-year period).

The section has effect as if the variation had been effected by the deceased or, as the case may be, the disclaimed benefit had never been conferred.

The Revenue set out their current practice in relation to variation of inheritances in RI 101 (February 1995). The main rules are that:

(1) the variation must be made in a written instrument;

(2) it must be made within two years of the relevant death;

(3) all those affected must give written notice ('an election') to the Board of Inland Revenue within six months of the date of the instrument (or such longer time as the Board may allow); and

(4) where the variation means that additional IHT is payable the personal representatives of the deceased must sign the election.

In the Revenue's view the automatic inheritance by survivorship by the surviving joint owner of jointly held assets are within the s 142 rules (RI 127 (October 1995)) because of the words 'or otherwise' in s 142(1)(a).

Intestacy arrangements can be subject to a variation by, in effect, incorporating a deemed will.

2.6:2 Multiple variations

There have been some cases in which a number of instruments of variation have been executed in relation to the same will or intestacy. The Revenue emphasise that these cases must be considered on their precise facts, but in broad terms their views will be as follows:

'(i) an election which is validly made is irrevocable;
(ii) an instrument will not fall within s 142 if it further redirects any item or any part of an item that has already been redirected under an earlier instrument; and
(iii) to avoid any uncertainty, variations covering a number of items should ideally be made in one instrument'.
Law Society Gazette, 22 May 1985, p 1454.

Following the decision in *Russell v IRC* [1988] STC 195 beware of trying to take two bites of the cherry. The case decided that once a deed of variation had been entered into, a further purported redirection to be treated as made by the deceased was not valid in respect of the assets in question, namely further redirections did not have this retrospective effect. Contrast this with the decision in *Lake v Lake* [1989] STC 865. In that case as the court was completely satisfied that the common intention of the parties when executing the first deed of variation had been that the assets specifically bequeathed should bear their own tax even though that deed referred to bequests being 'free of tax', an order for rectification of the first deed was accordingly made.

Reference should also be made to *Matthews v Martin* [1991] STI 418, where it was discovered that a deed of variation contained errors, but the discovery was not made until after the two-year period. The Revenue took the view that a deed of rectification would not be effective since the corrections would take effect only from the date of rectification. However, rectification by an order of the court would mean the original deed was varied as from the original execution date. The High Court approved and the application to vary the original deed was accepted and the order made. In the case of *Schnieder v Mills* [1993] STC 430 rectification was granted of a nonsensical clause whereby the intermediate income, as clearly intended, covered only the period from death to the date of the deed of variation, not for an indefinite period. See also *Racal Group Services Ltd v Ashmore* [1994] STC 416 on rectification.

A two-bite situation in practice:

(a) Execute a s 142 variation of certain assets into a s 144 two-year discretionary trust.

(b) The assets can then be redirected out of the discretionary trust without further IHT within the two-year period, (or up to ten years if the assets are within the nil rate band). See also **2.5:3**.

2.6:3 The variation can cover a wide range of circumstances including:

– divesting assets from a wealthy high IHT rate individual to the next generation (particularly to enable the nil rate band to be used);
– a life tenant releasing his interest in one part of the capital to the remainderman, and the remainderman releasing the other part to the life tenant absolutely;
– a redirection of the beneficial interest under will (for example a widow might renounce a life interest);
– converting 'tax free' legacies into 'subject to tax' legacies adjusted appropriately etc;
– Assume X dies leaving his entire estate worth, say, £300,000 to his widow,

and that within eighteen months of his death the value of his estate increases to, say, £500,000. If nothing is done this increase will pass to his widow. Maybe she does not need the extra £200,000. In that case, she might consider (a) entering into a deed of variation under which she takes a legacy of £300,000 with residue going to, say, her children and (b) making an election under s142(2). The value of her deceased husband's estate immediately before death would still be £300,000 and under ss38(1) and 39 all of this £300,000 would be attributed to the exempt specific gift to the widow, with the result that the entire value transferred on death should be exempt and £200,000 should (in the event, namely the increase in value) pass free of IHT to the children. Income tax problems would remain to the extent that if any income had actually been paid to the widow prior to the execution of the deed it would be treated as the widow's income for tax purposes (but this could be dealt with, eg by adjusting the legacy so that the widow was given enough to discharge her income tax liability).

As to further mitigation possibilities see **Appendix 6** items **5** and **6**.

Note that by virtue of FA 1995 Sch 18 para 5 this only applies to income actually paid to the donor of the variation not to income retained by the executors and paid to the new beneficiaries under the terms of the variation. Therefore it should now be possible to make a variation retrospective for income tax purposes as well as IHT and CGT, though only to the extent it has not already been distributed to the original beneficiary.

Consider combining this proposal with a transfer of the nil rate band to the children;

– where testator has made gifts in excess of the nil rate band to chargeable parties eg children, these chargeable parties redirect/vary the will in favour of surviving spouse who might subsequently make appropriate PETs. The Revenue are likely to attack such an arrangement under the *Ramsay* doctrine and/or s 268 and/or that the variation is for a consideration in money's worth (s 142(3)). In the latter case the children would have made a PET gift to mother, and mother's transfer would presumably not be a chargeable gift because made without donative intent under a binding obligation;

– extending 'the excluded property' s 48(3) benefit beyond a single generation where testator is non-domiciled. Thus the UK domiciled beneficiary varies the will whereby (a) he receives the assets by way of flexible life interest with remainders over (*or* the assets go into a discretionary trust in which the beneficiary can be a beneficiary because the assets are excluded property (s 48)) and (b) ensures the assets are non-UK situated (eg by interposing a foreign company). Result: assets remain excluded property beyond beneficiary's death. If a discretionary trust is used, no ten-year or exit charges should apply as excluded property.

Note that for CGT, the House of Lords has decided that it is the *beneficiary* (not the testator) who is treated as the settlor—CGT exemption therefore does not apply to remitted gains, if the trustees are or are treated as being non-resident, see *Marshall v Kerr* [1994] STC 638, HL. The Revenue confirmed the view that the decision in *Marshall v Kerr* has no application to IHT. Variations which meet all the requirements of s 142 will continue to be treated for IHT purposes as having been made by the deceased (RI 101 (February 1995)). For income tax there is no saving: income is assessable on the UK beneficiary—TA 1988, ss 673 and 739;

– varying the powers of executors, administrators and particularly trustees;

– correcting defects in a will.

2.6:4 Capital gains tax—TCGA 1992, s 62

There is also a power to alter dispositions on death for CGT but a separate election needs to be made to the Inspector of Taxes. Such a CGT election is usually made unless there are assets with losses; where it is wished to use up the small gains exemption; or where non-residents are involved. Consider the effect of *Marshall v Kerr*, see **2.6:3** above.

2.6:5 Elections

In case of a 'variation' (contrast a disclaimer) the election notice procedure applies. In some cases it can be appropriate for IHT not to elect. The effect of not electing is that the beneficiary making the variation is then himself making a transfer of value and this may involve a nil or lower lifetime IHT charge than if the deceased had done this and, as the law stands, after seven years the gift will not be included in the beneficiary's cumulative total. Where the relationship between the testator and the beneficiary is not an exempt one, eg parent to child, an election notice should clearly be made, otherwise there may be a double charge, ie once in the testator's estate and again on the transfer by the beneficiary effecting the variation outside s 142, ie as a gift by the beneficiary. Contrast the situation where there is an exempt disposition by a deceased, eg to his widow. If the widow's cumulative rate of IHT is lower (and bearing in mind that her gift can be a PET or chargeable at one half of the death rate), it will normally be better not to elect and have the gift taxed at her rate and not the deceased's—except where it is wished to use up the deceased's nil rate band. If the deceased's disposition is not exempt, eg to a child, an election notice should be given to avoid a double charge. As to CGT, an election notice should normally be given because of the CGT death exemption and market value uplift. If an effective election is *not* made, the IHT treatment is that of a normal transfer of value; for CGT the variation is a disposal.

2.6:6 Variations and disclaimers contrasted

The following distinctions should be borne in mind:

(1) In the case of a variation, the beneficiary redirects the destination of the disposition as he chooses. In the case of a disclaimer he has no choice and his disclaimer merely accelerates the subsequent interests, eg a disclaimed legacy may fall into residue. To overcome this negative character of disclaimers, the will could provide that in the event of any beneficiary disclaiming an interest, the disclaimed asset should fall into a suitable receptacle such as a flexible life interest trust with wide powers of appointment and advancement or a discretionary trust rather than merely passing to the person entitled in lieu.

(2) On a variation, *part* of a specific bequest or share of residue can be redirected. It is sometimes suggested that with a disclaimer the *whole* interest has to be disclaimed. It was reported, however, in *Tolley's Practical Tax* Vol 10, No 13, 28 June 1989 at p 102, that Bircham & Co had written to the Capital Taxes Office, putting the view that where the will showed an intention on the part of the testator that a donee should be free to disclaim part only of a single gift, then he could do so, and citing *Guthrie v Walrond* (1883) 22 Ch D 573. The Capital Taxes Office replied that disclaimer was a matter of general law. On the footing that *Guthrie*

represented good law, then the writer could confirm that s 142 would apply to a partial disclaimer. In reporting this correspondence, Bircham & Co made an additional point, that partial disclaimer may not be confined to cases where the will serves to authorise it. In cases before the courts donees had frequently sought to disclaim the burdensome part of a gift and keep the beneficial part, and it was not surprising that the courts had found a testamentary intention against this; but if the part subject to disclaimer was not burdensome, and was readily severable, it might be that disclaimer could take place. Support for this view came from the opinion stated by Lord Justice Maugham in *Dewar v IRC* [1935] 2 KB 351 at 370–371, that it would always be possible to disclaim part of a cash legacy. It would appear from this helpful correspondence, therefore, that a more confident approach can be adopted to partial disclaimers (see also **2.1:2**(2)). To put the testator's intentions of permitting and approving part disclaimers beyond any doubt a suitable clause for inclusion in the will could be as follows:

'I the testator HEREBY DECLARE that any gift or other benefit made under or in pursuance of this my Will or any codicil thereto may be disclaimed as to any part of such gift or benefit or as to the whole thereof. I accordingly authorise:—

(a) any person benefiting under this my Will or any codicil thereto; and
(b) my executors and trustees and any person acting in pursuance of their authority, to deal with and administer my estate in respect of any such partial (or full) disclaimer as hereby authorised.

In furtherance of this authorisation (but not otherwise) all gifts of money or share or shares of residue shall be deemed at any relevant time to be gifts of money in separate denominations of £1 each for the purpose of enabling any relevant beneficiary of this my Will or any codicil thereto to disclaim separate parts divisible in £1 units.'

NB. such a clause is included in the Step Standard Provisions (1st Edn).

It would also be possible to leave a beneficiary a series of separate staggered legacies or entitlements, each subject to different, deferred dates, so that the beneficiary could disclaim some of the (separate) legacies/gifts and retain others. Likewise entitlements to shares of residue could accrue at different times, eg 10; 20; 30 months from the testator's death. The beneficiary could also in reliance on the above clause disclaim a part only of one or more of these entitlements. See also para (1) above as to provision of a suitable receptacle for disclaimed interests.

(3) With a variation, it makes no difference that the beneficiary may earlier have received some benefit. In the case of a disclaimer, however, it is a condition that before the disclaimer he has received no benefit. Consider in this connection the use of the survivor provisions in s 92, eg, to enable a surviving spouse to disclaim his or her interest in a home effectively for IHT (ie, not having received any interim benefit), the gift of the home could be conditional on surviving the testator for the maximum period of six months within the section.

(4) A variation can benefit anyone, not merely another beneficiary or a member of the family. In the case of a minor beneficiary his interest can in no way be reduced without the court's consent.

For this reason, in the case of a testator giving a life interest, eg to spouse, the remaindermen should be restricted to the testator's children living at his death and not at the life tenant's death per stirpes (meaning: including his issue if he dies before the life tenant). In the latter case a variation of a testator's will by the remaindermen would be extremely difficult because of the contingent entitlement of future born issue.

2.6:7

Personal representatives can stand in the shoes of a deceased beneficiary who dies before the testator or within two years of the testator's death (see RI 101 (February 1995)). Within two years a recipient of the variation can himself effect a further variation if the original beneficiary elected. (The Revenue may try to challenge on the basis of multiple variation—see above.)

2.6:8   Excluded property etc

Section 142 applies to excluded property, but not to settled property in which the deceased had an interest in possession. Newly granted interests in possession under the will can be disclaimed or assigned. Joint tenancies can be the subject matter of a variation (but not a disclaimer) because the relevant assets are comprised in the deceased's estate (contrast former requirement of being competent to dispose): s 142. As joint tenancies cannot be disclaimed (*Re Schär, Midland Bank Executor and Trustee Co Ltd v Darner* [1951] Ch 280), appropriate assets held jointly, eg property, valuable chattels, should be severed into tenancies in common. Joint tenancies can, however, be an asset subject to a variation. In the appropriate variation, the joint tenancy should be severed so as to be in a better position to claim a valuation discount of between 10% and 15% and thereby increasing the assets within the nil rate band.

2.6:9   No consideration

A variation or disclaimer must not be for a consideration in money or money's worth (unless the consideration is another variation or disclaimer). For example the beneficiary effecting the variation must not be paid their costs or reimbursed income tax liabilities or have mortgage or other liabilities paid off.

2.6:10   Gifts with reservation

Where a testator has died and a beneficiary of the estate effects a variation eg by varying an outright gift to the beneficiary into a discretionary trust, the fact that the beneficiary is capable of benefiting from the varied gift, eg by being included as a discretionary object should not, it seems, constitute a reservation of benefit by the beneficiary because it is the deceased who is deemed to have created the varied gift, eg the discretionary trust.

2.6:11   Deeds of variation s 142 and the 100% [50%] business/agricultural property relief

Consider deeds of variation passing down these assets to non-spouses, eg children, grandchildren, or discretionary trusts (where the surviving spouse can be a beneficiary), rather than to a surviving spouse.

2.6:12 Income tax

This power to vary the destination of the estate operates for IHT and CGT only and not for income tax. In particular, if an adult gives up his share of the estate in favour of his minor unmarried children, he will be regarded as the settlor for income tax purposes (TA 1988, s 660B). Accordingly, to avoid the income from that share being treated as the settlor's, the income would have to be accumulated during the unmarried minority of those children.

Contrast the effect of court orders made under the Inheritance (Provision for Family and Dependants) Act 1975 which *are* retrospective to the date of death even for income tax purposes, unlike s 142 deeds of variation.

Although of great value therefore, in allowing second thoughts within the two-year period, s 142 is no substitute for regularly reviewing the terms of the will in the light of its relevance to all the circumstances during the lifetime of the testator. For example, an individual with such minor children should try to persuade his parent(s) to leave the share direct to the minors (ie to have a grandparent's rather than a parent's trust).

Moreover, any income due to the beneficiary (whether received or not) up to the date of the variation will be that beneficiary's income. Where a deed of variation is to be executed in favour of a charity, it should be done as soon as possible after the death because the charity, unlike the original beneficiary, will be exempt from income tax under TA 1988, s 505.

2.6:13 Stamp duty

Variations are exempt from stamp duty and adjudication requirements, provided the appropriate certificate is given under the Stamp Duty (Exempt Instruments Regulations) 1987 (SI 1987/516). Disclaimers are also exempt from stamp duty.

2.6:14 Tax planning and summary

In considering the effect of the variation:

(a) Take account of the identity of property and the needs of various beneficiaries. For example a widow is likely to need to own the dwellinghouse and liquid assets but may not need illiquid assets such as shares in the family company.

(b) Look at the incidence of IHT in particular as to whether to elect or not, the effect of the seven-year cumulation provisions and lifetime as opposed to death rates if there is no election—plus opportunities available for lifetime PETs. As a general rule for redirections by an exempt party under a will only elect in order to take advantage of nil rate band. If the original gift is to a chargeable party eg a child of deceased, do elect, because no extra IHT is involved. If extra IHT is involved consider likely interest charge. Beware of a further trap. If deceased dies with a free estate plus a life interest in assets, if he leaves the free estate to an exempt party, there is no aggregation with the capital supporting the life interest. However, if there is a variation so that the free estate is left to a chargeable party, extra IHT is payable on the death because of aggregation with the capital supporting the life interest. Following the Inland Revenue statement of 21 March 1990 (see *Law Society Gazette*, 9 May 1990, p 14) it appears that the aggregation will not normally apply to new life terminations cases after 21 March 1990.

(c) Consider allocating property entitled to business or agricultural reliefs to non-exempt beneficiaries.

Note that the former quirk advantage whereby a widow(er) is left a legacy which was allocated to business or agricultural assets has been countered (see FA 1986, s 105 (now IHTA 1984, s 39A); see **2.3:3** above).

(d) Try to allocate appreciating assets to younger individuals and depreciating assets to older individuals.

(e) Consider the cost involved including additional IHT (and interest thereon and income tax).

(f) Bear in mind that a deed of variation or disclaimer is not a substitute for IHT lifetime planning, particularly in the current voluntary PET era which may be relatively short-lived and may not survive now that a Labour government is in office.

Note also the likelihood of future restrictions on variations and similar arrangements by amending legislation as referred to in **2.1:2**(2) above, and under the re-elected Labour government.

2.7   GENERAL SUMMARY

This chapter shows how much can be achieved to preserve estates by the careful preparation of the will (including provision for disclaimers), by taking steps on variation of the will if need be, and how to prepare for the possible closing of that door. There is a need in current circumstances to prepare wills with the utmost flexibility, and still review them on a regular basis to keep them in maximum effectiveness, thereby averting the need for variations and disclaimers. In this context, the flexible life interest will as at **2.1:2** in favour of the spouse may be of particular relevance. In addition aim at 'dying tidily'—see the personal data sheet in **Appendix 7**.

2.7:1

A note on intestacy

The Law Reform (Succession) Act 1995 provides, in respect of deaths on or after 1st January 1996, that:

– If the widow(er) does not survive the intestate by 28 days, the intestacy rules apply as if such widow(er) had not survived the intestate. This will result in the widow(er)'s family not benefiting directly and also ensuring that the intestate's estate benefits from the IHT nil rate band as well as the widow-(er)'s.
– As regards issue entitled on an intestacy or partial intestacy under a will, such issue no longer need to bring into account lifetime gifts from the intestate.

Chapter 3

Husband and Wife

3.0 INTRODUCTION

This chapter deals with five aspects of estate planning for husbands and wives:

(1) the IHT exemption: general aspects;

(2) comparative estates of husband and wife and use of nil rate band;

(3) channelling of gifts and associated operations;

(4) matrimonial home and joint ownership;

(5) joint bank accounts.

3.1 THE IHT EXEMPTION: GENERAL ASPECTS

3.1:1 Importance

The inter-spouse exemption in s 18 is one of the cornerstones of IHT planning, and is referred to throughout this book. A fundamental aspect of IHT is that liability can be deferred until the death of the surviving spouse (unlike the old ED regime where duty was payable on the *first* death). Transfers between husband and wife whether during lifetime or by will are generally exempt from IHT subject to the domicile aspect dealt with in **3.1:3**. They each have their separate estates and availability of the nil rate band. Unlike CGT there is no requirement that the spouses are living together. Although 'spouse' is not specifically defined 'common law' spouses are not currently covered. On divorce, as opposed to separation, the exemption ceases to apply but relief is likely to be available under s 11: the topic (including court orders) is discussed at **7.12**.

Under s 18 it is only necessary to show that the value transferred by the one spouse is *attributable* to property which has become the property of the transferee spouse; so that it is not a requirement for exemption that the consequential loss to the transferor spouse must be exactly matched by the increase to the estate of the transferee spouse. This should normally give complete exemption even in cases where before a transfer the transferor spouse had control of say a family company (whether in his own right or as related property) and after the transfer he has not.

3.1:2

The exemption also applies where one spouse settles assets in trust for the other spouse by way of interest in possession. However the exemption is not usually available in the case of a discretionary trust where the trustees appoint to a beneficiary who is the spouse of the settlor (see **3.1:8** and **4.7:1**). Spouse exemption would still be available if the discretionary trust in question was a will trust and the distribution made later than three months but within two years of death. In this situation s 144 would apply. Note the trap that if the distribution is made within three months of death the exemption will not apply (*Frankland v IRC* [1996] STC 735 and *Harding v IRC* [1997] STC (SCD) 321) (see **2.5:3**).

3.1:3   Non-domicile aspect

If immediately before the transfer, the transferor but not the transferor's spouse is domiciled in the UK, the exemption is limited by s 18(2) to a maximum of £55,000 (the £55,000 is a cumulative figure taking into account any previous transfers). This is a *separate* fixed exemption (not subject to indexation under s 8) and does not reduce the UK spouse's nil rate band. It should be borne in mind in considering this £55,000 exemption that any gifts in excess of the exemption figure nevertheless constitute PETs. Moreover, the foreign domiciled spouse is in a position to make gifts of excluded property (**1.4:2**) outside the IHT regime. However here some care should be taken, for if excluded property is gifted to a UK domicilary its exempt status will, of course, be lost.

The various combinations of circumstances are summarised in the table below. Notice that the restricted exemption *only* applies where the transferee spouse is domiciled abroad and transferor spouse is domiciled in the UK. The widened definition of deemed domicile in s 267 (see **10.2:1**) applies in this context and therefore the transferee spouse, who might be non-domiciled for general purposes but is UK domiciled for IHT purposes, has the full exemption available. For example a change of domicile on emigration within the previous three years will not prevent the full exemption from applying.

Domicile of transferor spouse	Domicile of transferee spouse	Full s 18 exemption	Restricted exemption (£55,000)
UK	UK	Yes	–
UK	Abroad	–	Yes
Abroad	UK	Yes	–
Abroad	Abroad	Yes	–

Note: restriction *only* applies in the second case (although the excess is treated as a PET). Therefore where spouses both have the *same* domicile (wherever it may be), the full unrestricted exemption is available. Note a spouse *can* acquire a domicile separate from the other spouse (see **10.1:2**).

3.1:4   Conditions

The inter-spouse exemption is subject to certain conditions set out in ss 18 and 56 namely:

(1) The transfer or disposition must not take effect (presumably in possession) after any period, or when a prior interest terminates. For example, if a husband gives a life interest, say, to his brother and the remainder after such life interest to his wife, the exemption will not apply. If the gift were the other way round, however, this restriction would not apply. Further, it is provided that the exemption is not lost by reason only that the property is given to a spouse conditionally on surviving the other spouse for a specified period (s 18(3)(a)). This has particular relevance in the context of the survivorship clauses although they are in fact restricted to a six-month period (see s 92).

(2) The transfer or other disposition must not depend on a condition which is not satisfied within twelve months after the transfer (s 18(3)(b)). It is thought that if it is possible but not certain that the condition will be satisfied within twelve months, a 'wait and see' rule should be applied. This second rule would operate in respect of a condition that the surviving spouse acquires an asset for a third party, which is never in fact acquired.

If property is left to a person (whether surviving spouse or another) subject to a *condition* that the recipient must 'give' certain of his or her own property to another, it seems that this latter transfer is nevertheless a gift and not excluded by virtue of s 10. Although the 'transferee' does not intend to make a gratuitous disposition, as the *first* 'giver' did so intend, it is likely that both transfers are gifts having regard to the phrase 'a transaction intended' within s 10. Accordingly, to comply with the condition in s 18(3)(b) as between spouses the condition of making the second gift should not exceed the twelve-month period.

(3) The inter-spouse exemption does not apply to property given in consideration of the transfer of a reversionary interest, if that reversionary interest does not then form part of the recipient's estate (under s 55) because he has an interest in possession or future interest in the same settled property (see s 56(1)). This provision, intended to counter certain IHT avoidance techniques associated with dealings with settled interests, is of little practical planning effect, other than as a trap to avoid in considering the handling of settlements.

(4) Where a person acquires a reversionary interest in any settled property for a consideration in money or money's worth, the inter-spouse exemption does not apply on the termination of the prior interest (assuming, for instance, it was held by his wife) when the settled property passes to him as the new reversioner (s 56(2)).

3.1:5 Liability of transferee spouse

Section 203 provides that when a transferor has made a transfer of value to his spouse that spouse (to an amount equal to the value of such property at the time of its transfer) is liable for any IHT for which the transferor is liable, in respect of other transfers of value. This is designed to cover the case where the transferor might wish to avoid liability to IHT having made one or more chargeable transfers, by giving the rest of the assets to his spouse.

3.1:6 Pre-marriage

Prior to marriage the parties may wish to buy an asset such as a house and the wealthier party may wish to make a gift of the whole or a share in such asset to the other party. Except to the extent that general exemptions apply, this gift would be a potentially exempt, rather than exempt, transfer. A useful alternative might be for the wealthier party to lend the other party such additional funds so as to make the appropriate purchase and then after the marriage to forgive the loans, ie at a time when the inter-spouse exemption will apply. The waiver should be by deed to avoid the Revenue argument based on lack of consideration. The loan need not be on commercial terms (but it should be repayable on demand), as although the party making the loan could otherwise have earned interest on that money, the charge to IHT is (by s 3) simply on the decrease in the value of the transferor's estate (of which there is none), rather than on any increase which would otherwise have occurred.

3.1:7 Disposition for maintenance of family (s 11)

There are important exemptions for inter-family dispositions and particularly in respect of a former spouse, for example on divorce. Details are set out in **7.12**.

3.1:8 Definition of spouse v widow(er)

On a death, it is clear that the inter-spouse exemption operates in favour of a widow or widower because the estate is valued immediately *before* death (ss 4 (1) and 171). In certain other situations, the provisions of ss 53(4), (5) and (6) and 54(2) and (3) resolve the position by way of a compromise, ie benefits to a widow or widower are received as 'spouse' for up to two years following the death of their partner ('the settlor spouse'). Instances of the application of this rule are as follows:

(1) Section 54(2) and (3). Reverter to the settlor's spouse domiciled in the UK on the death of a beneficiary with an interest in possession. The reverter will only be exempt in favour of the settlor's UK domiciled widow if the settlor's death is within two years of the death of the beneficiary with the interest in possession, and if neither the settlor nor his spouse had acquired a reversionary interest in the settled property for money or money's worth; or where the circumstances are that a reversionary interest has been transferred into settlement after 9 March 1981.

(2) Section 53(4), (5) and (6). The same situation arises where the beneficiary with an interest in possession terminates his interest during lifetime.

It is difficult to understand the logic behind this compromise period of two years. Why should a widow or widower not be able to claim the inter-spouse exemption once the first spouse has been dead for more than two years? This illogicality is perhaps emphasised by the compromise which is not even applied consistently throughout the legislation. For example, in s 80, which treats property as not having become 'settled' where the settlor *or his spouse* retains an initial interest in possession, spouse is defined to include widow or widower without any temporal restriction.

Note, that there is no similar reverter exemption for a distribution charge out of a discretionary trust under the discretionary settlement provisions contained in IHTA 1984, Pt III, Ch III. This is perhaps not surprising as any distribution to the settlor himself would likewise be subject to tax.

3.2   COMPARATIVE ESTATES OF HUSBAND AND WIFE AND USE OF NIL RATE BAND

3.2:1

Before 15 March 1988, IHT was charged on an ascending scale comprising a number of successive rate bands. Steps were therefore recommended towards equalisation of estates between husband and wife and, to avoid the aggregation of the two estates and the entry into higher rates of IHT on the death of the survivor, the general advice was for the first to die to leave part of the estate covered by lower rates by will to non-exempt beneficiaries or trusts. As from 15 March 1988, however, the position fundamentally changed. After the nil rate band (£242,000 in 2001–02) there is only one single rate of 40% on death (half of that, 20%, for lifetime chargeable transfers). This means that, as a general rule, provided steps are taken to utilise the nil rate band on the first death, there is no longer any *current* advantage for IHT purposes in equalising the estates as between husband and wife (see **2.2:1**(3)). The re-elected Labour government may reintroduce the progressive rates of IHT.

3.2:2   Independent taxation of husband and wife

There is, however, a different need, in view of the introduction of independent taxation of husband and wife as from 6 April 1990, to ensure that each spouse has sufficient gross income (either from earnings, or from assets providing gross interest) to soak up the income tax personal allowance for each individual together with the married couple's allowance for one spouse. (Note in this context, however, that the allowance applies only if the claimant is a married man whose wife is living with him and was abolished for the under 65's with effect from 2000–01.) Then, after that, the less well off spouse (income-wise) ought to have income to take advantage of the lower and basic rate bands of income tax, which income can itself be net of basic rate. Since 6 April 1991 composite rate tax has been abolished (FA 1990, s 30 and Sch 5); as a result a married woman can receive bank and building society interest gross if she is a non-taxpayer, otherwise subject to deduction of basic rate tax. Although outright gifts without conditions between the spouses are successful in diverting income from one to the other, settlements where the settlor retains some interest (eg, interest in possession to spouse with reverter to settlor or remainder to children) will not achieve the aim, since the income will be deemed that of the settlor. The rule is that capital must accompany the income. Income from joint assets will be split equally between the spouses unless their beneficial interests are not equal *and* they make a declaration to the Inspector of Taxes of the correct shares. (They do not have to make a declaration, in which case the income will be split equally.) Furthermore, each spouse is entitled to his or her own annual CGT exemption, so that a judicious transfer of chargeable assets showing gains between the spouses can provide further savings if the assets are later sold. The spouses can, however, have only one main residence between them for CGT exemption.

Thus, for independent taxation, the requirement, subject to separate earnings by each spouse, is to arrange or transfer high income producing assets in favour of the less well off spouse to use up the income tax personal allowance and lower and basic rate bands; and assets with gains to benefit from the double annual CGT exemption. The adjustment of assets between the spouses is facilitated by the IHT inter-spouse exemption and the CGT inter-spouse no gain no loss rule (TCGA 1992, s 58). Note, however, in the case of capital gains tax the additional requirement that husband and wife must be living together.

Adapting to individual circumstances, the aim should be to accommodate these independent taxation requirements within the overall capital objectives for IHT as between husband and wife, notably the use of the nil rate band on the first death. One needs to add a word of warning that although currently the IHT concern over the respective size of estates of the spouses covers the nil rate band only, tax law and governments can change. If the one single IHT rate above the nil rate band reverted to a number of ascending rate bands, equalisation of estates might return. Flexibility, with any planning, is thus an important objective.

3.2:3   Use of nil rate band

In the current IHT circumstances of one positive rate of 40% above the indexed nil rate band (£242,000 in 2001–02) care should be taken, in the context of the estates of husband and wife, to ensure that the nil rate band is used for chargeable beneficiaries or donees. Not to use it costs £96,800 when added to the estate of the surviving spouse.

Where an individual would normally regard his spouse as the primary beneficiary, he might consider settling by will a sum equivalent to the upper limit of the nil rate band upon a discretionary trust so that the surviving spouse can have the benefit of the fund and at the same time the nil rate band can be utilised and not wasted. Distributions could be made in favour of the surviving spouse in case of need; and if they were of capital any exit charge under the discretionary trust regime in the first ten years would be by reference to the nil rate on the testator's death. Moreover, any distributions might be made by way of loan, which would normally expect to qualify as a deduction against the survivor's estate; or they could instead be income distributions subject to income tax.

The use of the nil rate band for a mini-discretionary trust in this way can be very effective. Furthermore, since the possibility of variation of wills may become severely restricted (see **2.1:2(2)**), a discretionary trust with a wide class of beneficiaries and wide powers may offer a flexible alternative (see **2.5:4**).

There are, however, seven points to watch in utilising the nil rate band for a discretionary trust. These are analysed in **2.5:3** and **2.5:4** above.

3.2:4

It should also be borne in mind in utilising the nil rate band as above that, because the nil rate band can normally be expected to increase annually by reference to the retail prices index (s 8), (even though any increase was negatived in both FA 1993 and FA 1994), the testator's will should reflect this fact to ensure that the gift matches the ceiling of the nil rate band when he dies. The gift in the will should therefore be of an amount equivalent to the upper

limit of the IHT nil rate band in force at the time of the testator's death under
IHTA 1984, Sch 1, as amended in accordance with the indexation provisions of
s 8. Such a formula, while most useful for cash gifts, cannot of course operate
in the same straightforward way in the case of specific legacies of assets,
particularly where business or agricultural reliefs are involved and changes in
values may occur.

3.2:5

In utilising the nil rate band the effect of such business and agricultural reliefs
(**9.0, 9.2**) is very important. Where relief is at 100% the benefit on top of the nil
rate band is unlimited. With relief at 50% the nil rate band can become
£484,000. Note, however, the trap with 50% (as opposed to 100%) relief under
a settlement on discretionary trusts if the assets are then distributed within the
first ten years under s 68 (see **4.3:6** below). As a general principle, because of
this multiplying effect on figures, business and agricultural property should be
given to chargeable parties rather than to the surviving spouse, to prevent it
being wasted. A further point to bear in mind, however, is that in the case of a
partially exempt estate as envisaged (ie because s 18 applies in whole or in part)
the business or agricultural property itself must be given, and it is not sufficient
merely to create a specific pecuniary legacy payable out of the business or
agricultural property. In this latter situation relief is denied on the value of the
pecuniary legacy and therefore (at least in part) lost (see s 39A(6)).

3.2:6

In many cases the family home forms the largest part of the joint estates of
husband and wife, and the survivor may need such cash or other liquid assets as
there are for living purposes. It is still possible to make use of the nil rate band
if the first spouse to die by will settles a cash sum equivalent to the nil rate band,
say, upon discretionary trusts for children and grandchildren (or absolutely),
and leaves the residue of the estate to the survivor. After the death the parties
(ie the executors and the surviving spouse) can come together and agree that
the cash gift should be charged on the matrimonial home, so that the surviving
spouse can continue in occupation. The charge could be registered at HM Land
Registry, but might be left as an informal one. See also **2.5:6**, proposal 4.

3.3   CHANNELLING OF GIFTS AND ASSOCIATED OPERATIONS

The art of timing (whether gifts are into settlement or outright) is for a donor
to make a PET or a chargeable transfer to use up the nil rate band while the
seven-year survivorship requirement is likely to be satisfied. Thus where a
husband and wife wish to make such gifts to others, for example their children,
it may be advisable to 'channel' the gifts through the spouse with the better life
expectation or who has not used up the nil rate band. On the face of it the
associated operations provisions of s 268 would appear specifically designed to
counter such channelling transactions. It was made clear, however, when CTT
was first being introduced, that in relation to outright gifts the associated
operations rules would be used only in blatant or culpable circumstances, or
where it was made a condition of the first gift that the other spouse would make
a further gift (Mr Joel Barnett, Hansard, March 1975, HC Deb, Vol 888, col
56).

It is considered that this assurance also applies to gifts into settlement, but the position is less clear cut having regard in particular to the exchange of correspondence between the Institute of Chartered Accountants and the Inland Revenue of September 1985 concerning *Furniss v Dawson* [1984] STC 153 reproduced in ICAEW Guidance Note TR 588 of 25 September 1985. The Revenue's response was as follows:

> 'I can confirm that we would not seek to disturb existing practices in relation to inter-spouse transfers. It should, however, be borne in mind that the circumstances of such transfers always need to be carefully examined to ensure, among other things, that the transaction has substance as well as form. (For example, an understanding between the spouses on the ultimate destination of the assets would be important in this connection.) In general the terms of the Press Release of 8 April 1975 remain valid as a description of the practice in this area.' (That Press Release, reproduced in Simon's Tax Intelligence dated 18 April 1975 at p 180, contained notes on the FA 1975: see at p 191 for the notes on the associated operations provisions of the then s 44, which reflect the Hansard statement referred to above.)

In certain circumstances it might be argued by the Revenue that the gift into settlement by a spouse, say a wife, who had received a gift from her husband, was a case where the wife was acting merely as a conduit pipe. In other words, that the husband never effectively alienated the property given. In these circumstances the husband might be regarded as the real and only settlor. Accordingly, various precautionary steps are recommended to reduce the effectiveness of any such Revenue contention. First, the initial gift by the husband should be recorded in a signed memorandum stressing that the gift is made to the wife as beneficial owner absolutely and unconditionally, eg as follows:

> MEMORANDUM and DEED that I the undersigned have this day of . . . . . . 200( )
> made a gift by way of [share transfer] of . . . of my Ordinary Shares of £1 each in the capital of . . . . .
> Limited to my wife [names] who has countersigned by way of acknowledgement and receipt.
>
> I RECORD AND CERTIFY that this gift is made as an outright unconditional gift to my wife for her sole absolute use and benefit.
>
> We Certify that this deed falls within Category L of the Stamp Duty (Exempt Instruments) Regulations 1987.
>
> IN WITNESS whereof the parties hereto have signed this Memorandum and Receipt as their DEED in the presence of the persons mentioned below this . . . . . . day of . . . . 200( )
>
> SIGNED and DELIVERED as a deed by . . .)
> [HUSBAND])
> in the presence of:)
>
> Witness:
> Address:
>
> Occupation:
>
> RECEIPT DATED . . . . 200( )
>
> I ACKNOWLEDGE receipt of the above gift upon the terms set out above.
>
> SIGNED and DELIVERED as a deed by)

[WIFE]   )
in the presence of:

Witness:
Address:

Occupation:

Second, the wife should receive independent professional advice if and when she creates her settlement, and any such advice should be recorded in writing. Third, the wife should not in any event settle all the assets (eg, shares or cash) given to her initially by her husband. Fourth, the wife's gift into settlement, if in fact she decides to make it, should be after a decent interval of time, one month at the very least. If possible (eg, in the case of cash) the wife should set up her settlement first, with the husband subsequently, as a separate decision and act, making a gift to the wife of a similar, but not the same, value.

Example
Mr A has made previous lifetime chargeable gifts totalling £242,000 gross. He wishes to make a gift of £100,000 gross into a discretionary trust for his son's family. This is a simple lifetime chargeable gift and the IHT (at half the death rate of 40%) would be £20,000. His wife whose estate is worth £200,000 has not used up any of her nil rate band. He suggests to her that she might wish to make the £100,000 gift, which she does at no cost to IHT. Mr A the following year decides to transfer £110,000 to his wife by way of exempt gift. It is considered that the wife's gift into the discretionary trust would not in practice be taxed as Mr A's under the associated operations rules of s 268.

3.4   MATRIMONIAL HOME AND JOINT OWNERSHIP

The matrimonial home is often the most important asset in a family and will most likely, in cases under review, have a value in excess of the nil rate band. This subject of the matrimonial home is treated under three heads:

(1) Mitigation of IHT generally.

(2) Types of ownership.

(3) Practical and procedural aspects (see also **7.4:1**).

Reference should also be made generally to **Chapter 7**: Gifts.

3.4:1   Mitigation of IHT generally

For IHT purposes, as between spouses, as in other cases, a life interest in an asset is treated in the same way as an absolute interest (the liability being based on the capital value on the death of the surviving spouse), and accordingly there is no difference for IHT between giving a life interest only in the matrimonial home to the surviving spouse and giving the property to the spouse absolutely. Moreover, for practical reasons it is the wish of the husband and wife in most cases that the survivor should have the matrimonial home absolutely. Accordingly when choosing the family assets with which to utilise the nil rate band, other assets may have to be chosen, such as shares in the family company. Indeed, there can be problems in seeking to use the matrimonial home in this way (although the risks seem to have been reduced following the commencement of Trusts of Land and Appointment of Trustees Act 1996). However, a number of points should be borne in mind. If the first spouse, for instance, leaves his interest in the home direct to the children, subject to a *right* to occupy in favour of the surviving spouse, it will probably give the survivor an entitlement to the use and enjoyment of the property equivalent to an interest in possession in it (see s 50 and *IRC v Lloyd's Private Banking Limited* [1998] STC 559), thereby shifting IHT on the house from the first death (exempt as passing to the survivor) to the termination of occupation by second. One is faced with an analogous problem to that raised by SP 10/79 whereby a beneficiary who is allowed by trustees of a settlement to occupy a house, part of the trust assets, on exclusive terms, will normally be regarded as having an interest in possession. Moreover, even if the house was left direct to the children, without the incorporation of conditions so as to secure occupation by the surviving spouse (which in any event seem not now to be necessary after the commencement of the Trusts of Land and Appointment of Trustees Act 1996 with effect from 1 January 1997), the CGT private residence exemption (TCGA 1992, s 225) would be at risk to the extent that all the children as owners did not live there. It may well be preferable, therefore, in many circumstances, to give the survivor the security of his or her own home absolutely, and look at other assets for nil rate band planning. However, see **3.2:6** for the possibility of charging a nil rate band legacy on the home; and **3.4:2** for the suggestion of leaving a half share by will to a discretionary trust where the widow is one of the trustees.

3.4:2   Types of ownership

There are four main types of ownership of the matrimonial home and this involves consideration of ownership in the sole name of one spouse or joint ownership.

(1) Sole ownership of husband.

(2) Sole ownership of wife.

(3) Joint holding as 'joint tenants'. This is the *only* form of co-ownership capable of existing *in law*, as contrasted with beneficial ownership, ie in equity. Under this method, by reason of the *jus accrescendi* rule, the survivor takes the entire interest absolutely by operation of law. Hence it is impossible (subject to severance which cannot be by will but, as a matter of practice can be by deed of variation) to make inter vivos or death dispositions to third parties because this interest accrues automatically to the survivor.

   A joint tenancy can be justified where it has been decided that the surviving spouse should have the entire property absolutely, a situation which, as appears from **3.4:1** is not unusual for IHT. Note that the difference between a joint tenancy and the other type of joint ownership ('a tenancy in common') is a mere matter of wording (see also **3.4:3**(4) re severance). If it can be shown that a holding as joint tenants was contrary to the true intention of the parties, the court *may* grant rectification (see *Re Colebrook's Conveyances, Taylor v Taylor* [1973] 1 All ER 132). However, as to the burden which must be satisfied in order to persuade the court to grant rectification, see *Racal Group Services Ltd v Ashmore* [1995] STC 1151, CA.

(4) Joint holding as 'tenants in common'. Since 1925 it is only possible to have a tenancy in common *in equity*. However, this is likely to be of no practical importance as the value of the property will be represented by the respective beneficial interests and not the bare legal title. This type of holding is frequently found to be the most satisfactory from the IHT and practical viewpoints. Each spouse has a separate, say, half share which he or she can separately leave by will or dispose of during lifetime.

A co-owner of a share is entitled at law to occupy the whole of the property in question (Trusts of Land and Appointment of Trustees Act 1996, s12). Accordingly, there used to be scope for planning by making, say, children co-owners along with their parents. The parents would simply make a gift of an undivided share of their interest in the home. Provided that none of the co-owners was debarred from occupation if they so wished, continued occupation of the whole property by the parents was thought not to give rise to problems in relation to the gift with reservation rules. This simple planning technique has however, been to some extent blocked by section 102B Finance Act 1996 introduced by Finance Act 1999. The gift of an undivided share of an interest in land is now deemed to fall within the gift with reservation provisions *unless* the donor provides full consideration for his occupation of the property or both donor and donee occupy the property together and the donor receives no benefit from the donee connected with the gift (see further **7.2** below where these provisions are discussed in detail).

Husband and wife as tenants in common should make provision in their wills concerning their shares in the property. As has been noted in **3.4:1** above, following the commencement of the Trusts of Land and Appointment of Trustees Act 1996 occupation of the family home by the surviving spouse should be secure even without conferring specific rights. That Act abolishes the old rule that interests in land exist behind a statutory trust for sale, imposing upon the trustees an ultimate duty to sell the land. Instead a simple trust for land is created. Sections 12(1) and 13(7) are of particular importance. Section 12 gives a person 'who is beneficially entitled to an interest in possession in land subject to a trust of land' a statutory right of occupation of the land that was purchased in the first place for his or her occupation. This will invariably be the case with the family home. The right is not, however, absolute, and is subject to restriction by s 13. Nevertheless, s 13(7) provides that the trustees cannot exercise their powers to exclude or restrict occupation by a person who is in occupation of land from continuing to so occupy unless he either consents or the approval of the court is obtained. Given that the underlying purpose behind ss 12 and 13 has been to give statutory effect to the opinion of Lord Denning in *Bull v Bull* [1955] 1 QB 234 it is thought likely that, should any application be made to the courts a more flexible approach will be adopted, and relevance given to factors such as the wishes of the person who set up the trust, as well as the welfare of any children. Before the commencement of the Trusts of Land and Appointment of Trustees Act 1996, the safest way of dealing with the family home was as follows. On the footing that the husband dies first he leaves his half share in the property upon discretionary trusts for the children and grandchildren; and he appoints his widow and a professional adviser, say his solicitor, as trustees. This appointment of trustees effectively prevents the widow's occupation of the house from being disturbed. Although this form of IHT planning may still be effective to achieve its purpose, in the light of the foregoing it is now thought to be an over-complication and risks attack by the CTO. In particular they may contend that the widow's occupation constitutes an interest in possession (particularly if the widow is a discretionary beneficiary). Of course, if there remains any doubt about these issues, it is better to leave the share in the house to the surviving spouse, and utilise other assets to take advantage of the nil rate band.

3.4:3 Practical and procedural aspects

When conveying (unregistered property-deed of gift) or transferring (registered property-deed of transfer) from the sole name of one spouse into the sole name of the other spouse or into the joint names of both spouses, whether as so-called joint tenants or tenants in common, the following practical points should be borne in mind.

(1)   Gift of matrimonial home to a donee other than a spouse

For IHT purposes, the reservation of benefit rules apply to gifts during lifetime (FA 1986, s 102 and Sch 20) and not to wills. If an owner makes a lifetime gift of his house, or part of it, and continues living there, the Capital Taxes Office are able to claim that by staying there after giving it away the former owner has reserved a benefit, so that the seven-year run off period for outright gifts does not apply (s 3A(4)), and nor does the percentage abatement of IHT on death within seven years of the gift (s 7(4)). The full value of the house remains in the total aggregable estate at death. There is in fact an exemption under FA 1986, Sch 20, para 6(1)(a) which rules out reservation if the donee leases the property back to the donor for full consideration. Such a gift would then be a PET. It is essential to negotiate arm's length terms for any tenancy or lease and for each party to be independently advised (see the Revenue letter dated 18 May 1987 to the Law Society in the *Law Society Gazette* dated 1 June 1988 at p 50). The Revenue take the view that full consideration is required throughout the period of any tenancy and the rent should therefore be reviewed at stated intervals, say every four years. They do, however, recognise that what is 'full' consideration must lie within a range of normal valuation tolerances and that any amount within that range can be accepted as satisfying para 6(1)(a) (see Revenue interpretation headed 'IHT gifts with reservation' in *IR Tax Bulletin*, Issue 9, November 1993 at p 98; also at [1993] STI 1409). There are other practical problems apart from reservation: the need for the donor to go on paying a full market rent as his income is perhaps becoming squeezed, and a continuing income tax charge on the rental for the donee. (Consider, in this context, the use of a grandchildren's accumulation and maintenance trust. The rental income could be distributed for the benefit of the grandchildren at a nil or low rate of income tax.) There would also be the question of rights of holding over occupation under landlord and tenant legislation. If, furthermore, a lease at a market premium was chosen instead of a continuing market rental there would still be the question of income tax on the premium as well as posssible rights of enfranchisement under the leasehold reform legislation. Finally, principal private residence relief from capital gains tax would not be available to the donee should he sell the property, on, say, the donor taking up residence in a nursing home.

One popular scheme used to be to take the matrimonial home and carve it into two interests: one, a lease under which occupation is retained; and the other, the freehold reversion subject to that lease which is given away. Usually the transferor would keep the lease (a wasting asset) in his estate, and make an outright gift of the freehold reversion arguing that in those circumstances there had been no reservation of benefit.

A variation of this scheme was recently considered and approved by the House of Lords in *Ingram v IRC* [1999] STC 37 (see also '"Carbolic Smokeball Protects Against Influenza" or Lady Ingram in the House of Lords' by Robert Venables QC Vol. 6 Issue 3 Page 177 Personal Tax Planning Review). In that case Lady Ingram transferred her property to her solicitor as nominee. The nominee then granted to Lady Ingram a lease – back in order that she could continue to occupy the property. The freehold reversion was subsequently transferred (at Lady Ingram's direction) to the trustees of Lady Ingram's children's trust.

Another variation of the "lease carve out" scheme was to grant the lease to the trustees of a life interest trust under the terms of which the settlor was granted an interest in possession, followed by a gift of the freehold.

These types of arrangement have now been largely blocked as an inheritance tax planning technique by section 102A Finance Act 1986 introduced by Finance Act 1999 with effect from 9 March 1999. A gift with reservation of benefit is now deemed to arise if (broadly) the donor or his spouse enjoys a right or interest which entitles or enables him to occupy all or part of the land or to enjoy some right in relation to the land otherwise than for full consideration in money or money's worth. Curiously, the provision does not apply if the right or interest in the land was granted or acquired before the period of seven years ending with the date of gift. Accordingly, there appears still to be scope for lease carve out provided any gift of the freehold takes place more than seven years after the creation of the lease under which the donor and/or his spouse will occupy. The result, therefore, is that effective tax planning using this method will now take fourteen as opposed to seven years to achieve.

It must also be remembered that even before the changes introduced by Finance Act 1999, there were a number of drawbacks with lease carve out schemes.

First, the donees would not normally benefit from the CGT main residence exemption; and since their acquisition value at the date of gift of the reversion would be low, the ultimate CGT would be likely to be high and to that extent negate the IHT savings. Second, there could be an income tax problem relating to lease premiums if the house was sold for any reason during the currency of the lease. Third, there is the danger that the Revenue might seek to apply the associated operations provisions of s 268 their argument being that the carving out of the lease and the subsequent gift of the freehold reversion were associated transactions. Fourth, if the donor, now occupying under the terms of the lease, outlives the duration of the lease, he must either leave his home or pay a full market rent to remain in occupation. Otherwise the original gift of the freehold revision will be treated as a gift with reservation of benefit under normal principles (ie within s 102) (these arrangements are now fully discussed at **7.2** above).

An alternative to the lease carve out scheme, which appears to remain effective in spite of the legislative changes contained in Finance Act 1999, is for husband and wife to retain the freehold and grant a long reversionary lease, eg for 300 years, at nominal rent. It is understood that this type of arrangement was accepted in principle as being an effective inheritance planning technique by leading council for the Crown in the *Ingram* case. The nature of a reversionary lease is that it commences at some time *in the future*. Accordingly, the long reversionary lease should be expressed to commence after the period the spouses would need to occupy the house. With care, the provisions of section 102A Finance Act 1986 should not apply for at least one of two reasons. First, it has already been noted that those provisions do not apply if the right or interest which enables the donor or his spouse to occupy the property was acquired before the period of seven years ending with the date of the gift. The 'gift' here is of the long lease, which comments in the future. The donor occupies, as he had always done, by reason of his owning the freehold. Accordingly, provided the property has been owned for at least seven years section 102A appears to have no application. Second, and in the alternative, section 102A does not apply if full consideration has been given by the donor for his right or interest in the property which entitles him to occupation. Once again, this right is the freehold. Accordingly, provided the property was purchased for full consideration, the revisionary lease scheme appears to be available even if the seven year exemption does not apply. The *only* effect that the new legislation appears to have had in relation to the reversionary lease scheme is in the case of a receipt of property by way of gift or inheritance within seven years.

Perhaps the main drawback with this arrangement is that s 149(3) of the Law of Property Act 1925 may render void any grant of a lease taking effect more than 21 years from the date it is granted, and 21 years might not be sufficient for occupation by the spouses. There is an argument that the 21 year limit only applies on a sale not a gift. Subject to that, this method, involving one transaction only, would be safe from associated operations; but would produce the same CGT disadvantages for the donees already discussed.

The Revenue might contend that a gift with reservation situation arises because possession and enjoyment are not bona fide assumed by the donee within the meaning of FA 1986, s102. It is considered that such a contention would be incorrect because the donee has the full benefit of a saleable and assignable asset.

Both in the case of the lease carve out and the reversionary lease, the ownership of the freehold and the leasehold interest should not merge, but be held by different parties.

Turning from these lease arrangements, it is possible for spouses to retain a share of the matrimonial home, perhaps a third or a quarter, and give the remaining share to their children (or possibly to the trustees of an accumulation and maintenance settlement) but the spouses and the other joint owners must all occupy the home and pay their proper share of the running costs. This method is based on a statement by Mr Peter Brooke, Minister of State HM Treasury, on 10 June 1986 (Standing Committee G Finance Bill) and is preserved in spite of the legislative changes applying to gifts of undivided shares of interests in land contained in section 102B Finance Act 1986. It may work very well in the case of an unmarried son or daughter, or even a married child living with the parents. If, however, the children already have their own home, the required element of occupation and sharing is missing. Furthermore, if the children did live there but later moved away, the parents would at that stage have to pay a full rent to avoid a reservation of benefit springing up. (Note the alternative of using a s 54 reverter to settlor exemption in **7.3**). This principle could extend to holiday homes and *pieds-à-terre*.

It might be feasible in some circumstances to base an arrangement on a gift of cash. The parents could give their son £100,000 cash outright. At a later stage he could make use of the cash to buy a house where they all might live. It would not be appropriate to use the cash to buy the parents' present home since the Revenue could attack the arrangement on the grounds of associated operations. (It would be simpler for the parents to give the son say a third of the house and for him to move in with them.)

It might also be possible for a son, out of an earlier cash gift, to purchase and settle a house on a parent for life (by way of interest in possession and PET) with the prospect of reverter to settlor exemption (s 54) on the parent's death (subject, however, as in the case of any relatively long-term planning, to changes in the law which might occur on a change of government). It would not be recommended for a spouse to leave the home in his will to a child on the understanding that the child would then make a s 54 settlement on the survivor, who would no doubt already be living there. Such an arrangement would be open to attack on grounds of artificiality.

Finally, a sale of the house by husband and wife to, say, an interest in possession settlement under which they are both entitled to full rights of occupation should be considered. The purchase price (which should be equivalent to the market value of the property) to be paid by the trustees should be left outstanding and secured on the property. The husband and wife then make a gift of the secured debt to, say, their children, or perhaps an accumulation and maintenance settlement. This gift would qualify as a PET. By reason of their interests in possession the husband and wife are deemed to continue to own the house. However, its value has been significantly reduced as a result of the secured loan. Provided that the terms of the loan note are drafted with care it is thought that a complete IHT saving can be achieved without the capital gains tax disadvantages associated with the lease carve out and reversionary lease schemes. This technique is set out and discussed in detail in **Chapter 7**. Proposals concerning the matrimonial home in a will and on death are discussed in **2.5:5**. Lease carve out and revisionary lease schemes as with the 'homeloan' scheme are discussed at greater length in **Chapter 7**: Gifts.

(2) Presumptions of advancement and resulting trust: intention as to beneficial ownership

Gifts between husband and wife are concerned with two competing presumptions of law in the absence of an express declaration of beneficial interests in the matrimonial home.

(a) Presumption of advancement This is the presumption that the recipient of an asset is to benefit. It can arise where the husband owns an asset and places it into his wife's name or jointly in the names of himself and his wife, or if he purchases an asset but has the purchase completed by a conveyance into his wife's name. However, the presumption does not apply between a man and his mistress (*Lawson v Coombes* [1999] 2 WLR 720). Further, the presumption does not operate where the transfer is from a wife to her husband (*Tribe v Tribe* [1996] Ch 107 at 118). Advancement can similarly be inferred where the donor purchases an asset in the name of his intended wife (provided that the marriage is duly solemnised and, it seems, that the transfer of the asset is conditional upon the marriage taking place),[1] and where a father places an asset in the name of his child or any other person to whom he stands in loco parentis. Failing evidence to the contrary, the law presumes that the husband

---

[1] *Moate v Moate* [1948] 2 All ER 486.

intends to benefit his wife (or child) but this evidence can be negated or rebutted by appropriate evidence as to the husband's intentions at the time of the transfer. An example can be seen in the case of *O'Neill v IRC* [1998] STC (SCD) 110. There, a father put money into an account in the Isle of Man which was a joint account in the name of himself and his daughter. It was held that because the existence of the account had been concealed from the daughter during her father's lifetime, who had retained de facto control over the account, the account had been set up as a sort of legacy, and the presumption of earlier advancement did not apply. However, the courts will not allow evidence of an improper purpose[1] to overturn the presumption such as an intention to defeat potential creditors.[2] *Pettitt v Pettitt* [1970] AC 777, [1969] 2 All ER 385, HL, is authority for the view, expressed subsequently in other cases (most recently *McGrath v Wallis* [1995] 3 FCR 661, CA), that it has in modern conditions become relatively easy to rebut the presumption (although it is still available to resolve the issue of ownership in the absence of evidence as to the spouse's true intentions at the time of the transfer), and that the presumption of joint beneficial ownership has more application as a general rule.[3] In *Webb v Webb* [1992] 1 All ER 17 a father had purchased foreign immovable property (a flat in Antibes) in the name of his son. The court rejected the presumption of advancement in favour of the son, declaring that there was sufficient evidence of the father's intention to retain the property for himself.

(b) Presumption of resulting trust This is the reverse presumption, namely that the recipient of an asset is *not* to benefit but merely to hold it on trust for the donor. The law on resulting trusts has recently been considered in detail by the House of Lords in *Westdeutsche Landesbank v Islington BC* [1996] AC 669.

The presumption applies where for example the wife owns an asset or contributes towards its purchase,[4] and the asset is placed into her husband's name or jointly between herself and her husband. Equity presumes that the husband is merely the nominee or trustee of his wife as to the appropriate share, unless the presumption is rebutted by appropriate evidence of the wife's intention to benefit the husband at the time of the gift. Moreover this aspect has been extended by way of imputing a constructive trust in favour of a common law wife in the case of *Eves v Eves* [1975] 3 All ER 768, CA. In this case a man and woman cohabited and had children. The house was purchased in the man's sole name although the woman did a great deal of work in repairing and maintaining the house and the garden. The court imputed a constructive trust in favour of the woman equal to a 25% interest. The concept of the trust, however, will not always apply to a man and his mistress as much as to a husband and wife. In *Burns v Burns* [1984] Ch 317, the Court of Appeal declared that where the home was bought in the name of the man alone without any substantial contribution by the mistress towards either the purchase price, the deposit or the mortgage instalments, then she is not entitled to

---

[1] *Gascoigne v Gascoigne* [1918] 1 KB 223.

[2] *Tinker v Tinker* [1970] P 136, [1970] 1 All ER 540, *Tribe v Tribe* [1995] 4 All ER 236, CA, but in *Bingeman v McLaughlin* (1973) 1 OR (2d) 485 the presumption was not rebutted since on the facts the creditors had not been delayed or harmed.

[3] See also *Jackson's Matrimonial Finance and Taxation* (6th edn).

[4] *Wray v Steele* (1814) 2 Ves & B 388 and *Snell on Equity* (28th edn) p 180 cited with approval in *Gissing v Gissing, supra*.

any share in the house, however hard she may have worked in other directions. The case contains a useful summary of the earlier cases and the common situations. If that case is considered out of line with earlier development, a step forward was taken in *Grant v Edwards* [1986] 2 All ER 426, CA, where a mistress was held entitled to a half share of the home. The case emphasised that the primary question is that of intention. Here there was an intention to share; and the true significance of contributions to the purchase price of the house or to the household expenses was an indication of the intentions of the parties as to beneficial ownership. However, to avoid the principle that equity will not assist a volunteer, the claimant must also demonstrate that she acted on that intention to her detriment. In *Turton v Turton* [1987] 2 All ER 641 an unmarried couple bought a house in 1972 with an express trust for themselves as joint tenants. They separated in 1975 and the house was sold in 1986. In the absence of any claim to upset it, the declaration of trust was decisive of the couple's respective interests (see *Goodman v Gallant* [1986] 1 All ER 311, CA). Moreover, the date of valuation of the claimant's interest was the date of sale, not the date of separation.

Another interesting issue arose in *Williams and Glyn's Bank Ltd v Brown* and *Williams and Glyn's Bank Ltd v Boland* [1979] 2 All ER 697. In each case the husband charged the matrimonial home to the bank without the wife's knowledge, the husband being the sole proprietor of the registered land. Each of the wives had contributed substantially towards the purchase price. The bank sought possession of the property but the Court of Appeal held that the respective wives had an equitable interest in the property which amounted to 'actual occupation' for the purposes of Land Registration Act 1925, s 70(1)(g) so that it constituted an 'overriding interest' to which the bank as mortgagees took subject, and they were therefore not entitled to obtain possession (cf the position in *Lloyds Bank plc v Rosset* [1990] 1 All ER 1111, HL, where the wife's contribution was *de minimis*).

This case was distinguished by the House of Lords in *City of London Building Society v Flegg* [1987] 3 All ER 435 where two parents (Mr and Mrs F) and their daughter and son-in-law (Mr and Mrs M-B) bought a house for their joint occupation. The Fs provided a little over half of the purchase price. The house was conveyed into the names of the M-Bs as beneficial joint tenants under a trust for sale and only they were registered as co-proprietors. In 1982 the M-Bs mortgaged the house unbeknown to the Fs. They defaulted and the building society sought possession. It was held that the Fs' rights took effect under the trust for sale but on creation of the charge their rights to occupy were overreached and thereupon switched to the capital advanced to the M-Bs and the equity of redemption, but subordinated to the legal charge of the building society. It is thought that, following the commencement of Trusts of Land and Appointment of Trustees Act 1996, although F would now have an interest in land, this would nevertheless remain a situation where the court would order sale under the jurisdiction conferred upon it by s 13. However, the way in which the court will in fact exercise this jurisdiction will have to be tested before any clear opinion can be given.

This case seems to have been distinguished from the other cases cited because there was more than one beneficiary living in the house. (See also articles by RT Oerton at (1990) New LJ 174 and Peter Cowell at (1992) SJ 439).

The following cases, although considering the old law may still be of interest in considering how the Court may in practice exercise its jurisdiction under

TLATA 1996, s 13. First, in *Barclays Bank plc v O'Brien* [1993] 4 All ER 417, HL, the indebtedness of the husband's company was secured by a charge over the matrimonial home jointly owned by husband and wife. The bank failed to warn the wife when she signed the security documents of the risk to the home. That failure fixed the bank with constructive notice of the husband's wrongful misrepresentation to her. She was therefore entitled to set aside the legal charge on the home securing the husband's liability. In contrast, *CIBC Mortgages plc v Pitt* [1993] 4 All ER 433, HL, was a case again of a matrimonial home in the joint names of husband and wife. The husband persuaded his wife to join in taking out a loan for £150,000 secured on the home which the husband wanted in order to deal on the stock market. The October 1987 crash intervened, and the husband could not keep up the mortgage payments. Although the wife had established undue influence by her husband, the lender was not affected by it because he had been told the purpose of the loan was to buy a holiday home and regarded the loan (paid into their joint account) as a normal advance to a husband and wife for their joint benefit. The wife's appeal was therefore dismissed. It is thought that these cases would be decided the same way, even under the new law.

Since there may be good estate planning reasons for placing the matrimonial home into the name of the other spouse or into joint names in order to arrange the estate between husband and wife while attracting the exemption of s 18, it is essential to avoid the operation of the resulting trust where the wife makes the gift or contribution. The instrument effecting the transfer, conveyance or assignment of the property, or an accompanying memorandum, must make the position clear, namely that a gift passing the full beneficial ownership is intended. Where the husband makes the gift it is also advisable that this intention is clearly indicated so that an advancement is not merely presumed but made express.

(c) Intention as to beneficial ownership Moreover, as the equitable presumptions referred to have become less operative, the question of deciding on the beneficial ownership of assets between the parties to the marriage, particularly as to the matrimonial home, has become largely a matter of determining the intentions of the parties. There have been a large number of cases before the courts in recent years turning largely on the facts and evidence of such cases, and it is not possible to state the law with any degree of certainty. Suffice it to say that as a general rule where one spouse, say the wife, has made a substantial contribution towards the purchase of the house either directly or indirectly, the court will apportion to her a beneficial interest in the property.[1] The principle has been extended to *business profits*. If a wife makes a substantial contribution to her husband's business and receives inadequate emoluments in return, she will be regarded as having an appropriate interest in the matrimonial home or the assets bought out of the profits (*Nixon v Nixon* [1969] 3 All ER 1133, [1969] 1 WLR 1676, CA). In the context of marriage breakdown, the Matrimonial Causes Act 1973, ss 23 and 24 give the courts a wide discretion to make financial provision and adjustment of property orders irrespective of how the beneficial interests are expressed, and s 25 of that Act imposes on the court a duty in deciding whether and in what manner to exercise its discretion and to

---

[1] For a more detailed analysis see *Jackson's Matrimonial Finance and Taxation* (6th edn).

have regard to all the circumstances of the case,[1] including among the specific matters mentioned, any contribution made for the welfare of the family.

The Matrimonial Proceedings and Property Act 1970, s 37 introduced further complications and uncertainty when considering improvements to the matrimonial home or other assets.[2] The section provides that a substantial contribution to improvements can vest in the contributor of the improvements a beneficial interest in that property.[3] The matter can be decided between the spouses and if as a result of this agreement the contributing spouse receives a realistic share, that should constitute a binding arrangement. The Matrimonial and Family Proceedings Act 1984 contains directions on the question of orders by the court. Under s 20 the court can make a lump sum order representing the value of the interest in the property of any party.

Liability to IHT is concerned with beneficial ownership and the uncertain application of the law referred to does give rise to difficulties, in particular, whether in any given case a spouse's contribution represents a material interest in the property, whether a gift has been made, or whether a resulting trust has arisen. This uncertainty can be avoided by the parties making their intention clear at the time the property is acquired.[4] In the case of *Heseltine v Heseltine* [1971] 1 All ER 952, CA, where the predominant motive appears to have been to minimise ED, such intention had not been sufficiently declared.[5]

(3)   Stamp duty

The consideration in the deed of gift or transfer is as a general rule not valuable, the consideration being expressed as the 'natural love and affection of the donor for the donee'. As a result of the Stamp Duty (Exempt Instruments) Regulations 1987 (SI 1987/516) any conveyance or transfer operating as a voluntary disposition inter vivos, ie as a gift, is not liable to ad valorem stamp duty, but is exempt provided an appropriate certificate is included in the instrument. But note the mortgage trap at (5) below.

(4)   Severance

If the property is held by husband and wife as joint tenants in law and in equity and it is desired to sever the equitable joint tenancy so that husband and wife become tenants in common in equity (thereby providing greater flexibility), a

---

[1] Consider also the so-called 'one-third rule' expounded by Lord Denning in *Wachtel v Wachtel* [1973] Fam 72, [1973] 1 All ER 829; and refer to (1974) SJ 431, 'The Matrimonial Home after Wachtel', S M Cretney.

[2] Note in particular the difficulties in assessing the *value* of improvements to the home discussed at (1975) New LJ 20 by Vivian Chapman.

[3] *Kowalczuk v Kowalczuk* [1973] 2 All ER 1042, CA, in which it was held that, where the husband had owned the property before his marriage, the wife's contributions had to be directly referable to the making of substantial improvements to the house or the payment of mortgage instalments.

[4] The court in *Leake (formerly Bruzzi) v Bruzzi* [1974] 2 All ER 1196 declined to go behind the terms of the trust deed which declare in whom the beneficial title vests but regarded such terms as conclusive of the parties' respective beneficial interests in the matrimonial home.

[5] Although this section is concerned with intention as to beneficial ownership of husband and wife, the courts are concerned more widely—see *Tinsley v Milligan* [1993] 3 All ER 65, HL, where the House of Lords showed their concern to respect the joint beneficial interest of two cohabiting women.

simple form of notice of severance suffices. An equitable joint tenancy can be severed by a joint tenant giving to the other joint tenant a notice in writing under the Law of Property Act 1925, s 36(2) (proviso) and s 196. This notice must be given during lifetime because a joint tenancy cannot be severed by will (although it can, in practice, by deed of variation under s 142). It is preferable for a severance to be agreed and signed by both parties.

(5)   Mortgages and other outgoings

Frequently the property is mortgaged; the mortgage may be either legal or equitable. Before a change can take place in the ownership of property subject to such a mortgage, the consent of the mortgagee must be obtained.

In the usual case of property subject to a mortgage with a building society or an insurance company little difficulty is experienced in practice in obtaining the mortgagee's consent to a transfer between spouses and therefore the method of transferring the property subject to the mortgage is normally adopted. Alternatively, there is nothing to prevent one spouse conveying or transferring to the other only the equity of redemption *without* the mortgagee's consent. There is, however, a nasty stamp duty trap to beware of. Ad valorem duty is still payable to the extent of the mortgage debt assumed by the donee (see the Inland Revenue's SP 6/90 of 27 April 1990).

The fact that a husband continues to pay mortgage instalments in respect of his wife's house or share therein should not give rise to any IHT charge because of the available exemptions, for example s 18 (inter-spouse) and s 21 (normal expenditure out of income). The same applies as to payment of other outgoings such as insurance, general rate, water rate, and ground rent if the property is leasehold.

However, there could have been difficulties in the husband obtaining tax relief on mortgage interest paid on his wife's house under TA 1988, s 354 unless he still had an interest in the property, although the Revenue have not usually taken this point. As from 6 April 1990 under independent income taxation a husband and wife may jointly elect that relief for qualifying mortgage interest paid by one spouse can be allocated to the other or shared (s 356B TA 1988).

(6)   Insurance

If there is any change in the ownership of the legal estate the relevant insurance company should be notified of such change and an endorsement obtained and annexed to the insurance policy.

(7)   Leasehold

Where the property is leasehold, particular attention must be given to the terms of the lease. Thus the prior consent of the landlord may be required (although this is unusual for long leases of say, 99 years); and in any event it is usually necessary to give notice to the landlord of any change of ownership of the legal or equitable interests or mortgage arrangements.

This section of Chapter 3 has been primarily concerned with a change of ownership of the matrimonial home. On the footing that prevention is better than cure, the decision as to the best method of owning the matrimonial property should, wherever practical, be considered from the outset and before a purchase is completed. In that case the spouses should produce their contributions to the purchase price from their separate funds, a record of this being retained. Otherwise complications can arise as to the actual beneficial ownership of the parties (see **3.4**(2) above).

Even where the spouses have modest means at the time of such purchase, the type of ownership from the IHT angle should be considered. The trend of earnings and wealth is usually upwards.

3.5 JOINT BANK ACCOUNTS

3.5:1

As a general rule, and subject as mentioned below, the use of joint bank accounts for substantial sums should be avoided as the law on the treatment of such assets can be uncertain. Where husband and wife have a common fund or pool of their assets, for example by way of a joint bank account, the husband's remuneration is treated as earned on behalf of both spouses being joint property and without regard to the amounts paid in or withdrawn by the party (*Jones v Maynard* [1951] Ch 572, [1951] 1 All ER 802). This presumption does not apply where it can be shown that the joint account was opened as a mere matter of convenience so that the beneficial ownership remained in one party (*Heseltine v Heseltine* [1971] 1 All ER 952 at 956, CA, per Lord Denning MR). Nevertheless, under the rules for independent income taxation for husband and wife, effective from 6 April 1990, the spouses are treated for the purposes of income tax as beneficially entitled in equal shares to income from joint property; that is, unless they enter into a joint declaration that either one or other is entitled absolutely or that they are entitled in unequal shares (TA 1988, ss 282A, 282B). However, in the case of large sums, it may be simpler and clearer for the spouses to have separate bank accounts (and similarly with building society accounts).

3.5:2

As between husband and wife the use of joint bank accounts for relatively small sums can however be recommended on two grounds. First as a matter of convenience for day-to-day living expenditure and secondly to prevent the sums in such accounts being frozen on the death of the first spouse. Substantial sums or assets should not, however, be placed on joint bank or other joint accounts between husband and wife, particularly in the context of **3.5:3**.

3.5:3

Where joint bank accounts are used for making gifts to third parties, serious IHT consequences can follow having regard to the uncertainty of the treatment by the Revenue and with particular reference to the following statutory provisions: s 272—the definition of 'property' as including 'rights and interests of any description'; s 5(2)—the inclusion in a person's estate of property, over which he has a general power of disposal; s 3(3)—the deeming provision whereby a chargeable transfer can occur by 'omission to exercise a right'; and s 268(1)—the inclusion in 'associated operations' of an omission (see also **1.3:1**). Moreover, on death money in the joint account will automatically pass to the surviving spouse as a matter of law through operation of the *jus accrescendi* principle discussed in relation to joint ownership of real property in

3.4:2. Remember that it is not possible to sever a joint tenancy by will (except by an instrument of variation under s 162).

An application of these IHT provisions could result in a double charge on transfers to third parties (for example the whole credit balance in a joint account could be treated as part of a deceased spouse's estate even though subsequently the surviving spouse made gifts (eg, PETs which became chargeable on the survivor's death within seven years) to third parties out of such account and can create anomalies as between the joint owners.

It is moreover important to counter any use of the joint account as a sort of testamentary disposition and 'will' substitute as a specific means of providing for the other joint owner on death. The reason, particularly with larger amounts, is the uncertainty of treatment for IHT described above (see for example *O'Neill v IRC* [1998] STC (SCD) 110 discussed at p 106 above).

3.5:4

It is also advisable for husband and wife to have separate bank accounts in the context of claiming the normal expenditure out of income exemption (see **7.10**), making annual exemption gifts (**7.8**) and £250 gifts (**7.9**), as well as making larger PET gifts to use up the respective nil rate bands of each spouse.

Chapter 4

Practical Aspects and Choice of Settlements

4.0 INTRODUCTION

As indicated in Chapter 2, the making of an appropriate will can lead to useful IHT mitigation; but as wills, by definition, only take effect on death, such mitigation is limited. The position of lifetime settlements requires careful consideration from the estate planning viewpoint. If already existing, should they be retained in their present form or in a varied form or be terminated? Should any new settlement be created?

Settlements still have many practical advantages. The settlor can choose trustees in whom he has confidence (he may even be a trustee himself); the beneficiaries can be selected with considerable flexibility or, in the case of charitable trusts, the trust's objects may include broad charitable purposes; and trusts can be established without the beneficiaries' knowledge, this confidentiality preventing any pressure being exerted on the trustees to release funds prematurely, and providing protection against spendthrifts and unstable beneficiaries.

This chapter treats the practical aspects of settlements under the following heads:

(1) definitions; creation; IHT liability;

(2) main types of settlement summarised;

(3) the discretionary trust regime;

(4) choosing the correct harmless settlement—*accumulation and maintenance*;

(5) choosing the correct harmless settlement—*interests in possession*;

(6) choosing the correct harmless settlement—*discretionary*;

(7) choosing the correct harmless settlement—*other varieties*;

(8) trust pitfalls;

(9) trust busting and variation: 1 by *consent*;

(10) trust busting and variation: 2 by the *court*.

4.1 DEFINITION OF SETTLEMENTS AND RELATED EXPRESSIONS (s 43); CREATION; IHT LIABILITY (s 201)

4.1:1

The IHT definition of settlement is wide, although not quite as extensive as for income tax or capital gains tax (see, for example s 660G Taxes Act 1988).

The term settlement for IHT is defined by s 43(2) (with some modifications for Scottish settlements by s 43(4)). It covers any disposition(s) of property, however effected, whereby that property is held in trust for persons in succession or subject to a contingency; or where that property is held on trust to accumulate income or with a power to make discretionary payments of income (whether or not there is also a power of accumulation). It also covers the position when property is charged to or burdened with a payment of an annuity or other periodic payment for a life or other limited or determinable period, but excludes situations where the charge or burden arises from a transaction whereby full consideration is paid in money or money's worth to the disponers. The expression 'full consideration' in this context may be compared with the dicta in the income tax cases of *Bulmer v IRC* (1966) 44 TC 1; *IRC v Plummer* [1979] STC 793, HL, and *IRC v Levy* [1982] STC 442, which consider commercial transactions where no element of bounty is intended, and which the courts have excluded from the wide income tax definition of settlement (including 'covenant, agreement or arrangement') contained in TA 1988, 660G(1).

Partnership assurance arrangements involving each partner taking out a policy in trust for the remaining partners are regarded as settlements for IHT. By concession (ESC F10), such partners' policies effected before 15 September 1976 are not so regarded (see also **6.3:5**).

Note that a lease of property which is for a life or lives, or for a period ascertainable *only* by reference to a death, or which is determinable on, or at a date ascertainable *only* by reference to a death, is treated as a settlement unless granted for full consideration in money or money's worth (s 43(3)).

Similarly the definition of settlor is widely (though not exhaustively) defined, including the person who directly or indirectly provides trust funds (as referred to *Crossland v Hawkins* (1961) 39 TC 493, CA, and *IRC v Mills* [1974] STC 130, HL—the 'engineer' of the settlement; and see *Butler v Wildin* [1989] STC 22 (nominal subscription for children's shareholding in development company which *parents* built up and *Swires Renton* [1991] STC 49. TA 1988, s 660B (income treated as parents') applied). As to wide definition of the term 'settlor', see also TA 1988, s 660G(1) and (2). In an IHT context the term does, however, have some limit. As noted by the House of Lords in *Fitzwilliam v IRC* [1993] STC 502, there has to be at least a conscious association of the provider of funds with the settlement in question, and it was not sufficient that the settled funds should historically have been derived from the provider of them.

The expression 'Trustees' includes the persons in whom the settled property is vested or who manage it (s 45).

4.1:2   The creation of a settlement

The IHT position on property transferred into settlement is straightforward. Transfers into an accumulation and maintenance or disabled trust or into an interest in possession (eg life interest) trust are singled out as PETs. A settlement on pure discretionary trusts remains a lifetime chargeable transfer; as also are other specialised settlements unless (eg, charitable trusts) they are given special treatment. A trust which gives the settlor an interest in possession does not entail a transfer of value as the settlor is treated as remaining beneficially entitled to the whole of the trust property. A trust giving an interest in possession to the settlor's spouse (having the same domicile) will be an exempt transfer (s 18).

4.1:3 The IHT liability for settlements (s 201)

The primary liability is on the trustees. Their liability is restricted to the trust fund itself and they remain solely liable until the due date for payment, normally six months from the chargeable transfer of value or chargeable distribution (for transfers after 5 April and before 1 October in any year see **1.7:6**). They can apply to the Board of Inland Revenue for a certificate as to their potential liability.

Secondarily liable are persons in whom the property or the income therefrom is vested (ie who have an interest in possession) or in whose favour it has been applied, or any person who is a settlor (while alive) in cases where the trustees are non-resident. This liability of a settlor of a non-resident trust is a very real one because the trustees are unlikely to submit themselves voluntarily to IHT: indeed to do so might constitute a breach of trust. The only satisfaction left to this unfortunate settlor is that the overseas trust fund will remain intact, whereas his assessable estate will be reduced.

4.2 MAIN TYPES OF SETTLEMENT

4.2:1 Interest in possession trusts (ss 49–57)

A beneficiary with an interest in possession has a specific right to the income or is otherwise entitled to the use or enjoyment of the settled property. In the case of a settlement including real property the beneficiary is given a statutory right to occupy (Trusts of Land and Appointment of Trustees Act 1996, s 12). This type of trust is sometimes called a 'fixed interest' trust or a 'strict settlement'. For IHT purposes a beneficiary so entitled is treated as beneficially owning the property in which the interest subsists, not merely an actuarial value of the life interest: (this is logical on the basis that the reversionary interest is generally excluded property). Accordingly as a general rule, subject to reliefs, exceptions and the application of the PET regime, when the beneficiary dies or makes a disposal of his interest in possession, there is an occasion of charge for IHT purposes—see **4.5** below. As to the meaning of the expression interest in possession see further **4.2:4** below.

4.2:2 Discretionary trusts (ss 58–85)

In the case of discretionary trusts (or, to be more precise, given that certain settlements which are discretionary in form, such as charitable and accumulation and maintenance trusts, are given favoured treatment and are excluded from the general discretionary trust regime, settlements containing 'relevant property'–defined in s 58(1)) the class of beneficiaries is usually drawn widely for example, children and grandchildren, their respective spouses, etc. and there is no interest in possession in all or any part of the property. On the tenth anniversary of the commencement of the discretionary trust, and on each subsequent ten-year anniversary, an IHT charge is levied on the value of the settled property, the rate of tax being reduced by 1/40th for each quarter during the previous ten years in respect of any part of the property where the discretionary trust regime did not apply because of changes in the form of the trust, for example, where an interest in possession subsisted during that period. Calculation of the tenth anniversary IHT charge is somewhat complicated. IHT is charged at three tenths of the 'effective rate'. The effective rate is found by first working out the amount of tax, at lifetime rates (the rate of which is one-half the normal scale in Sch 1, at present 20%) which would be charged on a transfer of value equal to the current value of the trust property made by a transferor with a cumulative total equal to that of the settlor in the seven years prior to making the settlement, to which is added the value of any property which left the settlement in the ten-year period.

The 'effective rate' is this figure expressed as a percentage of the value of property on which it is hypothetically charged. As already noted the rate at which tax is then in fact charged on the trust property at the tenth anniversary is then three-tenths of this effective rate. (For discretionary trusts set up before 27 March 1974 the effective rate is based on the current value of the trust property together with the amount of distributions made within the last ten years (but after 26 March 1974).)

There is also a proportionate interim or exit tax charge when property leaves the discretionary trust during the course of the ten-year cycle. This charge is a proportion of the full ten-year charge by taking 1/40th of the normal IHT rate for each quarter of a year which has elapsed since the last full charge and then applying that reduced rate to the full amount of the property. There are also provisions for a proportionate tax charge on property leaving the discretionary trust before the first ten-year anniversary. These interim levies are sometimes called exit charges.

There is no distinction made in the form of these tax charges between UK trusts and overseas trusts. For the detailed provisions see **4.3**.

4.2:3   Accumulation and maintenance trusts (s 71)

These are perhaps the most common 'harmless' trust, and represent a significant and relatively straightforward opportunity for IHT mitigation. They have many of the advantages and characteristics of discretionary trusts without the IHT disadvantages such as ten-yearly anniversary and exit charges. (See **4.4**.) As they were introduced by the then Labour government, the present government are unlikely to restrict their use.

4.2:4   Distinguishing interest in possession from discretionary settlements

In practice it can sometimes be difficult to distinguish between an interest in possession trust and a discretionary trust.

It has already been noted that the general framework of the IHT legislation draws a broad distinction between, on the one hand, settlements in which there is an interest in possession; and, on the other, settlements where there is no interest in possession and which, therefore, are subject to the discretionary trust rules. The legislation provides only limited help in distinguishing between the two. Section 51 sets out the IHT position when a person beneficially entitled to an interest in possession under a settlement disposes of his interest. Section 49(1) declares that a person with an interest in settled property is to be treated for IHT as beneficially entitled to the assets in which his interest subsists. Section 50(1) provides that a person entitled to income produced by a settlement is entitled to an interest in possession in the settled property. Section 50(5) equates an entitlement to the use and enjoyment of property to an interest in possession where there is no entitlement to income produced by settled property. These are all examples of interests in possession in what are sometimes termed 'strict settlements' or 'fixed interest trusts'. The IHT rules for discretionary trusts apply to those settlements where no interest in possession exists, and which are not otherwise excluded from the definition of 'relevant property' in s 58(1). It has already been observed that there are certain types of trust which, although discretionary in nature, receive favoured treatment, eg accumulation and maintenance settlements and trusts for the benefit of employees.

Subject to specially favoured settlements there are therefore two broad categories of settlement: fixed interest trusts, with an interest in possession, with one set of rules on the one hand and settlements without an interest in possession, with another set of rules on the other hand. Unfortunately, save as discussed in the preceding paragraphs, the legislation contains little help in understanding what an interest in possession comprises; and difficulties have arisen in practice in deciding on which side of the line certain cases fall.

The House of Lords in *Pearson v IRC* [1980] STC 318, [1981] AC 753 did a service, therefore, in introducing clear guidelines in the recognition of an interest in possession; even though the case did not give the ruling that some practitioners wished (and indeed the three to two decision in favour of the Revenue in the House of Lords reversed the Court of Appeal, which had unanimously approved the decision in favour of the taxpayers in the High Court). Opinions were therefore (and remain) somewhat divided, but at least there is now more certainty.

The issue in the case, very briefly, turned on the nature of the interest of beneficiaries who were entitled to the income of a fund subject to:

(1) a power of appointment over capital whereby the current interest of each beneficiary could be removed;

(2) the trustees' power to apply income towards the payment of taxes, fees and other outgoings; and

(3) the trustees' power to *accumulate* the income for a period of 21 years, rather than pay it out, as an accretion to the capital of the trust fund.

Was the interest, as the trustees claimed, an interest in possession because the beneficiaries had a right to the income unless and until it was taken away by the trustees in exercise of their power of accumulation or, indeed, their power of appointment over capital? In the context of the power to accumulate, it was conceded by the trustees that if there had been a *duty* to accumulate, then there would not have existed an interest in possession. The House of Lords (by a bare majority) found for the Revenue; that there was no interest in possession. They held that for there to exist an interest in possession the beneficiaries must have 'a present right to present enjoyment'. In this context there was no difference between a power to accumulate and a duty to accumulate. The power to accumulate prevented a present *right* to present enjoyment from ever arising.

A number of helpful principles emerge from the case, as follows:

(1) The existence of an overriding power of appointment over capital does not prevent there being a (possible) interest in possession. An overriding power of appointment was analysed as the right to *terminate* a present right

of present enjoyment, as opposed to a power to accumulate, which prevented a present right of present enjoyment from ever arising.

(2) The fact that the birth of further issue might cut down (or even defeat) a beneficiary's interest similarly does not prevent there being a (possible) interest in possession.

(3) Whether trustees exercise their power to accumulate income or not makes no difference to the decision whether the beneficiary has (or has not) an interest in possession. The mere *power* to accumulate prevents the existence of the interest in possession.

(4) The case shows that there may be apparent interests in income which are neither future interests nor interests in possession for IHT purposes.

(5) The power of trustees to pay taxes and other outgoings out of income is an 'administrative' (not a 'dispositive') power, which does not of itself prevent the existence of an interest in possession, represented by the receipt of net income.

(6) To constitute an interest in possession there must be a present *right* to present enjoyment. (There was no such right in the case of *Trafford's Settlement*, referred to below.)

(7) There was no such right in the *Pearson* case because the trustees could divert the subject matter by deciding to accumulate the income for the benefit of others.

The result of the *Pearson* case has accordingly been to introduce a fair measure of certainty in the previously difficult border areas. Moreover, for the beneficiary who is wealthy (namely has a substantial free estate) the *Pearson* case can be helpful in avoiding the aggregation of the trust fund with that free estate, a situation which applies for interest in possession trusts but not discretionary trusts.

It should perhaps be added, and it fits in with the thinking in *Pearson*, that an infant's contingent interest in a trust fund subject to powers of accumulation does not normally constitute an interest in possession.

The *Pearson* principle has been followed for income tax purposes in the case of *IRC v Berrill* [1981] STC 784. In that case additional rate income tax under TA 1988, s 686, was chargeable because the beneficiary's life interest in the income was subject to the power of the trustees to accumulate the whole or any part, and hence payable at the discretion of the trustees.

In *Stenhouse's Trustees v Lord Advocate* [1984] STC 195 the trustees had a power to advance the settled funds provided the beneficiaries had attained the age of 22. The trustees resolved to transfer to the three beneficiaries P, H and A their respective shares absolutely; but because A had not attained 22 the trustees resolved that payment out of the trust should not be made until each beneficiary gave an indemnity. They wrote accordingly to the beneficiaries on the same day. The Court of Session held that P and H became entitled to an interest in possession in their shares that same day. Their interests could be severed from that of A, where the trustees had acted ultra vires, so that A did not obtain an interest in possession.

Another interesting case was *Re Trafford's Settlement, Moore and Osborne v IRC* [1984] STC 236, where income was held under a discretionary trust for a class of beneficiaries which had not yet closed. There was only one current member of the class. However, because it was possible for a new member of the class to appear before current income fell to be distributed, the present sole member of the class did not have an interest in possession.

In the case of *IRC v Lloyds Private Banking Ltd* [1998] STC 559 Lightman J held that an interest in possession existed where a wife left her share in the matrimonial home, by her will upon the following terms: 'While my husband remains alive and desires to reside in the property and keeps the same in good repair and insured comprehensively to its full value with Insurers approved by my Trustees and pays and indemnifies my Trustees against all rates, taxes and other outgoings in respect of the property my Trustee shall not make any objection to such residence and shall not disturb or restrict it in any way and shall not take any steps to enforce the trust for sale on which the property is held or to realise my share therein or to obtain any rent or profit from the property'. Subject thereto the wife left her interest in the property to her daughter absolutely. The Special Commissioner had decided that an interest in possession had not been created for, as the husband and wife had been joint owners, the husband had the right to occupy the whole property in any event (subject, for example, only to an order of the Court under s 30 Law of Property Act 1925). Lightman J disagreed, and held that the words in the will were dispositive and conferred upon the husband a determinable interest in possession in the wife's half share of the property. Although as a joint owner the husband had the right to occupy the entire property, he did not have the right to exclusive occupation. His wife's will gave him this right. The decision in *Lloyd's Private Banking* has recently been applied in the Special Commissioner's decision, *Woodhall v IRC* [2000] STC (SCD) 558. See also *Faulkner (trustee of Adams, deceased) v Inland Revenue Commissioners* at **2.1:1**.

Trustees of a discretionary trust with a power to permit a beneficiary to occupy a dwelling house or to use furniture may, if they exercise the power, incur an IHT charge by giving the beneficiary an interest in possession (see the CTO's SP 10/79), and there is likely to be a further charge when that interest in possession terminates. Contrast the position if the trustees appoint the property to the beneficiary absolutely: on the basis that the beneficiary has an interest in possession by virtue of his enjoyment of the property, when he subsequently becomes absolutely entitled, there is exemption from IHT under s 53(2): see **4.5:1**. Contrast also the position if the beneficiary purchases (or is appointed) some small beneficial interest in the property which he is allowed to occupy. In these circumstances the beneficiary has a *statutory right* to occupy the entire property (Trusts of Land and Appointment of Trustees Act 1996, s 12). *Query* whether the trustees have given the beneficiary an interest in possession to the extent of their *share* by not allowing other beneficiaries to cohabit?

A gratuitous loan of trust property may be regarded by the Revenue as being equivalent to allowing the recipient of the loan the use and enjoyment of it and therefore amount to creating an interest in possession. However, in the case of a straightforward loan of money validly made out of the trust property at normal rates of interest the loan will be represented in the settlement by the corresponding debt due from the borrower just like any other investment or re-investment of the trust property and should therefore give rise to no IHT problems particularly if the loan is repayable on demand, as it should be (see also *CTT News* November 1981 pp. 262–263).

4.2:5   Discretionary trusts: the basic treatment

The IHT regime for taxing discretionary trusts contemplates two occasions for charging IHT: a general charge on the trust property at ten-year intervals, and a specific charge each time capital is distributed out of the settlement or the property ceases to be held on discretionary trusts (see **4.2:2** above).

4.3   THE DISCRETIONARY TRUST REGIME AND ANCILLARY PROVISIONS (ss 58–85)

4.3:1   Introduction

The present IHT regime for taxing discretionary trusts applies as from 9 March 1982 to 'relevant property', as settled property in which (apart from expressly excluded trusts, see below) *no qualifying interest in possession* subsists (s 58). (See **4.2:4** above on how to distinguish an interest in possession.)

Following the introduction of IHT by FA 1986 the treatment of discretionary trusts remained largely the same except as follows:

(1) reduction of cumulation period to seven years from ten years;

(2) reservation of benefit rules;

(3) knock-on effect of PETs becoming chargeable: see **4.3:6**.

The main purpose of the provisions is to maintain a broad balance between the weight of the IHT charge on property held in other ways (eg by individuals—although gifts into and out of discretionary trusts are not PETs).

Express exclusions from 'relevant property' (s 58):

(1) charitable trusts

(2) accumulation and maintenance settlements

(3) property held in a Treasury-approved maintenance fund

(4) superannuation schemes

(5) employees trusts

(6) protective trusts

(7) disabled trusts

(8) trade compensation funds

(9) excluded property

In respect of excluded property (assuming the settlor was non-domiciled on setting up the trusts) no charge arises where property becomes excluded on ceasing to be situated in UK; or if the beneficiaries are non-domiciled and non-ordinarily resident in the UK, where the trustees acquire exempt gilts by virtue of s 48(4). There can be a curious effect on excluded property where, although the settlor was domiciled outside the UK, there is an interest in possession to a UK-domiciled individual followed by discretionary trusts—see **10.3**.

A 'qualifying interest in possession' is one to which an individual (or a company whose business is to buy interests in settled property and acquired the interest from an individual for full consideration in money or money's worth) is entitled (s 59).

'Relevant property', therefore, refers to the generality of cases where assets and funds are held on normal discretionary trusts. A settlement may be composed of relevant property in *part only*, eg if the other part is held subject to an interest in possession.

Summary of discretionary trust regime:

Item/Charge	Data
(1) Entry charge	=settlor's transfer of value – subject to seven-year cumulation (10 years for transfers before 18 March 1986)
(2) 10-year anniversary charge	40 quarters: pro rata charge as appropriate. No credit for subsequent distributions. Rate=30% of lifetime scale. Top rate IHT is therefore 6% (=30% of top life rate of 20%)
(3) Interim (proportionate) charge=exit charge	Between ten-year charges at previous ten-year anniversary rate; time basis over quarters=maximum $30\% \times 20\% = 6\%$ NB effect of (2)+(3) IHT only on ten-yearly anniversary &/or interim charge (ie while in the trust). No other exit charge
(4) Aggregation—settlor	*Pre*-27.3.74 (= settlement's ten-year cumulation pre the ten year anniversary only) *post*-26.3.74. Full aggregation: (settlor's seven-year cumulation pre-ten-year anniversary and other related settlements of settlor)
(5) Valuation	Diminution in value! ss 3(1), 65(1)(b) NB sound barrier eg where shareholding control is lost
(6) Reverter to settlor/spouse	No exemption
(7) Accumulation and maintenance settlements	Still most favoured and a PET when created. No IHT when assets leave trust generally, except: a) depreciatory transactions b) property leaving trust to non-eligible assignee
(8) Special trusts	Charitable/accumulation and maintenance/superannuation/employee/disabled/protective; exempt while conditions satisfied but then subject to a tapered charge

4.3:2 The ten-year charge (s 61)—general

On the tenth anniversary of the date on which the settlement commenced and on subsequent ten-year anniversaries, a principal charge to IHT is levied on the *then* value of the relevant property comprised therein (as reduced by any available business or agricultural relief). The charge is three-tenths, ie 30% of the life rate of 20%=6%.

No date before 1 April 1983 could be a ten-year anniversary, so the first principal IHT charge takes place on the first ten-year anniversary after that, eg for discretionary trusts created before 30 March 1973 the first ten-year charge was 30 March 1993.

The commencement of the settlement (s 60) takes place when property first becomes comprised in it, which in most cases will be when it is first set up. Under s 80, where a settlor (or his spouse) has an interest in possession when the settlement is first set up, the property is only treated as having become comprised in the settlement when it becomes held on trusts under which neither the settlor nor his spouse have an interest in possession (except that this provision does not apply to settlements created before 27 March 1974— s 80(3)). References to spouse includes a widow or widower.

Also, when a settlor *adds* further assets to an already existing settlement, the addition constitutes a further settlement by the settlor. However in relation to both the above instances (ie the prior interest in possession and the addition) the ten-year anniversaries of the separate settlements are the same as that of the initial settlement. This is because, with regard to the prior interest in possession, s 61(2) expressly declares that the ten years shall run from the date of the original s 80 settlement; and because, with regard to the addition to the settlement, s 60 states that the commencement of the settlement (ie from which the ten years run: s 61(1)) is the time when property first became comprised in it, ie later additions do not signify. Thus, where a settlor makes an initial £100 settlement to get it started, and later adds further property, the ten years have already started running from the date of the settlement. There will of course be a reduction in the IHT rate of 1/40th for each quarter that the addition is not held throughout the ten years (see **4.3:4**). In connection with all references to pre-27 March 1974 settlements it is not a requirement that the trust was discretionary at the outset.

Discretionary will trusts commence from the death. (Beware of other settlements created by the will (except to a spouse), as they are 'related' settlements. The alternative should be considered of a bequest adding to a small lifetime 'pilot' trust—see **4.3:6** below.)

4.3:3 The ten-year charges—aggregation and the effective rate—post-16 March 1974 settlements, ss 64, 66, 67

In order to find the appropriate ie *effective rate* of tax on the discretionary settlement, a *notional chargeable transfer* is first taken (referable to the trust fund) consisting of the aggregate of:

(1) The 'relevant property' forming part or whole of that settlement, valued at the anniversary date. (The strict position is that the charge and the valuation occur 'immediately before' the anniversary.)

(2) As regards undistributed and unaccumulated income, the Revenue view (see Statement of Practice 8/86 dated 10 November 1986) is that such income is to be excluded from the ten-year and interim charges.

The rate of IHT chargeable on accumulated income is calculated as if it were an asset separate from the original trust property. Therefore such accumulated income only becomes settled property subject to the ten-year and interim charges, from the time the trustees become entitled to the income, not earlier.

If any sale of assets or investment switching may be in prospect, those transactions should take place before the anniversary so that the CGT incurred by the trustees is a liability which can be set against the IHT ten-year charge. Where the settlement has been made by a non-UK domiciled settlor, IHT is charged only on assets situated within the UK, and assets outside constitute excluded property. Accordingly, steps should be taken in advance of the tax date to see that the settled funds so far as practicable are invested outside the UK; or alternatively to consider whether the trustees of the non-domiciled trust should hold shares in an offshore investment company, so that those shares will be excluded property even if the underlying company (owned by the trustees) has investments in the UK.

(3) Other property, if any, subject to that settlement, in which an interest in possession has subsisted throughout the settlement period, valued at the commencement of the settlement, or immediately after it became comprised, ie **added** to—the settlement, or property held on special trusts otherwise expressly excluded s 58.

(4) The property comprised in any related settlement valued at commencement of that settlement (ie one made by the settlor on the same day as that settlement, other than charitable trusts). (See s 62.)

The effective rate of tax on that notional chargeable transfer, calculated at the *lifetime scale*, is then additionally ascertained by reference to a prior notional cumulative ladder, in order to represent chargeable transfers within the last ten years, and consisting of:

(a) the values of chargeable transfers made by the settlor in the seven years before the commencement of the settlement (ignoring transfers made on that commencement day), plus

(b) the full amounts subject to interim IHT charges in the ten years before the anniversary.

For the first ten-year charge for a settlement commencing pre-9 March 1982, the so-called 'distribution payments' under the old discretionary trust regime made out of the settlement post-26 March 1974 and pre-9 March 1982 and within ten years preceding that first anniversary charge fall to be included instead (s 66(6)).

There are provisions for adjustments to (a) above: broadly, on an addition of property the total *value* of the settlor's chargeable transfers in the seven years preceding the addition will, if it is higher, be substituted, in the calculation of the rate of tax, for the sum of his chargeable transfers in the seven years before the commencement of the settlement (s 67(3) and (4)).

Having thereby discovered the amount of tax on the notional aggregated chargeable transfer, the effective rate on that transfer is then expressed as a percentage by reference to the amount of tax on the aggregated transfer in relation to the transfer itself. The rate of charge on the relevant property in that settlement is then three-tenths of that percentage rate.

Example 1

Tom made a chargeable transfer of £50,000 on 1 May 1987 (having already exhausted his annual gift exemptions). On 1 July 1991 he made two settlements. £150,000 on settlement A on continuing discretionary trusts; £50,000 on settlement B upon trust for his wife for life (still living July 2001) with remainder on same trusts as in A (then exempt, s 18). On 1 July 2001 the IHT ten-year charge becomes payable on settlement A. The funds are then worth £260,000. The notional chargeable transfer is that £260,000 (settlement B is ignored since it cannot be treated as a related settlement since it has not yet 'commenced' and will not do so until the discretionary trusts come into being (ss 61(2) and 80)).

The notional chargeable transfer is made by a person with a cumulative total equal to that of Tom in the seven years prior to commencement of the settlement (ie £50,000). So the notional chargeable transfer is deemed to be made by a person with an unexpired nil rate band of £192,000. Tax attributable to the notional chargeable transfer is thus (£260,000 − £192,000) × 20% = £13,600. The 'effective rate' is £13,600 (tax chargeable) expressed as a percentage of £260,000 (the amount on which it is charged, ie 5.23%. The rate and IHT on the tenth anniversary of settlement A is therefore three-tenths of 5.23% = 1.57% of £260,000 = £4,082.

Example 2

Dick made gross chargeable transfers of £40,000 on 1 September 1983, £60,000 on 1 May 1986 and £20,000 on 2 February 1987. On 1 July 1991 he made a £140,000 settlement, half on discretionary trusts (worth £180,000 on 1 July 2001); half on trust for brother Harry for life (living 2001, with his interest in possession) with remainder as first half; and also a £50,000 accumulation and maintenance settlement on the same day.

IHT 10-year charge arises on 1 July 2001. Rate is 3/10ths of effective rate (as a percentage) on notional chargeable transfer of £180,000 (then value of relevant property); plus half of £140,000 (value at commencement of settlement of interest in possession property) plus £50,000 (value at commencement of related settlement) ie £300,000; which is added on top of cumulative ladder of £40,000 plus £60,000 plus £20,000, ie £120,000 (all gifts made by Dick in the seven years before the commencement of the settlement). The IHT on life rate scale on a transfer of value of £300,000 by a person who has already made chargeable transfers of £120,000 in the preceding seven years is £35,600. 'Effective rate' is 11.87%. Rate and tax on relevant property of £180,000 is accordingly 3/10ths of 11.87% = 3.56% = £6,408. No grossing up; this is a notional charge.

4.3:4 The ten-year charge—quarterly reductions on rate (s 66)

If the relevant property in the settlement at the anniversary date has for any proportionate period not been subject to the discretionary trusts throughout the whole ten years (eg because there was an addition to the settlement during the ten years or because there was an interest in possession for part of the time) IHT on that proportion of the settled property is *reduced* by *1/40th* for each successive quarter terminating before the property became subject to the discretionary trusts.

Example 3

The value of the relevant property comprised in a discretionary settlement on a ten-year anniversary on 27 June 2001 was £250,000. Full IHT thereon at an overall rate (ie 3/10ths of the effective rate) of 2.40% has been ascertained at £6,000 (after taking into account the settlor's cumulative total at the date of commencement of the settlement, together with the value of related settlements, as demonstrated by

Examples 1 and 2). £100,000 of the value came from an addition to the settlement on 1 January 2000. The rate of IHT on that addition is reduced by 34/40ths representing the completed number of quarters from 27 June 1991 (commencement of the settlement) to 26 December 1999, before the addition was made on 1 January 2000, so that the calculation of IHT becomes 6/40ths × 2.40% × £100,000 = £360. The IHT on the original settled property remains at 2.40% × £150,000 = £3,600, so the total IHT payable is £3,960.

4.3:5 The ten-year charge—limited aggregation and the effective rate—pre-27 March 1974 settlements, ss 66(6), 67(4), 68(6)

The calculation of the notional chargeable transfer to determine the effective rate for the ten-year charge on these pre-CTT/IHT settlements is modified, being *confined solely to the value of the relevant property in the settlement* plus the amounts in the ten-year cumulative ladder of that settlement. Other property in the same settlement with a subsisting interest in possession, and related settlements are omitted.

The make-up of the cumulative ladder is also different.

(a) If it is the *first* ten-year anniversary, the ladder consists of:

    (i) the amounts of distribution payments from the settlement under the old pre-1982 rules plus

    (ii) the amounts subjected to interim CTT/IHT charges (see **4.3:6**) all within the last ten years.

(b) If it is the *second or subsequent* anniversary, it is the amounts for interim IHT only.

Example 4

Mr X made a discretionary settlement on 1 January 1974 (ie a pre-27.3.74 trust). On 1 January 1984 (the first ten-year anniversary) the funds then subject to the settlement were worth £60,000. There had been distribution payments to beneficiaries of £10,000 on 1 December 1978 and £20,000 on 1 March 1980. There was also a sum of £40,000 which ceased to be relevant property on being paid out to a beneficiary on 1 September 1982. On the first ten-year anniversary the effective rate is 17.91% by reference to lifetime CTT of £10,750 on an aggregate of £130,000 less tax attributable to the first £70,000 representing the distributions and the payment out. The chargeable rate is three-tenths of that 17.91%, ie 5.373%. The ten-year anniversary CTT charge on the settled funds is accordingly £3,224 (£60,000 × 5.373%). On the second ten-year anniversary on 1 January 1994 the funds are worth £160,000 (and there have been no distributions etc since 1 January 1984). The charge is 3/10ths of 20% (lifetime rate) on £160,000 after nil rate band (then £150,000) = £600, an effective rate of 0.375%.

4.3:6 Interim IHT charges (ss 65, 68, 69)

IHT is charged *during* the ten-year cycles (ie between the full IHT charges on the ten-year anniversary dates) whenever any part of the property comprised in a discretionary settlement ceases to be 'relevant' (ie discretionary) property. This can happen when:

(a) the trustees make an advance of capital to a beneficiary, so that the property leaves the trust; or

(b) when under the terms of the settlement or in exercise of the trustees' powers of appointment, the terms of the trust are varied so that a beneficiary becomes entitled to an interest in possession; or

(c) (an anti-avoidance provision) if the trustees carry out a value-shifting (depreciatory) transaction which has the effect of reducing the value of the discretionary property unless no gratuitous intent exists (see s 65(1)(b), (6)).

Consequential loss (s 65(2)(9)). The amount on which the interim IHT charge is made is quantified as the amount by which the value of the relevant property in the settlement after the event is less than it would be but for the event. Note that this consequential loss formula occurs in the discretionary trust regime with the same effect as diminution in the estate of an individual under s 3(1) (see also **1.1:2**). Trustees are also subjected to an IHT charge similar to that under s 3(3), if they *omit to exercise* a right, unless they can show that it was not deliberate (s 65(9)).

Grossing up (s 65(2)(b)). If the IHT on an interim charge is paid out of the relevant property remaining in the settlement (ie not directly borne by the beneficiaries) the amount of the tax is added to the consequential loss in a grossing up operation. Contrast the notional ten-year anniversary charge when there is no grossing up.

Exclusions. No charge arises on a distribution out of the trust:

(a) in the *first quarter* from the creation of the settlement or ten-year charge (s 65(4)). (Therefore, if a distribution is made to a surviving spouse within this period, the inter-spouse relief is *not* available, and, in the case of a discretionary will trust s 144 could not apply (*Frankland v IRC* [1996] STC 735 and *Loveday v IRC* [1997] STC (SCD) 321.

(b) for *costs and expenses* fairly attributable to the relevent property (s 65(5)(a)).

(c) on a payment which would be *income* for income tax purposes in the hands of a recipient (or would be if he were resident in the UK) (s 65(5)(b)).

(d) for charitable purposes without any time limit (if temporary a tapering charge applies) (s 76).

Amount subject to interim charge (s 65)

The chargeable amount is arrived at on the basis of the consequential loss formula above, and is grossed up if tax is being paid out of the settlement funds.

Rate of interim charge before first ten-year charge

(a) *Post-26 March 1974 trusts* (s 68). The rate of IHT on the chargeable amount is found in a similar way to that for a ten-year charge (but not precisely in the same way) by taking three-tenths of the effective rate on a notional chargeable transfer consisting of the value at the *commencement* of the property in the settlement and any related settlement; which chargeable transfer is made by a transferor who is deemed to have made in the preceding seven years an aggregate of chargeable transfers equivalent to those made by the settlor in the seven years ending on the day of the settlement, ignoring transfers on that date; and this effective rate comes from the lifetime scale. The rate at which tax is charged is then that rate, multiplied by a fraction consisting of the number of complete quarter-years since the commencement of the settlement, over forty.

Example 5

George set up a £200,000 discretionary settlement on 8 January 1992. He had within the previous seven years made chargeable transfers totalling £70,000. Also on 8 January 1992 he set up a £65,000 settlement for a disabled relative. On 7 April 2001 the trustees of the discretionary settlement advance £20,000 to William absolutely. He finds the tax himself.

To find the rate, take the value of the settlement at commencement together with the commencement value of the related settlement: total £265,000. That is the notional chargeable transfer. This notional transfer is deemed to be made by a transferor with a previous cumulative total of £70,000, on the date of the advance to William. So, the notional transferor has an unused nil rate band of £172,000. Tax on this notional chargeable transfer (at lifetime rates) is therefore (265,000–172,000) × 20% = £18,600, giving an 'effective rate' of 7.02% (ie(18,600/265,000) × 100).

The rate of the advance of £20,000 is therefore three-tenths of 7.02% ie 2.11% so the IHT is £422. There are, however, only 32 complete successive quarters from the date of the settlement up to the date of the advance. Accordingly, the chargeable amount of £20,000 is taxed at 32/40 of 3/10 of 7.02% ie 1.69% = £338.

(b) Discretionary trusts are widely used in situations where no IHT is payable on creation of the trust because the trust fund is within the nil rate band. Moreover frequently this nil rate band can be 'grossed up' by the amount of the business or agricultural relief at 100% or 50% as the case may be. In this connection a note of warning has to be sounded—a trap for the unwary. Under s 68(4) and (5) in arriving at the rate on interim charges before the first ten-year anniversary, no allowance is made for any business or agricultural relief (note the references in those sub-sections to 'the property then comprised in it'). This does not matter where 100% BPR/APR applies ie the asset reduces to zero value, but it does matter where only 50% relief applies. Contrast this with calculating the amount of the 'relevant property' in the trust, ie at ten-year anniversaries where business/agricultural relief is given. It is only the rate that does not benefit.

This also applies to the £3,000 annual exemption(s) that may have been obtained on the creation of the discretionary trust.

Moreover this disadvantage only applies for interim charges before the first ten-year anniversary. At the first ten-year anniversary and at any time thereafter, whether by way of interim charges or ten-year charges, the rate does take account of business and agricultural relief through, so to speak, the back door, because the prior ten-year anniversary rate is the basis of all interim charges thereafter until the next ten-year anniversary.

Rate of interim charge between ten year charges (s 69)

(a) The effective rate that applied at the last ten-year charge will apply to the interim charge.

Example 6

The facts are those in Example 5. At the ten-year anniversary on 8 January 2002 the remaining funds subject to the discretionary settlement had grown in value to £240,000. To find the effective rate the aggregate is taken of the settled funds (£240,000), the value at commencement of the related settlement (£65,000), the chargeable transfers in the seven years preceding the date of the discretionary settlement (£70,000) and the amount of the £20,000 advance on which IHT had been paid in 2001. By taking the proportion of IHT of £32,800 on £395,000, the effective rate of 8.3% is produced. Three-tenths of that gives a rate for IHT on the anniversary of 2.49%, so that IHT of £5,978.71 is payable on the settled funds.

Example 7

Fred, who had made no previous chargeable transfers, created a settlement on 29 April 1983 having an initial value of £200,000 (£50,000 thereof being on accumulation and maintenance trusts). The ten-year charge arises on 29 April 1993 when the discretionary fund (excluding the A & M element) was valued at £300,000. Settlement finally wound up on 30 June 1997 when discretionary element worth £400,000.

Chargeable transfer:	£
relevant property	300,000
add A & M at initial value	50,000
IHT Payable at ten-year anniversary*	350,000
IHT on £350,000 =	40,000
effective rate $= \dfrac{40,000}{350,000}$	11.42%
3/10 thereof =	3.43%
£300,000 × 3.43%	10,290

IHI payable on distribution 30 June 1997

$$\text{IHT payable } = \frac{16\dagger}{40} \times 400,000 \times 3.43\% = \qquad\qquad £5,488$$

* nil rate band then £150,000
16†=completed quarters between April 1993 and June 1997.

(b) That rate will be *recalculated* (s 69(2)) if at the time of the interim charge the settlement includes relevant property ('new relevant property') which was not comprised in the settlement at the time of the preceding ten-year charge. The recalculation takes the form of adding the new relevant property (at the value when it became relevant property) to the property that was subject to the ten-year charge.

(c) Where an interim charge arises after the first ten-year anniversary, pre-27 March 1974 settlements are dealt with in the *same way* as post-26 March 1974 settlements, by reference to the effective rate at the last ten-year charge.

(d) The rate on the amount subject to the interim charge is again modified, by being multiplied by the number of complete quarters since the ten-year anniversary, over forty.

(e) No credit for IHT paid on a ten-year anniversary is given for interim charges and this applies whatever the date of creation of the settlement.

Knock-on effect of PETs becoming chargeable transfers

This can best be explained by an illustration:

Year 1   A makes a PET

Year 3   A makes a gift into a discretionary settlement

Year 5   the trustees of that settlement make an interim distribution (exit charge) to a beneficiary

Year 6   A dies. The amount of the exit charge is revised/increased because A's cumulative total has risen because the PET proves to be a chargeable transfer.

4.3:7   Liability of trustees

It was reported in the *Law Society Gazette*, 12 December 1984, p 3517, that the Law Society had taken up with the Revenue the question of liability of trustees where the settlor of a discretionary trust had been guilty of fraud, wilful default or neglect in matters which affected the rate of IHT (then CTT) on the trust. In their reply, the Revenue had confirmed that the trustees, once they had paid tax on a distribution, could apply for a certificate of discharge (see s 239). However, whether or not a certificate had been issued, the Revenue would not seek to recover the additional tax (eg on fraud by the settlor) from trustees personally where they had acted in good faith and had insufficient funds left in trust with which to pay.

4.3:8   Special cases (ss 70–76)

The IHT code for discretionary trusts contains special relieving provisions for certain types of trust—eg *accumulation and maintenance* trusts, *employee* trusts, *charitable* trusts, and trusts set up for a *mentally* or *physically* disabled person. Broadly speaking trusts of this kind are not liable to the periodic charge while they satisfy certain conditions, and payments out of such trusts are not taxable if made to certain qualifying recipients. However, when the trusts cease to satisfy the conditions or a payment is made to a non-qualifying recipient there is a charge to tax.

This charge is at a flat rate which tapers over time under s 70(6) (relating to charitable trusts but applied in other cases) as follows:

0.25% for each of the first 40 quarters
0.20% for each of next 40 quarters
0.15% for each of next 40 quarters
0.10% for each of next 40 quarters
0.05% for each of next 40 quarters.

Subject to a maximum rate of 30% (year 2025 earliest). The tapered charge will not be levied for periods before 13 March 1975. In the case of special trusts created after 12 March 1975, the charge will not be levied for periods before the date on which the trust was set up or converted into that form. For example a charitable trust set up in March 1975 (or earlier) to terminate in April 1996, (ie a charitable time trust) has subsisted for 84 quarters (21 years × 4). Therefore on termination the trust fund will be charged to IHT at $40 \times 0.25\%$ = 10% plus $40 \times 0.20\% = 8\%$ plus $4 \times 0.15\% = 0.6\%$: total 18.6%. A similar trust set up in May 1983 and terminating in June 1990 will be charged to IHT at 28 (quarters) − 0.25% = 7%.

No tapered charge arises during the period of any complete quarter when the property in question was excluded property.

4.3:9   Maintenance funds for heritage purposes (Sch 4, para 15)

The Treasury has the power to withdraw a direction that a trust should be treated as a maintenance fund if the facts, or the administration of the trust, so warrant. The tapered charge described above applies when property, for whatever reason, ceases to be subject to a maintenance fund.

4.3:10   Planning aspects for discretionary trusts

(1) Avoid related settlements (s 62) by arranging settlements to commence on successive dates. Problems arise if a testator wishes to create more than one trust under his will, one of which is discretionary. However, since a settlement 'commences' when it is first made, notwithstanding later additions (cf ss 60, 61(1) and 66(2)), it is possible to set up a series (on different dates) of small 'pilot' settlements (even £10 each) in the testator's lifetime. He can then merely leave property to each of the settlements in his will.

(2) The statutory references, eg s 65(1)(*b*) to the trustees making a disposition, appear to indicate that the associated operations provisions of s 268 may be applied to discretionary trusts (see s 272, defining a disposition to include a disposition effected by associated operations).

(3) The reverter to settlor or settlor's spouse exemption is available only to interest in possession trusts, not to discretionary trusts.

(4) Where property is *increasing* in value one should appoint as a general rule *before* the next ten-yearly anniversary because the previous ten-yearly anniversary fixes the effective rate. The contrary applies for decreasing values.

Example of increasing values

On 1 August 1992, a 10th anniversary of a pre-27 March 1974 discretionary trust value of trust property = £220,000 (assume brought forward cumulative total = 0).

The IHT rate = 3/10th of effective rate.

Lifetime scale on £220,000 = £14,000 effective rate is $\dfrac{14,000}{220,000}$

10-year anniversary charge = 3/10ths $\times \dfrac{14,000}{220,000} \times £220,000 = £4,200$

If 5 years later, on 1 August 1997 value of trust property increased to £450,000 and appointed on that date, the IHT =

Capital appointed £450,000

$$\frac{3}{10} \times \frac{20}{40} \times \frac{14,000}{220,000} \times £450,000 = £4,295$$

NB Appoint before next 10th anniversary, ie at former 10th anniversary effective rate.

Example of decreasing values

On 1 August 1992, a 10th anniversary, trust property = £400,000 IHT = £50,000 (life rate). Property is decreasing in value and on 1 August 1997 reduced to £250,000. Estimated reduction by 1 August 2002 = £100,000. If the property appointed on 1 August 1997 the IHT =

Capital appointed   £250,000

Charge on distribution is

$$\frac{3}{10} \times \frac{20}{40} \times \frac{50,000}{400,000} \times £250,000 = £4,687$$

NB If appointment deferred until after next 10th anniversary (1 August 2002) nil IHT as below nil band (which rate would apply to appointment of any property for the ten years thereafter even if property increases in value).

(5) The circumstances may be such that the trustees are able to pay the IHT on the ten-yearly charge and interim charges by instalments (see **1.5:2**); it may also then be appropriate to fund such instalments out of income which in certain circumstances might be treated as an income tax expense.

(6) Accumulation and maintenance and interest in possession settlements, in most cases, may well be the most appropriate family trust type, although the use of discretionary trusts, may be preferable where CGT holdover relief could not otherwise be obtained (see TCGA 1992, ss 165 and 260) and/or where maximum flexibility is desired. (See also **4.4, 4.5** and **4.6**.) Where a discretionary trust is contemplated because of the need to claim hold-over relief under TCGA s 260, problems can arise if the value of the property to be settled exceeds the settlor's unused nil-rate band (a charge at lifetime rates can arise). This charge might be avoided by giving the settlor, under the terms of the trust, a valuable right to call for the trust property back again, commencing after an appropriate interval. This type of management has been considered recently in *Melville v IRC* [2000] STC 628, and is discussed in detail in **Chapter 7** of this book–'Gifts'.

(7) See also general planning review of discretionary trusts at **4.6**.

4.3:11   Avoiding gifts with reservation of benefit provisions

The strategy is for any husband to make a gift to a trust under which wife takes an initial interest possession.

The mechanics of this ingenios idea (which appears to survive the extensive changes made by Finance Act 1999) are explained in **7.3:4**.

4.3:12   A summary on discretionary trusts which applies equally to A&M trusts. Discretionary trustees in receipt of dividend income after 6 April 1999 will be taxed less favourably than individuals. The reason for this is that in future, in accounting for tax under s 687 Taxes Act 1988 when a distribution is made out of the trust, although the distribution is still treated as an amount from which tax at the rate applicable to trusts (34%) has been deducted, the trustees are only entitled to set against this the tax *actually* paid by them upon receipt of dividend income and not the associated tax credit. The benefit of the tax credit is 'lost' within the trust. The full implications of this change are discussed in detail by Richard Vallat in his article 'Discretionary Trusts and the new dividend regime' (1999) Vol 7 Issue 1 *Personal Tax Planning Review* p 45.

4.4 CHOOSING THE CORRECT HARMLESS SETTLEMENT—ACCUMULATION AND MAINTENANCE (s 71)

Within the framework of the IHT legislation, there is considerable scope and flexibility in the use of appropriate 'harmless' trusts, of which the accumulation and maintenance trust ('A & M' trust) is perhaps the most frequently encountered example. Moreover, as these trusts were initially introduced under a Labour government, there is less risk of anti avoidance legislation; they also tend to be well received by clients.

4.4:1 IHT

The A & M trust can be described as a common or garden parent's or grandparent's trust—the signpost for the future. Between the years 1975 to 1980, more than one billion pounds worth of assets passed into this type of trust and it is likely to remain politically acceptable (in contrast, possibly, to the discretionary trust). Moreover, as already indicated in **4.1:2**, only an A & M trust and a disabled trust and after 16 March 1987 fixed interest trusts can benefit from the PET regime. Accordingly, the importance and application of A & M trusts has increased further since the introduction of IHT as from 18 March 1986.

Under the provisions of s 71, three basic conditions have to be satisfied:

(1) One or more of the beneficiaries will (ie must and see below) become entitled to the trust fund (ie the capital) or an interest in possession (ie income entitlement or right to use of property) on *or* before attaining a specified age not exceeding 25. Note the mandatory word 'will' and beware of any powers in the trustees or anyone else to diminish or exhaust the trust fund in circumstances that could conflict with such mandatory requirement. This is not a once and for all decision on creation of the trust, but must be kept in mind at all times throughout the life of the trust (see IR letter 8 October 1975). Note also that it is sufficient for the beneficiary in question to become entitled to the income or use of property, not necessarily the capital, by a specified age. This gives rise to considerable flexibility. For example, an A & M trust can provide for the beneficiary to have the income at 25 and the capital at a much later age, eg 40, coupled with the discretionary power of the trustees to advance capital in whole or part *earlier*. Alternatively, the beneficiary may *only* be given a life interest at say age 25 or earlier, with appropriate gifts over in reversion, but subject to a similar discretionary power of the trustees to advance capital in whole

or part. Note that the class of beneficiaries can be left open until the first beneficiary attains the specified age for an interest in possession (or capital) to vest and prior to this time the respective interests of the beneficences in the trust fund need not even be quantified.

(2) Pending the entitlement as above, no interest in possession exists, and the income is either *accumulated* or distributed for the maintenance, education or benefit of one or more of the beneficiaries.

(3) Not more than 25 years have elapsed since the commencement of the settlement (or, if the settlement was created before 15th April 1976, since that date), or the beneficiaries have a common grandparent (ie brothers, sisters, first cousins) subject to permitted substitutional gifts, ie *per stirpes*. This alternative requirement as to the existence of a common grandparent could be breached because the beneficiaries constituted a different generation (otherwise than on a *per stirpes* basis) or because the beneficiaries had different grandparents eg second cousins or because a 'peg leg' beneficiary had to be inserted initially–see below under '**Unborn beneficiaries**'. In those events it may be possible to overcome the difficulty by splitting the A & M trusts in two or more separate trusts by appropriate appointments.

Results

Assuming the three conditions of s 71 are (and remain) satisfied, the general position is that once the assets have been placed into the A & M trust, no further IHT is payable, ie the trust fund is IHT-exempt. Moreover, when the assets go into such a trust, this constitutes a PET and subject to the statutory conditions (see FA 1986, s 101 and Sch 19), IHT may be avoided or reduced. Thereafter, payments or distributions to a beneficiary in whole or part during or upon the termination of the A & M trust do not give rise to an IHT charge; for example when the beneficiary becomes entitled to, or to an interest in possession in, the trust fund on or before the specified age, or the death of a beneficiary before attaining the specified age. No ten-yearly or interim charge arises because the A & M trust is not subject to the discretionary trust regime being specifically excluded from the definition of 'relevant property': see **4.3:1** above.

Accordingly the use of an A & M trust has become fashionable in many circumstances, for example:

(a) as a PET or gift of business/agricultural property eligible for the 100% or 50% relief;
(b) by way of a *trust bust operation* eg of a discretionary trust of the nil band before the first or next relevant ten-year anniversary;
(c) as a capital tax free *fund* eg for private company shares or land;
(d) as a vehicle for death in service capital sums in an occupational pension scheme for a deceased working director who has recommended his children as beneficiaries to the trustees of the scheme. The A & M trustees might then use this liquid fund to buy other (illiquid) assets from the deceased's widow;
(e) to hold appropriate *life policies*;
(f) as a harmless type of *will trust* eg for grandchildren of the testator/testatrix.

Results—exceptional position IHT liability

Although in general terms an A & M trust once established is exempt from IHT, there are exceptional circumstances where IHT liability arises including the following:

First, expiration of the 25-year term if that is the applicable yardstick for the length of the trust (see above). It will be appreciated that the first time such a charge could have arisen is 15th April 2001. The special taper charging provision contained in s 70(6) will apply to the extent that at the end of the period of 25 years (if relevant), beneficiaries exist whose interests have not vested whether in income or capital, the trust then ceasing to be eligible for the favoured treatment. Thus if the whole of the trust fund remains unappointed there would be a tapered charge at the rate of 21% of the value of the trust fund at that time. This nasty trap can, however, be avoided; the moral must be to make the appropriate appointments, whether of capital or of income, prior to that date. For this purpose it may be appropriate to exclude the Trustee Act 1925, s 31 so that the vesting of interests in possession prior to the attainment of majority can be made. If an appropriate power is not contained within the settlement an application to the court to vary the terms of the settlement should be considered.

Secondly, under s 71(3) a charge in respect of depreciatory dispositions (value shifting) could be applied including circumstances where there was an omission to act unless without gratuitous intent. Such circumstances would include an uneven exchange where the trustees consciously make a bad bargain; interest free loans to non-beneficiaries; omission to take up valuable rights issues.

Thirdly, it is possible that an assignment by a beneficiary of full age before attaining an interest in possession could give rise to a charge; for example an accumulation and maintenance trust for Albert, income at age 25, capital at 30; and at age 23 Albert assigns his interest to his second cousin—a charge arises under s 70.

Fourthly, on the bankruptcy of the beneficiary in similar circumstances. It is considered, however, that as these two circumstances are outside the provisions of the settlement itself a charge might well be inapplicable.

Fifthly, on an actual advance out of the trust fund to a non-beneficiary, in the circumstances of the decision in *Re Clore's Settlement Trusts* [1966] 2 All ER 272, although a mere power to make such an advance would not itself breach the conditions of s 71. Indeed, as was indicated in *Clore*, such powers is implicit in the Trustee Act 1925, s 32, which will almost invariably apply, even if with modifications.

Where a charge does arise and the IHT is paid out of the trust fund, grossing up would apply.

A & M trusts normally contemplate the grafting on (conversion into) interest in possession trusts and their eventual termination. This will give rise to an IHT liability if still subsisting on death or a possible IHT liability as a failed PET if terminated prior to the life tenant's death, followed by his or her death within seven years. Therefore consider whether a discretionary trust *may* be more suitable in the long term, especially if the entry and ten-year IHT charges are nil or manageable and the trust assets are not contemplated to rise significantly in value or are to be retained. This could be achieved by giving the trustees power to terminate an interest in possession after it has arisen. The death of a beneficiary of a discretionary trust gives rise to no IHT and normally no CGT. As to the CGT holdover relief advantages of discretionary trusts, see **4.6:10**.

Further analysis—use of word 'will' s 71(1)(a)

As referred to above the condition that the beneficiary *will* become entitled to the capital or income at 25 years or under is a *mandatory* requirement. This was confirmed in *Lord Inglewood v IRC* [1983] STC 133, CA, and *Maitland's Trustees v Lord Advocate* 1982 SLT 483. Accordingly any overriding power to diminish the beneficiaries future entitlement must be avoided: the vesting of capital or interest in possession must not be capable of being defeated by any event other than death under the specified age and subject as qualified below. It is of course perfectly acceptable to vary the beneficiaries' respective presumptive interests while under the specified age provided that the trust fund will still be applied for the beneficiaries *as a class*. In the *Inglewood* case there was a trust for children at 21 or earlier marriage, but subject to a power of *revocation*. The trustees argued that at age 21 the children took an interest in possession and that the power of revocation could be ignored, the word 'will' merely referring to a state of futurity. The court disagreed contending that 'will' must mean that the power of revocation breached the provisions of the now s 71.

Specified age

Section 71(1)(a) requires the attaining of a specified age not exceeding 25 and strictly the reference to a 'period' would be insufficient but for the Revenue concessionary treatment (see *White v Whitcher* [1928] 1 KB 453, 13 TC 202 and Inland Revenue PR of 2 September 1977 also Extra-Statutory Concession F8).

Unborn beneficiaries

Section 71(7) requires the existence of at least one living beneficiary at the time that the trust is created. The inclusion of *unborn* beneficiaries is permitted so long as there is or has been a living beneficiary. This has given rise to the use of so-called 'peg-leg' beneficiaries whom it is not really intended to benefit at all but who act as the appropriate lever on which the trust can be founded. (If such peg-leg beneficiaries died before another beneficiary was born, this would not disqualify the trust.) A peg-leg beneficiary who was the first cousin of the intended beneficiaries might be suitable as there would then exist a common grandparent (see above). Illegitimate, adopted and step children are treated in the same way as children of the full blood (s 71(8)). If such inclusion is not intended by the settlor, an express exclusion is necessary.

An alternative method to overcome this difficulty is to establish the trust as a discretionary trust (preferably within the nil band) and then convert it into an A & M trust when one or more appropriate beneficiaries have been born.

Flexibility

A & M trusts are a species of discretionary trust: in particular, the trustees can appoint unequally among the available beneficiaries and there is no requirement that any one named or ascertained beneficiary need receive a proportionate share. In this context it is important, however, to avoid partial terminations of an interest in possession under s 52(1) which could give rise to an IHT charge under that provision. Accordingly, after attaining the specified age when a beneficiary becomes entitled to the income, the slice of capital of the trust fund supporting that income should be set aside for the beneficiary in question, because if it was reduced in favour of another beneficiary the charge under s 52(1) could arise if the beneficiary did not survive seven years. As the beneficiary is likely to be young and healthy the risk of dying within the seven year period will be small and could be cheaply insured against. The remaining trust fund can, of course, remain in its flexibly distributable form until another beneficiary attains an interest in possession when a similar setting aside of his share of capital must be made. Similarly, *after* attaining the specified age the beneficiary's share must not be capable of being *increased* because such a power would breach s 71 in that the other beneficiaries would not then necessarily become entitled by age 25. In other words, the settlement would no longer qualify for favoured treatment after the date upon which the first beneficiary attains the specified age, and from then on the normal discretionary trust regime would apply.

Where the trustees have restricted powers of appointment or revocation, it follows that the conditions of s 71 need not necessarily be breached, namely, if on any such appointment or revocation the result is that the trust fund is applicable to other beneficiaries satisfying the conditions of that section.

As regards another aspect of flexibility, most well drawn A & M trusts give the trustees wide powers including, for example, powers to enable beneficiaries to occupy property; take out insurances; carry on business; and hold non-income producing forms of investment. It has been argued that the mere existence of such powers breaches s 71, in that there is no certainty that any beneficiary will ever receive any income, ie interest in possession by age 25. It is understood that the practice of the CTO is that if the deed contains an appropriate 'self-denying ordinance', (ie that these powers will never be used to breach the conditions of s 71) the trust will still be capable of satisfying the section. A suggested wording could be along the following lines:

> 'None of the powers or provisions contained in this Trust Deed shall be exercised so as to (a) prevent any beneficiary entitled hereunder to an interest in possession (as defined in Inheritance Tax Act 1984 Part III) from being so entitled, or (b) prevent s 71 of the said Act (accumulation and maintenance trust requirements) applying to any of the trusts contained in this deed, if the said s 71 could otherwise apply.'

Note, however, that the efficacy of this clause has not yet been tested in the courts.

Such wide powers might also be regarded as creating and terminating an interest in possession: see generally *Dymond's Capital Taxes* 21.368–369.

Accumulations

Under the provisions of the Law of Property Act 1925, ss 164 and 165 as extended by the Perpetuities and Accumulations Act 1964 there are currently six permitted periods of accumulation, the most commonly used being 21 years from the date of the settlement. In this context, the trust deed may require specific wording to curtail as necessary the accumulations. For example, if on the creation of the trust one of the beneficiaries is already five years old, accumulations for him must not be permitted for the full 21 years as that would attempt to give him his entitlement beyond the required age of 25 years. In order to comply *also* with the vesting requirement at age 25 in s 71, the *shorter of* age 25 and the permitted accumulation period must apply to the A & M trust.

Section 71(1)(b) states that the income '*is to be*' accumulated. Accordingly a mere power to accumulate may be insufficient unless the trustees, in default of accumulation, are bound to apply the income for maintenance, education or benefit.

Where there is no specific provision as to accumulation or the accumulation period defined by the trust deed has expired, the implied right to accumulate under the provisions of the Trustee Act 1925, s 31 may apply up to the age of majority ie 18 (or 21 for pre-1 January 1970 settlements).

Note that a transfer to an A & M settlement is given PET treatment only 'to the extent that the value transferred is attributable to property which, by reason of the transfer, becomes settled property [subject to the A & M provisions]' (s 3A(3)). To be regarded as thus 'attributable', the transfer must be identified in the trust as settled property. Accordingly, the direct payment by the settlor of expenses on behalf of the trustees; the payment to a creditor in discharge of a debt owed by the trustees; the payment by the settlor direct to the life company of renewal premiums on a settled policy: these are all chargeable transfers (subject of course to the usual annual and normal income exemptions) and not PETs. Alternative routes should therefore be considered. Normally, on the footing that the trustees hold a bank account as part of the trust assets, a cheque—paid to the trustees and reflected in an increase in the credit balance—can be readily identifiable with an increase in the value of the settled property solely attributable to that cheque. The trustees are then free themselves to pay off their proper expenses and outgoings.

This aspect is of particular importance where the settlor pays premiums on trust policies.

The payment by a donor of school fees or buying a holiday is not a PET because no one's estate, the Revenue claims, is thereby increased and no property becomes comprised in the recipient's estate. The solution is for the donor to pay the donee cash, so that the donee, or someone on his behalf, then at a later stage pays for the schooling or holiday.

4.4:2 Capital gains tax

(1) 'Gifts' pre-14 March 1989

Having regard to the general holdover relief in FA 1980, s 79 etc it had been possible to defer any CGT payable on the creation, distribution or termination of the trust fund.

(2) TCGA 1992, ss 165 and 260

For 'gifts' on or after 14 March 1989 holdover deferral is restricted to:

(a) gifts of business assets (including unquoted shares in trading companies and holding companies of trading groups) (TCGA, s 165);

(b) gifts of *all* property which attracts IHT agricultural property relief (ie whether owner occupied or let and including 'hope', development value);

(c) gifts of heritage property;

(d) gifts to heritage maintenance funds;

(e) gifts to political parties;

(f) gifts on which there is an *immediate* charge to IHT, in particular gifts into discretionary trusts including the nil band and transfers chargeable at the nil rate because, for example, business property relief applies;

(g) occasions on which a beneficiary becomes *beneficially*, ie absolutely, entitled to trust assets held on accumulation and maintenance trusts (TCGA 1992, s 260(2)(d)), ie at a time when *no* interest in possession exists. Unfortunately this is of limited use, because most modern flexible type accumulation and maintenance trusts only provide that the beneficiary becomes entitled to *income* at the specified age, not capital, which remains in the trustees' discretion. It may be possible to advance the capital at the same time or before entitlement to income, arises, thereby satisfying that statutory requirement. Beware, that if an absolute appointment is made to a beneficiary with an existing interest in possesion a charge to capital gains tax may well arise *unless* the appointment is of 'business or agricultural assets' (see (a) and (b) above). A second possible solution may be as follows:

The beneficiary of the A & M trust as **settlor** settles/assigns as from an 'effective date' (and without apportionment) all his income interest under the trust to be held by the trustees on new trusts. Such income under the new trust **is** on A & M terms, eg with powers of accumulation and/or maintenance etc. From the date on which it is intended that the beneficiary is to receive the **capital** eg 25, this new trust collapses so that the A & M regime ceases and the beneficiary becomes entitled to the **capital and income at the same time** and therefore TCGA 1992 s 260(2)(d) is satisfied and the holdover claim is available. The assignment of the interest in possession is not a CGT disposal it is an assignment of an interest in *income* only.

In the case of holdover relief under TCGA, s 165 (essentially (a) and (b) above), the relief must, following the introduction of self-assessment, now be claimed on a specific claim form which the Revenue have produced (see further Help Sheet IR 295).

Where deferral is not available, payment of tax by instalments will be allowed for gifts of land, controlling shareholdings and minority holdings in unquoted companies (eg investment companies where holdover relief under TCGA, s 165 is not available), but not free of interest.

Moreover, the position of trustees, especially professional trustees, must be carefully considered, particularly where the trusts are likely to be 'exported'—see TCGA 1992, ss 80–98 and Sch 5.

In order to maximise the small gains exemption for a trust husband and wife should create *separate* (*not* joint) trusts. Thereby each trust will be eligible for this exemption, notwithstanding that for CGT purposes generally (and subject to independent taxation from 6 April 1990), husband and wife are treated as one person.

(3) CGT on disposals

On disposals the trustees of A & M trusts are liable to pay capital gains tax at 'the rate applicable to trusts' contained in section 686 Taxes Act 1988 (section 4(1AA) Taxation of Chargeable Gains Act 1992).

A former distinction between A & M trusts and interest in possession trusts whereby interest in possession trusts only suffered capital gains tax at 23% (the basic rate of income tax) was removed by Finance Act 1998. All trusts are now taxed at "the rate applicable to trusts".

4.4:3 Income tax

Under the provisions of TA 1988, s 686 to the extent that income is accumulated, A & M trusts are liable at the 34% rate, known as 'the rate applicable to trusts'. Accordingly it may be appropriate to distribute the income to low tax paying beneficiaries subject always to the provisions of TA 1988, s 660B (whereby if the settlement is by a parent the income is treated as his). The use of A & M trusts by grandparents may therefore be of particular significance as the provisions of s 660B do not apply.

In addition the other anti-avoidance provisions in TA 1988, Pt XV must be taken into account, including in particular s 660A settlements where settlor retains an interest (subject to the exclusions, eg reverter to settlor on death under the age of 25 where beneficiary has a contingent interest); the notorious ss 677 and 678—sums paid to settlor otherwise than as income and capital sums paid by body connected with settlement; and s 660B in relation to parent settlements as referred to above.

Upon the disadvantages associated with the receipt of dividend income by discretionary trustees see further **4.3:12** above.

As seven-year covenants of income from one individual to another no longer transfer that income for tax purposes, a capital settlement such as an A & M trust, remains the only effective method of achieving this.

Example: Life of an A & M trust

DATA:

Settlor: parent or grandparent

Beneficiary: child/grandchild

Entitlement: income at age 18

capital at age 30 (or earlier if trustees decide in their discretion to advance the whole or part of the trust fund Trustee Act 1925, s 32 to be extended).

NOTE: age 30 used for illustrative purposes only. The requirements of an A & M trust are satisfied provided the beneficiary becomes entitled to income by age 25, s 71(1). It is therefore usually better/more flexible to leave the appropriation of capital in the trustees' *discretion*. The settlor should write the trustees an appropriate letter of his wishes as to how such discretion should be exercised. This non-binding indication can, of course, be varied from time to time.

Trust fund: eg family company shares/property/investments.

A & M Trusts

TABLE: LIABILITY FOR THE TAXES

Relevant STAGE of the Trust/ AGE of BENEFICIARY	Inheritance Tax	Capital Gains Tax	Income Tax
1. START of TRUST—tax liability of settlor (beneficiary say age 2)	NIL—a potentially exempt transfer assuming 7-year survivorship and no reservation of benefit: see FA 1986, s 101 and Sch 19	YES—at income tax rates, UNLESS holdover election made by settlor (alone) TCGA 1992, s 165	from START until beneficiary age 18 (a) accumulated income: 34% or (b) income distributed for beneficiary's maintenance, education or benefit: (i) if parents' settlement = parents' income Income and Corporation Taxes 1988, s 660B (although tax payable by trustees) (ii) if NOT (eg grandparents' settlement treated as) beneficiary's income likely to be eligible for repayment claim—consider repayment claims for any income tax deducted at source

Relevant STAGE of the Trust/ AGE of BENEFICIARY	Inheritance Tax	Capital Gains Tax	Income Tax
2. Beneficiary AGE 18 (see data)	NIL—no transfer or deemed transfer of value. Between the ages of 18 and 30, the trust becomes an interest in possession type and if terminated, such termination normally constitutes a potentially exempt transfer: IHTA 1984 s 3A	NIL—no disposal and trust continues see TCGA 1992, s 76. If the interest in possession is subsequently terminated, there is a CGT disposal subject to holdover election by trustees and beneficiary TCGA 1992, ss 165	Beneficiary becomes entitled to the income (see data) and therefore his income for income tax purposes. See also Trustee Act 1925, s 31
3. Beneficiary AGE 30 (see data)	NIL life tenant becomes absolutely entitled to capital IHTA 1984, s 53	YES disposal for CGT unless held over TCGA 1992, ss 165 (s 260(2)(d) will not be applicable see **4.4.2**)	Assets become beneficiary's absolutely, therefore his income— no change since stage 2 above

4.5   CHOOSING THE CORRECT HARMLESS SETTLEMENT—INTERESTS IN POSSESSION (ss 48–53)

4.5:1   IHT

A person beneficially entitled to an interest in possession in settled property (and see the discussion on the *Pearson* case in **4.2:4** on what constitutes an interest in possession) is treated as beneficially entitled to the property in which the interest subsists. Therefore if an individual is entitled to the whole of the income, say as life tenant, the general rule, in the absence of reliefs and exemptions including the application of the PET regime, requires the whole of the trust fund to be assessed to IHT when such life tenant disposes of his interest during his life or when he dies. Moreover the value of the trust fund will be added to the individual chargeable transfers of the beneficiary concerned.

There is a pro rata liability for a partial interest. Where a persons entitlement is to income in a specified amount in any period such as an annuity, his interest in possessions is taken to subsist in such part of the trust property as produces that amount in that period. Artificial arrangements to reduce liability by raising or lowering the yield from the trust fund can be countered under the provisions in s 50(4), the Treasury maximum and minimum prescribed rates. Trustees are usually given power to vary investments. Therefore by switching into high yielding assets when the interest in an annuity is expected to terminate (with the resultant possible, PET, IHT charge), the annuity would represent a smaller share of the total income. Conversely, with a switch to low yielding assets, the balance of the income would represent a reduced share and therefore save IHT at the time when that balance was disposed of. The Treasury-prescribed higher and lower rates of yield are imposed to restrict this type of manipulation. Under the Inheritance Tax (Settled Property Income Yield) Order 2000 (SI 2000/174) the Treasury have taken the step of linking the yields to the FT Actuaries Share Index published in the *Financial Times*. For the higher rate, it will be the yield shown at the relevant date of Irredeemables in the FTSE Actuaries Government Securities UK Indices, and for the lower rate, the gross dividend yield of the All-Share actual dividend yield.

The use, occupation and enjoyment of trust assets such as a house can also constitute an interest in possession (s 50(5)) see also **3.4:1**, where SP 10/1979 is mentioned. It will be noted from the second paragraph of that SP, that the Revenue view is that no interest in possession is created by the grant of a lease at less than full consideration, although there will normally be an IHT charge on the diminution arising in the value of the trust fund.

As mentioned the termination of an interest in possession during life or on death would normally give rise to a charge on the capital supporting that interest subject to the PET rules, but there are important exceptions which should enable this type of trust to be used as an appropriate 'harmless' trust. These exceptions apply when the beneficiary becomes beneficially entitled, either absolutely, or to another interest in possession (in the latter case, unless the new interest has equivalent value to the former interest, there is pro rata exemption only under s 53(2) and s 52(4)(b); to the extent that the disposal is for a consideration in money or money's worth (see s 52(2)); to the extent that the trust property reverts to the settlor (s 53(3) and s 54(1)); to the extent that the trust property reverts to the settlor's spouse (or his/her/widow(er)) within two years of his/her death (s 53(4) and s 54(2)); and in respect of a surviving spouse where ED was payable on the first death. This last exemption applies in the case of a lifetime or death termination of an interest in possession where the first spouse died before 13 November 1974 (Sch 6, para 2)), and in these circumstances the trustees should aim for maximum capital growth of the trust fund as the fund will be exempt from IHT. This will involve important investment decisions, for example, that any cash deposits should be used to acquire appreciating assets. This transitional exemption will of course not apply to any new assets added to the trusts, as the application is in respect of switching investments. In this context consider a widow selling her home to the trustees and remaining with an interest in possession. The gain on the sale and the future gain while in possession will escape CGT (TCGA 1992, ss 222 and 225), meanwhile the widow receives liquid resources which she can spend or use for estate planning.

Example

Andrew Vickers died on 30 September 1970 and left £100,000 after payment of ED in trust for his wife, Agatha, for life, with remainder to their son. Agatha died on 30 June 2001, having made no lifetime gifts and leaving her entire free estate of £315,000 to her son. Andrew's will trust property was then worth £200,000.

On Agatha's death, IHT of £29,200 is payable on the free estate but the trust passes free of IHT to the son, ED having been paid on his father's death.

Had Andrew died on or after 13 November 1974, no ED or IHT would have been payable on the amount left in trust to Agatha (s 18) and IHT on her death would have been £109,200 on the combined total of her trust and free estate.

There is an anomaly in this retained ED surviving spouse exemption with regard to the related property rules in s 161 where, for instance, a widow has private company shares in her own estate, and she has a life interest under her husband's will (ED paid on his death) in a fund which includes shares in the same company. If her life interest terminates on her death, the husband's shares, though not liable to IHT, can nevertheless be brought in as related property in valuing the widow's own shares because Sch 6, para 2 provides that the husband's will trust property shall be 'left out of account' on the widow's death; but that does not prevent the husband's will trust shares, to which the widow is deemed to be beneficially entitled under s 49(1), from being brought in, when valuing her *own* shares, as related property. Contrast the position if the widow releases her life interest in her lifetime. Exemption of the husband's fund is then obtained under Sch 6, para 2, and no question of the valuation of the husband's shares or of her own at that stage arises. It may be appropriate for the widow to release part only of her life interest, eg sufficient of the shares in the husband's fund to bring the combined holding below 50% or, depending on other circumstances, some other level. However the release of her life interest, unlike termination on death, will give rise to a CGT charge where a beneficiary becomes absolutely entitled, under TCGA 1992, s 71(1), although this gain may be eligible for holdover relief under TCGA 1992, s 165 as appropriate unquoted shares (see **4.4:2** (2)) so it is a question of arithmetic. (On termination or death there can, exceptionally, be a CGT charge if holdover relief was claimed when the settlor placed the assets into trust, subject to any further possible holdover claim.) For the purpose of determining voting control s 269 provides that the interest in possession beneficiary aggregates his own beneficial holding with the trustees' holding. This is a corollary of the basic situation that if an individual owns shares in a company and is life tenant of a trust which also owns such shares, the shares are valued as if the individual owned both holdings.

The effect of the Revenue statement of May 1990 (see Butterworths *Orange Tax Handbook*, 2000–01 edn, p 15773 and **1.3:4**) is that on the lifetime termination of an interest in possession, the IHT charge under s 52(1) does not require the valuation to be aggregated on a pro rata basis, namely as to the individual's beneficial ownership and the interest in possession entitlement. They are to be valued separately. For example, if the estate owner holds, say, 40% of the ordinary shares in a company beneficially, ie outright, and 40% by way of a life interest, the two 40% holdings are to be valued in isolation on a minority basis; and not as part of an 80% controlling interest. Therefore, if an estate owner wishes to gift a controlling interest, it may nowadays be better to give two separate minority valued gifts, one beneficially/absolutely, the other by way of an interest in possession. It would be wise not to make the two gifts contemporaneously having regard to the application of the *Ramsay* principle (notwithstanding the present uncertainty surrounding its precise application following the decision of the House of Lords in *McNiven v Westmorland Investments* [2001] STC 237) and associated operations rules in s 268.

Interest in possession as PETs as from 17 March 1987

When IHT replaced CTT on 18 March 1986 it was anomalous that gifts into trust for beneficiaries under age 25 were PETs—ie exempt if donor survived the seven years without a reservation of benefit— even though an immediate right to income did not exist provided such trusts complied with the accumulation and maintenance trust requirements under IHTA, s 71. By contrast gifts into trust for beneficiaries over 25 who obtained an immediate right to income (ie an interest in possession trust) were chargeable transfers subject to lifetime rates.

Pursuant to F(No 2)A 1987, s 96, this anomaly ceased for lifetime transfers made on or after 17 March 1987. These amendments apply on three important occasions. First, upon the creation of such an interest in possession trust by an individual beneficially entitled to the relevant assets in favour of another individual (not being the settlor's spouse as such a transfer would be inter-spouse exempt under IHTA, s 18)—see IHTA 1984 s 3A.

Secondly, upon transfers or deemed transfers on the termination of such a trust where such termination is in favour of:

(a) an individual (not being the life tenant's or settlor's spouse, or settlor— these being covered by other exemptions). Such individual may benefit absolutely or become entitled to another interest in possession or;

(b) an accumulation and maintenance trust; or

(c) a disabled trust.

Third, in the case of depreciatory transactions (referred to in IHTA, s 3A (2), s 3A(6) and (7) and s 52(3)).

The results of the above are extremely important. Many donors are reluctant to make outright gifts even to beneficiaries who are over age 25. They are now able to take advantage of the PET regime *and* achieve this objective through the use of an interest in possession trust. Gifts into discretionary trusts and close company transfers under IHTA, ss 94–101 remain the main types of chargeable transfers.

However it must be remembered that the accumulation and maintenance trust still has an important advantage over the interest in possession trust. On disposal/termination for the former there is IHT exemption whereas for an interest in possession trust the seven-year survivorship period of the life tenant would apply.

Therefore, this does not cure the perennial problem of a testator who wishes to give his home to his children and give his widow a right to live there as long as she wishes. The new rules only help in these circumstances if the widow terminates that right more than seven years before her death.

Trust busting (see **4.9**) benefits from the new rules: thus where a life tenant and remainderman break the trust and divide the fund between them (eg on an actuarial basis), the part received by the remainderman has hitherto been liable to IHT under IHTA, s 52(2). After 17 March 1987 this liability ceases provided the life tenant survives seven years from the trust-bust.

Section 54A and s 54B anti-avoidance provisions

These provisions contain complex anti-avoidance rules. The aim is clear, namely to prevent loss of IHT where a settlor by way of a PET creates an interest in possession for a short term on the termination of which a discretionary trust arises. The loss of IHT would result if the life tenant's aggregation of previous transfers in the last seven years was lower than the settlor's, because the life tenant's termination would be the measure of the transfer of value, not the settlor's.

Section 54A applies where:

(1) there is a termination of an interest in possession on death or in lifetime; and

(2) the whole or part of the value transferred is attributable to property which became settled as a PET by the settlor on or after 17 March 1987 and within seven years before termination of the life interest; and

(3) the settlor is still then alive; and

(4) the trust fund then becomes settled property with no qualifying interest in possession (ie held on discretionary trusts).

In such circumstances IHT is calculated on the higher of:

(a) the normal charge, ie termination of the interest in possession aggregating the life tenant's chargeable transfers in the previous seven years;

(b) the aggregate IHT at the lifetime rates had the creation of the settlement not been a PET and taking into account the settlor's chargeable transfers within seven years preceding the creation of the settlement. In other words, the charge can be broadly on the basis of the settlor having created the discretionary trust.

Note that the mischief complained of is not caught where the initial settlement is an accumulation and maintenance trust under IHTA s 71 and in circumstances wherein an interest in possession thereunder is revoked and a discretionary trust substituted. By contrast, a disabled trust under IHTA s 89 is caught as such a trust is treated like an interest in possession trust when followed by a discretionary trust.

Note also that IHTA s 54A(2)(d) provides a let out from this higher rate anti-avoidance charge if the discretionary trust lasts for less than six months.

The trustees are primarily liable for the above IHT charge; hence the need for them to retain sufficient assets for up to seven years from the creation of the interest in possession trust. The settlor will, however, also be liable where the trustees have been non-resident between 16 March 1987 and the settlor's death. If the trustees were United Kingdom resident at the creation of the settlement and have been non-resident between 16 March 1987 and the relevant death, the settlor's liability does not arise.

4.5:2   Income tax

(1) As regards income tax, by definition a beneficiary who has an interest in possession must be entitled to the income as it arises and hence the income tax liability will depend on the beneficiary concerned, ie his rates and subject to his allowances. Also by definition there will be no power to accumulate, hence the rate applicable to trusts (currently 34%) as normally applies to accumulation and maintenance and discretionary type trusts is not in point.

(2) Avoiding the income tax surcharge.

This proposal relates to avoiding the rate applicable to trusts under TA 1988, s 686 in respect of certain beneficiaries of lifetime and will trusts; prior to them attaining interests in possession, and obtaining repayment claims. A problem arises where there is a minor beneficiary entitled to a gift contingently on attaining 18 or a later age. As the beneficiary only has a contingent interest in the income before the age of 18 two main disadvantages result. First, up to the age of 18 the trustees must pay income tax at the rate applicable to trusts; and secondly, there would be no possibility of repayment claims for the beneficiary, except insofar as the income is paid or applied for the beneficiary's maintenance, education or benefit. A possible solution is to give the beneficiary a vested interest in the *income* as soon as it arises, with the result that although he only has a contingent interest in the capital, the income will be regarded as his and consequently the trustees or the beneficiary will only be taxed by deduction at the basic rate and repayment claims may be made on behalf of the beneficiary. Accordingly the particular gift in the trust deed or will must provide that the beneficiary has a vested right to income before 18 (which income shall belong to the infant absolutely). A number of further difficulties arise if the gift is a gift by will such as a contingent *pecuniary* legacy which does not normally carry the intermediate income pursuant to the Trustee Act 1925, s 31. In that case the will must provide that the legacy should be set aside, invested and that the income produced by the investment of the legacy should belong absolutely to the beneficiary. This would enable the income tax advantages discussed above to apply also to the contingent pecuniary legacies. Having achieved these income tax advantages one must appreciate the possible risk, namely that the entitlement to income will operate as from the date that the trust commences to operate, and the infant beneficiary will have an interest in possession from then. Accordingly, should he die before he becomes entitled to the capital an IHT charge arises—but this can be easily insured against. Consider also the possible moral objections to giving perhaps significant amounts of income to one so young.

As to income tax anti-avoidance provisions applicable to settlements by parents for unmarried minors see TA 1988 s 660B.

4.5:3 Capital gains tax

(1) As regards CGT the mere fact that an interest in possession is granted to the settlor will not prevent the creation of the trust being a disposal for CGT purposes, although restricted holdover relief under TCGA 1992, s 165 may be available—see **4.4:2** above.

(2) Trustees of all settlements, whether discretionary or interest in possession, are liable to tax on their capital gains at the 'rate applicable to trusts' for income tax (currently 34%). A former distinction whereby interest in possession trusts were only taxed at 23% was removed by Finance Act 1998.

(3) It may be possible to 'wash out' CGT on a death in the circumstances outlined in **2.2:1**(3).

(4) TCGA 1992, ss 77–79

Care must be taken to ensure that neither the settlor nor his spouse has the capability of taking any interest in the settlement; otherwise the rate of CGT will be a maximum of 40% as opposed to the rate discussed at (2) above (see TCGA 1992, ss 77–79).

(5) TCGA 1992, s 67

(i) As to restriction of holdover relief see **4.4:2**

(ii) *'Unbalanced trusts'*: gifts between husband and wife etc.; changes were introduced in the income tax rules for income deriving from gifts between husband and wife and for some other settlements. The changes ensure that with independent taxation as from 6 April 1990, income from simple outright gifts of assets between husband and wife and also certain pensions allocated between them are taxed as income of the recipient. However the income will generally be treated as the *donor's* for tax purposes if, for example:

    (a) the donor has the right to get the asset back in the future, or to decide what the recipient should do with it; or

    (b) the donor uses a trust to give the income to his or her partner while retaining control over the capital, or passing the capital to a third party. Therefore in a common form life interest trust where a husband settles assets the income from which goes to his wife for life remainder as to capital to the children, the income is not the wife's for independent taxation purposes (see also TA 1988, s 660A(2)).

(iii) Deeds of variation under s 142 were to be very restricted for deaths after the Finance Act 1989 Royal Assent date. Although the Finance Bill provisions were abandoned, anti-avoidance legislation is a possibility in the future. The use of flexible life interests in favour of spouses with wide powers of appointment in favour of such spouses and/or other beneficiaries should to a degree overcome this problem. Such a course is therefore to be recommended.

(iv) Trustees need to watch the distinction between a distribution by a company of profits akin to a dividend in specie and hence income—to which beneficiaries interested in income are entitled—and a company reconstruction where what the trustees receive is capital to be added to the trust fund. In *Re Lee, Sinclair v Lee* [1993] 3 All ER 926, ICI decided to restructure its activities and placed its pharmaceutical interests into a new company Zeneca Group plc. They then demerged Zeneca, so that all the shareholders of ICI received shares in Zeneca. In the *Lee* will trust the testatrix had left ICI shares upon trust to pay the income to her husband for life, and on his death to her son absolutely. The court decided that the ICI transaction was a company reconstruction, with two capital assets (shares in ICI and shares in Zeneca) replacing one existing capital asset (shares in ICI). Accordingly, the trustees were to hold the Zeneca shares as capital of the trust fund. (For further analysis see the Case Note by Andrew Hitchmough at [1993] *British Tax Review* 406.) As for enhanced scrip dividends received by trustees of interest in possession trusts, see the Revenue SP 4/94 dated 17 May 1994.

4.6   CHOOSING THE CORRECT HARMLESS SETTLEMENT—DISCRETIONARY

Some estate planning aspects involving discretionary trusts

The introduction of the ten-year and proportionate (interim) CTT/IHT charging provisions in s 64 etc in place of the old periodic and distribution charges caused a revision of the earlier view in CTT/IHT planning that discretionary trusts in their pure form should generally be avoided or required justification in the particular circumstances of the case. For reasons already discussed where it is practical to use an accumulation and maintenance trust (s 71) this is likely to prove the *best* form of family trust. Subject to this the formation of a discretionary trust can still merit consideration for a number of reasons.

4.6:1   The burden of IHT

Provided that the settlor has not travelled too far up his own cumulative ladder, the IHT charges on discretionary trusts may well prove manageable.

Example A

Mr X has not made previous chargeable gifts. On 1 May 1991 he settles £71,000 on discretionary trusts (no IHT—nil rate band). On the ten-year charge in 2001 the trust property is worth £342,000. The IHT charge is £6,019.20 (nil rate band £242,000). If capital advances had been made *within* the ten years or the trust wound up, the IHT rate applicable would be calculated at 3/10 of the scale of IHT at the time of exit multiplied by 1/40 for every completed quarter to the date of charge from commencement. Based on £71,000 that inevitably produced a nil charge on exit.

Example B

Mr Y settles £200,000 on discretionary trusts on 7 April 1991, having made chargeable gifts of £242,000 within the previous seven years. On the ten-year anniversary in 2001 the trust property is worth £500,000 and the IHT charge would be £30,000 which is only 6% of the value of the property.

Even in respect of sizeable distributions, bearing in mind that currently the life rate is 20% (above the nil rate band) and with the ten-year charge at 30% thereof, the maximum ten-year charge can never exceed 6%; and if the property is eligible for the lower business or agricultural relief of 50%, the maximum rate is only 3%, and therefore the annual instalment payable over ten years is only 0.3% per annum.

A settlement which was not originally within the nil rate band can become a nil rate band trust as the nil rate band increases year by year.

4.6:2 Business property and agricultural reliefs and pitfalls

(1) Business property and agricultural relief are available on the initial transfer into the settlement, as is the £3,000 exemption (for the current year and if unused the previous year).

Thus, assuming the lower 50% BPR, an individual may make the following transfer within his nil rate band (£242,000 for 2001/02).

Gross	£496,000
50% BPR	£248,000
	£248,000
Annual × 2	£ 6,000
	£242,000

Both s 103 (BPR) and s 115 (APR) provide that for the purpose of the discretionary trust rules, references in the reliefs to value transferred by a chargeable transfer include references to the amount on which tax is then chargeable, and that references to the transferor include references to trustees.

So prima facie there is no problem. The hypothetical rate at which IHT is levied at the ten-year anniversary is, by s 66(4), calculated inter alia by reference to the value on which tax is charged under s 64. Section 64 charges the value of the property at the time of the charge. So BPR and APR are available because that is 'the amount on which tax is charged'.

However, this does not apply to exit charges within the first ten years. Here, the amount on which the charge is levied is the value leaving the settlement, which will qualify for BPR or APR but the hypothetical rate in s 68(1) and (5) is the value immediately after the settlement commenced of the property then comprised in it. This is outside the deeming provisions in s 103 and s 115 and so the hypothetical rate will be based on £484,000 and not £242,000.

This is an unpleasant pitfall, but is not a problem for the 100% discount, because the value of the asset is reduced to zero and therefore no business or agricultural relief is required.

(2) *IHT 100% business property/agricultural property relief and discretionary trusts*

The transfer of business or agricultural assets into such flexible trusts during lifetime or by will should undoubtedly prove among the best estate planning methods available. In particular:

(a) certain business and agricultural assets as outlined in (1) above will be able to be held in such trusts indefinitely with 100% relief and will not be chargeable at the ten-year anniversary dates nor any interim charges after the first ten-year anniversary charge. At the ten-year anniversary, the trustees will need to satisfy the relevant business or agricultural property conditions. Assuming the 100% relief applies (and any other assets in the trust are within the nil band), the ten-year anniversary charge rate will be zero, and that zero rate will apply until immediately prior to the next ten-year anniversary, even though the assets are no longer business or agricultural assets, eg the trust fund consists of the proceeds of sale.

An existing trap for the unwary remains relevant for the 50% but not the 100% relief. Under IHTA 1984, s 68(4) and (5) in arriving at the rate of interim charges before the first ten-year anniversary (but not otherwise) no allowance is made for any business or agricultural relief at the 50% rate. As to the 100% relief, the risk seems to have disappeared because the value of the asset for s 68 purposes is zero, and therefore there is no charge eg under s 65.

(b) for lifetime discretionary trusts, there is no CGT holdover relief restriction in connection with non-business assets—see TCGA 1992, s 260 (there may, of course be an IHT restriction in respect of 'excepted' assets—IHTA 1984, s 112).

Example

A discretionary trust has a ten-year anniversary charge on 1 May 2001 when its trust fund consists of £242,000 in cash and 26% of the ordinary share capital of Trading Co Ltd and a farm owned and managed by the trustees.

Any distribution of the trust fund in whole or part at any time before the next ten-year anniversary will be in effect free of IHT because under IHTA 1984 ss 68 and 69 the rate at the ten-year anniversary on 1 May 2001 is zero and that zero rate franks, ie applies until midnight of 1 May 2011.

Nor is this beneficial treatment affected or altered if after 1 May 2001 the business property or agricultural property is sold or otherwise disposed of (the claw-back provisions in ss 113A and 113B, and 124A and 124B are inapplicable, they could only apply if the settlor died within seven years of creating the trust).

Indeed the trustees should consider varying the trust so that one or more of the beneficiaries receives a life interest in the trust fund, because in that case on the death of the life tenant there would normally be a CGT exemption and market value uplift (see TCGA 1992, ss 62 and 73) and no IHT if the conditions for APR/BPR continue to apply. Note, however, that the life tenant would have to satisfy the time period requirements, eg two years for business property relief (ss 106 and 117(a)).

(3) *A double IHT relief using discretionary trusts* (See *Taxation*, 25 March 1993)

(a) Spouse 1 ('H') in his will leaves business/agricultural property to a discretionary trust in favour of the family including Spouse 2 ('W'). On H's death, BPR/APR relief obtained for the first time; plus CGT death exemption and market value uplift.

(b) H leaves W his investment assets or she owns such assets in her own right.

(c) W purchases at arm's length (eg under a market value option granted to her in H's will), the business/agricultural assets from the trustees.

(d) On W's death after two years from the purchase, her estate should also be eligible for the relief, ie second time. Consider insuring the two-year period. CGT exemption and market value uplift apply again.

(e) Ancillary aspects:

(i) Adapt for the farmhouse.

(ii) W could delegate management responsibilities if wished.

(iii) She need suffer no loss of income because she is a beneficiary of the discretionary trust.

(iv) Consider application of these arrangements by way of deed of variation—but more provocative and *Ramsay* implications.

Example

Mr Planner owns the following assets:

(1) Stock Exchange securities, building society and bank deposits £1,242,000

(2) A 30% holding in Adam Planner Ltd which manufactures widgets, the shares being valued at £400,000

(3) Planner Farm which Mr Planner has owned and farmed for many years, valued at £600,000

In his will Mr Planner leaves assets (2) and (3) to a discretionary trust in favour of his widow, children and grandchildren. He also leaves £242,000 of assets in (1) into the trust. The remaining (investment) assets he leaves to his widow, coupled with an option for her to buy the business and agricultural assets from the trust at market value.

Note: The nil rate band for 2001–02 is £242,000.

The effect:

(a) On Mr Planner's death, there is no IHT, and there is CGT exemption and market value uplift. Nearly £1¼m of investments have been transferred into a discretionary trust free of IHT and without any substantial CGT.

(b) On Mrs Planner's death, there is no IHT (assuming she survives two years from the exercise of the option and assuming that there are no surplus investment assets over the nil rate band), and no CGT and market value uplift.

4.6:3 Flexibility

A settlor who wishes to take advantage of his own seven-year-cut-off can form a discretionary trust and get his seven years running at a time when he is still not sure which of a number of possible beneficiaries should ultimately be absolute owners. Distributions out of a discretionary trust and their timing can be arranged with maximum flexibility. To the extent that such distributions are out of income, there is no IHT charge because such income distributions, assuming they are liable to income tax, are not chargeable IHT distributions (s 65(5)(b)) although there would then be a charge to income tax at the beneficiary's rate. Alternatively, if income is accumulated it takes on the character of capital and therefore does constitute a chargeable distribution for IHT purposes when it leaves the trust. See also *Carver v Duncan* and *Bosanquet v Allen* [1985] STC 356, HL.

4.6:4 Fragmentation

Discretionary trusts can be fragmented and the IHT levy substantially reduced. It is important to ensure that a number of separate settlements are created and (SP 7/84 not being relevant here) to ensure that this is so, the judgment of Lord Wilberforce in *Roome v Edwards* [1981] STC 96 gives the indicia of separate settlements (see also **4.10**).

Methods of fragmentation

A series of low value settlements on different dates, followed by additions on the same day to total the value of the nil rate band (currently £242,000) in all.

Example

	1 £	2 £	3 £	4 £	5 £
Initial settlement	500	500	500	500	500
Added property	45,700	45,700	45,700	45,700	45,700
	46,200	46,200	46,200	46,200	46,200
Cumulative total	–	500	1,000	1,500	2,000
IHT free growth	184,800	184,300	183,800	183,300	182,800
	231,000	231,000	231,000	231,000	231,000

The scope for IHT free growth in the second and subsequent settlements is less than that for settlement one because, of course, the creation of each preceding discretionary trust uses up part of the settlor's available nil rate band.

The IHT charge when adding the property, ignoring the annual exemption, will be nothing: this stems from s 66(5)(a), s 67(4)(a) and s 68(4)(b).

If the funds settled in this series comprise not cash, but CGT chargeable assets, eg shares in the family company, the separate fragmented disposals will be linked for CGT (the settlor and the trustees of each settlement being connected persons under TCGA 1992, s 286(3)) and, because the disposals are all within the six-year limit, the gain on each disposal will be by reference to the market value of the aggregate shareholding (TCGA 1992, ss 19 and 20). Beware, however, that the CTO may seek to attack this arrangement under the *Ramsay* principle or as associated operations. It is however thought that the associated operations provisions in particular should not be applicable. Those provisions apply only for the purpose of identifying the timing of a transfer of value. Section 60–commencement of settlement–does not operate by first identifying a transfer of value. It merely directs that the date when property first becomes comprised in the settlement is identified.

Further, the scope for challenge might be reduced by altering key features of each of the pilot settlements eg different trustees, administrative provisions, accumulation and perpetuity periods, class of beneficiaries, administrative powers etc. Avoid the use of merely nominal sums when creating the pilot settlement.

This remains an aggressive form of IHT planning, but provided adequate care is taken of the sort indicated, this is a technique which remains worthy of consideration.

On a more general aspect, remember that husband and wife each have their own IHT nil rate band and one spouse may be able to channel shares through the other spouse, although the Revenue have said they reserve the right to challenge this.

This arrangement can be adapted where 100% BPR/APR applies (see **Chapter 9**).

4.6:5

On the incorporation of a new company it may be worthwhile in certain circumstances to use new small discretionary trusts to avoid a 'related property' situation. For example:

discretionary trust 1 holds	26% of the shares
discretionary trust 2 holds	26% of the shares
discretionary trust 3 holds	22% of the shares
husband and wife together hold	26% of the shares
	100%

The shares held by the trustees will not be related with the husband and wife; and each holding will become eligible to the 100% business relief.

Note also that s 65(9) (the omission to exercise a right constituting a disposition) and the normal consequential loss formula on any disposition, apply with equal force to trustees as they already did for individuals. Therefore, trustees must, for instance, be prepared to take up favourable rights issues offered to them. Moreover, having regard to the application of the term 'disposition' to trustees of discretionary trusts, it appears that the associated operation provisions of s 268 will apply to these trusts. The use of discretionary trusts can be particularly appropriate in settling family company shares among a class of children so that the voting powers are retained in the trustees (of whom the settlor may well be one), as opposed to splintering shares among the individual beneficiaries absolutely. A disadvantage exists in that once the beneficiaries do have an interest in possession, the settlement becomes a fixed interest trust so that upon the death of a beneficiary there is an interest in possession charge under ss 49–50. However, consider the CGT death exemption and market value uplift (TCGA 1992, s 62).

Notice must also be taken of the income tax changes applicable to dividend income with effect from 6 April 1999. The broad effect of these changes is that in accounting for tax under s 687 Taxes Act 1988 on making a distribution out of the trust, while the distribution is still treated as an amount from which tax at 34% has been deducted, the trustees can only set against their liability tax *actually* paid to the Revenue upon receipt of Sch F income, and not the associated tax credit. In other words the benefit of the tax credit is lost. This new tax downside for discretionary trusts is discussed more fully by Richard Vallat in his article 'Discretionary Trusts and the new dividend regime' (Vol 7 Issue 1 *Personal Tax Planning Review* (1999) p 45).

4.6:6   Overseas situations

As regards a settlor domiciled outside the UK when the settlement is made, provided the assets are also outside the UK the settlement will be and remain excluded property for IHT purposes, the domicile of the beneficiaries being irrelevant (see **10.3** and **10.5**). Moreover, the unfavourable capital gains tax regime (contained in TCGA—s 86), whereby trust gains might be attributed to the settlor of a non UK resident settlement, will not apply. Trust gains will however be attributed to beneficiaries in receipt of capital payments (s 87 TCGA), unless the beneficiaries are either non resident or non domiciled at the relevant time.

4.6:7 Discretionary trusts in reversion

Reversionary interests are normally excluded property and therefore it is possible to have a discretionary trust interest in reversion without the ten-year proportionate discretionary trust charges applying (and without CGT provided the reversion is in a UK trust, TCGA 1992, s 85), whilst the interests are in reversion and before such interests vest.

4.6:8 For the elderly

Discretionary trusts may prove appropriate vehicles where it is wished to benefit elderly beneficiaries having regard in particular that such beneficiaries do not satisfy the condition of an accumulation and maintenance trust under s 71, and if an interest in possession trust was used there would be an early charge on the death of the beneficiary with that interest, subject furthermore to aggregation with that beneficiary's free estate. (There is of course no aggregation with a beneficiary's estate in the case of a discretionary trust.)

4.6:9 CGT and IHT—the second home etc

One use for discretionary trusts and CGT could be as to second homes given the holdover restrictions in TCGA 1992, ss 165 and 260. Consider the following steps:

(1) Father [and mother] transfer a second home into a discretionary trust in respect of which the son is a potential beneficiary. Note, however, that father [and mother] must both be excluded and, moreover, must not visit the house on a regular basis (see *Tax Bulletin*, November 1993), otherwise a reservation of benefit will arise, in which case the estate planning will have proved entirely ineffective. CGT holdover relief is available and hopefully no IHT payable because of one [or two] nil rate bands.

(2) The trustees allow/entitle son to occupy this home as his main residence. The entitlement should be after a period of say 3 months to enable the discretionary trust element to be evident—see below.

(3) Subsequently, on a sale by the trustees, CGT main residence exemption is available under TCGA 1992, s 225 and see *Sansom v Peay* [1976] STC 494. Alternatively, if trustees advance house to son, and he sells, CGT exemption applies under TCGA s 222.

Notes:

(a) During the 36 months preceding a disposal of the home, the main residence exemption can still apply even though not occupied during that period (TCGA 1992, s 223(2)).

(b) This suggestion could be adapted for other investment assets, eg portfolio shares.

(c) Beware if immediate occupation is assumed by the son. If it is, there are strong arguments that an interest in possession trust has been created irrespective of the trusts form (SP10/79). In these circumstances the disposal into the settlement will be a PET, but there will be a corresponding loss of hold-over relief. Occupation should be able to be avoided for up to 36 months without loss of principle private residence relief and, because the initial transfer was within the settlor's nil rate band, without triggering a change to inheritance tax. The date upon which occupation is to commence must not be pre-ordained.

(d) *Use of a failed accumulation and maintenance trust.*

Consider the following, provocative, proposal: a trust is created which would be eligible as a s 71 accumulation and maintenance trust but for a particular breach for example by including a non-eligible beneficiary, namely someone over the age of 25. This trust will therefore be a non-PET discretionary trust so that CGT can be held over without restriction. At a later stage the 'offending' beneficiary could be irrevocably *excluded*. Section 71 should thereafter apply. Note that if removal of the beneficiary is pre-ordained this form of planning must be considered particularly vulnerable

4.6:10 Flexible discretionary trust—CGT/IHT mitigation

In order to deal with investment type assets ('the assets') carrying unrealised capital gains, where it is not possible to holdover the CGT under TCGA 1992, s 165 (ie not business assets), it is suggested that a flexible discretionary type trust be used. This discretionary trust would, after a minimum of three months, terminate initially onto interest in possession trusts for the settlor ('the settlor') and then subsequently a further interest in possession or accumulation and maintenance trust for, say, his children or grandchildren from which he and his spouse would be excluded. Within this period there would be a time during which the settlor could claim back the trust fund or a part. The value of the settlor's retained interests are so substantial that there is little loss to his estate for IHT purposes.

It would, therefore, be an appropriate way of channelling assets to the children, minimising the payment of CGT and IHT. A variation of this type of arrangement has recently been considered, with approval, by Lightman J in *Melville v IRC* [2000] STC 628. The Revenue have appealed. This type of arrangement is considered in further detail in **Chapter 7**: Gifts.

4.6:11 IHT the ten-year bonanza

As regards the ten-year anniversary charge for discretionary trusts, the IHT rate continues throughout the period up to ie shortly before the first or next ten-year anniversary. This gives rise to tremendous opportunities for IHT planning. Take a striking example:

(1) Mr Discreet creates a discretionary trust on 1 July 1992 valued at £150,000 (the then nil band). He appoints Messrs Shrewd and Careful the trustees.

(2) On 1 June 2002 the trust fund is worth £150 million and Messrs Shrewd and Careful appoint the trust fund to Mr Discreet's two children absolutely; or

(probably preferably for CGT and other purposes) appoint the trust fund on flexible interest in possession trusts for those children. No IHT is payable because the original nil rate applies until midnight of 30 June 2002, when the trust fund has to be revalued and IHT (normally at 6%) paid if not previously distributed or resettled as above.

Awareness of this timing aspect is clearly of vital importance.

NB Unfortunately pre-CTT trusts ie created pre-27 March 1974, do not benefit from this historical valuation, but the distribution charge is based on the market value at that time (s 68 (6)).

4.6:12 IHT-mini discretionary will trust of the nil rate band

Discretionary trusts can also be used to enable a surviving spouse to enjoy the benefit of a fund without the penalty of wasting the nil rate band. (See **2.5:4**.).

4.7 CHOOSING THE CORRECT HARMLESS SETTLEMENT— OTHER VARIETIES

4.7:1 Inter-spouse settlements

This is mainly an extension of the inter-spouse exemption (s 18) and subject to the same conditions (see **3.1:4**). In particular a settlement created by one spouse giving the other an interest in possession is exempt on creation; but the reverter to settlor or settlor's spouse exemption does not apply for discretionary type trusts, although it does apply for fixed interest trusts. Note, that the term 'spouse' only includes 'widow' or 'widower' to a restricted extent (see **3.1:8**).

However, trusts of the reverter to settlor type may decline in popularity, in view of TA 1988, s 660A which provides that, unless the settlor has divested himself absolutely from the settled property, the income from it is still to be treated as the settlor's for income tax purposes. See also the CGT provisions of TCGA 1992, ss 77–79.

4.7:2 Trusts or dispositions in consideration of marriage (s 22)

Depending on the relationship between the donor/settlor and the parties to the marriage, differing amounts will be allowed as exempt transfers for IHT, namely £5,000, £2,500 or £1,000. Such dispositions may be by way of settlement provided the beneficiaries are restricted. The details are summarised in the table below.

Gifts in consideration of marriage (s 22)

1	2	3
Circumstances=gift (in favour of a party to the marriage) by:	*Exemption limits— outright gifts* *£5,000 £2,500 £1,000*	*If disposition is by settlement the exemptions in column 2 apply provided beneficiaries restricted to:*
(i) Each parent	√	parties to marriage; issue of marriage; spouse of such issue;

(ii) Each remoter ancestor	✓	certain persons becoming entitled on failure of trusts for any such issue;
(iii) Each party to the marriage	✓	subsequent spouse of party to marriage or their issue or spouse of issue; certain 'protective trust' beneficiaries. Trustee's reasonable remuneration allowed.
(iv) Any other transferor	✓	Beneficiaries restricted as above.

Gifts in excess of the exemption limits in column 2 will normally qualify as PETs.

The following points and examples should be noted in conjunction with the above table. The obligation to make the disposition must be made *prior* to and *in contemplation of the marriage*. The exemptions apply, not only to gifts by individuals, but also to the termination of an interest in settled property in consideration of marriage (s 57(1)–(4)). The life tenant has to give notice to the trustees.

Post-nuptial deeds of gift

It sometimes arises that a deed of gift is entered into *after* a marriage but in performance of a pre-nuptial agreement. This method should be used sparingly and subject to careful consideration of the following.

(1) Where a 'gift' remains uncompleted at the death of the donor no deduction from the deceased's estate can be made for IHT in view of s 5(5), which permits deduction of liabilities only where they are incurred for consideration in money or money's worth, ie, excluding marriage consideration. Contrast an agreement made in consideration of marriage, to settle specified property actually owned by the settlor which type of arrangement normally created a trust or lien of that property so that the exemption should apply even if the settlor died before transferring the property.

(2) For a gift to be exempt it *must* be made in contemplation of the marriage and is normally restricted to gifts made at the time or shortly *before* the marriage.

Very strict proof would be required where a gift is made *after* the marriage if it is alleged to have been made in consideration of that marriage.

(3) In *IRC v Lord Rennell* [1964] AC 173, HL (a case on the ED exemption) it was stated that the three requirements for exemption are:

(a) the gift must be made on the occasion of the marriage;

(b) it must be conditional on the taking effect of that marriage;

(c) it must be made for the purpose of or with a view to encouraging or facilitating the marriage.

Therefore a 'gift' taking place, say, several years after the marriage would not comply, especially as the donors would no doubt be retaining the capital and income in the meantime.

(4) The wording for IHT is less restrictive than it was for ED, having regard in

157

particular to the words in s 22(1), 'to the extent that the values transferred by such transfer'.

(5) The gift or settlement must therefore be made prior to and in contemplation of the marriage in question which must subsequently take place. Once a couple are engaged, the donor or settlor can make the arrangements. In the case of an outright gift, for example a cheque, the donor should evidence this by dated letter to the donee, making it clear that it is a wedding present. In the case of a settlement, the settlor can either arrange for the settlement to be created and the asset transferred into it before or on the wedding day or alternatively (but less satisfactory) marriage articles can be entered into before the marriage specifying the investments or assets proposed to be settled within, say, six months of the marriage. The trustees can be given the right to accept suitable alternative assets. Until these assets are in fact vested in the trustees, the exempt transfer will not have been made.

The £5,000 limit for a parent is available for each parent; therefore in respect of a bride and groom both of whose parents are still alive, an aggregate of £20,000 of exempt gifts are available. As in the case of other exemptions, the gift can be of cash or in kind up to the appropriate value.

It is likely, following the dicta in *Re Park (No 2), IRC v Park* [1972] Ch 385, CA (another ED case), that in the case of an absolute disposition in favour of a party to the marriage the *purpose or motive* of the transferor is irrelevant; and presumably where the disposition is by way of the permitted settlement provisions a sufficient intention of encouraging or facilitating the marriage will have been established.

There is a wide definition of 'child', including illegitimate, adopted and stepchildren. 'Parent' and 'ancestor' are also considered widely (s 22(2)). With respect to circumstance (iii) listed in the table, it is suggested that it would be preferable for the parties to wait until they are married and obtain the interspouse exemption (s 18) (meanwhile requisite payments could be covered by loans cancelled subsequent to the marriage). An excess above the stated limits is attributed to the transfers in proportion to the value transferred and will constitute either a PET, or a lifetime chargeable transfer and subject to grossing up if say on discretionary trusts (where the possible beneficiaries are restricted by s 22(4)). There is no grossing up in calculating the exemption limits.

Examples

Eric gave to his unrelated business partner David cash of £3,000 on David's marriage to Sandra. £1,000 would be exempt under s 22 and the balance subject to any other exemptions, would constitute a PET.

David was given £3,000 by his father, who also gave £3,000 to Sandra. £5,000 is free of IHT and the balance of £1,000 would be a PET, subject to any other exemptions.

David's grandmother was going to settle £5,000 on David and Sandra under a normal marriage settlement of which only £2,500 would have been exempt from IHT. She gave her husband £2,500 instead and each settled £2,500 under the marriage settlement, the whole of which was exempt; the Revenue did not consider this should be caught as an associated operation under s 268, but no doubt could have done.

David agreed to buy Sandra a Ferrari for a wedding present but prudently waited until after the wedding, which meant that the gift was exempt from IHT within s 18 instead of only £2,500 being exempt within s 22.

4.7:3 Life assurance policies written under MWPA and other trusts

The scope here is based on the appropriate use of exemptions and the avoidance of discretionary trusts. The subject is discussed in more detail in **8.3:2**.

4.7:4 Reverter to settlor settlements (s 53(3), (4) and (5) and s 54(2) and (3))

If an interest in possession comes to an end in the lifetime of the life tenant and during the settlor's life and on the same occasion the property in which the interest subsisted reverts to the settlor or settlor's UK domiciled spouse, IHT is not chargeable unless the settlor or the spouse has acquired a reversionary interest in the property for a consideration in money or money's worth. The exemption applies also to the settlor's widow(er) provided the termination is within two years of the settlor's death. There are similar provisions (s 54(1), (2) and (3)) excluding an IHT charge where there is a reverter to settlor on the death of a person entitled to an interest in possession. The rationale behind excluding the trust property from the life tenant's estate where there is a reverter to settlor becomes a little clearer when it is remembered that the creation of the settlement will have fallen within the gift with reservation provisions. The result, for inheritance tax purposes, is that the property never leaves the state of the settlor.

Examples

(1) Individual settles house on, say, mother for life: remainder to himself absolutely and he survives his mother. Exemption available. (This may often be a useful method of giving an elderly person an interest in possession without incurring a charge on the capital of the trust fund when the beneficiary dies—an event likely to occur after a relatively short time.) For example, a father could in his will leave his home (or, say, his half share) to his son to utilise the nil band. Son could, after father's death, death grant mother a life interest in the home reverter to himself.

(2) The same situation as (1), but the son does not survive the mother. Exemption not available and charge on son's death under the gift with reservation provisions.

(3) A grants B an annuity charged on land remainder to A. As for (1) or (2).

(4) A settles house on B for life, subject thereto to C for life, remainder to A. B dies 1993, C in 1995, A in 1997. Exemption not available on B's death because the asset did not revert to A 'on the same occasion' ie on B's death. The exemption is, however, available on C's death.

(5) But if in example (4) C dies in 1992, ie before B, the exemption will be available on B's death.

(6) S settles house on X for life with remainder to Y. S purchases Y's remainder in X's lifetime. The exemption is not available as the reversion has been purchased for a monetary consideration.

A reverter to settlor settlement may give rise to income tax difficulties, eg under TA 1988, s 660A.

Following the abolition of CGT dependent relative relief by FA 1988, s 111, consider the following: Albert gives Florence say, his mother, a life interest in a house which she occupies. When Florence dies, assuming Albert has outlived her, the property reverts to him free of IHT and CGT.

4.7:5   Pension schemes or funds (s 151)

IHT relief applies where appropriate income tax relief is available, for example, in respect of retirement benefit schemes, retirement annuity policies and personal pension arrangements, under TA 1988, Pt XIV. For IHT the death of a pensioner or annuitant gives rise to no IHT charge; likewise when such pension or annuity ends otherwise than on death. However, if the pension or annuity *continues* to be payable after the death (there might, for instance, be a guaranteed period of say five years for the pension), the value of the balance of the pension or annuity is taxable as part of the deceased's estate. It appears that if the pension scheme is so drawn as to provide for *separate* pensions for a dependant to *arise* on the death of a pensioner, the new pension is not taxable. But if a pensioner gives up part of his own pension to provide a deferred pension to anyone other than his spouse, that disposition may constitute a transfer of value (subject to s 11). Similarly a member's power or right to dispose of a lump sum, for example, by way of nomination, would be a chargeable transfer. Most funds accordingly have current rules which leave such disposal of lump sums on death in service of the member in the discretion of the scheme trustees among a wide class of beneficiaries comprising relatives, dependants and executors. The member may suggest to the trustees the person(s) he wishes to receive the benefit on his death, but this is not binding on the trustees, although normally they would follow the member's wishes unless there were strong reasons to the contrary. No IHT is payable in normal circumstances on the death in service benefit in these discretionary cases (see **5.3:4**). If, however, under the arrangements, the member's personal representatives had an enforceable right to the benefit, then it would be liable to IHT as part of his estate. See SP/E3 and SP 10/86 referred to in **5.3:4** which explains the matter. (There would be a similar situation in respect of accident insurance schemes, see Inland Revenue Press Release, 6 January 1976, and also s 12.)

Accordingly, for such schemes or funds, the ten-year anniversary and interim IHT rules relevant to discretionary trusts will normally not apply unless the benefits appropriated out of the scheme or fund are themselves settled on discretionary trusts.

4.7:6   Settlements for the benefit of employees, etc (ss 72, 75, 86 and 87)

These provisions give relief from IHT to trusts for benefit of employees if, during any period the property cannot be applied otherwise than for the benefit of a class of employees, their relatives or dependants or charities. During that period (a) an interest in possession in less than 5% of the property is disregarded and (b) a payment of the property is not a distribution of 'relevant property' (ie is exempt) unless made to a settlor or to certain defined participators, and exceeds £1,000. The rate of tax, if any, on distributions ignores aggregation with the settlor. The ten-yearly anniversary charges are inapplicable, and if a charge does arise, the tapering charge under s 72(2)(a) and (5), bringing in s 70(6), applies as referred to in **4.3:8**.

This relief will not normally apply to the so-called 'top hat' schemes, as they are usually for *individual* employees and therefore not 'persons of a class defined by reference to employment'.

The above provisions give relief while assets are *in* a settlement. Exemption is also available for assets going *into* such a settlement, subject to certain conditions. Under s 12 relief is available provided the contribution into the trust gave rise to a deduction for income or corporation tax purposes. This is particularly relevant in the case of a contribution into an employee trust by a close company where relief under s 13 (see below) is restricted because participators are included in the class of eligible beneficiaries. Care should be taken, however, over the possible application and effects of UITF 13. As an alternative to section 12, under section 13, where the disposition is by a close company, subject to complying with s 86 and participators being (broadly) excluded from benefit, exemption also applies. Where, however, the disposition is by an *individual* the exemption (under s 28) requires the trustees of the employees' trust to hold more than half the ordinary shares in the company and have voting control. There are restrictions on the trust making dispositions to existing or former participators (within ten years prior to the disposition) with the exception that persons entitled to, or entitled to acquire less than 5% of the issued share capital of any class, or who would be entitled to less than 5% of the company's assets on a winding up are ignored. CGT relief for such a transfer is given under TCGA 1992, s 239. It is considered that a trust for the benefit of the employees of a *group* of companies which otherwise satisfies the necessary conditions, enjoys the protection of s 86. The conditions for individuals remain so harsh as to make the exemption rarely applied in practice. If it is desired, however, to set up an employees' trust but retain control, some of the shares could be transferred to a new company in exchange for shares therein and all the shares in the new company transferred to the employees' trust. The disadvantage is that CGT rollover would be unlikely to be available on the share exchange under TCGA 1992, ss 135–137.

The relief under s 86 is still available (by virtue of s 86(5)) where there is a switch from one employees' trust to another within a one-month period and where the relevant conditions apply to both. Employees of certain newspaper publishing companies also become eligible.

4.7:7 Protective trusts (ss 73 and 88) and Trustee Act 1925, s 33

Background and information: ss 88 and 73

A protective trust is a trust for life, or any less period, of a principal beneficiary, which terminates on certain events such as the bankruptcy of that beneficiary or a purported sale or alienation of his interest. Thereupon the interest in possession comes to an end and the principal beneficiary together with his family become objects of a discretionary trust. The termination of the principal beneficiary's interest during the trust period was, under earlier CTT rules, exempt, giving rise to mitigation possibilities such as in *Thomas v IRC* [1981] STC 382. The rules were accordingly changed in 1978 so that the principal beneficiary's sale or alienation of his interest is disregarded and he is still treated as beneficially entitled to an interest in possession in the trust assets which, notwithstanding the sale or assignment, are now held on trusts to like effect as those in the Trustee Act 1925, s 33(1). 'Like effect' is treated by the Revenue as meaning 'not materially different from s 33(1) in their tax consequences' (SP/E7 (originally Revenue letter of 3 March 1976)).

Examples of 'like effect' include:

(a) *exclusion of spouse* from the class of discretionary beneficiaries;

(b) power to declare a *full life interest* (ie not merely a protected one);

(c) power to *advance capital* to the protected life tenant;

(d) that the protected life interest is *revocable* and that other trusts can be substituted.

Therefore if an individual sets up a protective trust in favour of himself and later purports to sell or alienate his interest, he would in fact have set up a discretionary trust of which he was entitled to income before such sale or alienation without having incurred IHT on its creation; but enthusiasm should be moderated, not only since the individual is deemed to have an interest in possession so that the assets are deemed part of his IHT estate, but also because of the income tax settlement provisions (TA 1988, Pt XV). If the settlor is also the principal beneficiary, there is no bankruptcy protection as applies in other circumstances.

Protective trusts have thus little merit for IHT planning, but may be useful for non-IHT practical reasons, eg the spouse of a Lloyd's member could give the member a protective life interest by will. It should always be borne in mind that a protective trust will usually add to a beneficiary's IHT estate or in any event not reduce it. A pure discretionary trust may also answer the practical problems, but consider the IHT (and CGT) implications.

A protective trust is capable of coming within the accumulation and maintenance trust provisions of s 71.

If the primary beneficiary had by mere divesting act triggered off a discretionary trust before the change of rules on 12 April 1978, there is under s 73 an IHT charge when the trust assets cease to be held on the substituted discretionary trusts (either because of the advancement of capital out of the trust other than to the primary beneficiary or because the trustees otherwise make some value-shifting disposition causing the value to go down).

CGT

When a protected life interest comes to an end on forfeiture there is *no disposal* for CGT purposes.

Income tax

On forfeiture of a life interest and automatic substitution of a discretionary trust, the rate applicable to trusts applies: TA 1988, s 686.

4.7:8 Trusts for the benefit of mentally or physically disabled persons (ss 74, 89)

Background and information

IHT relief is available in respect of a trust for the life of a mentally disabled person (as defined under the Mental Health Act 1983) and which contains no interest in possession, being for example, a discretionary trust, where not less than half of the settled property is applied during his life for his benefit: ss 74 and 89. A normal Trustee Act 1925, s 32 power to advance should not breach this requirement, although a wide power of advancement in favour of persons other than the disabled beneficiary may do so. The relief consists in deeming the disabled person to have an interest in possession in the trust assets, with the result that there is no IHT on a payment of capital to or for him but on an advance of capital to someone other than the disabled person, the termination of the disabled person's interest in possession constitutes a PET. The IHT position is therefore:

(1) property put into the trust by the mentally disabled person is an exempt transfer. For other settlors, eg the parent of the disabled person, the transfer is a PET;

(2) a payment out of the trust for his benefit is not a taxable distribution, ie it is exempt;

(3) when there is a payment/distribution out to someone other than the mentally disabled person, or the property ceases to be held for his benefit, or there is some reduction in the value of the trust estate because of a disposition by the trustees, the trustees have made a PET, and to avoid a charge the mentally disabled must survive seven years.

This relief has a wider application that might appear at first glance, as it extends to persons resident or present in the UK in receipt of an attendance allowance under the Social Security Act 1975, s 35, ie the disability can be mental or physical.

CGT: disabled trusts obtain the full small gain exemption as if the trustees were an individual (TCGA 1992, s 3 and Sch 1). For this purpose, half the income must be paid in favour of the disabled beneficiary; unless no income is appointed for the benefit of *any* other person.

4.7:9 Charitable trusts (ss 58(1)(a) and 70)

In relation to settled property held for charitable purposes only, the discretionary trust provisions including IHT liability for distributions and ten-year charges are excluded. But there is a special IHT charge where assets cease to be held on charitable trusts and are not applied for charitable purposes (other than meeting the normal costs or expenses of the trust) under s 70(2)—see **4.3:8**.

Moreover under s 76, payments or appropriations *by* discretionary trusts to such charities, or indeed to political parties, national museums etc are not liable to the interim IHT exit charge. Trusts are charitable if they are established for charitable purposes only (see further under **7.16**). This is restricted to UK established trusts or institutions (see *Camille and Henry Dreyfus Foundation Inc v IRC* [1956] AC 39, HL).

Charities can usefully be included as beneficiaries in a family trust to clear out income otherwise treated as the settlor's in a children's settlement (TA 1988, s 660B).

4.7:10 Certain compensation funds (s 58(1)(e), (3))

Certain compensation funds such as those administered by The Law Society and The Stock Exchange are excluded from the discretionary trust IHT regime.

4.7:11   Overseas trusts for excluded property (ss 48(3) and 267)

A trust fund will be excluded property provided:

(1) the assets are situated abroad, and

(2) the settlor was domiciled abroad when the settlement was made, (notwithstanding that the beneficiaries are resident and domiciled here).

Note: see generally, RI 166 of February 1997.

In the case of a reversionary interest which is situate abroad, this will be excluded property provided that the beneficial owner is domiciled abroad. The extended interpretation of domicile for IHT contained in s 267(1) only applies to property comprised in the settlement on or after 10 December 1974 (sub-s (3)). The test as to the time at which property is regarded as having become 'comprised' in a settlement appears to depend on when it was introduced and transferred into the settlement by the settlor, ignoring subsequent switches of property and reinvestment of proceeds of sale. In the case of an individual who is domiciled abroad with assets abroad, and who is considering taking up long-term residence or domicile here, it is vital that he should consider making trusts abroad before coming back, and leaving his assets in the overseas trust. If he has assets within the UK or wishes to sell foreign assets and reinvest in the UK, his overseas settlement should own shares in an overseas investment company; and it should be that company which owns the UK assets. Whether those assets inside the company are abroad or in the UK, the trust assets owned by the trustees will always be the shares in the overseas company, which will be excluded property. There is no lifting of the corporate veil for this purpose (see also **10.6:3**). Contrast the position of the UK resident taxpayer in *IRC v Brandenburg* [1982] STC 555. There the veil of incorporation was pierced in so far as the UK taxpayer as sole shareholder of a Jersey company was treated as being beneficially entitled to an interest in possession, not that company to whom the trust fund had, purportedly, been transferred.

It may be appropriate to utilise so-called 'limbo' trusts with a widely defined beneficiaries clause. (The decision in *Re Manisty's Settlement, Manisty v Manisty* [1974] Ch 17, [1973] 2 All ER 1203, confirmed that this is perfectly feasible.) In such a trust the settlor would have been domiciled abroad when the settlement was made; the trust assets would be abroad and to avoid the eventual IHT on their own estate, beneficiaries might become non-resident and non-UK domiciled at the time when the trust fund or an appropriate part was to be appointed to them or when the underlying company decided to make them a loan. One interesting suggestion in this context is that a trust might be set up by a non-resident non-domiciled friend with a small amount of capital and with non-resident trustees. The trustees would acquire shares in the trading company situated abroad to whom genuine orders are passed sufficient to enable the trust-owned company, on a proper commercial basis, to accumulate profits. The discretionary beneficiaries of the trust are overseas residents, possibly overseas charities, but there is power to add further beneficiaries. Bearing in mind TA 1988, ss 739–745, if a member of the taxpayer's family becomes non-resident at some time in the future, he can be added as a beneficiary and be paid a capital distribution, without incurring IHT. It is absolutely essential that the foreign settlor is not directly or indirectly reimbursed by the taxpayer because any such associated operations would undermine the whole arrangement, as the taxpayer would then become a settlor within the wide definition of s 44(1). In addition to TA 1988, ss 739–745, it is also important to consider the effects of TA 1988, ss 765–767 and TCGA 1992, ss 86 and 87 in such a scheme.

By way of summary, therefore, as regards excluded property, the interaction of the settlement provisions of s 44 and the beneficial ownership concept in s 6 (1) gives wide scope for planning. As regards settled property, it will be excluded property provided it is situated outside the UK and (a) in the case of a *reversionary* interest, the individual beneficiary (ie the person beneficially entitled to the reversionary interest) is domiciled abroad (relying on s 6(1)), the domicile of the settlor being then irrelevant; or (b) under s 48(3) the settlor was domiciled abroad at the time he made the settlement (in which case the domicile of the beneficiary is irrelevant whether he receives trust assets or makes a disposition of his interest).

Reference should also be made to Chapter 10 generally.

As regards CGT, the previous benefits applicable to non-UK resident trusts have largely disappeared, unless the individual is either domiciled or resident abroad.

4.7:12 Reversionary interests and their re-settlement

As indicated above (**1.4:2**), reversionary interests as defined in s 48 are generally excluded property. The Inland Revenue gave the following succinct definition (*Law Society Gazette*, 4 February 1976, p 89).

> 'A reversionary interest is excluded property if:
>
> (a) Wherever it is situated it has not been acquired for consideration and it is not expectant on the determination of a lease for life etc. granted otherwise than for full consideration, or
>
> (b) if the interest itself is situated outside the United Kingdom and is either
>
> (i) in the actual beneficial ownership of someone domiciled outside the United Kingdom, or
>
> (ii) itself settled property comprised in a settlement made by someone who was domiciled outside the United Kingdom when he made the settlement'.

Notice that the element of consideration mentioned in (a) above applies to *any* consideration in money or money's worth, however inadequate and acquired at anytime by the person entitled to it, or a person previously entitled to it. The fact that a reversionary interest is excluded property is a logical corollary of the basic IHT premise that an individual who has an interest in possession is deemed to own the capital supporting it. To subject the reversionary interest to tax as well, would involve a double assessment. Accordingly it is possible to resettle the reversionary interest, ie an interest that is not yet in possession, without a charge to IHT and if such resettlement is by way of an accumulation and maintenance trust under s 71 there will generally be no further IHT for the duration or on the termination of the resettled trust. This type of situation may be particularly appropriate where an individual has a reversionary interest subject to a life interest in favour of, say, his mother.

Where the reversioner is already wealthy, it will often be excellent IHT planning for him to resettle his reversionary interest in favour of, say, his own children.

Resettlement of reversionary interests must, however, be considered in the light of associated operations (s 268). Further, the device of a trust giving oneself an interest in possession, with a reversion to the spouse, where the spouse then gifts her reversionary interest, say, to the children, does not work. Neither would a trust in favour of one's spouse, with remainder to oneself. In neither case is the reversionary interest treated as excluded property (s 48(1)(b)).

Certain other IHT avoidance devices have been stopped, in particular where an interest in possession in property was created for a short period and the reversionary interest transferred as excluded property into settlement, followed by a tax free termination of the interest under the former much wider reverter to settlor or settlor's spouse exemption: the interest meanwhile having been acquired for its market value, which was nearly equivalent to the full capital value as the interest in possession was for a very short period, say three months. Nor does the exemption apply in the case of transfers between spouses or gifts to charities and certain public bodies where the assets are transferred in consideration of a transfer of a reversionary interest being excluded property not forming part of the estate of the person who acquires it. As to the enormous estate planning advantages in assigning a reversionary interest see **2.5:7** above.

4.7:13 Trading trusts

Tax advantages may be gained from operating a business through a trading trust.

An appropriate 'harmless' trust would be chosen, eg the accumulation and maintenance trust or interest in possession trust (see above). Trustees would be appointed, who would have a right to carry on a trade and appoint qualified managers, etc. They would be responsible for conducting the business for remuneration. Consider use of a limited partnership under the Limited Partnership Act 1907.

As to taxation the position would be that as the law stands:

(a) Trustees could benefit from the 100%/50% business/agricultural property relief (see Chapter 9). Subject to this, on creation if accumulation and maintenance or interest in possession trust used no IHT as a PET—provided seven-year survivorship and no reservation of benefit.

(b) The trustees would be assessable to income tax at maximum 34%. Contrast rates of tax for individuals/companies. Beware, however, application of s 660B TA in the case of an A & M trust, or s 660A TA 1988 where settlor or his spouse is included as a beneficiary.

(c) The distribution of the capital and income of the trust could be with the maximum flexibility, eg accumulating as capital or distributing as income according to the beneficiary's tax position if an A & M trust, taking advantage of lower rates of income tax.

(d) Many of the tax rigours would be avoided, eg transactions in securities (TA 1988, s 703); shortfall apportionments; benefits in kind.

(e) As to CGT the severely restricted holdover relief after FA 1989 may yet still apply on the creation and termination of the trust since business and agricultural assets are still covered by TCGA 1992, s 165. Disposals by the trustees will be taxed at 34%. But beware of possible applications of s 77 TCGA to deem gains to be those of the settlor. Further, the possibility of taper relief for business assets under section 2A and schedule A1 Taxation of Chargeable Gains Act 1992 should be considered. If available the potential charge on trustee disposals and/or attributed to the settlor under s 77 TCGA would be materially reduced. It should be borne in mind that full taper relief is applicable after only four years in the case of business assets.

4.8   TRUST PITFALLS

4.8:1   New discretionary trusts

There are circumstances, as mentioned in **4.6**, when opportunity should be taken for new discretionary trusts, but not without looking at all the facts and working out the arithmetic (including the ten-year anniversary charge and any interim IHT). In particular, remember that in ascertaining the rate for the ten-year charge, it is necessary not merely to look at the anniversary value of the discretionary trust property, but also to take into account the settlor's chargeable transfers within the seven years before the settlement was made; the value (on formation of the trust) of any property in the settlement in which there has been an interest in possession; the value (again on formation) of any property subject to a 'related' settlement, ie one set up on the same day as the settlement in contemplation (this, will apply usually to settlements created by will, but note that the order of lifetime creations is most important); together with the value of any advances out of the settlement in the ten years before the anniversary. In particular, because of the possible effect on aggregation, it is desirable to avoid related settlements and separate fixed and discretionary trusts in the same settlement.

4.8:2   Interests in possession

Having regard to the basic principle that the capital supporting the interest in possession is generally the basis of the IHT charge, one must beware in creating an interest in possession, for example, a life interest or annuity, particularly in the case of an elderly beneficiary. Similarly, avoid successive life interests with the IHT charge arising on each life tenant's death or termination of his interest. For the remaining scope for interest in possession, refer to **4.5**.

Remember also the importance of 'getting in first'. For example, in the case of an interest in possession trust, the interest in remainder may vest in a distant relative and the life tenant's next-of-kin, say his children, will be 'hoisted' with the aggregation of the trust fund with the life tenant's free estate when he dies. In this type of situation the life tenant should consider disposing of his free estate to his children in his lifetime and before the interest in possession terminates, thereby avoiding this aggregation. Note, however, the relaxation announced in May 1990 for lifetime terminations, referred to **4.5:1** above.

It is often much the better plan for a settlor to make a regular allowance to a poor beneficiary rather than to create an interest in possession in his favour, particularly where the instalments can be treated as normal expenditure out of income within s 21 (see **7.10** and **7.11**).

If a life interest is found to have been left by will to a beneficiary who is elderly or who does not need the income, consideration should be given to rewriting the will within two years of death under s 142; but note that although there are similar provisions for CGT and for stamp duty, any variation will for income tax purposes constitute a settlement by the beneficiary giving up his interest for the purposes of TA 1988, Pt XV.

4.8:3   Anti-avoidance provisions—depreciatory transactions (ss 52(3), 65(1)(b))

Transactions between trustees and beneficiaries or persons connected with beneficiaries, designed to depress the value of the trust fund, will be regarded as a transfer of value or a chargeable distribution as the case may be. This type of provision is particularly designed to counteract transactions involving an artificial sale and purchase price, interest-free loan arrangements (where repayment is not until a future specified date; loans repayable on demand are all right), artificial leasing arrangements, value shifting operations where, for example, the trustees agree to a change in the share structure of a company so that their own shares are depressed in value, and such devices as the conveyance of a perimeter strip—whereby a strip of land, say a yard wide, entirely surrounding the property, is transferred to a third party in order to reduce the value of the remainder (see also **1.1:2**).

Note that these anti-avoidance provisions do not apply if 'the transaction is such that, were the trustees beneficially entitled to the settled property, it would not be a transfer of value'. This envisages a commercial or business transaction on the part of the trustees as opposed to a mere gift, and other situations where the trustees sell or realise assets for a good reason, eg to enable a taxation liability to be met; and where no gratuitous benefit is intended. For discretionary, charitable and accumulation and maintenance trusts, ss 65(9), 70(10) and 71(5) specifically provide that a disposition can result from an omission to act unless not deliberate. This is in accordance with the 'general' transfer of value rules in s 3.

The question is sometimes raised in this context of a loan of money made by the trustees. First, it is clear that if the loan is repayable on demand there is no (or perhaps negligible) consequential loss to the trust. If the loan is declared to be repayable only at some date in the future, there will be a loss by virtue of a depreciatory transaction, since the present value in the trust of that future payment is a discounted sum only; and the difference will be subject to IHT. Secondly, unlike the case where a beneficiary is given exclusive occupation of a house and, as a result, acquires an interest in possession (see **2.5:6**), the loan of money does not produce an interest in possession in the borrower. The distinction can perhaps best be seen by comparing the house, to which the trustees still have legal title and which is still an asset of the trust, with the money which the trustees lend. That money thereupon belongs to the borrower absolutely, although he is under an obligation to repay an equivalent (not the actual) sum. A loan is therefore in essence a re-investment by the trustees. They have, by the lending transaction, ceased to own that money, having converted it into a debt due. The debt is now a trust asset, in place of the cash.

4.8:4   Trustees' liability for IHT on termination of an interest in possession

The trustees will be the persons primarily liable for the payment of IHT on the termination on death of an interest in possession under s 200(1)(b) subject to the limitation in s 204(2), ie, to the extent in broad terms of the property under their control or available to them.

In the case of the termination of an interest in possession during lifetime by way of a PET which becomes a chargeable transfer on the death of the former life tenant within seven years, the persons primarily liable are the trustees of the settlement (s 199(1)(c)) because, whether or not the settlement continued after the termination, the trustees will have had the trust assets vested in them 'after the transfers'. As the transfer has already taken place they cannot hold for anyone else. Any absolute beneficiary (s 199(1)(b)) or person with an interest in possession (s 199(1)(c)) will also be liable, but it is the trustees who hold the trust property, and if the settlement comes to an end on the lifetime termination of the interest in possession, the trustees will need to take steps, either by a retention fund or by watertight insurance, to provide for the potential IHT. The personal representatives of the former life tenant are also liable (in view of s 199(2)) but only secondarily because of the limitation in s 204(8). As to the CGT liability see TCGA 1992, s 71.

Historically, as to the general duty of care for trustees in connection with trust investments, note the case of *Barlett v Barclays Bank Trust Co Ltd* [1980] Ch 515 where bank trustees were liable in negligence to beneficiaries for not preventing two hazardous speculations. For trust companies and professionals the duty of care is higher than for individual lay trustees (see further Underhill and Hayton, *Law of Trusts and Trustees*, 15th edn, p 545 et seq.)

The duty of care to be exercised by trustees received statutory recognition in Trustee Act 2000. Section 1 of that Act provides that a trustee must exercise 'such care and skill as is reasonable in the circumstances having particular regard to any special knowledge or experience that he has or holds himself out as having and, if he is acting as a trustee in the course or furtherance of a business or profession, to any special knowledge or experience that it is reasonable to expect of a person acting in the course of that kind of business or profession'. The Act also contains extensive provisions dealing with the trustees' powers of investment.

4.8:5   The trustees paying the settlor's capital taxes

If an individual sets up a trust under the terms of which the trustees are to pay the IHT and/or CGT on the gift into settlement, then that trust may be ineffective for income tax purposes ie the income of the trust may be deemed to be that of the settlor having regard in particular to TA 1988, s 660A (income arising under settlement where settlor retains an interest) and s 677 (sums paid to the settlor otherwise than as income).

By concession for IHT purposes the Revenue's practice is not to take this strict view (SP 1/82, dated 6 April 1982).

Practitioners should appreciate, however, that this Revenue concession does not appear to apply as regards CGT where the primary liability rests on the settlor (TCGA 1992, s 282) to be contrasted with IHT (s 199(1)) where the liability is placed both on the transferor and the transferee. Where, however, the settlor takes advantage of the holdover provisions for CGT under TCGA 1992, ss 165 and 260, the Revenue will not apply the above settlement provisions of the Taxes Act (at least as from the date of submission of the holdover claim).

It is understood that if the trustees do not have a *power* to pay the CGT as expressed in the trust deed or some supplemental document or other evidence of agreement to pay the CGT, ie if the trustees just pay the CGT ad hoc, the Revenue will not seek to apply these income tax anti-avoidance provisions. In that event the trustees are in all probability committing a breach of trust, ie meeting a liability for which they are not responsible, but the Revenue would apparently not concern themselves on this point.

4.8:6 Anti-fragmentation provisions for discretionary trusts (s 81)

It is provided by s 81 that where property leaves one settlement and—unless some person in between takes an absolute interest—becomes comprised in another settlement, it shall be treated as still comprised in the first settlement. If, of course, anyone becomes absolutely entitled to the property in the interim, that absolute owner will be a new settlor. The aim is to discourage fragmentation of such trusts by rendering ineffective the transfer of property from one settlement to another so that all capital payments and dispositions by trustees are identified for computational purposes with the original settlement. Another effect is that if property is transferred out of a UK trust to a non-resident settlement the UK trustees of the original settlement remain *liable* for any IHT. (See further, on the application of s 81, Andrew Hitchmough and Conrad McDonnell, 'Irrelevant Property Settlements,' *Personal Tax Planning Review*, 1995/96, Vol 4, 79.)

4.8:7 Trustees' distributions

Are they income or capital? When trustees make a distribution of the trust fund it is often a grey area whether such distribution constitutes capital or income. It was hitherto always thought that the basic test was whether the distribution was income or capital in the hands of the *recipient* beneficiary. It seemed to follow from cases like *Brodie's Trustees v IRC* (1933) 17 TC 432 and *Cunard's Trustees v IRC* [1946] 1 All ER 159, CA, that the more regular the payments out of the trust, the more likely they would be treated as income in the hands of the beneficiary. Hence the advice was that if the trustees were intent on making a capital payment they should make it irregularly and for a clear capital purpose.

In *Stevenson v Wishart* [1987] STC 266, CA, however, it was held that a regular series of capital payments out of a discretionary settlement in order to pay medical and nursing home expenses of a beneficiary were still capital so far as the beneficiary was concerned. The Court of Appeal declared that if in their exercise of a power over capital, the trustees chose to make at their discretion regular payments of capital to deal with the special problems of the beneficiary's last year, rather than to realise a single large sum, that did not create an income interest. This decision appears to make the position somewhat easier. However, it is still safer to err on the cautious side. An irregular large payment will always look better and be more defensible than a series of small payments, particularly if there are no special problems as there were in the *Wishart* case itself.

Where a settlement is contemplated and regular payments out might be expected, consideration should be given to making a number of smaller separate settlements instead of one large one. A capital payment can be made on the first occasion out of settlement no 1, on the next occasion out of settlement no 2, and so on. A capital payment thereby occurs as regards any one settlement only at long intervals.

Note that having regard to the stringent CGT anti-avoidance provisions relating to the surcharge in TCGA 1992, ss 91–98, for CGT purposes it may prove beneficial to turn capital into income for non-resident trusts.

4.8:8   Trust deeds: change of practice: Inland Revenue press release 19 December 1990

The Inland Revenue have since 6 April 1991 changed the way in which they handle trusts for income tax and capital gains tax. Tax offices no longer in general ask, as previously, for a copy of every new trust document. Instead they will rely on the information shown by trustees, settlors and beneficiaries in their annual tax returns or repayment claims.

When a new trust is created, trustees will be sent a form asking for some basic factual information about the identities of the trustees and settlor and whether the trustees have power to accumulate income or distribute it at their discretion.

Practitioners should not be lulled into a false sense of security. To the contrary, if they have misinterpreted the type and nature of the trust, this may not be discovered for many years when additional assessments will be raised with possible interest and penalties. For example, an intended life interest may be subject to an (unintended) power to accumulate with the consequent higher rate applicable to trusts applying for income tax and CGT purposes.

As regards IHT, however, this practice does not alter the examination of deeds by the CTO as previously.

4.9   TRUST BUSTING AND VARIATION: 1 BY CONSENT

Under this first head, particular attention is given to methods of terminating or varying settlements with interests in possession followed by an absolute interest in remainder. As such methods depend upon the beneficiaries' consent, it is assumed that all the beneficiaries can consent to the arrangement being of full age and capacity, ie are *sui juris*.

There are six main circumstances set out in the tables in **4.10**, together with the relevant IHT consequences. In addition, consideration should be given to the possible application of the 100% business/agricultural property relief.

Finally, the following points should be noted regarding the tables which follow.

(1) Circumstance 1 (the division or partition method) could be particularly appropriate where it is wished to transfer *appreciating* assets to a remainderman at a stage where the life tenant may not survive the seven-year period for PET purposes. Moreover it may be possible to time the

partition during a period when the asset value is relatively low. The value of the gift to the remainderman is frozen at the time of the division/partition. The same applies to circumstance 2.

(2) Circumstance 3, enlargement by gift, is particularly important from an IHT planning aspect. The life tenant can acquire the remainderman's interest by way of gift free of IHT, and a life tenant should then be encouraged to make the maximum use of exemptions and reliefs and PETs and use the art of giving as described in detail in **Chaper 7**.

Example

Freeman is the life tenant of the Wagner trust. The remainderman Rogers gives to Freeman his reversionary interest in the trust, valued actuarially at £22,000. Freeman, as life tenant, is already treated for IHT as being entitled to the whole capital value of the trust, £100,000, in spite of the fact that the actuarial value of his interest is only £78,000. The transfer by Rogers is of excluded property and no IHT is payable.

(3) Circumstance 5, the release or surrender by a remainderman, for example to his children, can result in important IHT saving. This application will be particularly relevant in the case of a surviving spouse exemption where ED was paid on the first spouse's death. Where, say, a son who is wealthy in his own right is to obtain the residuary estate on the death of his widowed mother, if he assigns this interest, for example, to his own children, there will be no IHT on the assignment, as it is an acquisition by them of excluded property. Nor will there be a CGT charge if it is a disposal of an interest in a UK trust (TCGA 1992, ss 76 and 85), and, there should be no CGT on the death of the life tenant, having regard to the exemption on death (TCGA 1992, s 73).

(4) The ED decision in *Re Beit, Beit v IRC* [1951] 2 TLR 124; affd [1952] Ch 53, CA, may remain relevant for IHT planning. The arrangement in this case resulted in a settled fund becoming valueless on an annuitant's death. The facts were that under the testatrix's will, an annuity was payable out of the residuary estate and the trustees were directed to appropriate a specific capital value to meet the income liability, the remainder of the residue being exonerated. An arrangement was entered into between the annuitant, the trustees and the residuary beneficiaries, whereby the trustees applied a part of the residuary fund in purchasing from the residuary beneficiaries a covenant to pay an annuity of like amount to the trustees. The covenant by the residuary beneficiaries to pay the income to the annuitant became the sole security for its payment and it was further agreed that the trustees were thereupon free to distribute the remaining residuary estate. On the annuitant's death it was held that no ED was payable because the annuity had not been terminated. There had merely been an appropriation of a specified part of the trust fund in the form of the reversioners' covenants which became valueless on the annuitant's death. It may well be possible to apply this decision in contending that there is no termination of an interest in possession for the purposes of ss 51 and 52, and as the similar ED associated operations provisions were not applied, it would seem illogical that they should apply for IHT. The Revenue may, however, be able to contend successfully that for IHT the interest of the annuitant or life tenant has terminated without him becoming absolutely entitled, while the covenant is a retention of interest.

(5) For will trusts, note the important provisions relating to variations of wills, etc (s 142). (See **2.6.**)

(6) The following CGT aspects should also be noted:

    (a) minor variations *within* a trust—not a disposal (see SP 7/84 of 11 October 1984);

    (b) no chargeable gain accrues on a disposal of a beneficial interest under a UK trust (TCGA 1992, ss 76 and 85);

    (c) similar treatment for variation under Variation of Trusts Act 1958 (see **4.10**);

    (d) termination of life interest on death in respect of whole trust fund— exempt (but contrast the advantage of IHT lifetime rate or PET); partial CGT relief where life interest in part of trust fund. But if hold- over relief claimed by settlor on setting up trust under TCGA 1992, ss 160 and 265, that gain crystallises on the death (TCGA 1992, s 74);

    (e) a life interest in part—disposal only of *that part* of trust fund—subject to TCGA 1992, s 72(2)–(5);

    (f) s 52(1). On termination of an interest in possession, eg on partition, consider arranging that the beneficiary pays the CGT so that the CGT is a deduction against value transferred for IHT purposes.

(7) On making an advancement or appointment, the trustees may be able to alter or substitute the administrative and even the *dispositive* powers if that is for the overall benefit of the beneficiary in question: see the important case of *Pilkington v IRC* [1962] 3 All ER 622, HL; *Re Rank's Settlement Trusts* [1979] 1 WLR 1242 and *Re Hampden Settlement Trusts* [1977] TR 177.

4.10 TRUST BUSTING AND VARIATION: 2 BY THE COURT

In the former circumstances it has been assumed that the beneficiaries under the settlement have all been *sui juris* and of full age, so that the arrangements for termination or variation have been effected by consent of all the interested parties involved.

The sanction of the court is necessary where all the parties are not *sui juris* and/or of full age and cannot therefore give consents binding at law by reason of infancy or other disability, or because their identity has not yet been ascertained.

This second aspect can in appropriate circumstances (ie subject to the terms of the settlement) be overcome without application to the court, by means of advancements by the trustees of all the trust assets to the appropriate bene- ficiaries of the settlement. In that case, the CGT implications as to whether a disposal is constituted or not must be carefully considered. See the decisions in *Hoare Trustees v Gardner* [1978] STC 89; *Roome v Edwards* [1981] STC 96, HL; *Bond v Pickford* [1982] STC 403 *Swires v Renton* [1991] STC 490; and Inland Revenue SP 9/81, dated 23 September 1981 and SP 7/84, dated 11 October 1984. Where holdover relief is not available pursuant to TCGA 1992, s 165 or s 260, it may be appropriate not to create an entirely new trust by the advance in order that there is no disposal as the trust continues albeit in a different form, eg by making any appointment or advancement non-exhaustive.

TABLE: TRUST BUSTING/VARIATION WITH CONSENT

Circumstance	CGT	IHT	Stamp Duty	Remarks
1. Division of the interests in the trust = partition, eg between life and tenant and remainderman.	Yes—whole fund TCGA 1992, s 71(1) beneficiaries become entitled as against trustee subject to holdover claim possibly*	As to interest in possession (IP) terminating = PET. (The proportion taken by reversioner—not treated as a disposal by life tenant for consideration because s 52(2) says value of reversionary interest left out of account in determining adequacy of consideration.) But property taken by life tenant is exempt because he becomes absolutely entitled (s 53(2)), or 100% business/agricultural property relief may apply IHTA 1984 ss 103–114—see also 2 and 4 below.	£5 nominal	(a) This circumstance envisages a division normally on an actuarial valuation between the beneficiary with an IP, ie a fixed interest and a remainderman, ie with a reversionary interest. (b) Advantages to be obtained: (i) termination of life interest is a PET. In these circumstances the 100% IHT business/agricultural property relief may apply IHTA 1984 ss 103–114. (ii) remainderman to receive appreciating assets. (c) trustees accountable. CGT assumes trust ceases.
2. Release or surrender by life tenant to remainderman; cf 5	Yes—same principle TCGA 1992, s 71(1) subject to*	A PET	£5 nominal	Advantages as in (b) above. In these circumstances the 100% IHT business/agricultural property relief may apply. This method is particularly important from an IHT mitigation aspect where life tenant relatively young, and opportunities of subsequent PETs. In these circumstances the 100% IHT business/agricultural property relief may apply on subsequent transfers IHTA 1984 ss 103–114.
3. Enlargement by gift, ie life tenant acquires the remainder by gift.	Yes—same principle TCGA 1992, s 71(1) and TCGA 1992, Sch 7 as amended subject to*	No—a disposal of excluded property (s 48(1)).	Exempt if certificated (see **3.43** (3))	

Circumstance	CGT	IHT	Stamp Duty	Remarks
4. Enlargement by purchase. Life tenant buys the remainderman's interest.	Yes—same principle TCGA 1992, s 71(1) and TCGA 1992, Sch 7 as amended subject to*	A PET—by s 55(1) the reversionary interest will not form part of the life tenant's estate and he thus in effect makes a gift of the purchase price. He cannot rely on s 55(2).	1% ad valorem (if no certificate of value).	Reversionary interest not excluded property if acquired for consideration in money or money's worth. It is not possible therefore for the life tenant to reduce his estate—merely by buying up the reversion—but a PET transaction.
5. Assignment in favour of others by remainderman (reversioner's gift of his interest).	No—disposal of a beneficial interest under a trust exempt (TCGA 1992, s 76(1)) provided a UK trust (TCGA 1992, s 85).	No—transfer of excluded property (s 48(1)).	Exempt if certificated.	Circumstance 5 particularly suited for say, a son who is wealthy and will inherit capital on death of widowed mother who has a life interest under an estate duty (ED) type will. Gift of son's reversionary interests to his own children will be free of IHT. NB where settlor or spouse is entitled to the reversionary interest—not excluded property (s 48(1) as amended). NB act before interest vests in possession. But, a settlement for income tax within the anti-avoidance provision of TA 1988, Part XV.
6. Disclaimer of life interest not yet in possession, eg in case of B where trust provisions are to A for life, subject thereto to B for life, remainder to C.	No—not in possession TCGA 1992, s 76(1).	No—no IP and see s 142.	£5 nominal	

* Having regard to TCGA 1992, ss 165 and 260, CGT holdover relief is restricted for disposals on or after 14 March 1989 to a narrower class of disposals consisting in the main of business and agricultural assets (including unquoted shares in trading/holding companies); heritage property; gifts to political parties; and gifts on which an immediate lifetime charge for IHT arises (even if within the nil rate band)—see also **4.42** above.

175

4.10:1   Variation of Trusts Act 1958

Assuming the court's sanction is necessary, most variations or terminations of settlements are effected under the Variation of Trusts Act 1958 ('VTA') as the court's jurisdiction is thereby based on the broadest terms and subject to the widest discretion. Note, however, that this Act does not apply to Scotland or Northern Ireland although the Court's jurisdiction to vary is not confined to trusts to which English law applies. By VTA, s 1, the court can approve 'any arrangements ... varying or revoking all or any of the trusts, or enlarging the powers of the trustees of managing or administering any of the property subject to the trusts'. This does not, however, enable the court to override valid objections, or to dispense with any necessary consents. The trusts need not have arisen since the passing of VTA and the court's order can be of immediate effect or operative from a future date.

The predominant criterion is the 'benefit' of the person(s) on whose behalf the application is made. The trusts can be in respect of real or personal property 'under any will, settlement or other disposition'.

The court will not entertain an application where the beneficiaries are all of full age and sui juris as this must then be a matter of obtaining their consents (*Re Suffert's Settlement, Suffert v Martyn-Linnington* [1961] Ch 1) nor do discretionary objects as such have power to apply under VTA.

There are five different kinds of benefit that have been recognised in the many reported cases, namely: financial benefit; moral-social benefit; benefit by removing restriction on contingent interests; facilitating the general administration of the trusts; and widening of investment powers.

The majority of cases brought under VTA have been designed to reduce Revenue burdens, particularly ED but including also income tax, the former surtax and capital gains tax. Applications for CTT and now IHT purposes have included the breaking of discretionary trusts and the enlargement of life tenants' interests. Many of these various applications have been successful, but a notable exception was highlighted in the decision of *Re Weston's Settlements, Weston v Weston* [1969] 1 Ch 223, [1968] 3 All ER 338, CA, where unusually an application to transfer a trust to Jersey was dismissed as being 'a cheap exercise in tax avoidance', Lord Denning preferring to retain the trusts 'in this our England which is still the envy of less happier lands'.

In the rather similar circumstances of *Re Seales' Marriage Settlement* [1961] Ch 574 and *Re Windeatt's Will Trusts* [1969] 2 All ER 324 transfers of the administration of trusts abroad have been approved.

The reported cases have covered nearly all aspects concerning the variation and termination of trusts, including partitioning of the trust assets; resettlement of interests on discretionary or other terms; variation of provisions as to accumulation of income; inclusion and exercise of powers of advancement; widening of investment powers; transfer of trusts abroad and foreign administration; and many other aspects of 'trust busting' and variation.

The decision in *Re Robinson's Settlement Trusts* [1976] 3 All ER 61 is an example of a case involving CTT where the court's consent was sought for breaking a protective trust and where the amount to be received by an infant beneficiary, albeit that the entitlement was accelerated, was less than the net sum he would receive on the termination of the trust. Templeman J sanctioned the division of the trust subject to a ten-year with profits policy for £8,000 being taken out for the infant's benefit and payable out of the income of his share.

Procedure before the relevant court (usually the Chancery Division of the

High Court) is set out in Ord 93, r 6 of the Rules of the Supreme Court found in Sch 1 to the Civil Procedure Rules. The application is normally made by one or more interested beneficiaries, who join the trustees and any other beneficiaries. The application is commenced by claim form, and is heard in open court unless otherwise directed.

It should be stressed, however, that considerable scope is available by way of self help and with a little foresight and a carefully drafted trust deed many somewhat uncertain applications under the VTA should prove unnecessary. Thus specific power should be included in the trust deed to appoint foreign trustees. Indeed the balance of opinion indicates that the normal powers of appointment included in most trust deeds or implied under the provisions of the Trustee Act 1925 enable foreign trustees to be appointed without application to the court (see *British Tax Review* 1969, No 3, pp 193–194 and the unreported 1987 case of *Richard v Mackay* referred to in an article by R. Bramwell QC in *The Offshore Tax Planning Review*, Vol 1, issue 1, p 1). This is, moreover, supported to a certain degree by the decision of *Re Whitehead's Will Trusts, Burke v Burke* [1971] 2 All ER 1334, namely that there is no legal bar to the appointment of foreign resident trustees and that such an appointment is appropriate provided that 'exceptional circumstances' exist, for example, that the beneficiary is taking up residence in the foreign country. However, if out of an abundance of caution it is still wished to apply to the court, it is safer to make the appointment of foreign trustees and seek the court's ratification thereto rather than to ask the court to make the appointment itself; because whereas the court may be ready to ratify, they may be disinclined actively to appoint. If it is wished, in addition, to change the proper law of the settlement to a foreign country there is no doubt that in the absence of specific power in the trust deed, application to the court would be necessary. Specific power should therefore be included in the trust deed to cover this aspect as well and also to avoid any doubt arising as to whether the 'exceptional circumstances' as referred to above exist. If a settlement already has a foreign proper law this should be recited in the trust deed.

As to the possible disadvantages of appointing foreign trustees, see **4.1:3**. The appointment of foreign trustees might conceivably also breach the conditions of an accumulation and maintenance trust (see s 71), should the foreign law have no equivalent trust provisions, eg, on accumulation periods.

Still on a theme of self help to avoid the need for application under the VTA, draftsmen of modern settlements are generally aware of the desirability of going beyond the narrow powers of advancement in the Trustee Act 1925, s 32 and the need to include the widest powers of advancement extending over the whole of the settled funds including powers to appoint on new trusts or other settlements. However, in view of the restricted application of CGT holdover relief, mainly to transfers or business or agricultural assets or where inheritance tax is chargeable, it may be important in exercising any given power to show that a particular appointment does *not* constitute a new trust and is not therefore a disposal for CGT. (See in particular *Hoare Trustees v Gardner* [1978] STC 89; *Roome v Edwards* [1981] STC 96, HL; *Bond v Pickford* [1982] STC 403; *Swires v Renton* [1991] STC 490; and Inland Revenue Statements of Practice 9/81, 23 September 1981 and 7/84, 11 October 1984.)

4.10:2   Other jurisdictions

The VTA has become so predominantly used in any application for the court's sanction that other sources of the court's jurisdiction need be mentioned only briefly, including the following:

(1) the Court's inherent jurisdiction, where a compromise of rights in a genuine dispute is sought;
(2) Trustee Act 1925, s 53, enabling the court to appoint a person to convey property belonging to an infant who is beneficially entitled to the income or capital of trust assets;
(3) Trustee Act 1925, s 57, for issues relating to management or administration of trust property;
(4) Settled Land Act 1925, s 64, authorising any transactions affecting or concerning settled land (note, however, the gradual phasing out of the Settled Land Act introduced by the Trusts of Land and Appointment of Trustees Act 1996);
(5) Matrimonial jurisdiction, including maintenance of and financial provision for either party to a marriage and children in cases of divorce, etc (Matrimonial Causes Act 1973, s 24). The application of the Married Women's Property Act 1882, s 17 may be preferable to modern matrimonial legislation, because being merely *declaratory* cannot involve a CGT disposal, whereas orders under modern legislation may do so; transferring and settling property and varying matrimonial settlements; and title to or possession of property between husband and wife.

The jurisdiction of the court can often be of invaluable assistance to beneficiaries and trustees, particularly in the case of settlements created before our present tax structure was envisaged, and to counteract the increasing injustice of retrospective legislation.

Chapter 5

Transfer and Reorganisation of Business Interests—Companies

5.0 INTRODUCTION

This chapter is primarily concerned with unquoted, family controlled, close companies, and suggests ways of dealing with the threat of IHT in respect of lifetime transfers, and dispositions on the death of the principal shareholders. The main asset of an individual often consists of substantial or majority holdings of shares in such a company. In many family businesses the value of these shares can be a considerable embarrassment because, although the shares may well have a high face value, the holder reaps little if any benefit on this illiquid asset. The policy adopted is usually against declaring dividends, and the sale of the shares is unlikely if it is wished to retain the business in the family. If no adequate estate planning is undertaken, the result may well entail the break-up of the company or the sale of its shares on the death of the individual, for financial reasons. Moreover, break-up or sale may well be at an inopportune time, therefore detrimental not only to the individual's estate but also to the company, its other members, directors and employees. The need to gauge the impact of IHT not only on death but also on lifetime transfers highlights the difficulties involved in passing down a business from one generation to another in circumstances where there are valuable illiquid assets but not a great deal of available cash in the hands of individuals. Nevertheless, it must be said that the trend of the legislation has made the task considerably easier, notably under the PET regime, and then through the increase of business (and agricultural) relief to 100% and 50% (from 50% and 30%) as from 10 March 1992 together with the removal of the requirement that in excess of 25% be held in order to qualify for 'full' relief post-5 April 1996. This chapter outlines some of the main aspects of estate planning for these companies, namely:

(1) IHT planning for directors and shareholders;
(2) recipients of re-allocated shares, including gifts to members of a family and others; disposal by way of takeover or merger; and sale to financial institutions and the public by way of flotation;
(3) protection for the individual divesting shareholder.

In the case of gifts of business and agricultural assets where business or agricultural relief is involved, there can be some nasty clawback of relief where assets are disposed of without full rollover relief and in trust where changes have occurred: see **9.1**.

5.1 IHT PLANNING FOR DIRECTORS AND SHAREHOLDERS

Set out below are some of the possible methods which may overcome the obstacles and difficulties referred to above. The reader's attention is also directed to the wider issues in other chapters, including the art of giving (**Chapter 7**), insurance aspects (**Chapter 8**), special classes of assets including business and agricultural relief (**Chapter 9**), and emigration (**Chapter 10**).

Whenever a particular estate planning method is under consideration, careful attention must be directed to the anti-avoidance provisions outlined in **1.3:1**, particularly as regards associated operations (s 268), connected persons (s 270), restriction on freedom to dispose (s 163), related property provisions (s 161), tax charges in respect of future payments (s 262) and the close company transfer provisions (ss 94–102). In cases involving business and agricultural relief, the traps which can trigger off a clawback of the relief should be borne in mind (see **9.1**). The *Ramsay* approach to statutory construction, as recently explained by the House of Lords in *MacNiven v Westmoreland* [2001] 237, must also be born in mind.

It is also important to keep business asset taper relief in mind and to be wary of disposals that will bring a particular period of ownership to an end before maximum taper relief is available.

5.1:1 Sales versus gifts

Assets such as shares of a private company may be particularly suitable for making gifts either outright or into a favoured trust, first, if the 100% business relief is available for IHT, and secondly having regard to the possibility of CGT holdover. Capital gains on disposals by way of gift of family company shares fall into the small group of gains which can still be held over under the restrictive provisions of TCGA 1992, ss 165 and 260. The CGT relief covers shares and securities in trading companies, or holding companies of trading groups (defined as for CGT retirement relief (TCGA 1992, ss 163, 164 and Sch 6) where either:

(a) the shares or securities are neither quoted on a recognised stock exchange nor dealt in on the AIM; or

(b) (assuming the donor is an individual) the company concerned (and this here can include a quoted or an AIM company) is his personal company defined for retirement relief, ie, at least 5% of the voting rights are held by the donor; or

(c) there is a deemed disposal for CGT by trustees of a settlement of shares or securities in a trading company or of a holding company of a trading group and the trustees at that date controlled at least 25% of the voting right; and

(d) applies in any other case where business or agricultural property relief (even at the 100% rate) is available (TCGA 1992, s 260).

The donee might subsequently place such shares or some of them by lifetime chargeable transfers (eg, into a discretionary trust—CGT holdover being available without restriction because an IHT lifetime chargeable transfer is involved) at low minority value. Beware, however, of the minimum period of ownership requirements applicable for business property relief. Note that the Revenue accept that a gift qualifying for 100% business/agricultural relief (and hence of zero value for IHT) is still a chargeable transfer for TCGA 1992, s 260 holdover relief.

If the donor or his wife are receiving or continue to receive remuneration or pension benefits from the company, it might be possible that such transfer should constitute a reservation of benefit in the gift, thus turning it into a gift with reservation. Nevertheless it is unlikely that the Revenue will take this view if a service agreement is taken out as a preliminary step and which is reasonable in providing fixed terms for remuneration (albeit index-linked) and commission on a commercial basis, and similarly with pension provision, and is not open ended. A further safeguard would be to conclude this service agreement well before the gift of the shares, so that it can be argued that there is no reservation of benefit because the benefit, if any, from the service arrangements has been carved out prior to the gift. Reservation is not of course a problem for IHT if 100% business relief is available *and* maintained (in this context note that the days of 100% business property relief could be numbered). Such a lifetime disposal can be disadvantageous for CGT, as it sacrifices the death exemption and market value uplift.

There may still occasionally be circumstances when it is desirable to substitute an arm's length sale and purchase arrangement for a gift. Although potentially triggering a charge to CGT limited retirement relief may still be available to mitigate any capital gains tax charge (although this will of course be of decreasing relevance until retirement relief is finally fully phased out in 2003–04. A useful formula may be to agree to a sale of a parcel of shares at such value as shall be agreed by the Shares Valuation Division. This may then overcome the problem occasioned by the 'consequential loss' formula in s 3(1), the arm's length requirement of s 10 and the 'related property' rule of s 161. There are three hurdles to be overcome to take a sale of such shares outside the IHT provisions of s 3(1) and take advantage of s 10:

(1) no gratuitous intent in favour of *anyone*;

(2) the sale is at arm's length on such terms as might be expected to be made in a transaction at arm's length between persons not connected with each other;

(3) at a price freely negotiated at the time of sale or at a price such as might be expected to have been freely negotiated at the time of sale.

The Revenue may try to apply a 'double-standard'. For example, in a transaction between father and son for the 'sale' of a parcel of family company shares, notwithstanding that the value of the shares has been independently valued, for instance by the Shares Valuation Division, the Revenue may argue that the father would not have agreed to that transfer on those terms to a stranger. The then Chief Secretary (Mr Joel Barnett) (SCA 31 1975, col 493) suggested that the sale of part of the controlling holding of a private company's shares just sufficient to deprive the vendor of control would not be an arm's length transaction within the meaning of what is now s 10. This goes too far because an independent valuation should by definition take into account all available hypothetical purchasers deemed to be in the open market. The key question is how much the vendor would not only want but could expect to get for that parcel of shares if he were selling to a total stranger. (As to the other arguments marshalled by the Revenue, see **Chapter 7**.)

Clearly the main aim of this type of sale is to enable the estate owner to straddle the point at which the holding is turned from a controlling interest to a minority interest, ie to cross the 50% voting level—the owner will still be entitled (subject to satisfying the conditions) to 100% business relief if his shares are in an eligible unquoted or AIM company. For IHT such a transfer would reflect the loss of control, but if one is concerned with an arm's length sale price, one could try to argue that one should look at the percentage holding transferred without reference to the diminution in the transferor's estate. It would be necessary to watch the anti-fragmentation CGT principles of TCGA 1992, s 19, whereby two or more disposals to connected persons within six years may be added together for valuation purposes.

As an alternative it might be appropriate as a first step to sell a sufficient number of shares to an independent party, such as a financial institution, just enough to lose control. Thereafter the estate owner could be in a position to transfer minority holdings to members of his family at a minority valuation. This proposal has two serious reservations. First because s 10 refers to conferring a gratuitous benefit 'on any person' (ie the arrangement could be caught as an indirect gift to such member of the family); and secondly the arrangement could be attacked as an 'associated operation' under s 268 (see **1.3:1**). A further alternative whereby the necessary number of shares could be given to a charity or exempt body has been made difficult (s 161(2)(b)): these shares remain related property (see also **1.3:4** and **7.6:2**). With 100% business relief, however, such strategies are largely obsolete.

In considering sales versus gifts there are two other factors to bear in mind:

(1) The impact of business relief on a gift (**Chapter 9**).

(2) The fact that gains on sales of shares involve CGT whereas gains on gifts of unquoted shares in trading companies or shares in family companies (as defined) can be held over. (But a donee who has a held over gain retains it until he sells whereas a beneficiary acquiring on death obtains a new base value for CGT.) The absence of consequential loss in the transferor's estate for IHT must be weighed against the CGT on sale of the strategic shares at a worthwhile value.

It all comes down to a need to work out the alternatives and an appraisal of factors such as the availability of 100% business relief and, if not, whether the donor is likely to survive seven years (and the cost of insuring that risk).

5.1:2   Relief for business property (ss 103–114)

Clearly this relief at 100% or 50% of the value transferred (depending on the various applicable circumstances) is of fundamental and vital importance in estate planning for the shareholder of the family company and details of the relief are set out in **Chapter 9**.

One important factor is that the 100% relief for shares in an unquoted trading company, or company on the AIM, applies to all holdings, whatever their size so that the 100% relief is not lost in giving up over 50% voting control.

5.1:3   Hiving-off operations and parallel trading

Under this method, new developments or operations in a business would be syphoned or channelled to a new business with the existing business remaining static or contracting. IHT planning should therefore receive particular atten-tion on the formation of a business including the expansion of an existing business to new fields. The estate owner might have the controlling or other substantial interest in the existing business and little if any stake in the new business. The valuable contracts and connections might gradually be lost to the existing business and taken up by the new business. The estate would no doubt have 100% business relief for IHT on the existing company holding. However, one could mitigate the CGT position where the younger generation take up the shares in the new business at an initial stage when their value would be unlikely to exceed par value and build up their own IHT 100% relief. This idea may indeed be a practical method of handing on a business from an older to a younger generation indirectly, but practical difficulties could arise where the existing business had substantial fixed assets and particularly where those assets were charged for the working capital. Accordingly this method has particular relevance to know-how type businesses, or businesses with a sub-stantial goodwill value. Where these practical difficulties do exist it may be a possibility to undertake a hiving-off operation as to an appropriate part of the business. The Revenue could attack the arrangement if there was no adequate commercial basis; if need be in order to preserve commerciality, the operation can be accompanied by a royalty or other fee arrangement. A hiving-off operation of this type will operate more smoothly and be more likely to succeed if an existing business is considering a *new project*, and it is that project that is in fact started off in the new business to be carried on and owned by the younger generation. This is a variant of the principle that estate planning should receive particular attention when a new business is commenced.

5.1:4 Freezing operations, deferred and other special classes of shares

The aim of these operations is to freeze value in the hands of the owner, or even reduce it over a period, and permit excess value to accrue to other persons, eg the younger generation. **Under the present regime of 100% business property relief and holdover relief for capital gains tax much of what follows in this chapter may be treated as of largely historical interest, the much preferred course at the moment being a simple gift of shares.** What follows nevertheless remains in this book as time and again the practitioner will be asked to review tax planning effected in the past in the light of the present tax code. In so doing it is often vital to have an appreciation of what the earlier tax planning was trying to achieve, and how. In a freezing operation the share capital of a company might be divided into, say, two classes where the estate owner (who might otherwise have made a gift or settlement) retains the class (its rights being appropriately re-organised) which absorbs and contains all the *current* value of the company as to both the capital and income rights, without any or with limited growth prospects. A further new class would be created with little, if any, present value but containing the *future* growth and this new class would normally be allotted in the main to the younger generation or placed into an appropriate settlement, eg a discretionary settlement. Although s 98 aims at charging 'alteration' or 'extinguishment' of share rights, it is claimed that this freezing operation would not substantially reduce the value of existing shares. Care must however also be taken so as not to offend the value shifting provisions contained in TCGA in a mutation where hold over relief is not available.

A more sophisticated freezing operation could involve the formation of a new holding company to acquire all the shares in the existing trading company in which, say, the individual owns all the shares. The individual's children (or their trustees) could subscribe for a modest number of ordinary shares in the holding company at par, say, 100 such shares. The individual would then exchange all his shares in the trading company for, say, preference shares in the holding company with appropriate voting rights to preserve 100% business relief. The holding company would then own the trading company as a 100% subsidiary. The preference shares held by the individual would be likely to retain their par value, while the ordinary shares in the holding company, in the hands of the next generation, would reflect in their value all the growth in the underlying trading company. The question of excluding CGT on the individual's exchange of his shares in the trading company for the new preference shares is, of course, an important factor. Since the operation constitutes an exchange of securities within TCGA 1992, s 135, an advance application for clearance under TCGA 1992, s 138 is important. For IHT purposes, some effort should be made to ensure that the preference shares received fully reflect the market value of the individual's shares in the trading company. In particular the new holding should carry a dividend level fully in line with current returns. A variant might be to have loan stock instead of preference shares. A waiver must be by *deed*, as there is no consideration involved.

It must be said that while 100% business relief is still available and holdover relief for CGT a simple gift of shares by the estate owner is much the preferred course in any event.

A similar sort of idea (subject to the Revenue views (see below)) might be a bonus issue of deferred ordinary shares which have meagre rights during an initial period of years and will only gradually rank *pari passu* with the equity share capital, say, after a period of 10 or 15 years. (The actual period is one for discussion in the circumstances of the case. It may be appropriate for the rights to remain meagre until the end of that period whereupon the full rights will automatically accrue.) If the estate owner gives away these deferred ordinary shares shortly after the bonus issue, the gift will be at a low value for IHT and CGT purposes.

A further development of this scheme would be that at the end of the specified period, not only would the deferred shares attain full rights, but simultaneously the original shares would lose their own rights, so that the incidents attaching to each of the two classes of shares would change over. In this variant of the scheme, the value of the original shares would become negligible at the end of the period, instead of, as in the first version, retaining some value on ranking *pari passu* with the deferred shares.

However, in a letter published in the *Law Society Gazette* of 11 September 1991 the Revenue indicated that they had up to then taken a view that at the end of the specified period there would be no alteration of rights in the deferred shares within s 98(1)(b) even though there was an alteration in the company's share capital within s 98(1)(a). They had been advised that there was an alteration of rights in the deferred shares under s 98(1)(b). They proposed therefore—where deferred shares were *issued* after 5 August 1991 (*note: issued*, not where deferred shares took equal rights at the end of the period after that date under an earlier arrangement)—to claim IHT. The Revenue did not disclose the grounds of their legal advice in their letter. In any event, in a context where 100% business relief is now available, this arrangement, as with those already discussed, loses its relevance.

There are no IHT consequences on a waiver of dividends within a period of

12 months before any right to the dividend has accrued (s 15; see **5.1:7**); and a policy of waiving dividends may be sound tax planning where some of the shareholders are high taxpayers, while others, such as trustees at 34% or basic rate taxpayers are not. Some, such as charities and students, may not pay tax at all. The high taxpayers could waive their entitlement to dividends so that more dividends are available to the lower taxpayers. This method should give rise to no CGT charge. In practice the Revenue raise an assessment on the waiving shareholders as settlors if the beneficiaries of the 'trust' include minor or unmarried children of these high taxpayers, under TA 1988, s 660B. The use of separate classes of shares might be considered as opposed to dividend waivers, the low rate taxpayers having shares which entitle them to a high dividend yield. Consideration must however be given to the applicability of the value shifting provisions of TCGA. If applicable, care must be taken in creating the 'high dividend' shares with the intention of paying them to the low income taxpayers.

A disadvantage of waivers compared with having separate classes of shares (one class being held by, say, trustees) is the fact that waived dividends still produce a dividend history on the shares which could be used by the Shares Valuation Division as evidence for an increased valuation. Indeed it might be possible to have a minuted resolution demonstrating an intention on the part of the board and the company never to declare a dividend in respect of the class of shares held by the individuals, in the absence of unforeseen circumstances. Note, however, that long-term waiver of dividends may well give rise to an IHT charge under s 98 and or a deemed disposal for CGT under the value shifting provisions of TCGA 1992, s 29.

Where there are two classes of shares in issue, one class of, say, preference shares being entitled to all the declared dividend income, the other class of, say, ordinary shares having no entitlement to dividends, this would automatically decrease the value of the latter without an actual transfer of value. This is, however, subject to the general recommendation that waivers should be undertaken ad hoc and not more than one year at a time because a waiver covering several years could constitute a diminution in the individual's estate.

The existence of onerous contracts and arrangements, for example where the estate owner is the governing director or where pre-exemption provisions are contained in the articles of association, might be another method of reducing, containing or restricting the value of an estate owner's shares (but see, in particular, s 163, the value shifting provision of the CGT legislation, and **1.3:2**).

Where a controlling shareholder is considering transferring shares but is concerned about losing control, he could—as a first step—arrange to retain a single 'golden share' with rights personal to the holder which would give him overall voting control. Under s 269 control is construed as the control of powers of voting on all questions affecting the company as a whole. (Under s 269(4) where there are other shares with votes limited to the question of winding up, or shares of a specific class with votes only on matters relating to that class, control is determined by powers of voting on all questions except those specific matters.) Although the golden share would have a greater value than any of the other shares, its value as only a single share will not be great in real terms, especially if it had no rights (to dividends or on a winding up) other than for voting. It is possible that the Revenue might seek to attack such an arrangement on the grounds that the gift of the remaining shares was a gift with reservation. In any event, however, in an era of continuing 100% business relief, such a single share idea may be regarded as not only no longer relevant but also an undesirable complication.

On formation of a new company, or at an early stage in its life before share valuation became a concern, the possibility might be considered of having different classes of shares, each class having different rights, say, on voting, dividends, in a winding up. Such different classes might act as an aid in transferring shares down among the family, starting with 'junior' shares and passing through shares with 'medium' rights on to the 'senior' shares as a final step. The question of control of the company at any stage will be determined under s 269 (see above).

5.1:5 Splitting operations

It may be practical to separate the trading functions among the family. For example, a father might be responsible for the manufacturing side and his two sons dealing respectively with the supply and sale, and the parties could enter into arm's length restrictive criss-cross trading agreements. The result of this interdependence should be that each separate branch of the business will have a lower intrinsic value.

5.1:6 Watering-down operations

A favourite former method for reducing CGT and ED involved favourable rights issues whereby all the shareholders were issued with provisional allotment letters and the estate owner in question declined to take up his rights, whereas the younger generation eagerly took up theirs. This proposal looks unattractive initially for IHT, having regard to the provisions of s 3(3) whereby a deliberate omission to act, for example, a failure to take up favourable rights, can constitute a chargeable disposition. However, if the rights issue is commercially viable—and rights issues are usually subject to some discount—the proposal can continue to have practical importance for IHT. Moreover, the estate owner may omit to take up his rights for non-deliberate reasons, for example, lack of funds, absence abroad, etc, but cogent back-up evidence must be available. However, a simple PET gift of original shares is likely to be more straightforward.

Where the estate owner wishes to reduce his holding of ordinary shares but at the same time needs to maintain his income, a proposal on the following lines might be considered. A bonus issue is made on the ordinary shares in the company. The bonus issue consists of fully paid cumulative non-voting preference shares with a fixed ample dividend, but not participating in surplus assets on a return of capital or a winding up. The estate owner might then decide to give away the ordinary shares qualifying for 100% business property relief, but retain the preference shares with their dividend income. On the estate owner's death the preference shares if still retained should not have accumulated any further capital value.

5.1:7 Waivers of dividends (s 15)

A person who waives any dividend on shares of a company within 12 months *before* the dividend becomes due does not, by reason of the waiver, make a transfer of value. It appears to be accepted by the Revenue that the 12-month period ends in the case of a final dividend when it is declared in general meeting and in the case of an interim dividend when it is paid.

Thus for a final dividend declared on 31 December 1994, waiver would have to be made within 12 months beginning 1 January 1994. It appears that the Revenue would allow waivers of unascertained dividends and this practice is in line with the dicta in *Re Gulbenkian's Settlements (No 2), Stephens v Maun* [1970] Ch 408, [1969] 2 All ER 1173, whereby an individual appears able to disentitle himself from an unascertained right such as a right under a discretionary trust. The waiver must be by deed so as to overcome any Revenue contentions based on lack of consideration, and also with the view to reducing the force of any Revenue argument that for income tax purposes the right to receive a dividend gives rise to an income tax assessment, on the ground that receivability without receipt is nothing. Beware, however, that a long-term waiver may be considered to fall within the terms of s 98 (alteration of rights attaching to shares).

5.1:8 Waivers or repayment of remuneration (s 14)

Such waivers or repayment are similarly exempt from IHT, subject to certain conditions, namely that the remuneration would, apart from the waiver, have been assessed to income tax under Schedule E, and as a result of the waiver, or repayment the remuneration will not be treated as a deductible expense for income tax or corporation tax purposes or is otherwise brought into charge.

For this type of waiver it is also necessary that the document must be in the form of a deed, again to overcome any lack of consideration. In the case of a repayment of remuneration, some Inspectors of Taxes might insist upon an income tax liability thereon because there is actual receipt; and therefore, it is better if possible to waive future remuneration.

5.1:9 Purchase of own shares by unquoted trading companies (TA 1988, s 219)

The Companies Act 1985, s 162, enables companies, subject to conditions, to purchase their own shares. The redemption or purchase by the company of the shares will not be a taxable distribution, (and the shareholder will be liable only to CGT, if any) provided the company is an unquoted trading company or in a trading group and *either* the purchase of the shares is for the benefit of the trade (as opposed to tax avoidance) *and* various conditions are complied with (for example, the shareholder is UK resident; shares have generally been held for at least five years; and the shareholder's interest in the company is reduced substantially (as defined) as a result of the purchase); *or* the proceeds from the purchase of the shares are used to settle IHT. In the latter case s 219(1)(b) states that the whole or substantially the whole of the payment has to be applied by the person to whom it is made in discharging his liability for IHT charged on death, and is so applied within the period of two years after the death. It must also be shown that the IHT could not otherwise have been discharged without undue hardship. There is provision for the company to apply for advance clearance from the Board of Inland Revenue. Concerning the former requirement as to benefiting the trade, useful guidelines where clearance will normally be given are set out in SP 2/82, dated 3 August 1982, including most cases of a boardroom disagreement; an outside shareholder who has provided equity finance and is now withdrawing his investment; the proprietor of a company retiring to make way for new management; a shareholder who has died leaving shares in his estate and his personal representatives or the beneficiaries not wishing to keep them. The Revenue would normally expect the shareholder's entire interest to be purchased.

These provisions can be useful in cases of illiquid estates, where the main assets constitute shares in a family trading company. Even with the advantage of being able to pay by instalments, the death of a principal shareholder might otherwise necessitate the sale of the company (especially if the company is a property/investment company such that business property relief is not available) and these provisions may well assist in these circumstances. The provisions are also useful, for instance, where the shareholder who is selling can get CGT retirement relief. However, with top rates of both income tax and CGT at 40%, and retirement relief being phased out by 2003–04 there may well be circumstances where it is better for a shareholder to take a distribution from the company by way of dividend rather than have the company apply for clearance for a purchase of its own shares sometimes referred to as a negative clearance.

Moreover, it should be noted that for *all* distributions to trustees arising on or after 6 December 1996 on a purchase by a company of its own shares, that distribution is deemed to be income of the trustees to which TA 1968, s 686 applies. Accordingly, it falls to be taxed at the rate applicable to trusts.

5.2   THE RECIPIENTS OF RE-ALLOCATED SHARES

The shareholder in question, having agreed to reduce his holding, has a wide choice available, as to who should benefit thereby and what action to take. The clawback of business relief (**9.1**) and the two-year ownership rule (**9.6:1**) must, of course, both be watched. Possible recipients of re-allocated shares could include the following.

5.2:1   Spouse

The inter-spouse IHT exemption will apply s 18 (and see **Chapter 2** and **Chapter 3**.) In view of the automatic rollover on disposals between spouses living together (TCGA 1992, s 58) any question of obtaining CGT relief would be a matter for the transferee spouse.

5.2:2   Children and issue

This may give rise to an opportunity for 'skipping a generation'.

5.2:3   Trustees holding

This should be considered particularly where one of the appropriate 'harmless' trusts can be used, for example, the accumulation and maintenance trusts under s 71 (see **4.4:1**) and discretionary trusts. It is considered unwise to include the donor or his/her spouse among the discretionary class, as this will amount to a gift with reservation of benefit, and it is unlikely that the present very generous business relief will still be available in its present form at such time as the gift with reservation ceases (on death or otherwise). Note also the income tax disadvantages of so including the settlor/spouse (TA 1988, s 660A). For this reason also, interest in possession trusts for the donor and his/her spouse should be avoided. Moreover, by means of a judicious choice of trustees, an estate owner can in effect safeguard voting control of a company, ie in the knowledge that the trustees will normally vote as the estate owner would have done. Further, there is usually no objection to the estate owner being a trustee.

5.2:4   Employees

The appropriate IHT exemption while assets are in the trust should apply under s 75 (see **4.7:6**); and apart from this, an allocation to employees may constitute an arm's length transaction involving no gratuitous benefit or be exempt under the provisions of s 13. This provides for exemption when shares are transferred into such an employee's trust (see also **4.7:6**).

5.2:5   Charities

Private or other charitable trusts may be a useful method of holding a proportion of the shares of a family company, although this is not a viable method for losing control because the shares of the charity will remain related property with the transferors for five years.

5.2:6   Financial institutions

In contrast an allocation to a financial institution or merchant bank may be a useful method of avoiding control as well as finding cash for pending or future IHT liability.

With the increased interest over recent years being shown in fostering small and growing companies, a number of venture capital companies have sprung up, some connected with banks and financial institutions, who are interested and willing to take a stake in suitable circumstances. The proposals tend to vary, some requiring board representation in the company, others not, all of them naturally looking to their security, in some instances by the creation of preferential stock or shares. These institutions can be useful as a source of support for the company as well as providing funds for suitable expansion. Taking on an institutional partner in this manner can be a first step towards flotation. Although they have varying minimum values for the companies they wish to deal with, all of these institutions are looking for the strong, viable and potentially rewarding company proposition. Once the parties have agreed upon the basic terms, shares are normally purchased from the shareholder(s), thereby providing them with the requisite liquid funds, and further capital may be injected.

The normal activities of the venture capital market have been materially boosted latterly by positive changes from the government:

(a)   the Enterprise Investment Scheme, which has existed for income tax since its introduction by FA 1994, and was extended to capital gains tax by FA 1998 (replacing re-investment relief). Under the Scheme investors in unquoted trading companies can obtain income tax relief on investments of up to £150,000 in each tax year, as well as rolling-over capital gains. A word of warning however. The eligibility conditions are tight and extensive. In addition there is a widely drawn anti-avoidance code. Accordingly great care must be taken if use of the EIS is considered. A full discussion of the scheme is outside the scope of this work but the Revenue have published a booklet on EIS (see Press Release 28 July 1999; and see FA 2000, s 64 and Sch 17);

(b) the advent of a new type of investment trust, termed the Venture Capital trust, as a vehicle for investment in unquoted trading companies, with PEP-style benefits (freedom from income tax on dividends and CGT) for the investor (see TA 1988, s 842AA and Sch 15B and TCGA 1992, s 151A and Sch 5C).

Both of these avenues are worth exploring. However, the extent to which institutional investors will remain interested in purchasing an interest in the family company is some cause for concern following the abolition, for them, of the tax credit on dividends by F(No 2)A 1997.

5.2:7 'Takeover' and 'merger'

If a partial disposal of shares does not suit the individual, he may be interested in taking more extreme steps by selling or procuring the sale of all or a substantial majority of the shares in the company, thereby obtaining the necessary liquid, or easily realisable, assets to meet IHT in due course. Moreover by exchanging these shares for other shares, for example quoted shares, in a bona fide commercial arrangement, the CGT liability can be deferred (TCGA 1992, ss 135–138, providing for Revenue clearance in advance). These CGT sections also deal with schemes for reconstruction of companies and amalgamations. In a situation where there are associated companies with differing shareholders, a merger on commercial terms may result in removing control for particular shareholders in the associated companies. The merger must be without gratuitous intent in view of s 10 and must avoid the s 94 close company provisions.

5.2:8 Demergers

This is the opposite situation to takeover, amalgamation or merger. TCGA 1992, s 192 (for CGT) and TA 1988, ss 213–218 (income tax) contain provisions (hedged about by anti-avoidance conditions) whereby separate trading activities conducted by the same company or group can be segregated into separate independent companies or groups. The transactions resulting in the demerger are (if Revenue approval is given) exempt from CGT and some stamp duty, and any distributions are exempt from income tax. The provisions apply, for instance, where the shares of a company are currently held by two or more sides of a family who do not get on, and there are separate trading activities which can be divided up. Such a demerger can provide a more stable basis for future IHT planning (but watch the anti-avoidance provisions).

5.2:9 Flotation of company

A note of warning, first of all: business property relief will be restricted if not lost entirely (see further **Chapter 9**). However there are some advantages to be gained from going public and obtaining admission to the Official List of the London Stock Exchange at the appropriate time. There are three main advantages as regards IHT. First, the difficulties, delays and uncertainties in negotiating a valuation with the Shares Valuation Division that exist in the case of unlisted shares no longer apply. For listed shares, the practice is to value at a 'quarter up' from the lower figure of closing price on the day of the transfer of value or death (or nearest working day) shown in the London Stock Exchange Daily Official List; or midway between the highest and lowest prices which bargains were recorded on that day, if lower. Secondly, the realisation of shares to pay IHT becomes a much easier and speedier operation. It is true that the listing may itself increase the value of the shares and hence the IHT liability, but in appropriate cases the advantages referred to outweigh such a disadvantage. Thirdly, where shares and securities listed by the London Stock Exchange or holdings in authorised unit trusts are realised by executors or other accountable persons within 12 months of death at a genuinely lower level, they are, subject to conditions, able to claim that the total of the sale price should be substituted for the total of the date of death values of the investments realised (ss 178–189 and see **1.6:3**).

Part IV of the Financial Services Act 1986 applies to the listing of securities in the London Stock Exchange. In effect it provides the statutory framework under which the Stock Exchange controls the admission and regulation of listed securities in accordance with its manual, the 'Admission of Securities to Listing', known universally as the 'Yellow Book'. Part IV of the Act implements the relevant European Community directives which require the UK to regulate such matters in a particular way. Any company seeking admission of its securities to listing must therefore acquaint itself through its advisers with the current requirements of the London Stock Exchange. Among these requirements are certain stipulations regarding, for example, the size and profits record of the company as well as the proportion of the capital to be made available to the general public.

Only a small proportion of companies are therefore likely to qualify for a full listing on the London Stock Exchange. However, the London Stock Exchange also operates the Alternative Investment Market (AIM) to meet the needs of companies unwilling, or unable, to qualify for a full listing but desiring nevertheless a free market for their securities, whether to encourage investors, or for other reasons. The AIM is not regulated by Part IV of the Financial Services Act 1986 or by the Yellow Book. However the London Stock Exchange does enforce criteria for admission to the AIM and the statutory prospectus requirements apply. Details of admission to the AIM are obtainable from the London Stock Exchange or from its member firms. A company may well enter the AIM as a stepping stone to a full listing. The fact that AIM shares are 'unquoted' brings IHT business relief benefits—see **9.8:11**(2) and (3).

The future of the AIM is under review, although many practitioners feel a need for a junior market of this sort. Another alternative (sometimes as a preparation for a later flotation) is to introduce one of the specialist venture capital institutions (see **5.2:6**).

In planning the above re-allocation of shares, one must beware of a significant drawback: following official listing business property relief will no longer be available at the 100% rate (and only at 50% if the transferor had control of the company). This is probably sufficient to counter any of the possible so-called advantages described above.

5.3 PROTECTION FOR THE INDIVIDUAL DIVESTING SHAREHOLDER

5.3:1 Loss of voting control

This involves a difficult decision (and see **Chapter 9** as to business relief). A controlling shareholder who divests himself of shares carrying voting control has to ensure as far as he is able that the recipients of his shares (be they out and out donees or trustees) are sympathetic and reliable. Another safeguard would be to remain as trustee of family settlements of shares. Consider deferring when control passes by using the burnt-out share scheme in **5.1:4** but note the danger if 100% business relief is withdrawn, as is likely.

An effective way of giving reassurance to a former controlling shareholder now with a minority holding, who is concerned to be able to keep his directorship, would be for him to arrange, before he reduces his holding, that the articles of the company give him increased voting rights in respect of his shareholding so as to defeat any resolution being put to remove him from office. The increased votes in this one circumstance should be sufficient to protect him should his holding of shares go down to whatever level he might contemplate. The provision in the articles should also stipulate an upward movement in the voting rights should his colleagues, for instance, seek to issue more shares to nullify his present voting rights. This gives the transferor the knowledge and comfort that he cannot be ousted from the board against his will and his position as director is safe for as long as he wishes to retain it, preserving his ability to take part and have a full say in the running of the company. This form of voting provision in the articles was declared valid by the House of Lords in *Bushell v Faith* [1970] AC 1099. However, in an era of 100% business relief, the most prudent course is to avoid 'fancy shares' and keep the share structure of the company simple. On that footing, rather than giving weighted votes to particular shares, it may be more straightforward merely to have a shareholders' agreement whereby they agree to use their respective best endeavours to maintain the directors on the board of the company.

Interesting ways of seeking to keep family (or incumbent board) control in publicly listed companies have been developed over recent years. In one method a publicly quoted family company issued bonus preference shares with no voting rights (except in restricted circumstances). Family shareholders in need of cash could sell these preference shares without affecting voting control. The Americans have been particularly inventive with these 'poison pills'. One approach, for instance, where family control was under pressure, has been on lines such as to issue bonus B shares having ten time the votes of each original ordinary share. The B shares could be transferred only to members of the shareholder's family. To be transferred to anyone else, they had first to be converted to ordinaries. Thus a predator could get his hands only on ordinary shares with few minimum votes. For quoted companies in the UK, on the other hand, there are feelings that non-voting shares, for instance, are inappropriate in the present open era and work against the freedom of the market.

There are further pressures on unquoted private companies in the UK to keep the structure simple. If any restriction of share capital were contemplated, particularly if transfer of shares were to follow, it would be necessary to take into account TA 1988, s 703 (transactions in securities), as well as TCGA 1992, ss 29 and 30 (value shifting) and s 126 et seq (reorganisation of share capital). For IHT, s 98 (alteration of share capital) and s 268 (associated operations) would need watching, as well as business relief implications and gift with reservation danger.

5.3:2 Service/consultancy agreements

The divesting shareholder/director can be awarded an appropriate service or consultancy agreement on reasonable and adequate terms as to (index linked) remuneration, pensions, etc and this agreement can be for life. (However, it should be noted that under the Companies Act 1985, s 319 a service agreement exceeding five years requires approval of the company in general meeting.) For IHT and other tax reasons, the terms of the agreement should impose strict, onerous obligations on the individual. In particular, the remuneration ought not to exceed what can be defended as a reasonable return for services rendered (otherwise the excess might be treated as a company distribution and hence investment income, although currently, with no investment income surcharge, there would be no difference in the individual's income tax. There would, however, be the question of national insurance).

See **5.1:1** for the need to get the service contract firmly in place before any transfer of shares, in order to avoid any possibility of a gift with reservation.

5.3:3 Insurance and pension arrangements and pension schemes

Directors of limited companies and employees paid under Schedule E (other than controlling directors of investment companies) are eligible to join an occupational pension scheme. Tax relief is allowed in full for the normal contributions to a pension fund whether paid by the employer or employee. There is a maximum employee's contribution in percentage terms. The company's contribution will reduce the net assets and can therefore act as a further IHT planning exercise. From 8 October 2001, employers will be required — subject to some exceptions — to offer employees access to a stakeholder pension scheme. See the Stakeholder Pension Scheme Regulations 2000 and **6.3:3**.

The maximum pension under an occupational pension scheme which will receive the necessary Inland Revenue approval is, depending on length of service, two-thirds of final pensionable salary, with a widow's or widower's pension of two-thirds of his or her late spouse's pension, together with death in service life cover of up to four times salary. A tax-free lump sum may be taken on retirement up to a sum equal to one and a half times final pensionable salary in lieu of part of the pension under the commutation rules.

The field has been widened considerably by the alternative possibility of personal pensions, which may be taken out by the self-employed, and employees generally, including directors, under TA 1988, s 630 et seq. Whereas approved occupational pension schemes are concerned with limits on the size of pensions and other benefits emerging from the scheme, the personal pension regime works on a 'money purchase' basis; that is, there are limits on the level of tax deductible contributions being made into the pension plan by reference to fixed percentages, increasing with age, of relevant earnings; and at retirement the pension will be what the accrued fund will buy (and there is a right at that stage to take a proportion as tax free cash).

Under the FA 1989, however, with certain savings for existing members of approved occupational schemes, an indexed ceiling (£95,400 for 2001–02) has been imposed on the amount of qualifying remuneration. For occupational schemes this ceiling will determine the maximum two-thirds pension. Employing companies are free to arrange 'top-up' schemes over and above the ceiling, but these unapproved additions do not get the tax privileges of ordinary schemes.

Retirement annuity policies (RAPs) which were taken out by the self-employed or employees not in an occupational pension scheme (also known as s 226 policies, but see now TA 1988, s 618 et seq) were replaced by personal pensions, and no new RAPs have been allowed to be taken out from 1 July 1988. Those RAP contracts already in being, however, can continue to operate. Indeed, although the contribution limits for personal pensions are higher than those for RAPs (see the table in **6.3:4**), there is no indexed ceiling for qualifying remuneration on RAPs as there is for personal pensions. Accordingly, in the case of a very high earner, the permitted contribution to the RAP based on a percentage of the whole earnings may well be higher than the larger permitted contribution linked to the ceiling. It is possible for individuals to have both RAPs and personal pensions, and there are limitations on the respective contributions.

Following recent consultation the Inland Revenue have announced changes to facilitate improved flexibility in pension provisions. In particular the ability for Small Self Administered Schemes to defer the purchase of an annuity and in the meantime pay a pension by drawing down income from the schemes own resources have been extended. These arrangements will also apply to deferred annuity insurance contracts and for standing additional voluntary contributions schemes. The new method of income draw down will follow broadly the existing method used for personal pensions: Annuity purchase will be able to be deferred up to the age of 75 and income withdrawn from the scheme at levels up to a maximum approximating a level single life annuity (see further Personal Pension Schemes Update 8 [1995] STI 1359 and PSO Update 54 [1999] STI 1283].

5.3:4   Death in service benefits under pension schemes: use of rights

In a typical approved occupational pension scheme ('the scheme') an employee/director would be entitled to a maximum of four times final pensionable salary if he died before retirement. When the trustees of the scheme distribute the lump sum at their discretion this should be free of IHT because although the scheme is discretionary it is expressly taken out of the IHT settlement regime of s 58 by s 151 (see SP 10/86 following up SP/E3).

Accordingly, and subject to the s 3(3) problem mentioned in the last paragraph of this section, a member of the scheme has an excellent opportunity of mitigating IHT by recommending to the trustees that the lump sum should go to children, grandchildren or trustees on their behalf; or other parties to whom a gift of a lump sum on the member's death would incur IHT. If on the other hand the member recommends his widow, this is not particularly IHT effective because she would have been exempt from IHT in any event under the inter-spouse exemption. Moreover, if the lump sum is paid to her it will swell her estate for IHT purposes on her death and will not have taken advantage of skipping the generation as per the suggested route. Clearly one must temper any IHT mitigation motive with the practical aspect of whether the widow is adequately provided for. The widow could perhaps be 'compensated' by being left the free estate of the member; and for example if that estate includes shares of the family company, the beneficiaries of the scheme lump sum could use it (or trustees on their behalf) to purchase shares out of the lump sum, thereby making the widow liquid.

Another alternative might be to request the trustees of the scheme to advance the lump sum into a *new* discretionary trust in respect of which the widow (who would thereby be assured of income) as well as other members of the family etc could be beneficiaries. Unfortunately, however, the new discretionary trust would not be exempt under s 151 but would come within the settled property regime of s 58 and attract the consequent exit and ten-year anniversary charges.

Set out below is a suggested letter of request in respect of an approved occupational pension scheme.

DEATH IN SERVICE REQUEST FORM

To: The Trustees of the X Ltd

occupational pension
scheme ('the Scheme')

When exercising the powers and discretion given to you under the Scheme, I request, but without imposing any binding trust or obligation on you that you have regard to my undermentioned wishes in respect of any death in service or other lump sum benefits ('the lump sum').

1. The lump sum should be paid to the undermentioned in the stated proportions namely

   Names   % of lump sum

2. [In arriving at a final decision in respect of the payment/division of the lump sum, I would like you to consult my widow/widower [name] and take into account his/her wishes/requirements subject always to your overall discretion and the request set out in 1 above].

3. This request supersedes all previous requests made by me to you or your predecessors.

DATED   20

Signed

Note

In respect of the beneficiaries named in para 1, this could include trustees of an appropriate accumulation and maintenance, interest in possession or discretionary trust (as to this last see the above introductory comments).

It is of course perfectly possible to arrange for *part* of the lump sum to go to the widow to cover her needs and requirements and the 'surplus' to go for the benefit of children/grandchildren or other members of the family.

Some concern on the general tax freedom of discretionary lump sum benefits arose in late 1990 when it appeared that the Revenue might be contemplating the general use of the 'omission to exercise a right' provisions of s 3(3) to produce an IHT claim where an individual postponed taking his pension although entitled to do so, thereby leaving the discretionary lump sum still payable on his death. Fortunately, however, it became clear in summer 1991 that the Revenue intended to use s 3(3) only in extreme cases. The circumstances would exist where an individual is terminally ill, or uninsurable because of ill health, and either takes out a new pension policy assigning the death benefit into trust, or assigns the death benefit under an existing policy into trust, or pays excessive contributions into a policy already under trust. Even then, it appears the Revenue will not normally pursue the case if the evidence shows the individual was intending to make provision, if not for his own retirement, then in the event of early death, for his spouse and/or dependants, who take the benefit. This indication of Revenue practice upholds the general rule that discretionary lump sum payments on death before pension are free from IHT.

5.3:5 Small self-administered pension schemes

Small self-administered pension schemes have become more popular since the Inland Revenue Pension Schemes Office (the 'PSO') relaxed the rules on such schemes, ie those with at least some assets invested otherwise than in insurance policies or a current amount and with fewer than twelve members. The idea behind such a scheme is that the employing company pays a premium to the trustees of a pension scheme in the normal way, but the trustees include, for example, the directors of the employing company or partners of the partnership where the members are employees of a service company. The investment policy of the pension fund is therefore under the control of the trustees and the result is considerable flexibility in administration.

A small self-administered scheme must include among the trustees what is known as a pensioneer trustee, who is somebody approved by the PSO as being widely involved with pension matters, and his main purpose is to act as a safeguard in ensuring that the pension fund is not prematurely wound up and is used for the proper purpose of providing pensions.

There have been efforts to tighten up the investment requirements for small self-administered pension schemes. Under the occupational pension scheme legislation there is a provision restricting a pension scheme to a maximum investment of its funds in the shares of the employing company. Small schemes are however exempt from this requirement provided they meet two conditions:

(a) that all members of the scheme are also trustees of the scheme (along, of course, with the pensioneer trustee); and

(b) that the scheme rules require that before any employer related investment is made each member agrees to that investment in writing.

Rules specifically for small schemes (SI 1991/1614) were issued, taking effect from 5 August 1991, covering such matters as the maximum investment in the employing company, the ceiling on loans from the fund to the company, and containing a veto on any transactions between the fund and scheme members.

In addition, notification of a broad range of investment transactions will have to be made to the Revenue within 90 days.

5.3:6 Pre-emption provisions

If it is wished to limit the spreading of shareholdings outside the immediate family, pre-emption provisions can be introduced into the articles of association. By this method, before the shares can be transferred to non-members,

members must first offer their shares to the existing members at a fair price. The Revenue may bring in aid the provisions of s 163 'restrictions on freedom to dispose' where an IHT valuation advantage is sought. Nevertheless such pre-emption provisions should in practice assist in reducing share valuations. In the case of *IRC v Crossman* [1937] AC 26, [1936] 1 All ER 762, HL, it was decided that although one must assume a free market exists *apart* from the pre-emption provisions, the hypothetical purchaser when registered will hold the shares subject thereto. Pre-emption provisions in the articles of association attach, of course, to the shares and affect all shareholders, present and future, unless and until the articles are changed. An alternative way of producing the same effect for the time being is the conclusion of a shareholders' agreement whereby the present shareholders agree to give each other pre-emption rights over the shares. Such an agreement is personal to the shareholders, although the Revenue may still resort to s 163.

5.3:7   TA 1988, s 703

A share arrangement may involve a transaction in securities which results in a defined tax advantage (see TA 1988, ss 703–709) so consider whether it would be appropriate to apply for clearance under s 707. The Revenue tended to be more lenient in granting a clearance if the proceeds of a scheme were required to meet pending ED commitments. This was, moreover, substantiated in the House of Lords decision in *IRC v Goodwin* [1976] STC 28, where it was held that making provision for ED in order to safeguard family control constituted a bona fide commercial reason and therefore no (what is now) s 703 liability existed. The distinction made at the court of first instance between commercial and financial reasons was not followed although the House of Lords was not decisive as to whether there can be a difference between financial and commercial reasons, its decision being mainly based on upholding the Commissioners' finding of fact. This case involved the issue of capitalised redeemable preference shares as an ED funding scheme and the basic principles and policy are likely to be followed for IHT. While the 100% IHT business relief era continues this aspect becomes of less importance.

5.3:8   Loans to pay IHT (TA 1988, s 364)

Interest on a loan to personal representatives applied in paying the IHT on an application for a grant of representation to the deceased's estate is allowed for income tax purposes, subject to a maximum period of one year. There is no income tax relief for interest on loans to pay lifetime IHT.

Despite 100% business relief, IHT has to an extent made it more difficult for a business to be passed down from one generation to another. One of the aims of this book, and particularly of this and the next chapter, is to indicate the means and methods by which this common intention can be accomplished.

Chapter 6

Transfer and Reorganisation of Business Interests—Partnerships and Other Firms

6.0 INTRODUCTION

Partnerships have long been a popular medium for trading and holding assets and this is likely to continue. In particular, a partnership does not suffer from the dual liability to CGT suffered by a company, once on its assets and again on the shares in the shareholders' hands. For the professions, partnerships have long been the main, if not the only method of carrying on business. Nevertheless, although a new business normally starts off as a partnership (if not conducted by a sole trader), it is later usually and by natural progression converted into a company, often for non-tax reasons, the main motivation being limited liability. Shares in a company are, moreover, easier to deal with, transfer, and settle on trust than a share in a partnership. A company shareholding may benefit from being valued as a minority holding, whereas in the case of a partnership, a share, however small, is based on the net asset value. However, the introduction of the PET regime has given a certain flexibility in dealing with partnership interests, provided care is taken to avoid falling into the gift with reservation traps which are found in this field.

FA 1994, ss 178–218 and Schs 19 and 20 provided the first part of the revolutionary income tax and CGT changes as to *self-assessment* and the introduction of the *current year income tax basis* for the preceding year basis. The main provisions apply from 1997–98, and will apply particularly to the self-employed. The complex, detailed provisions are clearly outside the scope of this book. For detailed analysis see Tolley's *Self-Assessment* 2001–2002 by Jan Matthews and Nigel Eastaway

This chapter treats partnership and other business interests in four main sections:

(1) general principles relating to IHT with ancillary references to other taxes;

(2) IHT planning for partnerships and businesses;

(3) protection of an outgoing partner;

(4) partnerships of 'relatives'.

6.1 GENERAL PRINCIPLES RELATING TO IHT

6.1:1

For IHT, there are very few specific provisions applying to partnerships (for example, s 107(3), s 277(6)(b)) and the general principles, particularly as set out in ss 3 and 10, apply.

IHT can apply to partnership situations, especially family partnerships, in the following situations:

(a) on formation;
(b) on a variation, eg introduction of partners, change in profit/capital shares etc;
(c) on a lifetime gift of a partnership share of capital or profit;
(d) on retirement;
(e) on death while still a partner;

This chapter contains frequent references to business and agricultural property reliefs. It should be read in conjunction with **Chapter 9**, which explains these very generous reliefs in more detail.

6.1:2   CGT application

Reference should be made to the important SP/D12 originally dated 17 January 1975 on Revenue practice in relation to CGT and partnerships (as extended by SP 1/79 (retired partner: lump sum as well as annuity) and SP 1/89 (CGT rebasing and indexation)). Although they do not have the force of law, the statements are generally helpful to the taxpayer. Thus in normal circumstances, so long as the partners are not relatives and the balance sheet figures (eg for goodwill) are not increased, there is no CGT on the introduction or retirement of a partner, or on a change of profit sharing ratios, except to the extent that a monetary consideration changes hands. Even then there is no CGT if that consideration is the introduction of capital or the withdrawal of capital or annuities within the specified limits. The moral is not to revalue assets prior to a profit sharing ratio change; instead it may be appropriate to make adjustments on a subsequent sale, ie by sharing the proceeds unequally. These rules are modified where partners are 'connected' by family relationship: see **6.4**. The principle in the statement (as extended) may be followed for IHT although one must not assume this too readily because for CGT any benefit is often merely a deferral, for example, where an incoming partner acquires an asset at a lower base value than the market value. For IHT purposes, on the other hand, the Revenue aims at assessing *each* transaction representing a transfer of value.

Finance Act 2000 extended both the amount and scope of business asset taper relief. If a business asset has been held for at least four years, and that period began after 5 April 1998, only 25% of the gain will be chargeable. This means an effective rate of capital gains tax of 10%.

Shares in a trading company held by an individual will now be business assets if one of the following conditions is met:

(a) the company is unlisted;
(b) the individual is an employee; or
(c) the individual holds 5% or more of the voting rights.

Note, however, that taper relief will be restricted if the period of ownership began before 6 April 2000 and the shares did not qualify as business assets under the rules applicable before that date.

Other assets held by an individual will be business assets if used for the purposes of a trade:

(i) carried on by that individual;

(ii) carried on by a partnership of which that individual is a member;

(iii) carried on by a company whose shares (or whose holding company's shares) would have satisfied the business asset requirements set out above; or

(iv) carried on by the individual's employer and used for the purposes of the individual's office or employment.

There are also detailed provisions, similar to the above, for determining when assets held by trustees and personal representatives will qualify as business assets, and a number of anti-avoidance provisions. Reference should be made to a detailed work on capital gains tax.

6.1:3 Reciprocal arm's length arrangements

These arrangements should give rise to no IHT consequences on the basis that, having regard to the existence of reciprocity, no gratuitous benefit is intended. This should apply to many aspects of a partnership, including repayment of capital, and rights relating to pensions, annuities, and consultancy, likewise the writing out of goodwill. Many of these rights are contained in the partnership agreement from the outset, on an arm's length basis, available to all the partners, and a partner's entitlement at a particular time is usually merely a question of chance or 'the luck of the draw'. In the absence of special provisions in the partnership agreement, the actual book values should represent the assessable values.

In each case where partners are 'connected' as relatives, the onus is, however, much more heavily on the taxpayer to demonstrate commerciality (see **6.4**). With a view to discharging this onus, whenever a partnership transaction is undertaken involving a relative, it is preferable to offer (or have offered) a stranger similar terms. However, where it is desired to make an outright gift, care must be taken in relation to partnerships that transfers constitute PETs and cannot be construed as gifts with reservation. First, on a question of timing, if a gift, eg of a tractor, is made and subsequently the donor goes into a farming partnership with the donees of the tractor this constitutes a reservation of benefit. Contrast the situation where the donor is already in partnership and then makes the gift of the tractor which is already used by the partnership—in which case there is no reservation. Reference should be made to the *Munro* and *Chick* cases in **6.2.5** below. Those cases both concerned gifts of land and, the distinction just highlighted used to be as valid in relation to gifts of land as it remains in the case of the chattels referred to in the examples. However, save in very limited circumstances in the case of land the planning opportunities afforded by these decisions appear to have been stopped by s 102A FA 1986 (introduced by Finance Act 1999). This provision is discussed more fully at 7.2–7.4 above. The limited circumstance where s 102A would appear not to apply in the case of the second example given, is if the partnership (the agreement regulating which gives the donor the right to occupy the land following the gift) was entered into more than seven years prior to the gift of the land (section 102A(5) FA 1986).

Problems can also arise where there is a *partial gift*. For example the donor gives the whole of the partnership capital to the donee but retains, say, half the profit entitlement; this probably constitutes a reservation of benefit. It may be possible to counter any such Revenue contention by segregating the partnership shares of capital and profit on the basis that they are *separate assets* and can therefore be the subject of separate gifts.

The aim should be to carve out and freeze the interest which the donor wishes to keep, and make an outright gift, without reservation, of the rest: see **6.2:5**.

Moreover, any capital sum accruing to the estate on death would of course be chargeable as an asset held on death s 171(1). Remember, in this regard, that a 'buy and sell' agreement or a similar arrangement under the partnership provisions whereby the partner's estate is contractually entitled, not to a direct interest in the partnership assets themselves, but to a purchase price, should be avoided because there is no business relief (see **5.1:2** and **9.11:15** and the unobjectionable alternative of the *option* method).

As to the application of business/agricultural property relief, see **Chapter 9.**

6.1:4   Application of 'free loan' provisions

In many cases, one or more of the partners is the owner of the freehold or leasehold premises used by the partnership and allows these premises to be used at less than a commercial rent. Apart from the application of the lower 50% business property relief (and not even this drawback in the case of farmland), no other IHT consequences arise out of this 'free use of asset' type of arrangement if the owner partner can re-occupy at will. A long-term lease arrangement at a low or nil rent could, however, constitute a diminution in the owner's estate for the purpose of s 3(1), on the footing that the estate is left with the discounted value only of the asset, not its full value, unless the owner takes a larger share of the partnership profits in lieu of rent.

6.1:5   Restriction on freedom to dispose (s 163)

Reference to this anti-avoidance provision has already been made (see **1.3:2**) and it is likely to have particular reference to partnerships, including arrangements in partnership agreements where favourable options are granted and also artificial restrictions relating to goodwill. Consider, however, bringing in aid the reciprocity argument referred to in **6.1:3**.

6.1:6   Position of an outgoing partner

The rights of an outgoing partner are normally set out in the partnership agreement on a reciprocal basis and should therefore give rise to no IHT liability.

A partner should consider retaining *some* share in the partnership rather than retiring, having regard to business/agricultural property relief; for example as to capital 'invested' in the business.

The effect of retirement on BPR was recently illustrated by the Special Commissioner's decision in *Beckman v IRC* [2000] STC (SCD) 59. See also the discussion of the Limited Liability Partnerships Act 2000 at **6.2.11** below.

6.1:7   Dispositions allowable for income tax or corporation tax (s 12)

Such dispositions are exempt for IHT. There is no longer any requirement as to carrying on a trade or business and the exemption covers approved or comparable pension and retirement schemes and certain dwelling house rent free arrangements for employees etc.

6.2   IHT PLANNING FOR PARTNERSHIPS AND BUSINESSES

Several proposals have already been dealt with in the previous chapter and can be adapted appropriately. References to these aspects are therefore given by way of heading only. Furthermore, there are many other general planning possibilities available and these are dealt with elsewhere, particularly in **Chapters 7** and **9**.

6.2:1   Relief for business property (ss 103–114)

The scale of reductions of the value of business property transferred, frequently 100%, is analysed in **Chapter 9**. Property consisting of a business or interest in a business is covered and business includes profession or vocation.

6.2:2   Applying and adapting the ratio of *A-G v Boden*[1]

It might be regarded as a commercial arrangement, not giving rise to any gratuitous benefit for a partner to transfer his share in the partnership in consideration of having to work less hard, hence outside the IHT charge. *Boden*'s case was decided for ED, but the Revenue practice is to follow this decision for IHT. Although this type of arrangement is of historical interest only where 100% APR/BPR is available, it remains of importance where only 50% relief is available or, in the case of BPR, where the provision excluding land dealing and investment business is offended.

The *Boden* 'scheme' is as follows. Where an elderly partner, for example, a father, wishes to dispose of shares in the partnership to a younger partner, for example, his son, it is normally possible to avoid payment of IHT on the value of the goodwill attaching to such shares by taking advantage of the ratio decidendi of *Boden*'s case. The facts of this case were that a father who had taken his sons into partnership disposed of his shares to such sons to take effect on death, the sons paying nothing for goodwill (the other assets were paid for at a proper valuation). The partnership agreement provided that the father was not required to devote more time and attention to the business than he should think fit. On the other hand, the sons were bound to devote their full time. Accordingly this advantage that had accrued to the father was considered by the court to constitute full commercial consideration for the passing of the goodwill in the shares (ie a bona fide purchase within the relevant position) and no ED was therefore payable on the value of the goodwill on the father's death.

As stated, this position should also apply for IHT purposes on lifetime transfers or dispositions on death.

A suggested partnership clause to give effect to this *Boden* scheme could read as follows:

> 'During the subsistence of the partnership each partner other than [senior partner] shall devote his whole time and attention to the partnership business but [senior partner] need not devote more but shall devote not less than [one-third] of his time and attention to the partnership business.'

Although the *Boden* scheme had particular reference to avoiding ED on

---

[1] [1912] 1 KB 539.

goodwill there is no logical reason why the principle should not be extended.[1] The Capital Taxes Office are more likely to succeed in resisting such an extension where 'relatives' are involved (and see **6.4** below).

A *Boden* scheme can usefully be effected in stages, for example:

Stage 1—where senior partner is required to work full time.

Stage 2—he disposes of *part* of his profit share and partnership interest in exchange for merely giving such time and attention as is necessary for the partnership; or say four days per week.

Stage 3—in exchange for a further disposal of his partnership interest he merely has to give such time and attention as he thinks fit; or say 2 days per week.

The form suggested above can be adapted for use in such stages by reducing the minimum time to be devoted by the senior partner at each stage.

A subtle use of the *Boden* principle may enable the partner to remain engaged for substantially the whole of his time for the purposes of this s 628, and yet gain the *Boden* advantage of working less hard than the remaining partners.

There should normally be no stamp duty on a *Boden* arrangement. A gift or voluntary disposition is not liable to stamp duty, nor subject to adjudication, provided it is certified in the appropriate form (see Stamp Duty (Exempt Instruments) Regulations 1987, SI 1987/516); although ad valorem stamp duty at 1% continues to be payable on a conveyance or transfer on sale. It would appear that a *Boden* document, although not a voluntary disposition because the son gives full consideration, does not constitute a sale transaction either, so that no stamp duty is payable.

6.2:3 'Accruer' arrangements

The Revenue have confirmed that business property relief is available for 'accruer' arrangements (which are not treated as buy and sell arrangements), and where the deceased partner's estate is paid on a valuation or formula basis (see *Taxation Practitioner*, 10 April 1997, p 10).

6.2:4 Absence of covenants in restraint of trade

Partnership businesses are often dependent on the efficiency and merit of the individual partners and this applies particularly to professional partnerships. The goodwill is theirs (ie 'dog' goodwill) and *they* constitute the goodwill in contrast to goodwill which is attached to the premises or location of a firm ('cat' goodwill). For the zoological classification of customers and the type of goodwill they generate, see *Whiteman Smith Motor Co Ltd v Chaplin* [1934] 2 KB 35. Accordingly, covenants in restraint of trade restricting competition should only be included in partnership agreements if absolutely essential for other, non-tax, reasons (eg, if there is concern about a possible future disagreement; but in that case, the parties should consider carefully whether they want to become partners). From an IHT viewpoint, the absence of any such provision will greatly help in resisting an assessment on the value of a partner's

---

[1] See for example *A G v Ralli* (1936) 15 ATC 523 where ED assessment on partnership reserve funds was avoided.

goodwill because if any partner can set up in competition virtually next door without restriction, little if any value can be apportioned to goodwill. By way of exception, if a *Boden* scheme is to be relied on, a restrictive covenant can be imposed on the junior partners leaving the senior partner free, thereby strengthening the taxpayer's argument by 'feeding' the consideration moving from the junior partners. At a later stage the junior partners should consider excluding the covenant.

6.2:5 Reallocation of shares in the partnership: carving out an interest to avoid reservation

The ownership of a partnership as in the case of a company is normally based on shares in that partnership.

The holding by a partner of an interest in the partnership usually determines and represents his interest in the capital, profits (and losses), and the right to surplus assets in a winding-up. Thus a re-allocation of shares from a more senior partner to a more junior or newly introduced partner may effect useful IHT planning. A more subtle re-arrangement can be undertaken if the three elements of capital, profits and surplus assets are separately treated. Thus the disposing partner may wish to retain a high ratio of the profits but be perfectly ready to dispose of his interest in the capital and surplus assets. In that case the partnership is reorganised so that profits are divided between the partners in ratios unconnected with the capital shares. Income tax considerations may conflict with this IHT planning.

It would be claimed that this re-allocation of the partnership interests is on a reciprocal, arm's length basis without any gratuitous intention as referred to in s 10.

Problems for IHT could arise in the case of this sort of partial gift, eg where the donor gives the whole of his share of partnership capital to the donee, but retains say half of the profit, because the retention of the profit interest could constitute a reservation of benefit. The same difficulty arises with other types of partnership freezing operations where the donor transfers capital assets, which are intended to appreciate in the hands of the donee, but retains a high profit share; or where the donor makes a gift of the farm (land and buildings) but continues to occupy the farmhouse. (He might in this latter case be able to 'carve out' and keep the farmhouse, and make a separate outright gift of the land. But beware here the possibility of losing agricultural property relief on the farmhouse—the CTO take the view that to qualify for relief both farm-house and farmland they must be in common ownership). In this general context, it might be of assistance if the partnership agreement were drafted so as to segregate the shares of capital from the shares of profit. It might then be possible to contend that the donor had carved out and retained his interest in the high profit share; and that the gift was of the capital share only.

Similar gift with reservation situations may exist in two further situations. First, where a partner makes a gift of working capital and, or accrued profits to another partner, eg a child or relative and that recipient partner allows that capital and, or accrued profits to remain in the partnership free of interest. The donor partner can certainly be said to derive and have reserved a benefit. The solution would be for the recipient partner to charge a commercial rate of interest on the capital so re-introduced by him. Secondly, it may be dangerous for new partners to indemnify existing partners (who transfer shares to the new partners) as to liabilities outstanding when the new partners join, because existing partners could thereby be said to reserve a benefit. It may be possible to counter this argument on the basis that the indemnity is part of the overall commercial deal.

Problems with reservation of interest can also arise in partnership cases where a donor at a later stage after the gift re-acquires an interest in the subject matter because reservation then commences. Two contrasting cases illustrate the trap. In *Munro v Stamp Duties Comr* [1934] AC 61, PC, the father's interest in the partnership was already in existence when he made a gift of land. It was therefore a successful case of carving out and there was no reservation of benefit. On the other hand, in *Chick v Stamp Duties Comr* [1958] 2 All ER 623, PC, the father made an absolute gift of land to his son. Later the father, the son and another formed a farming partnership, and the son brought the land into the partnership. This constituted a reservation of benefit. (It would now be possible to overcome this reservation by entering into a commercial lease: FA 1986, Sch 20, para 6(1)(a). See also the discussion at **6.1.3** above concerning gifts of land in the light of the new s 102A FA 1986.)

6.2:6   Reverting to employee status

A somewhat sophisticated and revolutionary proposal is that when a partner reaches, say, his mid-fifties, he should revert to an employee status. This could have dual advantages. First, for IHT there would be no 'capital' asset on his death. Secondly, while so employed, the individual could benefit from appropriate pension arrangements such as a personal pension scheme (see **5.3:3**). This is of course subject to application of business/agricultural property relief—see **Chapter 9**.

6.2:7   Hiving-off operations and parallel trading

See **5.1:3**.

6.2:8   Splitting operations

See **5.1:5**.

6.2:9   Incorporating a partnership

Subject to careful consideration of the many other Revenue aspects of turning a partnership into a limited company (and also the relative impact of national insurance charges), such a step may be appropriate for IHT planning, for example:

(1) shares in the company can thereafter be transferred in appropriate parcels, taking advantage of available exemptions;

(2) incorporating a partnership and selling minority shareholdings or undertaking 'watering-down' operations along the lines discussed in **5.1:6**;

(3) approved pension schemes can be implemented along the lines indicated in **5.3:3**.

For some professional partnerships, for example, architects or stockbrokers (if they still maintain their independence), a limited or unlimited company could be used. As regards CGT the taper relief implications must be born in mind. A disposal will bring to an end the individual's period of ownership. His interest in the company will need to be held for a further four years before he will have the opportunity to benefit from full business taper on the heldover gain. The company itself cannot obtain relief. Instead it is still entitled to an indexation allowance.

To obtain holdover relief, the conditions set out in TCGA 1992, s 162 will have to be strictly complied with. In particular, *all* the assets of the partnership (with the sole exception of cash) must be transferred to the new company and to the extent that the consideration is in shares in the new company, there will be a deferral of the CGT liability. Note also that the company acquires the business together with its assets at *market value*. This creates considerable scope for planning as subsequent disposals can be made by the company with little (if any) liability to tax being triggered. An alternative route would be to gift assets into the company utilising the holdover relief for business assets under TCGA 1992, s 165; in this case it would not be necessary for *all* the assets (other than cash) to be transferred although the company would in this case inherit the gain. An appropriate half-way house might be to set up a service company for the partnership and make appropriate disposals of shares in that company. Such service company would normally deal with the administrative and property holding functions of the partnership making an appropriate arm's length profit, say, between 5 and 10% on the expenditure incurred by it. It should, however, be borne in mind that, whereas premises owned by the partnership would obtain 100% business relief, a holding of shares in the service company could, arguably, not qualify for relief on the basis that that company falls within the exception for investment companies contained in s 105(3). Regard must also be given to TA 1988, s 770 as to artificial prices between 'associated persons'; and note *Stephenson v Payne, Stone, Fraser & Co* (1967) 44 TC 507 (excessive profits made by the service company may not be a deductible expense for the partners yet be taxable on the company). One of the main disadvantages of incorporating a partnership is that a company suffers double CGT, once on the company and again on the reflected value in the shares; another is the income taxation of distributions in seeking to get cash out of the company; although with lower personal income tax rates this is not as difficult a problem as it used to be. Loans to participators of a company are also subject to charges to tax (TA 1988, s 419).

6.2:10 Limited partnerships

Such partnerships are formed under the Limited Partnership Act 1907 and have over the years had restricted application, although they have been used to an extent in film production ventures and oil and gas exploration. Moreover TA 1988, s 117, which nullifies *Reed v Young* [1985] STC 25, CA, disallows deduction as income tax losses of non-recourse borrowing in limited partnerships generally. Nevertheless, such partnerships still have a useful role, and in utilising them (which would avoid the rigours of close company legislation) there must be at least one general partner who is subject to full unlimited liability, although such general partner might be a limited liability company. As regards the limited partners, their contribution to the partnership represents their ceiling liability and they can assign their shares but may not take part in the management of the business. (It is claimed that the limited partners can nevertheless be 'active' for the purpose of TA 1988, s 833(4)–(6), so that the income is earned income.) Given this vehicle, the IHT planning aspects described in **6.2** can be adapted, and it might also be a useful method of introducing trustees of appropriate harmless trusts, such as the accumulation and maintenance trust, as the limited partners (see **4.4:1**). Such trustees should be given wide, flexible powers, but without breaching the IHT conditions. It may be appropriate for the trustees themselves to be limited companies.

6.2:11 Limited Liability Partnerships Act 2000

This Act introduced a new corporate entity. A limited liability partnership is treated as a company for most company law purposes and its members' liability is limited. For tax purposes, however, it is largely treated as a partnership. Its separate existence as a corporate entity is ignored and the income and capital are treated as owned by the individual partners. Assets held outside, but used in, the partnership are treated for inheritance tax purposes—including APR and BPR—just as the assets of a traditional partnership. The incorporation of a limited liability partnership will not interrupt ownership for the purposes of these reliefs. See *Tax Bulletin* 50 (December 2000). Limited liability partnerships became available from 6 April 2001.

6.2.12 Setting up a family partnership

Where a new enterprise is being started up by parents with their children, it may be expected that the parents will contribute the bulk of the capital. By careful drafting of the partnership agreement it would be possible to arrange, on the one hand, that profits and losses are divided out as may be agreed, and on the other, that capital profits, on sale or on revaluation of the partnership assets, be shared between the children only. The aim would be to freeze the value of the parents' interest and permit the capital growth to pass to the children.

6.3 PROTECTION OF AN OUTGOING PARTNER

In the more traditional and bygone partnership era, a retiring partner usually looked to the continuing or new partners for a substantial payment of capital payable either by a lump sum or by instalments and used such sums in his retirement and for his widow's benefit.

This method is now relatively unusual, not only for the practical reason that so few persons can provide the necessary capital, but also because, as indicated in **6.2** such payments are expensive for tax reasons, particularly IHT and CGT.[1]

Therefore the trend is to replace capital or goodwill payments by payments for consultancy, pensions and/or annuities, and insurance arrangements.

6.3:1 Consultancy and pension payments to the outgoing partner

On retirement of a partner it is fairly common practice to retain him as a consultant and show this position on letterheading, etc, 'below the line'. A

---

[1] There may still be limited retirement relief available against capital gains tax in the short term (ie until 2003–04 on a reducing basis) (TCGA 1992, s 163 and Sch 6 as amended).

consultancy agreement should be entered into whereby the consultant is paid fees on an agreed basis (for example, £xx per month).[1] Payments to consultants are sometimes expressed as an 'agreed share of profits' because the continuing partners do not wish to commit themselves to a fixed sum irrespective of the partnership's profitability in any year. This method has the advantage of a built-in protection against inflation, but the danger is that such 'consultant' might be deemed for certain purposes still to be a partner, having regard to the definition of a partner in the Partnership Act 1890, ss 1 and 2. Protection against inflation can be more appropriately covered by inserting a clause pegging the consultancy fee and, if wished, any pensions, to the general index of retail prices. These payments should never be *charged* on profits but merely be enforceable by way of personal covenant, because a charge might give rise to an assessment to IHT as an interest in possession settled property under s 51(1).

If a consultancy agreement is not for life, on its termination the consultancy payment can be substituted by a pension which would normally be somewhat less than the previous consultancy payments. Pension provisions can also be included for the consultant's widow or widower.

These arrangements should be unobjectionable for IHT purposes on the consultant's death, on the basis that they are reciprocal, arm's length arrangements not extending any gratuitous benefit.

If payments and other fees of the consultant exceed the VAT registration threshold (currently £54,000 per annum), he will have to register for VAT and charge VAT to the firm when billing for his services. It may be possible to avoid these VAT complications by making the consultant a salaried employee taxed under Schedule E (however, there would then be other difficulties such as a stricter test for allowable expenses, national insurance, wrongful dismissal legislation, etc, which should be balanced against the disadvantages of VAT registration).

The complications of VAT and (to a lesser extent) the treatment of partnership pensions as earned income within certain limits (see TA 1988, s 628) means that consultancy arrangements are somewhat less popular than previously. Whether an ex-partner should be kept on as a consultant or be paid a pension now depends largely on the commercial circumstances of each case.

6.3:2 Annuities/pensions to widows, widowers and dependants of the outgoing partner

As mentioned above these annuities are a practical alternative to capital or goodwill payments. Moreover in most cases the payment of the annuities should not give rise to any IHT results. A letter from the Revenue was

---

[1] To enable such payments to be allowed as 'earned income' for income tax purposes the amounts paid should not be excessive (see TA 1988, s 74) and references to transfers of shares in the partnership should be kept completely separate and outside the consultancy agreement: see *Hale v Shea* [1965] ALL ER 155, 42 TC 260. Notwithstanding the abolition of the investment income surcharge, earned income can remain an advantage over unearned eg as income supporting pension provision (see **6.3:3**) although in the context of independent taxation earned income (unlike the assets producing unearned investment income) cannot be transferred between husband and wife.

published in the *Law Society Gazette*, 2 July 1975, p 699 (but not considered important enough to qualify as a Statement of Practice) as follows:

'In the normal case where the partnership agreement can itself be regarded as a commercial transaction the agreement to pay the annuity would itself be covered by the provisions of [s 10] as would the actual payments as and when they became due. The commencement of the annuity on the death of a partner would not itself be an occasion for charge although his share of the partnership would normally be a part of his estate.'

Notwithstanding the above, it is still advisable to secure the payment of such annuities by *personal* covenant not charged on the partnership assets. The consideration for the annuity could then be the cross-covenant by the other partners and not the passing of goodwill, thereby it seems avoiding any IHT problem. Continuing annuities should wherever possible be *separate* and distinct and not continuous or for joint lives, as this may further assist in resisting any IHT possibility (in the case of husband and wife this would not normally be relevant having regard to the inter-spouse exemption).

This type of arrangement will be particularly suitable in the case of the older members of the partnership who have not paid sufficient premiums under a retirement annuity or personal pension scheme (as considered in **6.3:4**) to provide a reasonable income in retirement. It may therefore be necessary to continue to provide an income out of the partnership by means of pensions or annuities from the firm. Such pensions, in order to qualify for tax relief, are paid as charges on the paying partners' earned income less income tax at the basic rate. Under TA 1988, s 628, a pension paid to a retired partner or his dependants under the partnership agreement or any supplement thereto, is treated as earned income within limits. The main limit is 50% of the average of the partner's profits for the best three (so far as he is concerned) out of the last seven years prior to the partner's death or retirement during which he was required to devote substantially the whole of his time to acting as a partner.

There were provisions for linking the threshold for the investment income surcharge to the retail prices index. To the extent that the payments are treated as investment income of the recipient, the payments are deductible from the investment income of the payer. (Again, this will be relevant only if investment income surcharge should be re-introduced.)

If it is decided to pay partners' pensions from the firm it is sensible to agree them in advance, and record the fact in a supplementary agreement or in the partnership minutes, to take advantage of this provision and the income tax requirements of TA 1988, s 660A(9).

One considerable disadvantage of paying partners' pensions out of the future profits is that the retiring partner is dependent on the continued success of the firm after he has left it and can no longer influence its fortunes. It may also be difficult to introduce new partners where the liability to pay former partners is considerable. It may be necessary to provide that in no circumstances will the total of all pensions exceed say 20% of the profits in any one year. This of course increases the risk which an outgoing partner bears.

It is generally much better therefore to provide pensions so far as possible by means of retirement annuity and personal pension schemes rather than out of future profits. Against this, however, must be balanced the as yet unknown effect of the abolition of the tax credit for institutional investors by F(No 2)A 1997. An exception could also be made where any annuity from the firm is paid to a partner who has previously paid for or built up and then written off his goodwill. The goodwill written off and the annuity could be linked under TCGA 1992, s 37(3), which could charge the capitalised value of the annuity payments to CGT as well as income tax. This would only apply, however, if the annuity is more than can be regarded as reasonable recognition of past services to the partnership. An annuity of two-thirds of the average of the best three out of the last seven years is regarded by the Revenue as reasonable for a full-time partner with ten years' service (SP/D12, originally dated 17 January 1975, para 8; and note that SP 1/79 extends the practice to a lump sum paid in addition to the annuity).

Accordingly, wherever possible, pensions from the continuing partners should be restricted to such 'goodwill' situations, and to the older partners who have been unable to fund adequate retirement annuity arrangements. For the younger partners, their pension arrangements should be via existing retirement annuity policies or personal pension schemes and appropriate mandatory obligations can be written into the partnership agreement (see **6.3:4**).

6.3:3 Stakeholder Pensions

From 8 October 2001, most employers with five or more employees will be obliged to provide access to a stakeholder pension scheme for all of its employees.

Stakeholder pensions provide greater flexibility than personal pensions because contributions can be increased and decreased without penalty and because the link between earnings and contributions has largely been removed. However, some members of occupational pension schemes—in particular controlling directors and those earning more than £30,000 per annum who participate in a defined benefits scheme—are not entitled to a stakeholder in addition.

6.3:4 Retirement annuity policies ('RAPs') under TA 1988, Pt XIV Ch III and Personal Pension ('PP') schemes under TA 1988, Pt XIV Ch IV

Until 30 June 1988 partners were normally eligible to take out RAPs under the provisions now included above, being self-employed and in non-pensionable employment. However, from 1 July 1988 RAPs were superseded by the new wider-ranging personal pension legislation. Partners and others who took out RAPs before that date can still keep them up (assuming the terms of the policy allow it); and, subject to the contribution limits, can take out by way of 'top-up' new PP plans to run alongside them. New partners are limited to taking out PP arrangements.

Although the two regimes, RAPs and PP arrangements, have a common aim in building up pension benefits, there are significant differences as well as similarities in the way they operate. The following salient points should be noted:

(1) The maximum contributions in each case are based on a percentage of net relevant earnings. The RAP scale is less generous than the PP scale. However, the PP contributions unlike the RAP ones are subject to an earnings ceiling (which is index-linked). For 2001–02 for example, this ceiling is £95,400. A partner with an existing RAP whose earnings are above that ceiling may well be able to contribute higher actual amounts to the RAP than into a PP plan.

Maximum contributions: the age is at the beginning of the tax year

1987–88 onwards		*1989–90 onwards*		*2001–02*
RAP		PP		
Basic	$17\frac{1}{2}$%	Basic	$17\frac{1}{2}$%	Up to £3,600 for
Age 51–55	20%	Age 36–45	20%	qualifying
56–60	$22\frac{1}{2}$%	46–50	25%	individuals
61 or	$27\frac{1}{2}$%	51–55	30%	
more		56–60	35%	
		61 or	40%	
		more		

Where individuals have concurrent RAP and PP arrangements the maximum contributions are reduced accordingly (TA 1988, s 655). The effect is that the RAP contributions must be within the RAP limits above. If the individual wished to make PP contributions as well, the total contributions under the two contracts would have to fall within the PP limits (subject to the prevailing earnings cap).

(2) The allowable premium paid is in each case treated as a deduction from the payer's income and therefore benefits from tax relief at the payer's top tax rate.

(3) The premiums are in each case invested in a gross (ie, tax-free) pension fund. In the case of RAPs this will be a fund administered by an insurance company or friendly society. There are, however, a number of insurance companies which have been prepared to market group arrangements for partners of a particular firm.

On the other hand, PP arrangements are available not only to partners and other self-employed people but also to employees on specifically individual schemes. Persons wishing to effect PP plans are not limited to the traditional insurance providers, but can choose schemes run by banks, building societies and unit trusts.

(4) The date of retirement in the case of an RAP can be selected at any time within the age band 60–75. Under a PP scheme the retirement age band is 50–75. There is no need for actual retirement in either case. Although the PP age band looks generous, the build-up of the fund and the benefits it can provide are likely to be much less at 50.

(5) On taking his retirement the PP plan-holder can generally take 25% of the fund as lump sum tax-free cash. The RAP rule fixes the maximum lump sum on retirement as three times the annuity available from the rest of the fund after the cash has been taken and, depending on age and sex, this is likely to produce a somewhat more favourable result than the PP 25% rule, except that RAPs taken out on or after 17 March 1987 are subject to the upper limit tax-free cash limit of £150,000. The rationale appears to be that the contrasting PP lump sum where the upper limit has been abolished will be kept to a reasonable amount by the effect of the ceiling on earnings eligible for contributions.

(6) In both RAP and PP arrangements any lump sum benefit payable on death before retirement to beneficiaries at discretion will normally be free of IHT (and see **5.3:4** as to planning). In contrast, where the contributor's personal representatives have a legally enforceable right to the sum, or the contributor had the power immediately before the death to nominate the

sum to anyone he pleased, IHT will be chargeable (see SP/E3 originally published September 1975; and also ss 151(2)–(4) and 5(2)).

(7) Both arrangements allow the additional provision for a pension on the death of the contributor before his retirement payable to his spouse or other dependant.

(8) In both cases it is possible to take a reduced pension at retirement which will continue to provide a pension for the widow or widower.

Finally, as contributions are allowed in full for income tax and are invested in a tax-free fund, both the RAP and the PP arrangements are very sensible investments for an individual unable to participate in an occupational pension scheme.

Clearly the earlier in a partner's career such a pension is taken out, the longer the period of funding and better the terms available from pension companies. It is quite common nowadays for partnership agreements to require partners to contribute the maximum or a proportion of allowable premiums into such an existing retirement annuity or personal pension scheme and this can be coupled with provisions for a compulsory retirement age. In times when capital or goodwill payments are impracticable, such early retirement planning is to be encouraged.

Following consultation last year the Inland Revenue have recently announced measures to improve flexibility in pension provision. Detail of the changes are contained in PSO Update 54 ([1999] STI 1283). Broadly, the changes are as follows:

(1) A facility for approved money purchase schemes and buy out contracts to defer the purchase of an annuity and in the meantime pay pensions by income drawdown. This has for some time been possible in the case of small self administered schemes, however the rules applying in that situation are being made more flexible in that the amount of pension taken will be able to be less that the full amount. The method of income drawdown will follow broadly the existing method used for personal pensions.

(2) A relaxation in the current position in relation to additional voluntary contributions.

(3) Partial retirement, allowing main scheme retirement benefits to be paid at any age between 50–75 without the necessity for full retirement by an employee. This last proposal is likely to be delayed for some time as the PSO feels that further consultation is necessary in the light of perceived problems with the interaction with Social Security law.

6.3:5 Cash options under approved annuity scheme (s 152)

Where under either a retirement annuity contract or a personal pension scheme, an annuity becomes payable on a person's death to a spouse or dependant of that person, and a capital sum might at the deceased's option have become payable instead to his personal representatives, the deceased is not to be treated as having been beneficially entitled to that sum, with the result that it escapes liability to IHT.

6.3:6 Life assurance

One of the main problems of a professional partnership is the provision of sufficient cash to repay the capital accounts of an outgoing partner on his death or retirement. Even though there are difficult problems, especially with uneven, larger and changing partnerships, partnership life assurance can often help in these circumstances. It is important to bear in mind the basic practical aims of such assurance, which are:

(a) to provide cash in the right hands at the right time;

(b) to ensure the equitable division of cost among the partners;

(c) to avoid liability to IHT. The greatest problems come with trust policies (see below) where the Revenue regard the IHT discretionary trust regime as operating; in other cases the arm's length and reciprocity principles may be relevant in the context of s 10; or one of the other exemptions such as normal expenditure (s 21); great care should be taken in advance of the implementation of any arrangements;

(d) to avoid liability to CGT (normally the exemption under TCGA 1992, s 210 will apply);

(e) to ensure that any arrangements are flexible and will allow for resignation of partners or the addition of new partners.

There are various means of trying to achieve these ideals.

(1) Trust policies

Each partner insures his own life for the benefit of his other partners absolutely. A separate policy is usually effected in favour of each partner and these policies are payable at the life assured's retirement date or in the event of his death enabling the continuing partners to repay his capital. Trust policies for a large partnership usually involve a multiplicity of policies which can be somewhat inconvenient. Moreover, the IHT dangers of breaching the reciprocity provisions of s 10 must always be watched.

(2) Life of another policy

Each partner effects a policy on the life of his other partners to provide the wherewithal for his share of the outgoing partner's capital account. The market value of policies on the lives of the surviving partners would be part of the deceased partner's estate for IHT. If there is a wide disparity of ages it may be difficult for a young partner to pay the premiums required on the lives of the senior partners, but term assurance could play a part.

(3) General

Whether the actual policies are endowment, whole life or term depends on whether the actual retirement dates are known with precision, and whether the retirement cover can be afforded. Term assurance may be of great help but would only cover death before the usual retirement date. A mixture of policies may be required.

In conclusion, therefore, it is noted that financing retirement by life assurance can have various advantages. Reciprocal arrangements can be made as described above, which should constitute commercial arrangements between the partners provided the consideration moves directly between them and there are no trust policies within the IHT charge for discretionary trusts or gifts with reservation. An extra twist would be to consider a 'dread disease' provision in any such policies, to cover not only the death but also the serious illness (and hence the enforced early retirement) of a partner. Moreover the payments received under life assurance policies are normally exempt from CGT under TCGA 1992, s 210.

Upon the maturity of a life policy, the beneficial owner of the cash proceeds may then invest in an annuity and depending on his age at that time, a large proportion of this annuity, constituting in effect a return of capital, will be tax free, under the provisions of TA 1988, s 656, and only the interest proportion will be taxable. Retirement annuities and personal pensions on the other hand are fully taxable upon the recipient as earned income except to the extent that the limited lump sum commutation rights are exercised.

6.4 PARTNERSHIP OF 'RELATIVES'

IHT planning in partnerships is made more difficult where partners are 'connected persons' within the definition of s 270 by reason of being related. Relatives for this purpose include spouses, father, mother, children and issue, brother, sister, uncle, aunt, nephew and niece and such relatives' spouses. By virtue of the interaction of ss 270 and 10, any disposition between 'relatives' is in effect presumed to be a gift and the onus of rebutting this presumption is on the taxpayer (see also **1.1:2**).

The onus will be satisfied if it can be shown that the 'relative' is being treated no more favourably than would be a 'stranger'. On any partnership rearrangement involving a 'relative', it is therefore good tax planning to introduce a 'stranger' on the same or similar terms, if this is otherwise possible; or be able to show that terms previously reached with 'non-connected' partners were on the same or a similar basis.

In the case of non-related partners, they are not 'connected persons' 'in relation to acquisitions or disposals of partnership assets pursuant to bona fide commercial arrangements'. Accordingly, in these circumstances it is normally possible to show that there was the appropriate element of bona fide commercial arrangement and reciprocity, thereby avoiding any IHT liability.

Similarly there should be no gratuitous benefit giving rise to an IHT assessment where an individual transfers an asset or pays a sum in consideration of an actuarially equivalent annuity. Moreover, if this annuity comes within the ambit of TA 1988, s 660A(9) (for example, defined payments under partnership agreements), the annuity should be fully deductible for all rates of income tax by the payer. Before implementing this suggestion, careful consideration should be given to the CGT implications in TCGA 1992, s 37(3) because the consideration for disposal of the asset could be measured by the capitalised value of the annuity subject to SP 1/79 dated 12 January 1979.

Chapter 7

Gifts: The Art of Giving, including Use of Exemptions

7.0 INTRODUCTION

This chapter considers how to make gifts in a IHT efficient way. It highlights some of the pitfalls of the legislation and deals specifically with the gifts with reservation of benefit provisions. The following topics are covered:

- planning the correct type of gift with particular reference to the nil rate band; and potentially exempt transfers ('PETs');

- gifts with reservation with particular reference to the family home, *Ingram* and FA 1999;

- other planning aspects of gifts;

- the donee paying IHT rather than the donor;

- gifts versus sales;

- gifts versus loans;

- gifts in value not exceeding £3,000 per annum (s 19);

- £250 per annum gifts to any number of separate donees (s 20);

- normal expenditure out of income (s 21);

- gifts in consideration of marriage (s 22);

- dispositions for maintenance of family (s 11);

- gifts of excluded property (s 5(1));

- the former mutual transfer relief;

- dispositions allowable for income tax and corporation tax (s 12);

- charities and political parties (ss 23 and 24);

- gifts for national purposes (s 25 and Sch 3);

- gifts for public benefit (now repealed) (s 26);

- voidable transfers (s 150), etc;

- deathbed situations;

- gifts by cheque.

7.1 PLANNING THE CORRECT TYPE OF GIFT

7.1:1 A reminder of the gift rules

Under the present regime there are effectively 3 main rates of inheritance tax: The 40% rate which is chargeable on death, the 20% rate chargeable in respect of lifetime transfers of value (where the transferor does not die within 7 years of the transfer), and 0% chargeable in respect of chargeable transfers up to a value of the applicable nil rate band.

The general rule is that the tax is immediately chargeable. Thus a gift of £100,000 to a discretionary trust or to a public company by an individual who has exhausted his nil rate band is immediately chargeable at the 20% rate. The deemed transfer of value made by participators in a close company when the close company makes a transfer of value is also immediately chargeable to tax: see s 94.

Not all transfers of value are immediately chargeable however. As explained in Chapter 1 certain transfers of value are only chargeable if the transferor dies within 7 years after the date of the transfer of value. These transfers are referred to as 'potentially exempt transfers' (PETs). A PET is a 'transfer of value' (see below) made by an individual after 18 March 1986 to:

(1) another individual;

(2) a settlement in which another individual has an interest in possession;

(3) to another individual (either absolutely, or to a settlement in which the individual has an interest in possession) where the individual making the transfer makes the transfer of value because his interest in possession has terminated (see s 52);

(4) an accumulation and maintenance trust within s 71; or

(5) a disabled trust within s 89.

The cessation of a gift with reservation is also a potentially exempt transfer: For further discussion on the concept see **Chapter 1**.

The 'transfer of value' must itself satisfy certain conditions. In the case of (1) and (2), the value transferred by the transfer of value must be attributable to property which becomes comprised in the estate of the individual mentioned in (1) or (2), or, if this is not the case, the estate of the individual mentioned in (1) or (2) must be increased in value by virtue of the transfer and the charge is potentially exempt to the extent of the increase in value of the individual's estate.

In the case of (4) and (5) the value transferred must be attributable to property which, by virtue of the transfer, becomes settled property to which s 71 or s 89 applies. Again the transfer of value is potentially exempt only to the extent that this condition is satisfied.

These conditions are illustrated by the following examples.

(a) An individual settlor of an accumulation and maintenance trust within s 71 meets the debts and liabilities of the trustees, eg the settled property includes a policy of insurance and the settlor pays the premium.

(b) An individual settlor releases the trustees of an accumulation and maintenance trust from a debt.

(c) An individual transfers assets to a company whose shares comprise the settled property.

(d) An individual pays the school fees of his grandchildren, or purchases a holiday for his father.

In the case of (a) to (c) there is no PET because the value transferred by the settlor is not attributable to property which becomes comprised in the settlement by virtue of the transfer. In the case of (d) there is no PET because no other individual's estate is increased by the transfer of value.

The solution is to arrange the gift so that a PET is made, if that is the intention. For example, in the case of (a) or (b) the settlor could settle cash and leave the trustees to satisfy the trust debts, and if he wanted to transfer assets to the company he could route them through the trustees. In the case of (d) the individual could gift the cash to the parents (a PET) leaving the parents to arrange the school fees. In the case of holidays, the individual could give the cash to his father so that he can purchase the holiday himself.

Using the gift rules

Lifetime PETs enable the individual to effect a substantial saving of IHT on his death. No charge arises immediately, and none arises if he survives 7 years. After 7 years, the amount of the gift also drops out of the transferor's current reckoning and cumulative total for future gifts. Even if he dies within 7 years of the date of the gift a saving may be made if the date of death is at least 3 years after the date of the gift. If the transferor does die within the 7-year period the value of (what is now) a chargeable transfer is the value at the date of the gift. Therefore, it is advisable to give away appreciating assets. In the case of depreciating assets there is a fall-back in s 131(2). This rule allows the transferee, should the value have gone down by the date of the transferor's death, or should he have sold the asset at arm's length at a loss in the transferor's lifetime, to substitute the reduced value as the taxable amount. In relation to this see **7.1:5**. Remember the possibility of insurance if there is a risk of the transferor dying within the 7-year period.

However, making a PET is not always good tax planning.

First, a PET may avoid an immediate IHT charge arising at the date of the gift, but it will not reduce the value of the transferor's estate on death if a benefit is retained in the property given away so that the gift with reservation of benefit provisions apply: see FA 1986.

Secondly, chargeable assets included in the IHT estate receive a free capital gains tax uplift on death. This is lost if the asset is given away to a trust (other than a trust in which he has a life interest), or to some other person or persons. This may mean that gifts should be made to the person about to die, not by him. One circumstance where this might be appropriate is where an individual is near death and his spouse owns chargeable assets which have appreciated in value. If the estate of the deceased, including these assets would be within the nil rate band, the spouse could gift them to the spouse who is near death. The assets will then pass under his will to his surviving spouse free of IHT but with a free uplift in market value for CGT. If this is done the moment before death, it might be said that the assets did not truly form part of his estate within the meaning of IHTA 1984: see *Westmoreland* and *Ramsay*. However, it is thought that there are no associated operations.

Thirdly, a gift to a connected person (or indeed a disposal at undervalue otherwise than at arm's length) is a chargeable event for capital gains tax. Suppose that 5 years ago, an individual purchased a holiday home for £100,000. It is now worth £300,000, and he gifts it to his adult child. No IHT arises because he has made a PET. But he will be immediately liable for capital gains tax at up to 40% on a deemed chargeable gain of £200,000 (subject to any reliefs). Furthermore, if he reserves a benefit in the house by using it otherwise than for full consideration, the gift with reservation rules may apply so that his estate is charged to IHT on the value of the house notwithstanding the gift (see **7.2:1**).

Possible solutions

One can approach this problem in one of two ways. The first is to make a PET (to avoid the IHT) and then rely upon CGT reliefs. For example, the transferor could have made a gift of an exempt asset for capital gains tax such as a principal private residence, chattels, a car, or cash. Or he could have given assets which qualified for 100% business asset holdover relief under TCGA 1992, s 165. A full discussion of exempt CGT assets is beyond the scope of this book.

The more interesting approach is to make an immediately-chargeable transfer for IHT purposes (apparently triggering an IHT charge) so that s 260 holdover relief is available. This approach is very flexible because chargeable CGT assets may be given. For example, if the transferor's gift fell within his available nil rate band, or if he was able to claim 100% agricultural or business property relief, he could make a gift to a discretionary trust. There would be no IHT charge at the date of the gift on the gift to the discretionary trust. Although the IHT charge is nil, he has not made a potentially exempt transfer and he may therefore claim s 260 holdover relief, and defer the CGT charge (possibly indefinitely).

Melville schemes

What if the value of the immediately-chargeable transfer of value exceeds the nil rate band and qualifies for no IHT reliefs? One answer is to make an immediately-chargeable transfer of value to a discretionary trust, so that s 260 holdover relief is available, but depress the value of the chargeable transfer so that the IHT is kept to a minimum. The High Court and Court of Appeal decision in *Melville* is an example of this. In *Melville* the transferor made a gift of property to a discretionary trust. Under the terms of the trust after 3 months he became entitled to a right to direct the trustees how to deal with the settled property, including the right to direct the appointment of the whole trust fund to himself. This was a valuable right (discounted by the fact that he might die within the 3-month period and so not acquire the right at all). Its existence meant that the transfer of value made by him was very low. Therefore, full holdover relief was obtained with a small IHT charge. The case is to be appealed. The critical issue is whether or not the right is 'property' for the purposes of IHTA 1984. The High Court found (without much difficulty) that it was, as did the Court of Appeal. However, while it is unknown whether the House of Lords will consider the case, the argument could be sidestepped by attaching the right to something that has long been accepted to be 'property' for IHT purposes, such as an interest under the trust. This scheme can be combined with the scheme for gifting the holiday home at **7.1:2**.

The order in which gifts are made is also a factor which will affect the efficacy of planning by making gifts. See further **7.1:4**.

Some of the main points mentioned above are further explained in the following three examples.

Example 1 (showing potentially exempt transfer and taper)

Estate of £592,000.

Assume gift (for example outright to individual) of £292,000 made in the seventh year before death and death occurring in 2001–02.

	£		£
Inheritance tax payable at death rate on first £292,000 (being the potentially exempt transfer)			
First	242,000	=	Nil
Next	50,000 at 40%	=	20,000
			£20,000

	£		£
But as donor died in the seventh year the tax after taper relief is £20,000 × 20%		=	4,000
Inheritance tax payable on remaining estate at death	£300,000 at 40%	=	120,000
Inheritance tax on potentially exempt transfer			4,000
Total inheritance tax			£124,000

Note:

		£
If gift in sixth year: inheritance tax on £20,000 × 40%	=	8,000
If gift made in fifth year: inheritance tax on £20,000 × 60%	=	12,000
If gift made in fourth year: inheritance tax on £20,000 × 80%	=	16,000
Otherwise, inheritance tax on first £292,000		20,000
Inheritance tax on next £300,000 (as above)	=	120,000
Inheritance tax on £592,000		£140,000

Example 2 (showing chargeable transfer and taper)

If the gift made in the **seventh year before death** had been into, say, a *discretionary* trust (no interest reserved):

		£
Inheritance tax payable on creation = £292,000 at one-half death rate (one-half of £20,000)	=	£10,000
But taper charge at death rate (as above)	=	£ 4,000

219

£

(No repayment of inheritance tax involved.
   Payment of £10,000 stands)

If death in the sixth year

Inheritance tax on creation	=	£10,000
Tapered death charge rate (as above)	=	£ 8,000

(No repayment of inheritance tax involved.
   Payment of £10,000 stands)

If death in the fifth year

Inheritance tax on creation		10,000
Tapered death charge rate (as above)	=	£12,000

Additional inheritance tax due (£12,000 less £10,000 already paid)		
Death charge with credit for inheritance tax paid	=	£2,000

If death in the fourth year

Inheritance tax on creation	=	10,000
Tapered death charge rate (as above)	=	16,000
Additional inheritance tax due	=	£6,000

If death in the third or subsequent year

Inheritance tax on creation	=	10,000
Untapered death charge rate	=	20,000
Additional inheritance tax due (half death charge)	=	£10,000

Chargeable transfers and PETs made within seven years of the PET in question which have become chargeable provide special problems.

The complexities of the legislation are illustrated by the remarks of Mr Powell, as reported in *Hansard*, 10 June 1986 at column 401:

'At present, because the seven-year period brings the potentially exempt transfer into the taxation net where the transferor dies within seven years and the potentially exempt transfer cumulates with the gifts made by the transferor in the previous seven years, the effect is that the transferor's chargeable disposals within 14 years of his death are affected by the inheritance tax as opposed to those within three years of his death, with cumulation ten years back, making 13 years in all, under the capital transfer tax system. So for those caught by the tax the new law is slightly worse than the old law.'

The 'knock-on' effect is illustrated in Example 3 as follows.

Example 3

1 October 1988	PET	£200,000
1 April 1992	Chargeable transfer	£100,000
3 June 1995	PET	£400,000
11 November 1997	Chargeable transfer	£300,000
1 September 2001	T dies leaving estate of	£500,000

In April 1992, no chargeable transfers had been made in the previous seven years. Therefore, the full nil rate band applicable at the time (£150,000) was available and no tax was payable on the chargeable transfer of £100,000.

On 11 November 1997, there were cumulative chargeable transfers in the past seven years of £100,000. The tax payable on the November 1997 transfer of £300,000 was:

£115,000 @ 0%	£0
(ie nil rate band of £215,000 less £100,000 of cumulations)	
£185,000 @ 20% (lifetime rates)	£37,000

Tax Paid: **£37,000**

Adjustments to be made on death:

(1) In relation to the potentially exempt transfer of £400,000 on 3 June 1995 (which has become chargeable following T's death within seven years)

Cumulations:		
1 April 1992		£100,000
Total		£100,000
Nil rate band available	£154,000	
Less cumulations	(£100,000)	
Nil rate band remaining available	£54,000	
Tax payable on £54,000 @ 0%		£0
Tax payable on £346,000 @ 40%		£138,400
20% taper on transfer more than 6 but less than 7 yrs before death		£27,680

Additional tax payable re PET on 3 June 1995   **£27,680**

(2) In relation to the chargeable transfer of £300,000 on 11 November 1997

Cumulations:		
1 April 1992		£100,000
3 June 1995		£400,000
Total		£500,000
Nil rate band available	£215,000	
Less cumulations	(£500,000)	
Nil rate band remaining available	*None*	

221

Tax payable on £300,000 @ 40%	£120,000
80% taper on transfer more than 3 but less than 4 yrs before death	£96,000
Less credit for tax paid on lifetime transfer	(£37,000)
	£59,000

Additional tax payable re chargeable transfer on 11 November 1997	**£59,000**

(3) Estate on death

Cumulations:

3 June 1995		£400,000
11 November 1997		£300,000
	Total	£700,000

Nil rate band available	£242,000	
Less cumulations	(£700,000)	
Nil rate band remaining available	*None*	
Tax payable on £500,000 @ 40%		£200,000

No taper relief

Example 3 illustrates four important benefits provided by the IHT legislation.

(a) the chargeable gift is valued at the time it is made, not the value at the date of death. This is useful for appreciating assets and represents a built-in 'freezing' operation. However, difficulties will arise in valuing a gift retrospectively and there is a risk that the Inland Revenue may try to apply 'hindsight' to the valuation. In addition the valuation for capital gains tax purposes can be on a different basis;

(b) the presumed lower indexed rates of inheritance tax operating on the death apply;

(c) for cash flow purposes there is no inheritance tax payable until the survivorship condition is breached. Whereas the advantages in (a) and (b) also apply to non-potentially exempt chargeable gifts, this third advantage is peculiar to potentially exempt transfers.

These IHT advantages must clearly be weighed against any CGT charges which may result from the proposed transactions.

(d) where the donor of a PET dies, the possibility of quick succession relief should be borne in mind by the executors who may have to wait up to seven years to see if the PET becomes chargeable by the death of the donor. Note the possibility of insurance.

7.1:2   Use of the nil rate band (s 7)

An estate owner should ensure that he takes advantage of the nil rate band and keep this under review because s 8 provides for indexation of all rate bands annually, unless Parliament otherwise determines. The increase in the retail prices index in December in each year is to apply to the rates of chargeable transfers made on or after 6 April in the following year. Although the PET regime, where no IHT is immediately payable and none will be provided the donor survives seven years, has considerably improved the outlook for making gifts, for many people the nil rate band may represent a practical limit on IHT planning. It has already been emphasised (**2.2**) that in a will where it is proposed to take advantage of the inter-spouse exemption, one should at least ensure that the nil rate band is used by making some gifts under the will to other beneficiaries. The nil rate band can be useful for making lifetime chargeable transfers (eg, a settlement on discretionary trusts) where, although no IHT is payable because of the nil rate band, holdover for CGT can be obtained. Always remember, however, that such holdover will stop CGT taper relief and the donees start a new period. Although, if the four-year qualifying period for business asset taper relief is reduced to two years as promised by the Chancellor, this may not matter.

A discretionary settlement within the nil rate band could be a useful vehicle for the owner of a second home with a significant capital gain not eligible for CGT private residence exemption and whose market value is less than, or equal to the owner's available nil rate band. The owner could transfer the property on discretionary trusts claiming holdover relief for CGT. The trustees of the settlement could permit a suitable beneficiary, eg the son, to occupy the property as a main residence. Then, on a sale of the property they could claim full CGT exemption under the terms of TCGA 1992, s 225 (and see *Sansom v Peay* [1976] STC 494). Alternatively, if the trustees advance the house to the son claiming holdover relief (which is available because of the exit charge) and the son sells he will obtain full CGT exemption under TCGA, s 222. Consider combining this scheme with a variant of a *Melville* scheme if the house is worth more than the available nil rate band. See **7.1:1**.

7.1:3   Use of seven-year cumulation rule (s 7(1))

Coupled with a positive attitude to the use of PETs, careful utilisation of the seven-year cumulative ladder can produce staggering results. Seven-year cumulation is really a misnomer. If the donor dies having made a PET just within seven years which is therefore now chargeable, that gift is aggregated for its own ladder with chargeable transfers within the seven years preceding its own date, making 14 years in all. Nevertheless, a wealthy husband and wife both aged 55 might use the nil rate band and make lifetime chargeable gifts (possibly also entitled to CGT holdover relief) of £242,000 each (together £484,000). They could repeat that exercise at age 62, and if they died after 69, they would each have a further nil rate band—a grand total of £1,452,000. If the 50% lower business or agricultural relief was available, that figure would double to £2,904,000. With 100% business or agricultural relief the amount would be unlimited. In addition, if they had started making PETs in their fifties the saving could be considerably increased. But even at a more modest level, there is a surprising standard of saving which can be achieved, particularly if consistent use is made of the annual and normal income exemptions.

This aspect is further illustrated in the table below.

The 8-year cycle at its
best (no previous gifts)

Year(s)	Individual transferor	Reliefs/exemptions		Total	Cumulative Total
		Nil rate band	Annual		
		£	£	£	£
1	Husband	242,000	6,000	248,000	248,000
2–7	Husband	—	18,000	18,000	266,000
8	Husband	242,000	3,000	245,000	511,000
1–8	Wife	484,000	27,000	511,000	1,022,000

Notes:

(1) If all property transferred qualifies for the lower 50% business/agricultural property relief the cumulative total could be £2,050,000. If 100% relief, then unlimited.

(2) The nil rate band for 2000–01 is £242,000 per individual.

(3) The table assumes that the individuals concerned start year 1 with a clear slate, ie with no cumulation of chargeable transfers and without having used up the annual £3,000 exemption in the year preceding year 1.

The above table can be summarised in a different way:

Nil rate £242,000×2	484,000
Annual exemption £3,000×8=	24,000
add assumed shortfall carried forward £3,000×1=	3,000
	511,000
plus like amount, for the other spouse	511,000
	1,022,000

Notes **1–3** above apply as before.

7.1:4 Order of gifts

As IHT is a cumulative tax, the nil rate band will be taken up by earlier gifts (whether lifetime chargeable gifts or PETs becoming chargeable). Accordingly, as a general rule, one should make early gifts to those whom one wishes to benefit the most, for example, one's children and issue, so they are either first on the cumulative ladder, or are first to drop out after seven years. Gifts with 100% business/agricultural relief do not show up at all on the ladder.

There is one anomalous feature relating to lifetime chargeable transfers where the donor dies within seven years and IHT has to be recalculated on the death rate, with the benefit of taper relief. Under s 7(5), tapering relief cannot be given if the result would be that IHT on death is less than the tax paid in the lifetime. This means that with the death rate at 40%, and half of that rate paid at the lifetime rate 20% the gift can never get the benefit of taper relief in the earliest two years of the seven-year period (ie the sixth and seventh years) where the reduction in rates is to a percentage of 40% for the sixth year (that is 40% of the death rate of 40% = 16%) or 20% for the seventh year (20% of 40% = 8%). Since both 16% and 8% are below the half rate of 20% paid on the gift in lifetime no reduction can be made. Where, however, lifetime chargeable transfers are limited to the nil rate band, and PETs are made thereafter rather than before, that anomalous result ought not to arise. If the lifetime gift has been within the nil rate band, no taper relief is available, as the applicable rate is zero!

If two or more gifts are made on the same day, s 266 prescribes their order. The transfers are treated as made in the order which produces the lowest value chargeable (s 266(1)). This rule was important for lifetime chargeable transfers made on the same day, some grossed up and some not, in former times when there were a number of increasing rates. Subject to that, the transfers are treated as one so they share proportionately the total tax (eg, if they use up all or part of the nil rate band and go up into the taxable band): s 266(2).

As a general rule, if a donor is contemplating an immediately chargeable gift into a discretionary trust plus PET gifts, the discretionary trust gift should be made on an earlier date so as to ensure that the nil rate band attaches to the gift into the discretionary trust and periodic ten-year charges and interim charges are kept down to the minimum.

Another appropriate order of giving, where the nil rate band is in point and PETs can drop out after seven years, could be as follows.

(a) Cash gifts, ie where the reliefs in (b) and (c) below will not apply.

(b) Gifts where the instalment basis is available under ss 227, 228 and 229 namely, land and buildings; certain shares and securities; businesses or interests therein and timber (see **1.5**).

(c) Followed by assets which will receive the 50% business or agricultural reliefs so that those reliefs will benefit from the full rate of IHT.

(d) In theory, gifts with 100% business or agricultural relief, provided the conditions for relief are maintained, can be left till last since they will not be subject to IHT if death intervenes.

7.1:5 Making gifts now which are likely to appreciate and vice versa

There is another reason why the correct timing of gifts is of crucial importance. This was first mentioned at **7.1:1**. The IHT planner will be primarily concerned that an asset should be transferred at a time when its potential value has not been reached or is in a temporary trough, since the values of both PETs and lifetime chargeable gifts are frozen at the date of gift. For example, a business might be suffering from a temporary dip in profitability; the market for the asset in question may be currently depressed, for example, property or shares; or the asset may have a built-in acceleration factor (see, for example, the deferred ordinary share bonus issue discussion in **5.1:4**, or the gift may be of a foal which may one day become a Derby winner). A subsequent increase in value after the gift has been made will not affect the IHT liability so that the question of whether the gift is covered by the annual £3,000 exemption (see **7.8**) is decided on the value at the date of the gift. Consider also the reverse position, ie that one should *retain* an asset with a current high value which is likely to depreciate, for example, a lease retained by the estate owner.

7.2   GIFTS WITH RESERVATION OF BENEFIT—THE RULES AND SOME POINTERS (FA 1986, s 102 AND Sch 20)

7.2:1   The general rule in FA 1986, s 102

Section 102 of the Finance Act 1986 is an anti-avoidance provision. It applies in relation to gifts of property (including land) made on or after 18 March 1986. It applies to an individual ('the donor') who gifts his land, shares, cash and other property to, say, his children or the family trust where:

(a)   possession and enjoyment of the property is not bona fide assumed by the donee (ie the recipient of the gift) at or before the beginning of the relevant period; or

(b)   at any time in the relevant period the property is not enjoyed to the entire exclusion, or virtually to the entire exclusion, of the donor and of any benefit to him by contract or otherwise.

The 'relevant period' is the period ending on the date of the individual's death and beginning seven years before that date, or if it is later, on the date of the gift. For example, where a donor makes a gift ten years before his death which satisfies (a) or (b) above, the relevant period is the seven years before his death. But where the gift was made four years before his death, the relevant period is that four years.

Its effect is that the property disposed of is a 'gift with reservation of benefit' (commonly referred to as a 'GROB' or 'GWR') and is treated for the purposes of IHTA 1984 as property to which the individual was beneficially entitled immediately before his death: FA 1986, s 102. The gift is therefore ineffective to reduce the value of his IHT estate.

The proper scope of s 102 is not easy to grasp on first reading. In **7.2.2** onwards, the meaning and relevance of the important terms are considered. An explanation is also given of how s 102 applies in special circumstances such as gifts into settlement, and gifts of property which is then sold or replaced by the donee. A pleasant surprise is that, although the provision appears to cover any possible benefit retained or enjoyed, there are limits on its application— see, for example, the decision of the House of Lords in *Lady Ingram* [1999] STC 37, and the statutory exceptions explained at **7.2.10**. Furthermore, although FA 1999 reversed *Ingram*, FA 1999 provided its own opportunities for tax planning.

7.2:2   'property'

The limits on the term 'property' were considered in *Lady Ingram v IRC* [1999] STC 37.

Lady Ingram v IRC

In 1987 Lady Ingram made a gift to her children of the freehold interest in Hurst Lodge subject to a leasehold interest which she retained. The leasehold interest was created by two steps, first, a conveyance of her house and land to a nominee, secondly, a grant of a lease for 20 years with a covenant only for quiet enjoyment by the nominee to Lady Ingram. The purpose was to enable Lady Ingram to continue to occupy Hurst Lodge by virtue of the lease without making a gift of the freehold with reservation of a benefit within section 102 Finance Act 1986.

The House of Lords held that Lady Ingram had made an effective gift of the freehold reversion in which no benefit had been reserved. In reaching their conclusion they provided invaluable confirmation as to the scope and meaning of the gift with reservation of benefit provisions.

They confirmed that the provisions apply only if a benefit is reserved in 'property' given away. For this purpose 'property' is not an object with a physical existence such as Hurst Lodge. It is a specific interest in that object. In Lady Ingram's case it was the freehold reversionary interest in Hurst Lodge. It followed that Lady Ingram did not reserve a benefit in the property she gave away, even though she continued to enjoy Hurst Lodge by virtue of the lease. She simply gave away one interest in Hurst Lodge in which she reserved no benefit and retained another interest in Hurst Lodge which entitled her to remain in residence.

The House of Lords thus adopted the approach and analysis of the estate duty cases on the original gift with reservation provisions (contained in the 1894 Finance Act). Lord Hoffmann relied in particular upon *Munro v Stamp Duties Comr* [1934] AC 61.

Their Lordships provided a further insight into what constitutes reserving a benefit. Both Lord Hoffmann and Lord Hutton emphasised that the provisions were concerned with the substance of the gift, not its mere conveyancing form. In the High Court Ferris J had held that whatever the conveyancing form, '*In terms of substance, Lady Ingram had held her beneficial interests from the very same moment that the trustees and beneficiaries had the property subject to those interests*'. The House of Lords agreed. So long as the equitable obligation to hold the freehold subject to the leasehold arose as soon as the freehold was vested in the trustees, the gift by Lady Ingram comprised for the purposes of section 102 only the freehold reversion.

The emphasis on the substance of the gift is noteworthy for two reasons. First, it means that Lady Ingram's scheme would have been effective even if a lease granted by a nominee to a principal was invalid (it was not). Secondly, it rejects dicta of the Court of Appeal in *Nichols v IRC* [1975] STC 278 to the effect that a conveyance of land subject to an obligation to grant a lease back is a gift subject to a reservation of benefit.

7.2:3   'virtually'... 'no benefit by contract or otherwise'

There is an argument that the phrase 'or otherwise' must be construed *ejusdem generis* with the phrase 'by contract...' so that it refers only to some enforceable legal right (see *A-G v Seccombe* [1911] 2 KB 688). However, the term 'otherwise' is just as likely to refer to any method which is not contractual, such as an informal arrangement. Indeed, it is widely considered that a benefit is reserved where a donor continues in occupation as a result of an act of kindness by the donee. It is likely that the odd casual visit by the donor will not prevent the donee enjoying the property to 'virtually' the entire exclusion of the donor. Generally, however, it would be prudent to err on the side of caution here. See also the Revenue's Interpretation at RI 155.

7.2:4   Substitutions and accretions: Sch 20, paras 2 and 3

Where property changes hands after the initial gift there are complicated rules (based on the estate duty provision, FA 1957, s 38) to determine whether the original subject matter of the gift can be traced and substituted by other assets and valued accordingly. These substitution rules are intended to prevent a simple anti-avoidance trick, eg A gives Blackacre to B; B exchanges it for Whiteacre which A occupies. The rules mean that A has reserved a benefit by occupying Whiteacre.

However, if the donor gifts cash to his child who buys a holiday home in which the donor is allowed to holiday, the gift of cash cannot be traced into the holiday home. Likewise if the subject matter of A's gift (Blackacre in above example) is sold for cash by donee. This is subject to *Ramsay* and the rules for 'associated operations' although these rules should not be capable of re-characterising the transaction—see *IRC v Brandenburg* [1982] STC 555 at 564b.

7.2:5   Special rules for settled property

Where a donor makes a gift by way of *settlement*, the type of asset is immaterial: it is the property *comprised* in the settlement that is material. The donor should be excluded from the class of beneficiaries and if there is a power under the settlement to add to the class of beneficiaries, the trustees should be expressly prevented from adding in the donor (see CTO correspondence, *Taxation* 9, January 1987, p 291). The suggestion in **7.3:4**. that the donor make a gift of cash to his child who may purchase a holiday home would therefore not work at all if the cash were given not to the child outright but to a settlement.

7.2:6

A gift can be caught under the GWR rules in circumstances where the donor reserves a benefit, eg the donee does not take up exclusive possession, only *after completion of the gift*, (see in particular the *Chick* decision (referred to in **6.2:5** above).

7.2:7   GWR wrinkles

The reservation does *not have to emanate from the gift itself* but can be by way of *collateral* arrangements made by or on behalf of donee, eg payment of a covenanted sum to the donor. It is considered, however, that some associated connection with the gift would be required—see *Stamp Duties Comr of New South Wales v Permanent Trustee Co* [1956] AC 512, PC; *A-G v Worrall* [1895] 1 QB 99, CA.

It is *immaterial* that the benefit reserved is small and *not commensurate* with the value of the asset itself or even that donor is unaware of the benefit (except as to the reference to 'virtually' in s 102(1)(b)). Thus, a gift by a donor of a 1,000 acre farm could be brought back into the estate by s 102 simply because the donor was permitted at a later stage to occupy one room of a small cottage on the edge. Here the donor should pay demonstrably full consideration for his benefit; see Sch 20 para 6.

It is also immaterial that the benefit reserved to the donor is not *detrimental* to *donee*.

It has been argued that a trust for a settlor's children that indirectly benefits him, eg paying school fees, constitutes a gift with reservation. This is probably incorrect on the basis that the benefit is too remote or indirect, and s 11 should in any event exclude any claim.

7.2:8   Full consideration

Where the donor gives full consideration in money or money's worth there would normally be no reservation. There is a specific rule to this effect for land and chattels in Sch 20, para 6(1)(a) (see **7.2:10**(2) below); and the rule ought to hold good for other types of assets in general circumstances. Steps should be taken by means of a regular review to ensure that full consideration continues to be paid. Revenue guidance on the meaning of 'full consideration' can be found in *Revenue Tax Bulletin*, November 1993, p 98.

7.2:9

The cessation of a reservation of benefit is itself treated as a potentially exempt transfer by the donor. Therefore, provided that a benefit *ceases* to be reserved outside the seven-year period, no IHT or additional IHT will be payable. It is likely that such cesser is easier to arrange in the case of a series of gifts rather than a large single gift: Sch 20, para 1.

7.2:10   Statutory exceptions to s 102

(1) Gifts which are exempt transfers

The reservation of benefit charge does not apply to certain *exempt transfers* as listed in s 102(5) although the exemption provisions have their own built-in requirements and restrictions. The £3,000 annual exemptions; and normal income gifts are *not* included in the list. The Revenue in their guidelines (see **7.2:3**) take the view that where there is a GWR, and the reservation ceases so that the gift at that point becomes a PET, there can be no £3,000 exemption when the reservation thus ends. The £3,000 exemption will be available against other gifts made in that year. The scheme at **7.3:4** uses the spouse exemption under s 18 to avoid a gift with reservation of benefit on a gift of a holiday home to a trust. The scheme could also be used in relation to insurance policies issued on the life of an individual. Such policies are exempt assets for CGT purposes in the hands of the original owner, and 5% of the value may be encashed each year tax-free. That 5% income will be available for the benefit of the donor if the need arises. Meanwhile the valuable asset is held on trust outside his estate.

(2) Full consideration in money or money's worth

Schedule 20, para 6 sets out circumstances where the GWR rules do not apply; but the conditions are onerous. For example, in the case of land and chattels the retention of a benefit by the donor is disregarded if the donor is in actual occupation or actual possession and pays full consideration in money or money's worth. The need for actual occupation or possession precludes subletting by the donor. In their guidelines (see **7.2:8**), the Revenue underline the point that full consideration is required throughout the period, and that regular reviews of rent should take place. However, they recognise that normal valuation tolerances must be recognised in deciding what is 'full' consideration for para 6(1)(a).

The donor's occupation of *land* is expressly disregarded under para 6(1)(b) if it results from:

(a) unforeseen changes in circumstances (merely getting old is not itself unforeseen); *and*
(b) the donor is unable to maintain himself through old age, infirmity, etc; *and*
(c) it represents a reasonable provision by donee for care and maintenance of donor; *and*
(d) the donee is a relative of the donor or his spouse.

These cumulative conditions are onerous. They contrast sharply with the Revenue's interpretation of how short the visits of a donor should be after the gift of a house in order to satisfy the 'virtually' *de minimis* test in s 102(1)(b). Some of these limits could well be challenged in specific cases.

If the donor wishes to rely on the exception in Sch 20 para 6, consider a 'commercial lease' (FA 1986, Sch 20, para 6)—pursuant to which the donor pays a full arm's length rent for the lease or tenancy retained. Such a rent would need to be reviewable upwards say every three or five years in the light of changing conditions and preferably inflation, and certified by a qualified surveyor. The creation of such a new source of taxable, non-deductible income can be very disadvantageous (although the taxable receipt problem may be solved using a grandchildren's accumulation and maintenance trust under s 71). Moreover, the estate owner's income will be reduced. The proposal may be more acceptable for an older estate owner (ie where there would be less emphasis on rent reviews). Note, however, that although the gift with reservation rules will not apply, the PET 7 year requirement will apply. Instead of a rent, consider a 'one-off' premium which satisfies the full consideration condition.

7.2:11 Avoidance of double charge: s 104

The structure of IHT means that in certain circumstances the same property can be charged twice and entered twice into the cumulation of chargeable transfers as a result of a transferor's death. The Board have made regulations (SI 1987/1130) which provide for relief in these circumstances.

Regulation 5 provides for the avoidance of a double charge where there is a transfer of value by way of gift of property which is or subsequently becomes a chargeable transfer, and the property is (by virtue of the provisions relating to gifts with reservation) subject to a further transfer which is chargeable as a result of the transferor's death. As under regulation 4, whichever transfer produces the higher amount of tax as a result of the death remains chargeable and the value of the other transfer is reduced by reference to the value of the transfer which produced that amount. However, this reduction in value does not apply for the purposes of any discretionary trust charges arising before the transferor's death if the transfer by way of gift was chargeable to tax when it was made. Further, provision is made for credit to be given on account of any tax already paid on the transfer by way of gift against so much of the tax payable on the other transfer as relates to the value of the property in question.

Example

A gives B a house, but reserves the right to continue to live in it, and does so until he dies five years later. There is a charge on the gift from A to B because it is within seven years of death, but because this is a gift with reservation the house is also charged as part of A's death estate.

7.2:12

There is no statutory clearance as to the application of the GWR rules. Some comfort may be gained from the Inland Revenue Statements of Practice, in particular see Revenue Interpretation 55 (also in the *Tax Bulletin* No 9 of November 1993 at p1409).

7.3 GIFTS OF AN INTEREST IN LAND

Consider this example in relation to s 102. The donor owns a freehold house. She grants a 20-year lease of the house to a nominee for herself. Then she gives the freehold subject to the lease to her child. The donor carries on living in the house by virtue of the lease.

The facts in the example are essentially those of *Ingram*. The House of Lords held that the donor's gift is not caught by s 102 because she remained in occupation by virtue of the property retained (the lease), and not by virtue of the property given away (the freehold subject to the lease).

Finance Act 1999 introduced s 102A into FA 1986 with the intention of blocking the *Ingram* scheme. It applies where an individual disposes of an interest in land by way of gift on or after 9 March 1999.

7.3:1 The rule in s 102A

Where X disposes of an interest in land by way of gift and s 102 does not apply, the interest in land is property subject to a reservation of benefit (so that the value of the gifted property remains in the donor's IHT estate) if:

(a) X or his spouse enjoys a right or interest, or is party to an arrangement, in relation to the land; and

(b) that right interest or arrangement entitles or enables the donor to occupy all or part of the land, or to enjoy some right in relation to all or part of the land, otherwise than for full consideration in money or money's worth.

The best example of s 102A is *Ingram*: Section 102 did not apply and she enjoyed an interest in relation to the land (the 20-year lease) which entitled her to occupy otherwise than for full consideration in money or money's worth.

7.3:2 Application of s 102A to the reversionary lease scheme

But consider the reversionary lease scheme. The donor grants a 999-year lease over his principal private residence to his children's trust (from which he and his wife are excluded). The lease is to commence in 10 years on the basis that the donor has an actuarial life expectancy of 9 years. (In any event the period should be less than 21 years to avoid Law of Property Act 1925, s 149(3) if a rent is to be paid). The period is also fixed to avoid the risk of the grant constituting a deemed settlement under IHTA 1984, s 43. Does X's retained freehold interest entitle or enable X to occupy all or part of the land, or to enjoy some right in relation to all or part of the land, 'otherwise than for full consideration in money or money's worth'? The answer is surely 'No'. Although the Revenue would no doubt argue that the occupation must itself be for a rent notwithstanding that full market value was given for the right to occupy on acquisition of the house.

There are other issues which should be briefly mentioned: Section 268 (associated operations) may be avoided by gifting the freehold retained under the will to someone other than the holder of the reversionary lease. The grant of the lease itself is not an associated operation because it is a single transaction. There is a capital gains tax problem because the children's trust has an increasingly valuable asset which does not qualify for PPR relief—but see the scheme referred to at **7.1:1** using holdover relief from a discretionary trust.

7.3:3 Exceptions to s 102A

There is an exception to s 102A where:

(a) the right, interest or arrangement does not and cannot prevent the enjoyment of the land to the entire exclusion, or virtually to the entire exclusion, of the donor; or

(b) the right, interest or arrangement does not entitle or enable the donor to occupy all or part of the land immediately after the disposal, but would do so were it not for the interest disposed of; or

(c) the right or interest was granted or acquired before the period of seven years ending with the date of the gift.

Exception (b) is important because it disapplies s 102A in a case where the donor grants a 20-year rent-free lease to B by way of gift. In such a case there is a gift of an interest in land and in relation to the land the donor enjoys some right or interest (rights under the lease and as freeholder). The exception applies because those rights do not entitle or enable him to occupy the land immediately after the disposal, but would do so were it not for the interest disposed of.

The effect of exception (c) is that the *Ingram* scheme still works if a gap of 7 years is left between the date of the purchase of the freehold and the grant of the freehold subject to the lease. Likewise, the reversionary lease scheme (see **7.3:2**) still works if a gap of 7 years is left between the date of purchase of the land and the date of the grant of the lease (so that it may be unnecessary to rely upon the argument that full consideration has been given—if indeed it has).

Note that although s 102A refers to the donor's spouse this does not mean that the donor reserves a benefit in gifted land by virtue of his wife receiving a benefit. Rather it is intended to prevent the donor granting a 20-year lease to his wife, then occupying the property by virtue of her lease.

Variant of the Ingram scheme with a 7-year gap

A common (and simpler) example of an *Ingram* scheme involves a grant of a lease over the principal private residence to a life interest trust of which the grantor is life tenant. This is a potentially exempt transfer for IHT and an exempt disposal for CGT purposes. The lease is for nil rent and its length is based on the grantor's life expectancy (but less than 21 years). The grantor gives the freehold subject to the lease to a children's trust from which he and his spouse are excluded. The grantor thus remains in occupation in consequence of property (the leasehold interest) retained but receives no benefit in the property (the freehold subject to the lease) given away. This IHT scheme still works if a gap of 7 years is left between the grant of the lease and the gift of the freehold subject to the lease: see FA 1986, s 102A(5).

There is a capital gains tax problem when the children's trust sells. This is because no individual has occupied the trustee's interest in land as a principal private residence, but it has increased in value just as the lease has reduced in value. To avoid the associated operations provisions it is prudent to gift the lease under the will to a person other than the children's trust. It is considered that *Ramsay* will not apply here to block the scheme.

7.3:4   Other statutory exceptions to ss 102 and 102A

The exception for exempt transfers to spouses in s 102(5) is applied to ss 102A and 102B by virtue of s 102C(2). Thus, X could give his holiday home to the trustees of a settlement to hold on interest in possession trusts for his wife for six months and subject thereto on interest in possession trusts for his children. The trustees have a power to advance capital or income to X and his wife. Since the whole value of the property gifted is attributable immediately after the transfer of value onto the trust to the spouse's estate, s 18 must apply, and the gift with reservation provisions must be disapplied. There should be no associated operations (s 268) if the spouse's interest in possession terminates automatically since, arguably, it is not an 'operation'. Even if it is, s 268(3) does not appear to undo the benefit of the scheme.

The Inland Revenue take the view that there are two gifts here so that the exemption does not prevent a gift with reservation of benefit arising in the children's interest in possession. In the author's view this is contrary to the language of FA 1986, Sch 20, and to basic trust law principles. It is also irrelevant because the application of s 49 to a gift to an interest in possession trust for the spouse means that the exemption applies to the whole value of the property gifted. Therefore, even if there were two gifts made at the date of settlement, the exemption applies to both.

This scheme has now been litigated in the Special Commissioners: at the time of writing the decision was unknown.

7.3:5   Avoiding s 102A by avoiding gifts of land

(1)   Gifts of cash

A parent could consider making an outright gift of cash to his child (but with no strings attached). If the child purchased a house in which child and parent live s 102 would not apply because of FA 1986, Sch 20 para 2(2)(b). Section 102A would not apply because there is no disposal of an interest in land. Avoid settling the cash: FA 1986, Sch 20(5).

It is probably too risky for the child to purchase the house in which the parent is living. A suitable length of time should be left between the gift to the child and the purchase of the property from which the donor may benefit.

(2) Lifetime debt scheme

The scheme: X sells his principal private residence to his life interest trust for full market value. The purchase price is paid by the issue of a loan note (or by set-off against a loan from X to the trustees). X gifts the loan note to a life interest trust for his children or an accumulation and maintenance trust for his grandchildren. X is wholly excluded from benefit under this second trust.

X remains in occupation of his home by virtue of his life interest under the trust. The value of his IHT estate must be considered in light of the deeming provision in IHTA 1984, s 49. Strictly, s 49 deems him to be beneficially entitled to the 'property' in which his interest subsists. The PPR is 'property' but the debt is not. This is a concern but it may be sufficient that the trustees have a lien over settled property for the payment of such trust debts which would affect the market value of the property. The concern disappears if the settled property is encumbered: s 162(4). But this puts X at risk of making a gift of an interest in land.

This scheme should avoid s 102A because, unless the debt is secured by a mortgage on the house at the date of the gift, there is no gift of an 'interest in land'. Furthermore, the purchase price is paid by the trustees albeit by the issue of an IOU, or by set-off against a loan to X. This means that there is no vendor's lien over land for an unpaid purchase price which, if given by X, could amount to 'a gift of an interest in land'.

The scheme should also avoid s 102 because X gives away a debt with a fixed repayment date (eg one month after the death of X). If the loan was repayable on demand and the donee failed to demand repayment, X would reserve a benefit in the debt by virtue of FA 1986, Sch 20 para 6(1)(c) and IHTA 1984, s 268 (the debt representing the land for the purposes of s 268).

The sale of the property to X's trust will give rise to a stamp duty charge on the whole value of the property. The charge may be avoided by letting the sale rest in contract.

X's occupation of the PPR as beneficiary means that the trustees can qualify for PPR relief on any gain on a sale of the property. There is also a free uplift in the market value of the property on the death of X if TCGA 1992, s 72 applies. The gift of the loan note is a disposal to a connected party for its (deemed) market value. However, any gain is exempt under TCGA 1992, s 251. The repayment of the debt will be a chargeable disposal by the second trust, but the debt will have a base cost as a result of the earlier (exempt) disposal.

This scheme only reduces the value of X's estate by the value of the debt at the date of death. Note that FA 1986, s 103 is not relevant. For an imaginative analysis of this scheme see *Taxation* 2 August 2001 pp 456–7.

(3) Fixing a GWR with 'reverter to settlor'

Suppose X has inadvertently reserved a benefit in his settlement of the family home. To eliminate the GWR, he could appoint the house to the son absolutely. The son (if he so decides) could then settle the house onto interest in possession trusts for the parent and subject thereto for himself. There is no IHT on the parent's estate on death (assuming the son survives the parent) because of the reverter to settlor exemption: IHTA 1984, s 54. Furthermore, if the trust does not come to an end on the death of the parent but instead the settlor acquires an interest in possession, the house also obtains a free CGT uplift in market value (under TCGA 1992, s 72). Note that there may be

CGT and IHT on the appointment to the child. The son must acquire his interest in the house absolutely; otherwise the original settlement may be deemed to continue (in which the father has retained a benefit): s 81. *Ramsay* may apply to the construction of the phrase 'beneficially entitled' in s 81 in such a way that if he were bound to resettle it, then he fails to be 'beneficially entitled'. The son must therefore be given a genuine choice, and should be separately advised.

7.3:6   The rule in s 102B FA 1986

Finance Act 1999 extends to gifts of an undivided share of an interest in land, for example, where the sole freeholder gifts half of his interest to another.

Section 102B applies where an individual disposes of an undivided share of an interest in land by way of gift. In that case, the share disposed of is property subject to a reservation; and section 102(3) and (4) FA 1986 apply, except where:

(a) the donor does not occupy the land; or

(b) the donor occupies the land to the exclusion of the donee for full consideration in money or money's worth; or

(c) the donor and the donee occupy the land; and the donor does not receive any benefit, other than a negligible one, which is provided by or at the expense of the donee for some reason connected with the gift.

Where s 102B applies, ss 102 and 102A do not: s 102C(6). So, if X's son lives with him, X could give 90% of his share of the freehold to the son. The son should not contribute in any way to the father's share of the upkeep and expenses. Section 102B will apply, not ss 102 or 102A, but there is no GWR because of (c). If the child moved out he could charge X a rent (see (b)), or settle his share onto interest in possession trusts for X and subject thereto for himself and then his children. This latter scheme relies upon the reverter to settlor exemption for the father. The child may also benefit under TCGA 1992, s 72 (increase in market value) if the trust continues after his father's death.

Concluding points

A stamp duty charge will not arise on any gift of property such as land. However, if the land is subject to a mortgage or debt which is assumed by the donee, for stamp duty purposes the amount of the debt is treated as consideration so that the conveyance will be stampable with ad valorem duty: SA 1891, s 57 and see Statement of Practice 6/90 dated 27 April 1990. Possible solutions are: (a) the donor remains liable for the debt: but this must be made clear in the terms of the gift; (b) repay the mortgage and let the donor mortgage in his own name. However, the two transactions must be independent to avoid a *Ramsay* attack; and (c) where the facts permit, the donor could make a series of gifts each under £60,000. Each gift must be genuinely independent of the other gifts.

Finally, where the donor gives away his family home, or an interest in it, consider whether it will adversely affect his rights to community care and assistance from the local authority. The area is complex (and fortunately outside the scope of this book) however a starting point is the National Health Service and Community Care Act 1990 and the Health and Social Services and Society Security Adjudications Act 1983.

7.3:7   Settlor as trustee and GWR

(1)   General rule

It is generally acknowledged that a trustee's duties are entirely of a *fiduciary* nature, since his sole duties and functions is to safeguard the interests of the beneficiaries. Thus, as a matter of trust law there is normally no objection to the settlor being one of the trustees (possibly even the first named). In *Oakes v Comr of Stamp Duties of New South Wales* [1953] 2 All ER 1563, the Privy Council stated 'if property is held in trust for the donee, then the trustees' possession is the donee's possession for this purpose, and it matters not that the trustee is a donor himself' (see also *Stamp Duties Comr of New South Wales v Perpetual Trustee Co Ltd* [1943] 1 All ER 525 and *Oakes v Comr of Stamp Duties of New South Wales* [1953] 2 All ER 1563; also 1986 STI, p 606 at para 15).

This section considers the affect of the settlor being trustee in the context of the Inheritance tax GWR rules.

For the purposes of income tax and capital gains tax one should consider excluding the settlor and spouse of the settlor from any benefit under the trust whatsoever.

(2)   Trustees' remuneration

A trustee should receive *no remuneration* at all from the trust if he or she is also a settlor of the trust. Otherwise the settlor may be reserving a benefit in the property gifted. There is however a possible let out for *reasonable* remuneration under IHTA, s 90 (exemption for a trustee receiving an annuity of a reasonable amount having regard to the duties/services performed). It is understood that the CTO favour this interpretation.

(3)   Position where settlor/trustee is a paid director of a company whose shares are settled (see also exchange of correspondence with Revenue reported in Law Society Gazette *1 June 1988)*

Such a situation may also constitute a gift with reservation. Moreover, if the trust deed gives specific dispensation for such entitlement (and from a trust law perspective it is better if it does) this could merely emphasise the existence of the gift with reservation. If there is no dispensation the trustee would strictly hold such remuneration on behalf of the beneficiaries—see *Barrett v Hartley* (1866) LR 2 Eq 789 and *Re Sykes* [1909] 2 Ch 241, CA.

The reservation of benefit danger is greatest where a settlor settles shares in a company onto a trust (whether or not he is a trustee) and then obtains a paid position as director or employee of the company. Arguably the fact that he is able to receive payment which derives from settled property means that he has reserved a benefit in that property. The problem is particularly common in cases where the owner of a small family company wishes to settle his shares onto trust, but continue running the business.

The practical solution is to avoid the argument and have in place a service agreement which agrees the remuneration, and the position, independently from, and prior to, the gift of the shares to the trust. The remuneration should be set at a reasonable rate. The settlor then has a credible argument that the remuneration is simply consideration for a service provided to the company and no 'benefit' is received or reserved. The remuneration should not be open ended, but if flexibility is required, consider a fixed amount pegged to the cost of living index and/or subject to a reasonable commission on profits arrangement.

If it is not possible to arrange a service agreement prior to the creation of the trust, the settlor should definitely obtain no more than reasonable remuneration for work done. To be on the safe side the settlor should not be remunerated at all.

(4) Position where settlor settles some shares in a company and retains other shares beneficially

Again it could be dangerous from a gift with reservation viewpoint for such a settlor to be a trustee—particularly the first named trustee with the voting power. The danger is especially apparent if the settlor's beneficial holding and the trust's holding together constitute control, ie the 'marriage' value benefit.

This position is dangerous from a GWR point of view even if the settlor is not a trustee.

Where 100% business/agricultural relief applies, GWR problems should disappear (see **Chapter 9**).

7.3:8 Remuneration/pension arrangements

Remuneration/pension: are these benefits reserved to a 'donor'? (s 102, Sch 20). Consider this also in the context of the company making additional voluntary pension contributions; and generous 'redundancy'/compensation payments. See *Oakes v Comr of Stamp Duties of New South Wales* [1953] 2 All ER 1563.

The requisite arrangement for remuneration or pension provision should be made as far in *advance* as possible prior to the gift of the shares to avoid any Revenue argument that there is a reservation of benefit. If the arrangements were made *subsequent* to the gift there would prima facie be a gift with reservation.

The arrangements should also be made on a commercial/arm's length basis (*Copeman v William Flood & Sons Ltd* (1940) 24 TC 53 and *LG Berry Investments Ltd v Attwooll* [1964] 2 All ER 126).

7.3:9 Partnership situations

Gifts made out of partnership interests in the context of the GROB provisions are dealt with at **6.2:5**.

7.3:10 Paintings and other valuable assets

Keeping paintings etc in one's house after giving them away is likely to be a gift with reservation of benefit even where the donor is acting as a caretaker. It is also probable in such cases that possession and enjoyment have not been assumed by the donee (s 102(1)(a)). The solution could be to pay an arm's length rent, or a single capital premium.

7.3:11 Variations (IHTA, s 142)—avoiding the GWR rules

Where a testator has died and a beneficiary of the estate effects a variation, eg by varying an outright gift to the beneficiary into a discretionary trust, the fact that the beneficiary is capable of benefiting from the varied gift, eg by being included as a discretionary object, should not, it seems, constitute a reservation of a benefit by the beneficiary because it is the *deceased* who is deemed to have created the varied gift, eg the discretionary trust.

7.3:12   Health warning

Throughout, the practitioner must be aware of two main caveats.

First, the application of the 'associated operations' provisions—s 268. Remember, however, that merely because two operations are associated does *not* necessarily entail an IHT charge. Section 268 is merely a definition section and does not itself constitute a charging section: a charging provision would additionally be needed as is in fact the case with GWRs (Sch 20, para 6(1)(c)). Nor can associated operations change the nature of a transaction.

Secondly, the possible application of the *Ramsay* doctrine as laid down in *WT Ramsay Ltd v IRC* [1981] STC 174, HL; *Furniss v Dawson* [1984] STC 153, HL, and now confirmed as a principle of statutory construction by the House of Lords in *MacNiven v Westmoreland* [2001] STC 237. See **1.8**.

7.4   OTHER PLANNING ASPECTS OF GIFTS

7.4:1   Avoiding gifts *donatio mortis causa*

Such gifts are those made in contemplation of the death of the donor and therefore are conditional and only take effect on the donor's death; and can include land as well as personalty (*Sen v Headley* [1991] 2 All ER 636, CA). Moreover, these gifts are automatically revoked if the donee predeceases the donor or if the donor recovers from the illness. It would therefore seem that the donor retains such an interest as would make it a gift with reservation. The amount of IHT is thus not affected.

It follows that donors should observe two criteria:

(1)   never make a gift *donatio mortis causa* unless it is genuinely desired that the gift should lapse on recovery;

(2)   if it is wished to make an unconditional gift on a deathbed or in an illness and the gift is likely to be exempt only if made during lifetime (eg the annual £3,000, normal income gift, marriage or an exempt £250) (**1.4:1**), the presumption that the gift is a *donatio mortis causa* should be firmly rebutted. For example, the donor could accompany the gift with a letter to the donee to the effect that the gift is unconditional, is to take effect forthwith and is not dependent on the donor surviving or any other contingency.

7.4:2   Creating a benefit without a transfer

It has already been noted that 'an omission to act', notwithstanding the anti-avoidance provision of s 3(3), may still constitute a planning opportunity in appropriate circumstances (see **5.1:6**). Another possibility would be the provision of opportunities; for example, instead of an estate owner acquiring an adjoining field which would greatly add to the value of his existing land, the adjoining field might be purchased by, say, his son (but not the estate owner's wife having regard to the related property provisions of s 161). Similarly, there exist the hiving-off and splitting operations mentioned in **5.1:3** and **5.1:5** (Remember that hiving-off operations should be commercially based, eg, with a licensing or commission arrangement, to avoid any possibility of a transfer of value by the company under s 94(1)). It appears that the entering into of a guarantee would not of itself constitute a disposition on creation, although a call under such guarantee might well give rise to a liability; in any event the associated operations provisions would have to be carefully considered.

It would appear that farmers passing their farms on to the next generation frequently place a covenant on the land preventing its development. The aim is to require consent for development from non-farming family members, who are likely to give their consent only if a capital sum is paid out of the development proceeds to them. The CTO have confirmed that the imposition of such a restriction does not constitute a GWR (S G Ilett in *Tolley's Practical Tax*, 12 May 1993, pp 79–80).

7.4:3   Assuming burdens

Where the transferee of an asset assumes in return equivalent or appropriate obligations, the transaction may be one which confers no gratuitous benefits within the context of s 10; and on the footing that there is no gift, there cannot be a gift with reservation. For example an ageing parent may transfer a property or an interest therein (say his or her residence, exempt from CGT whether transferred for consideration or not) to a child in exchange for that child assuming the burdens of maintaining and caring for that parent for the remainder of his or her life, including provision of accommodation, care, sustenance and provision of nursing and medical facilities. In such circumstances the arrangements should be recorded by an appropriate arm's length binding agreement.

A parent may take his child into partnership, and their respective covenants on time and attention to be given to the business could take advantage of the *Boden* decision (see **6.2:2**). As a caveat, it is sometimes argued that the assumption of a liability can still be a 'disposition' having regard to the reference in s 3(1) to diminution in the estate. However, s 3(1) first of all defines a transfer of value as a disposition, and a disposition is generally regarded as a transfer of property or a payment over of cash. Moreover, under s 5(3) and (4), a liability is taken into account in valuing an estate only in so far as it has been incurred for valuable consideration.

7.4:4   Some gifts may be better made in kind than in cash

This is a matter of valuation. For example, instead of the parent making a cash gift of, say, £15,000 on a daughter's marriage, only £5,000 of which would be exempt (the balance being a PET), such parent might have bought furniture, retained and used it, possibly for a short time, and then given it to the daughter, ie at its second-hand value of, say, £5,000. Similarly, instead of giving cash to enable someone to buy a new car the donor could buy the car himself and then give the asset. Clearly the associated operations provisions of s 268 will have to be carefully considered.

7.4:5   The character of exemptions

Exemptions are generally, but not always, separate and cumulative. The annual £3,000 exemption and the marriage gift exemption are both separate and cumulative. If a father gives his daughter £15,000 on her marriage, the gift is exempt to the extent of £5,000 (marriage: s 22) plus £3,000 (annual: s 19), leaving £7,000 as a PET (unless normal income expenditure applied). By persuading his wife to make similar gifts, the £15,000 could be covered. Moreover, both the £3,000 and the marriage exemptions are available for settlements where there is an interest in possession which the life tenant terminates (in his lifetime, not on death). Thus, if the father in the example above had a life interest under a trust he could terminate his interest in £8,000, enabling the marriage and annual exemptions to be claimed by the trustees (s 57): see also **7.12**.

On the other hand, the £250 exemption for outright gifts to any one person in the year (s 20) applies only where the total of gifts to that person does not exceed that sum. The exemption is not available in order to exempt £250 out of a larger gift to that person (s 20(1)). Nor is this exemption available to trusts.

The exemption for normal expenditure gifts under s 21 available to individuals only, operates separately and apart from the other exemptions.

7.5   THE DONEE PAYING IHT RATHER THAN THE DONOR

7.5:1

In the case of a lifetime chargeable transfer, there are advantages to be gained by the donee paying IHT rather than the donor. These advantages include the following:

(1) instalment basis of certain assets is only available in respect of lifetime gifts if the donee pays the IHT (s 227(1)(b) and for further details as to instalments, see **1.5:2**);

(2) there is no grossing up if the donee pays the tax (s 162) (see **1.2:5**);

(3) certain expenses incidental to a transfer are deductible from the value transferred where the donee pays the tax (s 164). Although not defined, these expenses should include such items as costs of valuation and professional fees for transferring the asset;

(4) capital gains tax (s 165) is deductible from the value transferred if, but only if, it is paid by the donee (whether IHT is paid by the donor or donee). Therefore if there is a lifetime chargeable transfer and the donee contemplates an early sale, do not claim the CGT holdover (available for lifetime chargeable transfers) because this will lose the possible CGT deduction against the value transferred for IHT purposes. On the other hand, if CGT holdover relief is claimed, and there is a later CGT disposal of the gifted asset by the donee, there will be an allowance against the chargeable gain on that disposal for the lesser of (a) the IHT on the donor's gift to the donee (including any further IHT on a subsequent variation) and (b) the amount of the gain on the donee's disposal (see TCGA 1992, s 165(10) and s 260(7)). The IHT can therefore wash out the

donee's gain but not give him a loss. Accordingly, where the donee is intending to retain the asset for the time being, it may be worthwhile, even if there is only a very small gain for CGT on the donor's gift, to elect for holdover relief, to enable the IHT on the donor's gift to be allowed against a possible large gain on a later CGT disposal by the donee. However, always take into account that holdover stops the CGT taper relief period from running.

7.5:2

Having established the right to pay by instalments in respect of a chargeable lifetime gift because the donee pays the IHT, an extremely useful method of funding the IHT is for the donor then to proceed to make exempt gifts to the donee regularly in order to enable him to pay the instalments in whole or part although there should be no undertaking to do so. Such exempt payments could include the £3,000 annual exemption and normal expenditure income gifts, etc. This suggestion affords a key planning opportunity in those cases (particularly—subject to the question of business or agricultural relief— business and agricultural assets, see **1.5**) where IHT can be paid by interest free instalments. Moreover the Inland Revenue have confirmed in the *Law Society Gazette* for 1 March 1978 that this proposal would not be regarded as an associated operation. Accordingly, annual exemptions can be used to help to fund the IHT on very substantial gifts (notably, since the advent of 100% business or agricultural relief, of land). Where sums in excess of the annual exemptions are required, the donor could make a loan (interest free and repayable on demand) to the donee, which loan could itself be released or waived in stages by means of annual or other exemptions; but note that any release or waiver should be effected by deed because of the lack of consideration. Alternatively, the donor could make PET gifts.

7.5:3

Having regard in particular to s 199(a) and (b), which places an equal liability for IHT on the transferor and transferee, it is the generally accepted view that the Revenue must accept IHT whether the donor or the donee tenders it and in particular the Revenue cannot require the donor to pay rather than the donee in order to obtain the greater amount of tax on the grossed-up basis. Nevertheless it is sound practice that when it is intended that the donee should pay the tax, this is recorded in a binding form between the parties (note also the inclusion of an appropriate indemnity). This is particularly relevant for PET gifts in case the PET becomes chargeable. The receipt of the covenant should not constitute a gift with reservation. A suggested form of covenant is set out below, and as there may be no consideration for such covenant it should be in the form of a deed (no stamp duty).

To [Donor]

I THE UNDERSIGNED hereby acknowledge receipt from you this day of [brief details of the asset given] ('the gift') and confirm and agree that the gift is conditional on the covenant, hereby made by me as donee, to pay any IHT, CGT and any other taxes or imposts whatsover due and payable on or in respect of the gift by the due date(s). AND I will effectually indemnify you against all claims, demands, actions, proceedings, costs, interest, charges and expenses in respect of or in any way arising out of or in consequence of the said liability to IHT, CGT or any other taxes or imposts whatsoever.

This covenant undertaken by me shall bind my legal personal representatives and shall likewise be enforceable by your legal personal representatives.

Dated   20

SIGNED AND DELIVERED AS A DEED
BY [DONEE] IN THE PRESENCE OF:

7.6 GIFTS VERSUS SALES

7.6:1

Straightforward purchase and sale at arm's length between unconnected persons transactions do not attract any potential IHT liability because they confer no gratuitous benefit within the context of s 10. However, great care is required in respect of transactions between connected persons, because the relationship might well suggest the possibility of bounty.

7.6:2

In many cases it may be practical to substitute an arm's length sale and purchase arrangement for a gift, thereby avoiding any IHT results. Before deciding on a sale rather than a gift, however, there should be weighed in the balance the amount of CGT on a sale compared with the restricted possibility of deferment of CGT on a gift (see TCGA 1992, ss 165, 260). Remember also that on a sale, as contrasted with a gift no business or agricultural property reliefs are available. A useful formula, if a sale is considered preferable, might be to agree to a transfer of an asset at such price as shall be the value agreed for stamp duty and the other revenue purposes, by the Shares Valuation Division in the case of a private company's shares or the District Valuer in the case of land.

Moreover, this procedure of selling should overcome the problems occasioned by the consequential loss formula and the 'related property' rules where assets are held by husband and wife or there has been a transfer by either of them to a charity or exempt body (see **7.16** to **7.18**). An arm's length sale would also avoid any question of gift with reservation. It would also constitute an effective freezing operation.

This proposal could be particularly relevant where an estate owner wishes to transfer shares in a private company which will lose him control.

Where transferors are in reasonably good health and gift term assurance cover is available, PETs may be a better proposition than a sale; particularly for family trading company shares where business relief is available for IHT and holdover relief for CGT. Consider the arithmetic; and note the strict requirements of s 10 for sales and the possible application of s 268 (associated operations). Moreover, the PET regime is available even though in the case of family company shares the donor is losing control. The gift is a PET in respect of the larger loss to donor value, as contrasted with the benefit received by the donee, although the significance of this loses its relevance if 100% business relief is available.

7.6:3   Wasting operations

This proposal of arranging a sale might, however, be combined with a 'wasting operation'. An asset could be purchased by, say, a son from his father in consideration of an actuarially calculated annuity. This transaction should not constitute a transfer of value under s 10 and the father will have no chargeable asset in his estate as there is full consideration made. For income tax purposes this is known colloquially as a 'reverse annuity operation'; and under TA 1988, s 125, the annuity instalments have normally to be paid gross without deduction of tax and do not constitute a charge in computing the taxable income of the payer. Under the old law exceptions to this general rule where annuities continue to be paid under deduction of basic rate tax include annuities under partnership agreements, in return for the transfer of a business and annuities in consideration of the release of an interest in settled property in favour of a subsequent beneficiary (which still remains (TA 1988, s 125(3)(b)). In the case of these exceptions, provided that the annuities can be shown to have been made for valuable and sufficient consideration, the whole of the annuity instalments will be deductible from the payer's income under TA 1988, s 660 (now repealed), as a charge for income tax purposes, and will be tax deductible for higher and additional rates of income tax.

7.6:4   Exchanging assets and services

Where there is an equality of exchange (ie the assets exchanged are of equivalent value), the transaction should result in no IHT (even though it may involve CGT and stamp duty). Where the assets are not exactly equivalent, an appropriate cash balance should be paid. This method of exchange could be particularly appropriate where a depreciating asset held by a younger generation is exchanged for an appreciating asset held by an older generation, assuming at the date of exchange the assets have equal value.

7.6:5   Creation of a tenancy and associated operations

The creation of a tenancy, say, to a relative such as a son, followed by a gift of the freehold reversion, is likely to be caught by the associated operations provisions in s 268. The following proposals should not, however, be subject to such associated operations and being an arm's length arrangement should be outside the IHT net entirely. First the freeholder, say the father, creates a tenancy in favour of the son at full market rent (including adequate rent review clauses, say, every three or five years). The father later decides to sell the freehold reversion to his son at its investment value *but* after a period exceeding three years from the creation of the tenancy. Note that by virtue of s 268(2) the grant of a lease for full consideration is not associated with any operation effected more than three years later, although there would necessarily follow the tenancy. Even though effective for IHT, such an arrangement might have to be rejected because of the income tax liability on the rent received (see also **3.4:3**).

7.7   GIFTS VERSUS LOANS

Where an individual makes an interest free loan of cash, or allows another the free use of any asset, such as a property, no IHT liability arises on the notional interest, or rent, etc, forgone. The possibility of an interest free loan to a prospective beneficiary can be extremely useful as a 'freezing' operation, and the concept has been taken up by life companies as the basis for a continuing albeit restricted form of the inheritance trust, discussed at **8.3:11**. The face value of the loan is still an asset of the lender's estate because of the liability of the borrower to repay (s 166), but the borrower can utilise the cash to buy an appreciating asset, or go into business, or merely to earn himself interest; and the lender's estate is meanwhile remaining static.

However useful those loans are, they should not take precedence over the use of gifts within the nil rate band or the use of PETs combined with the seven-year cumulation cut off, annual and other exemptions (which could be used to release a borrower from repayment of part of the loan), and transfer of appreciating assets.

Loans by trustees of settlements can also be a useful means of making cash available to beneficiaries without necessarily incurring an IHT charge. If such loans are on favourable terms, for example, repayable at the end of a fixed period, an IHT liability can arise as a depreciatory transaction, see ss 52(3) and 65(1)(b) and **4.8:3**. The question is sometimes raised whether a gratuitous loan of trust property may be regarded as equivalent to allowing the recipient of the loan the use and enjoyment of it and therefore amount to creating an interest in possession. This is not so, because in the case of a straightforward loan of money validly made out of the trust property the loan will be represented in the settlement by the corresponding debt due from the borrower just like any other investment or re-investment of the trust property and should therefore give rise to no IHT problems. Contrast the position where the trustees allow a beneficiary exclusive use of a trust asset, eg a dwelling-house. Unlike the loan, where the trustees have used the cash to acquire a new asset consisting of the debt due, the trustees still hold the house as a trust asset, and the beneficiary does have an interest in possession (see **4.2:4**).

Whenever loans are made, they should be on terms providing for repayment on demand. If the loan is not repayable until the end of a stated period, the Revenue are likely to contend that the lender has replaced his ready cash by a debt due for repayment at some future date; and that the difference between the amount of money advanced, and the present discounted value of the debt, produces a diminution in the lender's estate and constitutes a transfer of value for IHT within s 3(1).

Care should also be taken to ensure that the debt owed to the trustees is sited offshore if the settlement is intended to be an excluded property settlement.

Where loans are subsequently released or waived, perhaps taking advantage of annual exemptions, the release or waiver should always be carried out by deed because of the absence of consideration. It appears that the CTO will not accept that a loan has been waived unless effected by deed, relying on *Pinnel's Case* (1602) 5 Co Rep 117a and *Edwards v Walters* [1896] 2 Ch 157, CA. The Law Society revenue law committee have indicated their view that, while the Revenue's contention is not unassailable, unless and until the contention is confirmed or rejected by judicial authority, it must be prudent for clients undertaking IHT planning involving a loan and subsequent waiver to effect the waiver by deed to ensure that the estate of the lender is reduced (*Law Society Gazette*, 18 December 1991, p 40; see also at STI (1992) p 30). The same point is involved in waivers of dividends (**5.1:7**) and waivers of remuneration (**5.1:8**). There are stringent anti-avoidance provisions for IHT in respect of artificial loans (FA 1986, s 103).

7.8 GIFTS IN VALUE NOT EXCEEDING £3,000 PER ANNUM (ss 19 AND 57)

7.8:1

Transfers of value by a transferor in any one fiscal year (ie 6 April-5 April) are exempt to the extent that the values transferred by him do not exceed £3,000. A larger gift can be exempted *pro tanto*, so that a gift of £10,000 could be exempt on the first £3,000, leaving (unless other exemptions were also available) a PET transfer of £7,000. The exemption applies only to lifetime transfers, but is separately and additionally available to other exemptions, subject to compliance with the various conditions. However, the Revenue take the view that the annual exemption cannot be used in respect of a GWR in the year that reservation by the donor ceases so that it then becomes a PET.

The exemption can also be used on the lifetime termination of an interest in possession in settled property (s 57). The life tenant has to notify the trustees of the availability of the exemption within six months of the release on the prescribed form 222 available from the Capital Taxes Office. The life tenant is deemed to be the transferor; and he has of course only one £3,000 exemption per year to cover both gifts out of his own estate and terminations of interests in possession.

7.8:2

There is a right to accumulate this exemption for one further year to the extent that it has not been used in any year. The exemption for the year of transfer must be used completely before any unused part for the previous year, and if any part left over from the previous year is not used in the current year, it is lost, for example:

Year	Gift £	Amount of exemption available £	Carry forward £
to 5 April 1999	2,400	3,000	600
to 3 April 2000	2,700	3,600	300
to 5 April 2001	4,000	3,300 (not 3900)	Nil

As in the year to 5 April 2000 a £2,700 gift has been made, there is only a £300 carry over and the £600 accumulation from 1999 has been lost.

Note that under s 19(3A) the annual £3,000 exemption is set against an immediately chargeable transfer and not against a PET made earlier in that year. If the PET becomes chargeable by the death of the donor within seven years it is treated for the £3,000 exemption (no other purpose) as having been made later than the immediately chargeable gift, which keeps the exemption.

7.8:3

Subject to the special rule in s 19(3A) (see **7.8:2** above) earlier transfers are exempt before later ones although transfers made on the same day are treated pro rata; but as regards PETs the £3,000 annual exemption is available first against chargeable transfers and then against PETs which become chargeable (see s 19(3A)).

In considering the planning aspects:

(1) these £3,000 gifts should be made *regularly* so as to ensure that the exemption with the right to accumulate for one year only does not lapse. Husband and wife together can give away £60,000 under this exemption over ten years; and a couple liable at the 40% rate, by failing to do so, would be giving £24,000 to the Treasury rather than their beneficiaries. It will be appreciated that the exempt gift need not be in cash but can be in assets, such as shares of a company, interests in a property, or a loan account representing the appropriate value;

(2) the gift should be made, and *shown* to be made out of *capital* rather than income so as not to reduce the 'normal expenditure' exemption;

(3) the exemption has particular relevance and use for funding life assurance (see **8.0**) and for annual waivers along the lines indicated in **7.7** above;

(4) as between husband and wife it may be appropriate to 'channel' assets from one spouse to the other who can thereupon pass on the appropriate gift, eg to a child (see also **3.3**). The terms of a particular gift should always be recorded in writing and where cheque payments are made such cheques should be presented not merely endorsed over;

(5) consider adding assets into an appropriate trust, such as the accumulation and maintenance trust (see **4.4:1**);

(6) it is not enough to create a liability (even by deed) over one's assets in favour of the prospective beneficiary or write him an 'IOU'. There has to be a consequential loss to the estate under s 3(1); and since under s 5(5) a liability can be taken into account only if it has been *incurred* for consideration in money or money's worth, the creation of a liability to pay in these circumstances is not effective;

(7) if the asset gifted is a loan or capital account with a company or partnership, the correct method is to proceed as follows, in order to ensure that there is a properly completed gift. Assume that A has the loan account and he wishes to give B the benefit of it:

(a) The firm gives a cheque to A, and A acknowledges receipt. A's loan account is closed.

(b) A pays the cheque into his own bank account and it is cleared.

(c) A writes a letter to B informing him he wishes to make a gift of £x and encloses his cheque for that amount in B's favour.

(d) B pays the cheque into his own account and it is cleared.

(e) B writes a cheque in favour of the firm and accompanies it with a letter saying he is lending the firm the relevant sum. The firm opens a new loan account in favour of B.

Note that a payment by cheque takes effect only when it is cleared (see **7.21**).

(8) FA 1986, s 102(5) excludes most exempt transfers from the gift with reservation rules. To this there are two notable exceptions: the £3,000 annual exemption and the normal expenditure out of income exemption (see **7.10** below). It would appear therefore that if a gift with reservation exists these exemptions cannot qualify. The Capital Taxes Office take the view that the normal income exemption can never apply to a gift with reservation. Furthermore, the Revenue take the view (see their November 1993 interpretation guidelines (RI 55) referred to at **7.2:1** above) that the annual £3,000 exemption cannot apply to a gift with reservation should the reservation cease in the donor's lifetime whereupon a PET is then treated as made. This is a change from their former view.

Example

On 1 September 1987 A gives his son B his holding of 20,000 shares in publicly quoted XYZ plc. B allows A still to have the benefit of the dividends. This arrangement ceases on 10 January 1997, A being henceforth excluded, and a PET is treated as made at that time. On 2 March 1997 he makes a gift on discretionary trusts which is a lifetime chargeable transfer. The annual £3,000 exemption cannot be used against the gifted shareholding becoming a PET on 10 January 1997 but is available against the lifetime chargeable transfer on 2 March 1997 (along with any unused part of the 1995–96 annual exemption).

7.9 £250 PER ANNUM GIFTS TO ANY NUMBER OF SEPARATE DONEES (s 20)

7.9:1

A transferor can make any number of separate £250 outright gifts to separate donees in any year to 5 April. Such gifts can be in cash or kind and would cover the normal type of entertainment expenditure disallowed for income tax purposes and hence would not strictly be available under the exemption of dispositions allowable for income tax, etc (s 12(1)). As the gifts must be *outright* they cannot be used for placing assets *into* settlements.

7.9:2

The £250 exemption cannot be used to exempt part of a larger gift (s 20(1)) and only covers donees who have not received more than £250 from the transferor in the year. Thus if a donor gives £3,250 to a donee, the first £3,000 can be exempted under the annual exemption (**7.8** above); but the £250 exemption cannot be used for the balance. One way of coping with this for, say, a husband and wife with a son and daughter would be for the husband in the present year, to give £3,000 to the daughter and £250 to the son, and the wife vice versa. In the next year they can switch the gifts over. Remember, moreover, that this value is not the value of the property gifted, it is the diminution in the transferor's estate.

7.10   NORMAL EXPENDITURE OUT OF INCOME (s 21)

7.10:1

With the top rate of income tax at 40% a number of taxpayers can take advantage of this useful exemption. A gift will benefit from the exemption if, or to the extent that, it complies with certain conditions, ie:

(a) the gift was part of the *normal expenditure* of the transferor, and

(b) that (taking one year with another) it was made out of his income, and

(c) that, after allowing for all transfers of value forming part of his normal expenditure, the transferor was left with sufficient income to maintain his usual standard of living.

7.10:2

The following comments on these conditions may be noted:

(1) *Facts and circumstances.* The question whether gifts constitute normal expenditure must be answered according to all the facts and circumstances of each particular case and is a subjective test. For example, if a widower, with children grown up, frugal tastes, and no mortgage, regularly saved a high proportion of his income it appears that to give away this proportion would be part of his normal expenditure. Another individual, albeit with a higher income, but with large family commitments and outgoings and no history of savings, may be unable to claim any gift as normal expenditure, as such gift would reduce his standard of living. In the case of a wife who does not contribute to any material extent to the joint standard of living, a higher proportion of her income should, following independent taxation, be capable of ranking as her normal expenditure.

(2) Following dicta in *A-G for Northern Ireland v Heron* [1959] TR 1, a case on the similar ED 'normal and reasonable' exemption, the payments need not necessarily be repetitive, the test of normality being a qualitative not quantitative test. Thus although it seems that a pattern of continuity must be established, a single first premium paid under an insurance policy or the first instalment under a deed of covenant may well satisfy this test, on the basis that a payment under a contractual or legal obligation may well indicate an intention of regularity. As one is now concerned with an annual, lifetime tax, it is possible for the Revenue to some extent to adopt a wait and see attitude to this exemption, although their practice is to apply the exemption broadly usually without the need to undertake an annual analysis of the annual income except in the larger or borderline cases. The Revenue regard 'normal' as meaning habitual (ie conforming to the 'norm' of giving which the transferor has established). The Revenue do not as a matter of practice seek a return of normal income gifts where they are clearly exempt; but in cases of doubt it may well be advisable to return the gifts to the Capital Taxes Office and claim exemption for them at the same

time, if the circumstances appear appropriate. In any event, it can be useful to keep a record of such gifts in case evidence is later called for (see **7.10:3**).

The term 'normal expenditure' has now been interpreted in the High Court in *Bennett v IRC* [1995] STC 54, Lightman J held that in the context of s 21, the term 'normal expenditure' connoted expenditure which at the time it took place accorded with the settled pattern of expenditure adopted by the transferor. The existence of such a settled pattern might be established either:

(a) by reference to a sequence of payments by the transferor out of past expenditure; or

(b) by proof of a prior commitment or resolution adopted by the transferor regarding his future expenditure.

The facts in *Bennett v IRC* were as follows. Mrs Bennett's husband bequeathed, by his will, his shares in a family company and the residue of his estate on trust to pay the income to his widow Mrs Bennett for her life and subject thereto to his three sons, the taxpayers. Following certain transactions the income of the trust increased enormously. Nevertheless Mrs Bennett lived modestly until her sudden death on 20 February 1990. In 1989 she executed a form of authority addressed to the trustees authorising them to distribute equally between her sons 'all or any of the income arising in each accounting year as is surplus to my financial requirements of which you are already aware'. Payments were made of £9,300 on 14 February 1989 and £60,000 on 5 February 1990.

Lightman J held that the evidence established that Mrs Bennett had made a considered determination for the rest of her life to give to her sons all her surplus income from the trust beyond what she reasonably required for maintenance, and that her determination had been implemented by the execution of the authority requesting the trustees to act accordingly and their so acting. Mrs Bennett had therefore adopted a pattern of expenditure in respect of the surplus income, and the payments to her sons had been made in accordance with that pattern and were accordingly within the meaning of s 21.

Lightman J made a number of additional points. First, that if a prior commitment or resolution is shown, a single payment may be within s 21. Secondly, a commitment towards paying annual premiums on a life assurance qualifying policy gifted to a third party could be a suitable example for s 21. Thirdly there is no need to show that the expenditure is reasonable although it may go to show that as a matter of evidence the relevant pattern of payments exists. An example of how not to get relief is *Nadin v IRC* [1997] STC (SCD) 107. Mrs Nadin gave away £271,000. Her gross income for the year was £18,605. There was no prior commitment nor any settled pattern of expenditure. The special commissioner, said the evidence pointed to abnormal expenditure. This case looked doomed on the facts and it was.

(3) As regards the test that the payment must be 'out of income' there is in fact no specific requirement that this means after tax. Nevertheless, in so far as PAYE is deducted from salaries and other Schedule E emoluments, and the general practice for those with investment incomes is to pay the assessed tax out of income as a regular and inevitable outgoing, it follows

that looking at the net of tax income merely reflects the general view of what is available income. However, if an individual goes abroad to work for three or four years, suffering little or no tax, he clearly will have little need to take tax into account. With the advent of independent taxation of husband and wife, some transfer of income producing assets to the wife may take place for income tax purposes; and this will enhance her ability to make normal income gifts. Furthermore, where a wife has surplus income and the husband's income is sufficient to maintain the family, separate bank and other accounts should be kept so as to identify the wife's surplus available income. It has already been noted (**1.3:7**) that the capital element of a purchased annuity is not regarded as income for IHT purposes. Withdrawals within the annual 5% allowance from single premium policies, as well as withdrawals above that limit which may be liable to higher rate income tax, are still capital withdrawals from a capital asset, and are not available for normal income gifts. Otherwise income refers broadly to income on accounting principles. As capital gains are not the transferor's income, it is not necessary to take into account capital gains tax. The exemption covers normal *expenditure*; and expenditure connotes payments regarded as expenses or *money* spent. Gifts qualifying for exemption may therefore be expected to have a cash basis out of income. Gifts by an individual of stocks and shares out of his estate, or of furniture out of his house, will not count; although regular cash gifts which in fact enable the donee to purchase shares or furniture on an instalment basis may well do.

(4) Exemption is granted to 'the extent that' income is available. This means that if, for instance, an individual is paying heavy premiums on a single very large trust policy, the exemption can apply to a proportion of the premiums representing his available income; and the balance of the premiums will be liable to IHT. This ability to split a single gift and exempt one part but not the other removes any need to effect a number of separate staggered policies to ensure that the entire premiums on perhaps the first and second policies are exempted if not the others. Thus in the case of single large premiums (or other large regular gifts) the Revenue will allow a due proportion, ie 'to the extent that'. (The practice of staggering policies may however be advisable for other reasons, see **8.2:1**.)

(5) There is a further favourable aspect in the reference to 'taking one year with another' in the context of available income. This appears to mean that if an individual, such as an artist or a businessman in hard times, has a widely fluctuating income, the fact that in any one year he has insufficient income should not be a bar to claiming the exemption, when over the years his income can be evened out.

(6) As regards the third condition (maintenance of usual standard of living) the individual should not be obliged to realise capital assets in order to supplement his income. On the other hand 'exceptional' expenditure can be ignored because it does not reduce the 'usual' standard of living. A loan account credit with a company, on which PAYE has been paid, gives scope for claiming the exemption when the loan is available for repayment to the individual.

(7) As to the gift with reservation position, see **7.8:3**(8).

7.10:3 Procedure

Negotiations with the Revenue will be assisted if at the time that the gift was made the appropriate circumstances and intentions were recorded by an appropriate memorandum on the following lines:

MEMORANDUM that I the undersigned have this   day of
      20   made a gift of £   to

I RECORD AND CERTIFY that this gift is part of my normal expenditure and [taking one year with another] has been paid out of my income. My current and anticipated requirements of life are of a modest nature and this gift together with other similar gifts that I have made and intend making in the future will leave me with sufficient income to maintain my usual standard of living.

                            Signed.............................

RECEIPT (on duplicate)
I ACKNOWLEDGE receipt of the said sum of £

DATED   20

                        SIGNED ....

Note: The above words in square brackets should if possible be deleted, even though they are included in s 21. The exact meaning of these words is uncertain—see above.

Example

(1) Mr A, aged 70, has a net income after tax of £24,000 pa made up of earned income by way of pension and income from investments. Mr A's residence is free of mortgage and he is able to save a regular monthly sum of £600 = £7,200 pa. Mr A has been making regular monthly gifts of £400 (equals £4,800 pa or 20% of his net income) divided as to £200 to his sister and £100 each to his son and daughter. The Revenue would no doubt accept that such gifts were part of Mr A's normal expenditure. He could thus still make full use of his annual £3,000 exemption.

(2) Mr B, aged 45, has a net income after tax (taking one year with another) of £35,000 pa. He is unable to make any regular savings because his income fluctuates having regard to the profitability of his business, and as he has outstanding commitments on account of mortgage, insurance, education and other liabilities. He is making an allowance of £1,500 per quarter to his son-in-law, who is still training, by dipping into capital.

In this example the Revenue might wish to disallow at least a part of such an allowance as not being part of Mr B's normal expenditure out of income. (The £3,000 annual exemption might also be relevant.)

Since the exemption depends so much on individual circumstances it is not possible to be dogmatic on any particular example, and no special significance attaches to the fraction of income gifted.

Practitioners are recommended to give detailed consideration to this exemption of an individual's normal expenditure, because it represents a useful method of IHT planning and one which can be applied easily and simply in the appropriate circumstances, especially if a particular gift does not come within the PET regime.

7.11 GIFTS IN CONSIDERATION OF MARRIAGE (ss 22 and 57)

There are two statutory restrictions, first, as to the persons within the marriage consideration, and secondly as to the allowable amount of such gifts or settlements. Full details are given in **4.7:2**.

The marriage exemption can also be used on the lifetime termination of an interest in possession. The life tenant has to notify the trustees of the availability of the exemption within six months of the release on the prescribed form 222 available from the Capital Taxes Office.

7.12 DISPOSITION FOR MAINTENANCE OF FAMILY (including arrangements on divorce) (s 11)

7.12:1

The following dispositions are not transfers of value:

(1) for maintenance of the spouse or ex-spouse;

(2) for maintenance, education or training of the child;

(3) for maintenance or care of a dependent relative.

7.12:2

In view of the existing inter-spouse exemption (s 18) this exemption has particular relevance to 'ex-spouses', ie as regards financial arrangements on the breakdown of the marriage, particularly on divorce.

Where there are alterations or variations of a maintenance order or agreement between the parties, the method employed can be of fundamental importance. So long as the *original* court order or agreement is varied or amended, the IHT exemption of s 11 will apply; but if it is by way of a *new* order or agreement, it is unlikely that the exemption will apply.

Apart from s 11, however, it is probable that a financial arrangement made on a divorce or separation is not in any case a gratuitous transfer and is accordingly excluded from IHT charge under s 10.

As regards children the definition is wide and includes illegitimate, adopted, and step-children. In certain circumstances, the exemption is available for someone who is not in fact the child of the parent but in the care of the person making the disposition. The exemption can extend beyond the age of 18 if the child then continues in full-time education or training.

The Revenue interpret the section as applying only to lifetime gifts and not available on death although this interpretation is not obvious from the section. As to scope for this relief; and as to safety valves in wills (see **2.2:1**).

7.12:3

The s 11 exemption could apply to a non-domiciled spouse.

As regards education policies for IHT these will be exempt by virtue of s 11 if provided by a parent, but education policies by grandparents and relations other than parents will usually give rise to an IHT charge (for further details see **8.3:8**).

At first sight the section might be thought to be a useful way of placing sizeable amounts inter vivos into a family settlement free of IHT provided the beneficiaries are confined to the defined categories. In particular under s 11(5) where an identifiable part of the property subject to a disposition (ie specified assets forming part of the total property disposed of) satisfied the conditions of s 11, that part may be exempt, the remainder of the property comprised in the disposition being taxable. However, the Revenue practice is to treat the section very restrictively, confining its use to the narrow purposes and period in the section and denying relief in so far as the trusts stray at all over the edge.

7.12:4

Clearly if a particular gift fails the s 11 exemption test, the gift may nevertheless qualify as a PET.

7.13 GIFTS OF EXCLUDED PROPERTY

The main category of excluded property is property situated outside the UK where the person beneficially entitled to it is an individual domiciled outside the UK. Therefore, in the case of a gift of cash from abroad, the overseas donor should open a bank account outside the UK in favour of the donee who can then remit free of IHT. Conversely, if the donor sends a cheque here which is cashed here, the gift will no longer be one of excluded property. In the case of settled property, the criterion is that the settlor was not domiciled in the UK at the time the settlement was made and the trust assets are abroad (but for reversionary interests, see **4.7:12**). In the case of an individual domiciled abroad with assets abroad who is considering re-acquiring a UK domicile, that person should settle those assets abroad *before* he or she returns to the UK. In addition, if the size of the case warrants it, and the trust will contain sizeable UK assets, the trust should own the shares of an offshore investment company (which is situate outside the UK and hence will continue to be excluded property in the hands of the trustees); and the investment company should own the assets including those in the UK. A reversionary interest is excluded property, unless it has been acquired (at any time before by the present owner or a predecessor) for a consideration in money or money's worth, unless it is one to which the settlor or his spouse is or has been entitled; or it is under a lease for life not granted at a rack rent.

Accordingly, estate owners may wish to concentrate on gifts of this type of asset, as discussed further in **4.7:11** and **4.7:12**.

7.14 MUTUAL TRANSFERS (the former ss 148–149)

A gift back by a donee to the donor within ten years from the date of the donor's transfer of property up to the value of the donor's chargeable transfer was exempt from the then CTT provided it was made within the donor's lifetime and increased the value of the donor's estate, or his spouse's, or was made within two years after the donor's death, or 1 April 1975 if later, and increased the value of the estate of the donor's widow or widower.

This exemption was abolished in respect of transfers after 17 March 1986 by FA 1986, s 101, and Sch 19, para 25. Where relevant, readers are referred to the authors' *Practical CTT Planning* 3rd edn, p 219.

The mutual transfers exemption formed the basis of the scheme carried out in *Hatton v IRC* [1992] STC 140 and *Fitzwilliam v IRC* [1993] STC 502, HL (see **1.3:1** and **1.8**).

7.15   DISPOSITIONS ALLOWABLE FOR INCOME TAX OR CONFERRING RETIREMENT BENEFITS (IHTA, s 12)

Such dispositions are exempt from IHT if allowed in computing the disponer's profits or gains from income tax or corporation tax purposes, or would be so allowable if there were any such profits taxable in the UK. The exemption is extended to contributions to approved or comparable pension and retirement schemes and to certain rent-free accommodation for employees such as servants, gardeners, etc.

7.16   CHARITIES, POLITICAL PARTIES AND HOUSING ASSOCIATIONS

7.16:1

Gifts to charities are entirely exempt from IHT and whether made in lifetime or on death. Moreover the exemption applies where property is given to a charity by way of a capital payment out of a discretionary trust, and note the special treatment in **4.7:9**. Under s 70 the discretionary trust provisions do not apply to charitable trusts except and until property ceases to be so held.

Note that the related property provisions of s 161 extend also to charities and public bodies (see **1.3:4**).

This exemption is, however, subject to certain conditions set out in s 23(2)–(5) for charities partly by way of anti-avoidance and partly to ensure complete vesting. In particular, it should be remembered a deferred gift to charity is not exempt (s 23(2)(a)), a conditional gift is not exempt unless the charity becomes absolutely entitled within 12 months of the transfer (s 23(2)(b)), and a defeasible gift is not exempt unless it becomes indefeasible within 12 months (s 23(2)(c)).

The conditions in s 23(2)–(5) also apply to ss 24, 24A, 25, 27 (gifts to public bodies), and did apply to s 26 (now abolished).

Where the value transferred (ie the loss to the transferor's estate as a result of the disposition) exceeds the value of the gift in the hands of the charity, etc, the Revenue take the view that the exemption extends to the whole of the value transferred (Statement of Practice E 13).

The exemptions under sections 23 to 27 are all subject to section 56 which excludes exemption in certain situations involving settled property, reserved rights or reversionary interests. Section 56 prevents, inter alia, the avoidance of IHT by A settling property on himself for life, remainder to his son where A assigns his life interest to a charity to be used as an intermediary before the benefit passes to A's son.

7.16:2

'Charity' has the same meanings as in the Income Tax Acts (see TA 1988, s 505). Registration as a charity with the Charity Commission under the Charities Acts 1992 and 1993 is not a necessary requirement for tax relief, but is very desirable as it is conclusive evidence that a charity exists so long as the registration lasts. In order to be registered, the charity must be established by UK law.

7.16:3

Gifts to political parties whether during lifetime or on death are wholly exempt. To qualify for exemption the party must have obtained at the last general election either two members elected to the House of Commons or one member and not less than 150,000 votes given to their candidates (see s 24).

7.16:4

Note that where an estate is divisible between a charity or political party or other exempt beneficiary and other beneficiaries who are not exempt, the burden of IHT on the chargeable proportion falls on the non-exempt beneficiaries (s 41) (but note the effect of the *Benham* and *Ratcliffe* decisions outlined in **2.4:3** above).

Example

A testator dies 1 May 1999 leaving an estate of £1,015,000, having made no previous transfers. By his will he leaves a legacy of £100,000 to a registered housing association (exempt), a legacy of £291,000 free of IHT to his daughter and the residue as to two thirds to his son and one third to charity (exempt). In order to find the amount of IHT chargeable:

(1) Gross up the legacy of £291,000 to the daughter as if it were the only transfer ie take the nil rate band of £231,000 and multiply the balance of £60,000 by $\frac{10}{6}$ (= £100,000) to get the gross figure of £315,000.

(2) Work out the chargeable part of the estate with that grossed up legacy of £315,000. The residue is £1,015,000 less legacies of £100,000 to the housing association and £315,000 to the daughter. The son's two thirds is £400,000. The chargeable part of the estate is £715,000.

(3) IHT on an estate of £715,000 is £193,600. The daughter's legacy is now grossed up again by multiplying by $\dfrac{A}{A-B}$ where A is the estate and B is the tax on it.

Thus £291,000 $\times \dfrac{£715,000}{£521,400}$ = £399,050.62 which is the daughter's re-grossed

up legacy.

(4) Finally, recalculate the chargeable estate using the daughter's re-grossed up legacy of £399,050.62. The son has two thirds of (£1,015,000 less (£399,050.62 plus £100,000) ie £343,966.23. The chargeable part of the estate is now £399,050.62 plus £343,966.23, ie £743,016.85 on which tax is £204,806.74. The housing association and the daughter take their legacies of £100,000 and £291,000 respectively. The residue (ignoring costs) is £1,015,000 less £391,000) ie £624,000. The charity takes one third, ie £208,000, leaving the son to bear the burden of tax on his two thirds so that he takes £416,000 less £204,806.74, ie £211,193.26.

Note that s 41 applies 'notwithstanding the terms of any disposition', so that the terms of a will or other disposition cannot override the operation of the section. The point applies to any exempt beneficiaries (see **3.2** as to inter-spouse transfers).

7.16:5

Gifts made after 13 March 1989 to registered housing associations are also exempt transfers (see s 24A). The anti-avoidance legislation applying to charities and public bodies in IHTA, ss 23–26, also covers gifts to housing associations, for example, that the donor must gift his entire interest.

7.17   GIFTS FOR NATIONAL PURPOSES (s 25 AND Sch 3)

Gifts to certain national institutions as listed are wholly exempt transfers for IHT. These include the main museums, the National Trust, etc, the Nature Conservancy Council, local authorities, government departments and universities in the UK (as to works of art, see **9.14**). A similar relief is available for CGT at TCGA 1992, s 257.

7.18   GIFTS FOR PUBLIC BENEFIT (s 26)

The exemption for gifts for the public benefit, ie gifts to various non-profit-making organisations as approved by the Treasury has been abolished for transfers made after 16 March 1998. With respect to transfers made before this date. The particular asset being transferred to such non-profit-making organisations may consist of land, buildings, contents, as well as maintenance funds given as a source of income for the upkeep of such exempted property or works of art, etc. The Board of Inland Revenue may have required undertakings in respect of the preservation of the property and access to the public (ss 30(1)(b), 31(1)(d)). If the exemption is not claimed it may well be possible to negotiate a relatively low rate of death value, having regard to the cost of upkeep for example, in the case of historic buildings.

A similar relief was available for CGT (TCGA 1992, s 258).

7.19   VOIDABLE TRANSFERS (s 150) AND INHERITANCE (PROVISION FOR FAMILY AND DEPENDANTS) ACT 1975 (s 146)

Relief is provided by s 150 for IHT where the whole or any part of a chargeable transfer has by virtue of any enactment or rule of law been set aside as voidable or otherwise defeasible. This could apply for example in the case of bankruptcy or undue influence, or where a court rules that the donor had no or a defective title. However, it does not appear to apply if the parties elect to set a transfer aside or the Court rules that damages should be paid in lieu of setting the transfer aside. In such cases the transfer has not been 'by virtue of any enactment or rule of law been set aside'.

The principle is extended by s 146 to the Inheritance (Provision for Family and Dependants) Act 1975 in respect of deaths after 6 April 1976. Under s 2 of that Act, the court may order inter alia lump sums and or maintenance payments to be made in favour of a wide class of dependants (which includes 'common law' wives) when an individual has not made reasonable provision for them in his will or in accordance with the intestacy rules. The property affected by such order is for IHT purposes to be treated as if it had devolved on that individual's death subject to the provisions of the order. Moreover, under s 146(8) the principle covers circumstances where such order stays or dismisses proceedings under the Act on terms. Under s 10 of that Act, the court can require a donee who has received a gift in money or assets from a donor within six years prior to the donor's death, to 'return' the gift in whole or part to the donor's dependants; and any IHT paid is repaid with interest and if not yet paid ceases to become payable. Interest paid to the taxpayer is tax free (IHTA, s 236(3)). In respect of settlements or variations thereof, there are corresponding reliefs against capital payments and termination of interest in possession charges.

A claim under the Act must normally be commenced within six months of grant of probate and personal representatives must be careful not to distribute the estate whilst there is a possibility of a claim being made. Testators should be made aware of the effect of the Act when drawing up their wills; it may be appropriate to leave with the will, a letter setting out the testator's reasoned motives for the particular provision he has made, and/or omitted to make.

Under abortive proposals in the Finance Bill 1989, the 1975 Act was to become the restricted yardstick of what could be achieved by a variation under s 142, but these proposals were dropped.

7.20 DEATHBED SITUATIONS

No individual should leave his IHT planning to his deathbed, but some of course do. There is very limited scope for artificial arrangements such as were once common, and a deathbed marriage of convenience to secure the spouse's exemption may not have a wide appeal. Nevertheless there are a number of steps which can be taken to reduce the burden of IHT or to facilitate further advantageous post-death planning.

First, advantage should be taken of the exemptions available only during lifetime (see **1.4:1**). For example, if an individual is life tenant of a fund passing on his death to strangers, he can ensure his own family receive the full benefit of the nil rate band by making PETs to them in lifetime, which become chargeable on death and earlier in the cumulative ladder, leaving the settled fund to bear the full rate of IHT on cumulation after his gifts. Make sure that gifts by cheque are completed (**7.21**); and that all gifts are outright ones, and not *donatio mortis causa*, which are conditional upon the expected death taking place (**7.4:1**).

Other important reliefs which have application on death are noted elsewhere, including business relief, agricultural relief (**9.0**), and woodlands and works of art (which exceptionally have no stipulated period of ownership). Check also in the case of partnerships or private company shares that there are no 'buy and sell' arrangements which would exclude business/agricultural relief (**9.11:15**).

If there is time, make one or more small discretionary settlements (**4.6:3**); and let the client settle assets by his will on those trusts. This should also prevent operation of the related settlement provisions. It is also possible to create a settlement giving one's spouse a revocable interest in possession and, subject thereto, upon discretionary trusts; with the result that on revocation of the spouse's interest the rate of IHT will be determined by the spouse's cumulative ladder (s 80). Distributions within two years of death are at present treated as made under the will (s 144) and this allows more extended thoughts on destination. There is also the two-year precatory trust under s 143 (see **2.5:5**).

If there is no time for a fresh will, consider the planning possibilities available in the two years after the death through a deed of variation or disclaimer of the will or intestacy under s 142 (see **2.6**).

Should the healthier spouse (say the wife) have chargeable assets showing large capital gains, they can be transferred to the other during lifetime in order to obtain a new base value for CGT on his death, and they can return to the donor exempt from IHT under his will.

The ailing spouse could also leave his assets to the surviving spouse, thereby obtaining CGT exemption and market value uplift. Thereafter, the surviving spouse may be in a position to make PET gifts to members of the family. Indeed, this may be the correct general formula to adopt where assets show a high CGT liability (eg, a low or nominal base value) and holdover relief is no longer available. See also **2.2:1** as to leaving the bulk of one's estate to the surviving spouse.

One method whereby a testator before his death might at the same time benefit both a charity and an individual is being put forward. The suggestion makes use of s 143 whereby, if a legacy is bequeathed by will to a legatee with a non-binding request that the legatee should transfer any of it to other persons, and the legatee carries out the request within two years of the death, the legatee's transfer is treated for IHT as having been made by the testator. If the request was in favour of a charity the benefit is then exempt from IHT. However, for purposes other than IHT, the transfer has been made by the original legatee. He therefore appears able (assuming sufficient taxable income) to take advantage for income tax of the gift and provisions of FA 1990, s 25, whereby a gift of an unlimited amount can be treated as a net amount and qualify for tax relief. Thus where a testator leaves say £750 to X with a non-binding wish that X should give it to charity Y the following results would if successful apply. IHT of £300 would be saved; the charity would receive £750 net and reclaim basic rate tax of £250 as on a gross gift of £1,000; and X would seek to reclaim higher rate tax of £150—a total tax saving of £700 on the sum of £750 given in the testator's will. But see **2.5:9** above for a note of warning about the use of Gift Aid and ss 143 and 142.

It was thought that it would similarly be possible to arrange a variation of a will under s 142 to produce such a non-binding legacy. However the Special Commissioners in *St Dunstan's v Major* [1997] STC (SCD) 212 decision upheld the Revenue view that FA 1990, s 25(2)(e) would disqualify such a scheme. This subsection excludes relief for gift aid where either the donor or any person connected with him receives a benefit in consequence of making it, on the grounds that the IHT saving is such a benefit. However, the benefit contemplated by s 25(2)(e) appears to be one provided by the donee charity itself. Furthermore, while a variation operates from the death for both IHT (see **2.6:1**) and CGT (see **2.6:4**), it does not do so for income tax purposes, a point upheld by the Special Commissioners in *St Dunstan's*. Accordingly therefore, where a beneficiary of the estate, say the testator's son, enters into a variation unilaterally, without reference to others interested in the estate, providing for s 143 charitable gifts out of his *own* interest (and thereby serving to reduce it), there should be no question of any prior general arrangement among beneficiaries generally which might vitiate the son's claim for income tax relief under the gift aid provisions on the subsequent charitable donations by him. See **2.5:9** for further discussion.

Finally, consider this scheme. A UK-domiciled individual purchases interest in an excluded property settlement for £1m. He makes no tranfer of value because the purchase is at full market value. Although he now owns an interest under a trust worth £1m, its value will not be included in his chargeable IHT estate on death because it is excluded property. There may be stamp duty implications however.

7.21 GIFTS BY CHEQUE

Finally in the art of giving it should be borne in mind that a gift by cheque is not completed until it is paid *and* cleared. Until then, it is simply a revocable authority to the bank which can of course be withdrawn by stopping the cheque. In *Re Owen, Owen v IRC* [1949] 1 All ER 901, the decision turned on whether gifts by cheque (drawn outside the statutory gift period but cashed within) were subject to ED; and it was held the gifts were completed only when the cheques were honoured, so that the gifts were made within the statutory period and were liable to ED. *Owen* was quoted with approval in *Parkside Leasing Ltd v Smith* [1985] STC 63 where it was held the date of entitlement to income for Sch D Case III purposes was not the date the payee received the cheque (even though drawn on the Bank of England and therefore possibly as good as cash) but the date the cheque was cleared, which was in the next accounting period. The same principle was applied in *Barclays Bank plc v Bank of England* [1985] 1 All ER 385 which makes it clear that when a presenting bank (ie that of the payee) receives from him a cheque for collection, its responsibility to him is discharged only when the cheque is physically delivered to the payor's branch for decision whether it should be paid or not.

This principle that a gift by way of cheque takes effect only when cleared should be kept in mind where time limits are approaching. It could be relevant, for example, at each yearly stage of taper relief if the time spent in clearing the cheque made the time of the original gift a few days late. It could also be relevant in respect of the running of the seven-year period for PETs and the renewal of the nil rate band.

Chapter 8

Life Assurance and other Insurance Schemes

8.0 INTRODUCTION

Life assurance has a vital role to play in IHT planning, and it is a fact that, despite the flexibility of the PET regime, the presence of IHT makes lifetime giving more difficult, so that making a gift has to a great degree become a conscious, deliberate act, embarked on only after careful thought and advice. In this atmosphere, a relatively simple means of mitigation or cushioning the effect of IHT is to be found in many cases by way of either life *assurance* whereby the beneficiary of the policy is *assured* of the benefits at an event *certain*, for example, the end of a specified period or earlier death; or by contingency *insurance* whereby the beneficiary is *insured against* a contingency such as death before a particular date. Examples of life assurance include whole of life and endowment in each case with or without profits. Examples of life insurance include term insurance, level or decreasing, and convertible term insurance, which can be *converted* into life assurance. In addition, there are the special uses of life assurance in such products as new style inheritance trusts, which can play a useful role in planning.

The chapter will deal with insurance planning under five heads:

(1) the IHT liability on policies;

(2) aims and uses;

(3) the traditional insurance arrangements;

(4) insurance and the PET regime;

(5) traps for the unwary.

This chapter cannot explore thoroughly the varied possibilities and ways in which insurance schemes can be of benefit and detailed advice should always be taken from an independent financial adviser who should be an authorised independent intermediary. As a result of the Financial Services Act 1986, the Financial Services Authority are responsible for making sure that all persons engaged in carrying on the business of investment (which is widely defined, and includes life assurance and pensions) are authorised, under the regulatory regime. The objectives are to ensure that all persons so authorised observe high standards of integrity, act with due skill, care and diligence, and deal fairly with their customers. An independent financial adviser (an 'IFA') who is authorised by the appropriate regulatory body (look at his stationery) is not tied to one company's products but is under an obligation to consider and advise on the choice of available products in the market. A 'tied agent' (or company representative) on the other hand is restricted to offering only those products as are supplied by the life office or company to whom he is tied, although he too is under an obligation to give suitable advice in relation to the range offered by his employer.

8.1 THE IHT LIABILITY ON POLICIES

8.1:1 Upon death

Where a policy becomes payable on death, the principles in s 171 apply so that IHT is charged on the proceeds of the policy. For example, if an individual takes out a life policy on his own life, for the benefit of his own estate (generally a poor planning idea), pays the first premium and then dies, IHT will be payable on the policy proceeds. But if he takes out a policy on the life of another person and then dies, leaving the other person living, then the market value of the policy has to be accounted for in his estate. In these days when 'second-hand' policies are readily marketable through specialist firms, the market value could expect to be greater than the surrender value from the life office (particularly if the life assured was known to be in poor health). However, should the life assured die soon after the proposer's own death, it is nevertheless still only the market value of the policy at his death that needs to be included in the proposer's IHT estate.

8.1:2 Lifetime transfers (chargeable and PETs)

The minimum value of a transfer will be the total premiums paid less any surrenders, the aim being to prevent low artificial values on the surrendering of policies—see s 167(1) and note that s 167(2) prevents these artificial rules from applying on death. These rules do not apply to term policies of three years or more; and unit linked policies which are valued at the value of the quoted units if less than the premiums paid. This basis of assessment will apply where a policy is taken out by an individual who pays the premiums though the policy is written in trust for dependants absolutely: the value in their hands is linked to the premiums paid. The gifts of premiums are likely to be covered by the available exemptions (see **8.2:1**). This basis will also apply where an individual assigns the benefit of a policy by way of gift or where there is a termination in whole or part of an interest in possession in a trust policy under s 52.

It is often stated that the normal value is the surrender value (if greater than the premiums paid) but this is incorrect, as the market value is to be used which cannot be less than, but could well be more than, the surrender value.

8.2 AIMS AND USES

8.2:1 Using lifetime exemptions

These exemptions have already been outlined in **1.4:1** and **7.9–7.14**. For the purpose of insurance planning the following exemptions will have particular relevance.

(1) The £3,000 per annum exemptions (s 19).

(2) The normal expenditure out of income exemption (s 21). The proceeds of many policies written in favour of dependants under the Married Women's Property Act 1882, s 11, or otherwise on trust are exempt from IHT if and to the extent that the premiums constituted the transferor's 'normal expenditure' within the context of s 21. Moreover, this view is

strengthened by the reasonable attitude adopted by the Capital Taxes Office whereby the payment of one premium alone is sufficient evidence of an intention of normal (ie habitual) expenditure, provided only that the policy is capable of lasting a number of years. It has been noted in **7.10** that this IHT exemption is particularly generous in that it is available 'to the extent that' the necessary conditions are satisfied. Where therefore there is doubt how far the exemption may cover payment of premiums, it is not necessary to have several staggered policies in order that exemption can be given to one or more of them, leaving premiums on the others liable to IHT. Large premiums on a single policy can, if need be, qualify for normal exemption in part. Moreover the condition that the expenditure must be 'out of income' is read subject to the words 'taking one year with another'.

(3) Gifts in consideration of marriage (s 22).

Each of these exemptions (£3,000; normal income; marriage) are separately available, being mutually exclusive.

Using these exemptions with insurance arrangements has two important advantages as contrasted with making other exempt gifts. First, it provides a ready incentive and a regular method of enforced saving; secondly, there is protection in that the problems arising from a premature death are overcome. For example, an estate owner may plan to transfer to his children a significant holding of shares piecemeal over a period of years, each transfer being covered by his available exemptions. Should he die before the anticipated actuarial life span, the IHT liability crystallises on the balance of the shares. By contrast, if the liability in respect of the share holding is funded by way of life assurance on his life, the insurance moneys will be payable if his death occurs before his actuarial life span has been exceeded. For example, a man aged 50 next birthday could take out a 15-years with profit endowment policy in favour of his children for a premium of £2,000 per annum which would give immediate life cover of £25,000 and could produce £50,000 at the age of 65 which would enable his children to buy the shares or other appreciating assets from him or from his estate on his premature death. These figures are by way of illustration only and would depend on current economic conditions and interest rates. It should always be borne in mind that the life assurance industry varies, different companies having different products and different strengths, eg a company might be extremely good and competitive in an area it has concentrated on (say ten-year endowment) and not so competitive in another area in which it is less interested (say term assurance). It is advisable, therefore, to consult a good independent financial adviser.

8.2:2 Deferring IHT between husband and wife

As previously emphasised (see **2.1**), it is possible, after utilising the nil rate band, to postpone the IHT liability on the death of the first spouse until the death of the surviving spouse (s 18). As indicated in **8.3:1**, appropriate joint life and last survivor policies are specifically designed to fund this liability.

8.2:3 Flexibility of funding

There are many other occasions when IHT liability will arise that can be appropriately funded, including the death of the first spouse having left assets to the children direct, or where it is wished to have funds available on an endowment basis for a gift intended to be made in the future. A better alternative to the latter proposal could be to write the endowment policy in trust, paying regular premiums, exempt as normal income gifts, so that the benefit is already in the hands of the donee(s) (otherwise the maturity proceeds will pose a problem as a large gift). Apart from husband and wife cases, it is frequently simpler in the case of a single person, eg an unmarried aunt or uncle wishing to benefit nephews and nieces but where the principal asset is the residence, to effect a whole life policy in favour of the beneficiaries. The way to look upon policies written in trust is that the estate owner is creating an IHT-free pool of money for the beneficiary(ies), who then either have ready cash towards payment of IHT on death or, the preferable alternative when an endowment matures during lifetime, have the funds to buy appreciating assets from the estate owner himself.

Another possibility for funding is, when a donor makes a PET gift, to cover by insurance the IHT risk on the donor's death within seven years. There are policies on the market which, if death should occur, provide appropriate sums, reducing with taper relief after three years, from which to pay the IHT (see **Appendix 8**). It is advisable, however, not to be too rigid with the amounts insured under these policies, but allow some margin for eventualities, particularly where the gift consists say of freehold property where the Revenue might argue for a higher value. The policy should of course be effected for the benefit of the donee(s).

8.3 THE MAIN AVAILABLE INSURANCE ARRANGEMENTS

8.3:1 Joint life last survivor policies

These policies are designed for husband and wife to cover the IHT liability arising on the death of the surviving spouse, ie that spouse's estate including the assets received from the other spouse who died earlier. Thus to obtain the important cash flow advantage of deferring IHT until the death of the survivor, a husband and wife may decide, subject to use of the nil rate band, to leave each other virtually everything and fund the IHT liability by such a joint life and survivor policy written in trust for their beneficiaries. Moreover, life offices have introduced considerable flexibility into these and other policies, including options for guaranteed future insurability (whereby no future medicals are required) and options for inflation proof indexing. The Revenue accept joint life last survivor policies as qualifying policies (within the meaning of TA 1988, Sch 15, Pt 1, in particular) under certain conditions set out below. Although life assurance premium relief was abolished in respect of qualifying policies effected as from 14 March 1984, the qualifying status is still important to preclude the higher rate tax charge arising on the maturity or surrender of a non-qualifying policy. The qualifying policy status will apply in particular where the premiums are paid until the survivor's death, or until the first death with a minimum of ten years' premiums. The former alternative is the most common and enables the cost of the premium to be kept to a minimum and with a particularly favourable maturity value.

A point of view is sometimes expressed that the emphasis on these joint life and survivor policies is overplayed. It is pointed out that the premiums payable are in effect based on a whole life policy for the *younger* life, ie the premiums payable for a joint life or whole life policy on the younger can often be similar. Nevertheless the whole life policy on the younger may well be preferable, say in the case of a husband even with normal health for his age and a younger wife in healthy vigour. If the older party dies first, as anticipated, a joint life and survivor policy would not in any case have matured; and if the younger dies first there is the acceleration of the payment of the policy moneys which could then be paid to or for the benefit of the children earlier than would otherwise be the case. The single whole life policy is, moreover, more flexible, for example as to encashing or (normally a better alternative) selling such a policy with current bonuses. Nevertheless, it has to be remembered that the premiums on a joint life and life of survivor policy will normally be cheaper than those on a single life policy. It is necessary to consider the arithmetic in the circumstances of the case.

8.3:2   Married Women's Property Act or other trust policies

An individual can propose for a policy to be written under trust either by statute (Married Women's Property Act 1882, s 11) or by making express provision that the policy on his life is held in trust for a stipulated class of beneficiaries, such as the spouse, children or other members of the family. The premiums can be funded from income or capital and, as explained above, in many cases it is possible to obtain complete IHT exclusion by use of one or more of the available exemptions. It is often appropriate to write this type of policy on the basis of joint life and survivor, using the proceeds maturing on the death of the surviving spouse to cover IHT on the combined assets then passing. It may be useful to effect a trust policy to mature on the death of the first spouse to die, either to fund IHT if for any reason it was desired to give children benefits over the nil rate band (where the surviving spouse is well provided for); or, perhaps more usually, to establish a discretionary fund to provide benefits for the surviving spouse if need be.

The trust could comply with the conditions for children's accumulation and maintenance trusts (see **4.4:1**), so that no further IHT is payable when the policy moneys arise in the trust. Even though there may be no actual income arising from the trust policy, the condition that the beneficiaries must become entitled to an interest in possession in income or capital before 25 is satisfied by allowing s 31 of the Trustee Act 1925 to apply. A power to advance the policy moneys to an outsider, for example, a widow, breaches the IHT conditions of these trusts, although a power to allocate money unevenly between the beneficiaries themselves is normally unobjectionable.

Alternatively, the policies could be effected by the proposer in trust for one or more beneficiaries absolutely and indefeasibly thereby avoiding the settlement provisions. If it is wished to make provisions by way of a class gift, for example to existing children and children born before the eldest attained 18 or 21, with s 31 of the Trustee Act 1925, as amended, applying, there is no interest in possession until the contingency is fulfilled. (There will of course be interests in possession between 18 and 21.) Thereupon the membership of the class closes, the introduction of new-born children *within* that period will not give rise to any IHT liability, and the conditions of the accumulation and maintenance trusts are met. In respect of the death of a beneficiary *after* attaining the specified age and before the policy matures, an IHT charge will arise under s 52(1) on the basis that there is a partial termination of an interest in possession.

These policies are often written on a with profits or unit-linked basis but consideration should be given to the alternative of a without profits policy with guaranteed insurability, whereby the assured is entitled to take out extra cover within limits and at stated intervals without the need for a further medical. This enables the assured to reassess his individual and family circumstances periodically.

It is also possible to write the policy in favour of the beneficiaries, so that they have an interest in possession, but at the same time retaining an overriding power of appointment among a class consisting normally of the beneficiaries together with the spouse of the proposer of the policy; so that, if circumstances change, the interest in the policy can be appointed to the spouse of the settlor, the reverter to settlor's spouse exemption (applicable in trusts where there is an interest in possession under s 53(4); although not available in the case of discretionary settlements) excluding potential IHT on that event. Note that the settlor himself cannot be included among the discretionary beneficiaries because the retention of this interest would make the policy trust into a gift with reservation. The Revenue do not regard the inclusion of the settlor's spouse among the discretionary objects as a reservation of benefit to the settlor, unless any actual payments to the spouse were utilised, for instance, in paying household or other expenses for which the settlor was responsible. (See the *Law Society Gazette*, 11 Feb 1987, pp 385–6; and see also Stg Committee G Finance Bill, 10 June 1986, cols 419–420.) Although the interest of the settlor's spouse will bring the case within the settlements provisions of TA 1988, Pt XV, Ch III, there will be no income tax consequences because there is no income.

It is possible, where there are likely to be changing views on prospective beneficiaries, to write the policy on normal discretionary trusts for a wide class (again including the spouse of the settlor as some protection for the future) but the price of greater flexibility will be IHT anniversary and exit charges unless (as may happen in many cases) the nil rate band applies. In normal circumstances, however, the interest in possession would be the recommended one.

Two points have been raised about the payment of premiums on trust policies which should be mentioned. The first is whether on a strict interpretation of FA 1986, s 102(2), the payment of a renewal premium direct to the life company by the settlor/donor could be treated as a gift with reservation since possession and enjoyment had not been assumed by the trustees. The Capital Taxes Office have confirmed in reply to insurance body enquiries that they would not take this point of itself to constitute a gift as one with reservation.

The second point arises out of s 3A(3) whereby in dealing with favoured trusts PET treatment on gift applies 'to the extent that the value transferred ... becomes settled property'. The Revenue take the view that second and subsequent premiums paid by the settlor/donor to the life office qualify as PETs only to the extent of the additional surrender value which the premium adds to the policy, and the balance is an immediate lifetime chargeable transfer. The same result applies to interest in possession policy trusts under s 3A(2). Most such premiums will be totally exempt anyway under the annual and normal income exemptions, so that no problem arises. To the extent that the premiums are not thus exempt, however, the Revenue take the view that full PET treatment on the premiums will be obtained if the settlor/donor, instead of paying the premium direct to the life office, makes a transfer to the donee/trustees. In the case of premiums that are too large to qualify for annual or normal income exemption, therefore, the normal route might be for the trustees to open a bank account to receive the cash transfer from the donor, so that the trustees can pay the premium to the life office themselves.

8.3:3 Endowment assurance

Endowment assurance, whereby a capital sum is received after a given period of years or earlier death, is particularly appropriate when written under trust, say, for children or for grandchildren (on accumulation and maintenance trusts) to build up an IHT-free fund by way of gift. A policy maturing in, say, 10–15 years' time may be suitable. The proceeds if maturing on the expiry of the policy period will be useful to the beneficiaries for school fees or for other general purposes. If maturing on the earlier death of the life assured they will be available to cover IHT, either on gifts passing to beneficiaries over the nil rate band or on PETs made to them by the donor within seven years of the death. If the transferor wishes to preserve his flexibility, a better alternative is a trust policy with a reverter to settlor's spouse possibility (see **8.3:2**).

8.3:4 Life of another policies

These continue to be important. Under such a policy one individual (say the wife) insures the life of another (say the husband's), the latter being the life assured. Provided the person taking out the policy has an insurable interest and pays the requisite premiums from his or her own resources, there should be no IHT payable on the death of the life assured, subject to the anti-avoidance provisions of ss 263 and 268. (As between spouses it would not matter who paid the premiums because of the inter-spouse exemption.)

Two main aspects must be borne in mind in effecting these life of another policies.

(1) Insurable interest

The Life Assurance Act 1774 provided that no insurance was to be made on lives by persons having no insurable interest in the life assured. An individual has an unlimited interest in his or her own life and in the life of a spouse. Elsewhere insurable interest must be based on pecuniary interest. The table below summarises, therefore, the main categories where an insurable interest exists.

Person effecting the policy	Life assured	Restrictions of insurable interest
Individual	Own life	Unlimited
Husband	Wife	Unlimited
Wife	Husband	Unlimited
Creditor	Debtor	Amount of debt
Parent	Child	Only if and to the extent that a *pecuniary interest* exists
Fiancé	Fiancée (or vice versa)	The measure of damage resulting from monetary loss should engagement be terminated
Employer	Employee	Value of services ('key man' insurance)

267

Employee	Employer	Extent of remuneration
Partner	Co-partners	If and to the extent that on a death the continuing partners must purchase the share of goodwill or repay capital and current accounts
Trustees	Beneficiary	If and to the extent that settlement permits plus pecuniary interest (normally the likely amount of any tax on beneficiary's death)
Mortgagee	Mortgagor	The value of the loan plus costs, etc
Donee of gift or beneficiary or trustee under settlement	Donor/settlor	Prospective liability to IHT on gift or settlement (trustee must be empowered)

If an insurance is effected without the requisite element of insurable interest, the policy is null and void. However, it is unlikely that a reputable life office would seek to avoid payment on the grounds that insurable interest had not been adequately proven. In practice life offices need confirmation of insurable interest before accepting a proposal on a 'life of another' basis and, if satisfied initially, it is not necessary for the insurable interest to continue even though the assurance is a continuing contract.

Moreover, the question of insurable interest can easily be overcome by the life assured effecting the policy for his own benefit and, after payment of one or possibly two monthly premiums, assigning the policy by deed to a beneficiary. The assignee will then have a proper interest in the upkeep of the policy. Any question of IHT will be restricted to the premium(s) paid by the life assured initially plus any further gifts to enable the assignee to proceed with the policy (it is likely that there will be exemptions available to cover these).

The investment clauses in a settlement should always be drafted to include powers to enable the trustees to effect, invest in and keep up policies; and in the absence of insurable interest, the policy can be effected by the life assured and assigned to the settlement trustees (as in the previous paragraph).

It is of course always possible for an individual to effect a policy on his own life (unlimited insurable interest) *in trust* for beneficiaries.

(2) Payment of premiums

The person effecting the life of another policy, or the assignee of a policy effected by the life assured, may well pay the premiums; but if the life assured pays them, he will for IHT purposes be making successive transfers of value as outlined in **8.1:2** above, although subject to the available exemptions referred to in **8.2:1**, as well as the inter-spouse exemption.

(3) Application

Life of another policies will have particular application in respect of the liability on the donee in the case of lifetime gifts (both chargeable and PETs) where the donor dies within seven years; in that event the donee is responsible for any (additional) IHT by reason of the death and the donee should therefore consider insuring the donor's life in respect of this liability (see also **1.2:1**).

There is also the problem that if A takes out a policy on his life written in trust for B, B may not know that the policy is in existence and so will not insure against the increased liability due on the premiums (assuming exemptions do not cover) paid in the seven years before death. A should therefore tell B (if he wants B to know that the original policy exists). The same position arises in respect of inter vivos trusts where the trustees may decide to take out such a policy on the settlor's life to take account of any IHT or increased IHT on death within seven years. Life of another policies may also be relevant to other parties in the context of the seven-year statutory period. Where, for instance, a transferor has given away his house worth £250,000 on 1 August 1997 before moving to an old people's home and has a remaining estate of £50,000 and a life interest in possession in a trust fund worth £100,000, the reversioner of the trust fund may on current rates suffer IHT at 40% if the transferor does not survive 1 August 2004, dying within seven years of the £250,000 gift so that it is subject to cumulation on the death; and insurance of the transferor's life to cover this liability should be considered (see **Appendix 8**). Life of another policies can also be written in trust for dependants such as issue (in that case a children's accumulation and maintenance trust or an interest in possession trust should be used). The death of the life assured does not give rise to any IHT (he is merely the subject of the insurance policy), although the death of the owner of the policy before the life assured will give rise to an IHT liability on the *market value* of the policy at that stage if he had an interest in possession in the policy, but not an under-age beneficiary or an accumulation and maintenance trust.

8.3:5   Term insurance

As an alternative to the life of another policy, term insurance by donees or certain trustees may be appropriate to cover the risk of the donor dying within the seven-year period (see **8.3:4** and **Appendix 8**). Term cover is also relevant where an individual decides to acquire an overseas domicile and it is wished to insure against death within the minimum period that it takes to acquire such overseas domicile, namely three years (see s 267). A convertible term insurance will enable the donor to convert the term insurance into a whole life insurance if he so wishes without the need for a further medical. The exemption of this type of term insurance under s 167(3) has already been noted.

In undertaking this type of insurance there are two golden rules: first, the donor/settlor should never himself effect the insurance for his own benefit because the proceeds would then become part of his own estate. Secondly, only allow the settlor to write the policy in trust for the intended donees if it is possible to bring in aid one of the appropriate exemptions such as normal income expenditure. Doubt about insurable interest may, however, necessitate the proposal being made by the donor/settlor (at least initially, followed by assignment to the beneficiaries).

Although term assurance is comparatively cheap, sickness and accident insurance is even cheaper, but again should be set up so that the benefit remains outside the estate of the individual concerned.

8.3:6   Back-to-back arrangements and associated operations

This type of scheme has already been referred to in **1.3:7** and covers circumstances where an individual purchases one or more annuities to enable him to take out one or more life policies written in trust and where the annuity payments feed the premiums for the life policy. Since for IHT the capital element of a purchased life annuity cannot be regarded as income for the normal expenditure exemption (s 21(3)), the scope is restricted. The arrangement may still commend itself, however, where the annuity is purchased out of capital of an estate above the nil rate band since the purchase is 'subsidised' at 40% by IHT being no longer payable on the top slice of that estate representing the purchase price. Note also the terms of s 263 summarised in **1.3:7**. If s 263 applies to an annuity purchase coupled to a whole life policy the IHT position would be restored and the plan wholly ineffective. However, the Capital Taxes Office are prepared to accept that the two contracts are not 'associated operations' if the whole life policy is shown to have been underwritten on the basis of medical evidence without reference to the annuity. The easiest way to demonstrate that the two contracts were not 'associated' would be to take up the annuity and the policy with separate life offices. If the same life office is used, it is vital for the policy to have been issued and the premiums fixed on the basis of full medical evidence.

Purchased life annuities are split for income tax purposes (TA 1988, s 656) into a capital element and an interest element on the basis of tables agreed with the Revenue. Each annuity instalment is thus divided between the capital element on which no income tax is payable (it is considered as a part return of the purchaser's original capital purchase price), and an interest element which is taxable. Life offices will quote the capital and income elements if asked. Women, of course, have a greater expectation of life than men, and see **Appendix 3**.

With appropriate planning it may be possible to pay liabilities out of capital, so leaving more income available for the normal expenditure rule.

8.3:7 Pension and other arrangements

These have been outlined elsewhere, particularly as to superannuation arrangements and director's death in service (**5.3:3** and **5.3:4**), and retirement annuities stakeholder and personal pensions (**6.3:2** to **6.3:4**). In most cases death in service lump sums and accident policies will be free of IHT.

8.3:8 Education insurance

In an age where it is becoming virtually impossible to pay school fees out of income, single premium education insurance policies have proved popular and can be combined with IHT saving. Although the value of education may be intangible the loss of the capital is now the normal measure to which any IHT liability attaches in view of the consequential loss formula in s 3(1). However, for parents taking out such a policy, the capital sum used will normally be exempt under s 11 for a different reason, ie because the payments will not be treated as transfers of value, being for the maintenance, education or training of a child by the parent under sub-s (1) (and it is also arguable that no gratuitous benefit is conferred under s 10, the parent being under a moral and possibly legal obligation to provide the education). A person having the care of a child can obtain similar exemption under sub-s (2). Education policies taken out by other persons such as grandparents or uncles and aunts will fall within the scope of IHT. For those individuals it may be possible to fund the policies out of income utilising the normal income expenditure exemption or other exemptions and reliefs, such as the £3,000 per annum exemption and the nil rate band.

Another way a grandparent has been able to help towards the costs of a child's education (or indeed generally) is by means of a deed of covenant in his favour (usually covered by the normal gift exemption), enabling the child to recover the tax so deducted from the Revenue. Tax relief for such 'non-charitable' deeds of covenant made on or after 15 March 1988 has been abolished (FA 1988, s 36) although relief for existing covenants can continue. Grandparents can still of course make regular normal income gifts, and the payment of premiums on educational policies is a reasonable route.

As a general rule, the parent or settlor of the education policy should forgo the right to surrender it from the moment of payment, otherwise if death occurs before the policy starts paying out, the capital sum would normally be regarded as being an asset of the estate, the estate owner retaining a 'general power' over the capital sum within the meaning of s 6(1).

Moreover, education policies are normally flexible, covering relevant aspects as to transferability, scholarships, death of settlor, abolition of school fees or if the child does not go to a private school.

As an alternative, education policies can be planned out of income, normally by way of a series of flexible endowment assurance policies which are started when the child is very young and mature at intervals during his time at school. The younger the child, the longer the time before the fees become payable, and the more advantageous the policy terms. A period of ten years or more will allow the maximum benefits to be obtained from a series of endowment assurances where the premiums are payable regularly out of income, the policies maturing to produce fees in the relevant future years. If capital is available, funding arrangements can be made to provide the premiums. Since premiums can vary from time to time (reflecting current investment conditions and interest rates), details of the going rate for the time being should be obtained via an independent financial adviser or direct from school fees specialists. Naturally, the maximum benefit can result from a policy taken out immediately on the child's birth.

8.3:9 Annuities and home income plans

It may be worthwhile considering the purchase of an annuity from a life office in the case of an elderly person (or couple) who are short of income. The disadvantage is that the purchase moneys disappear out of the estate, but if the estate is over the nil rate band, the loss is reduced by the 40% IHT otherwise payable; and annuities can be capital-protected, giving a guaranteed return if early death occurs. The rate of the annuity depends on age and current economic circumstances and interest rates, and an escalating annuity can be chosen giving an increase each year, although the starting annuity rate for the same capital will of course be smaller. Since the Revenue regard the bulk of the instalments from a purchased life annuity as representing a return of the capital, income tax is payable only on the minor income proportion (TA 1988, ss 656–658).

Another possibility where income is required by the elderly is the annuity home income plan. This arrangement enables an individual (or more than one person, eg husband and wife, or sisters) to realise capital on the security of the family home, at least 90% of which has to be used for the purchase of an annuity. Again, the greater part of the annuity instalments will escape income tax as a return of the capital, and only the interest part will be taxable. The interest on the mortgage has to be paid out of the annuity payments; but it can be an interest-only mortgage, and interest relief is still available at the basic rate of income tax on a home income loan of up to £30,000 (TA 1988, ss 353(1G)(b) and s 365). On death the mortgage is paid off out of the sale proceeds from the home. Under the tax rules the borrower and each of the annuitants has to be over 65 at the time the loan is made, although annuitants need to be older to generate worthwhile income; and the mortgage interest should be at a fixed rate to preserve the gap. The question is whether the extra income is worth the restriction of the mortgage on the home. The home has to be in the United Kingdom or the Republic of Ireland.

The home income plans that have really caused concern have been those where elderly people have raised large loans on their properties out of which they have invested in a unit-linked single premium investment bond. The aim was that the income from the bond would be more than sufficient to pay the mortgage interest and the capital value of the bond would go up. However, at the end of the 1980s, when interest rates rose, the value of houses fell and the capital invested went down, the individuals faced disaster—see *R v Investors' Compensation Scheme Ltd, ex p Weyell* [1994] 1 All ER 601 for a cautionary tale (see also Court of Appeal, (1994) Times, 30 June). Such schemes have effectively been banned and potential borrowers are well advised to restrict themselves to schemes issued by SHIP (Sale Home Income Plans) an association of providers of home income schemes.

Prudence would dictate that the elderly should be very chary of mortgaging their home, and that they should seek to improve their income in other ways.

8.3:10   Fragmenting discretionary trust policies

It is possible to fragment life assurance policies so that each one represents a nil band value. On that basis there should be no disadvantage and considerable advantage as regards flexibility in using the discretionary trust form; in particular a further generation could be skipped. For this purpose each policy should be taken out at least one day apart (preferably longer) and the beneficiaries under the various trusts should differ to some degree. The Revenue regard the initial premium as constituting the creation of the settlement but see the last paragraph of **8.3:2** as to the payment of second and subsequent premiums.

8.3:11   Insurance and the PET regime

The FA 1986 not only introduced IHT and the PET regime with its increased flexibility in the making of gifts, but also stopped a number of old insurance arrangements. PETA plans (that linked pure endowment with regular withdrawals and term assurance providing the benefit for the donee) were stopped by Sch 20, para 7. The deferred premium policy (small first premium in lifetime; covenant to pay second large premium after death, but (then) deductible against the estate; in trust for the beneficiary) met up with s 103(7) disallowing the premium deduction. Finally, the old style inheritance trust was stopped under the gift with reservation provisions of s 102 (with a saving for existing cases in s 102(6)).

The old style inheritance trust in its simple form consisted of a settlement set up by an individual whereby he settled a small sum of cash on flexible trusts (in essence for donees absolutely with an overriding power of appointment for persons including the settlor). He then lent a substantial sum to the trustees of the settlement, interest free and repayable on demand, and the trustees used the money to buy single premium policies. The trustees then took annual 5% tax free withdrawals from the policies, and paid them over to the settlor in part repayment of the loan, providing him with a regular flow of cash. On death the trust fund consisting of the policies less the outstanding loan belonged to the donees. (There was a variation known as the reverse loan trust which need not concern us.) Under s 102 the arrangement became categorised as a gift with reservation, and appeared to have died.

New style inheritance trusts have evolved out of the new legislation. The first arrangement (normally termed a retained interest trust or a split trust) proceeds as follows. The individual effects a single premium policy on the joint lives of himself and his wife and the life of the survivor. He declares trusts over the policy whereby he carves out and retains a proportion, say 40%, of the beneficial interest for himself and his wife jointly; and the balance is held for children who have an interest in possession subject to an overriding power of appointment among a class including the settlor's wife (but not the settlor) as one of the possible beneficiaries. The husband and wife receive the 5% annual tax free withdrawals made by the trustees out of the policy. These withdrawals are measured against the whole policy but deducted only against their retained proportion. If the retained proportion becomes exhausted, and especially after the husband's death depending on the widow's needs, appointments can be made out of the children's proportion back to her. Because the purchase monies for the policy have come from her husband, there is no gift with reservation by him if appointed sums are paid (in his lifetime) to his wife provided she does not use the sums to pay off liabilities (eg housekeeping) for which he is responsible or otherwise give him some benefit out of the moneys. On the footing that he is excluded, he has made a PET.

It is noteworthy that this first new style inheritance trust does not contain the feature of the settlor's loan which figured in the old style trust. The reason appears to stem from doubts raised by FA 1986, Sch 20, para 5(4), which at first sight seems to catch property derived from a loan to the trustees of a settlement. However, the Revenue have confirmed that FA 1986, s 102 and Sch 20 apply only where there is a gift with reservation. Thus, if there is no question of reservation, as there should not be in the initial version of the new style trust as outlined above, there is no place for para 5(4). Accordingly, it follows that the donor is able to lend moneys, interest free and repayable on demand to the trustees of a new style trust out of which they could buy further policies.

It was no doubt such thoughts as these that have prompted the appearance of a second new style inheritance trust arrangement. This version is on the lines of the old style trust but with two new features. The first feature is to set up the trust so as to avoid any question of reservation to the settlor: either with a small sum of cash from which he is rigidly excluded; or by means of an 'empty' settlement where the trustees have no assets until the settlor makes the loan; or (in at least one case) by an initial nominal charitable gift to create the trust into which the interest free loan is made. Subject to setting up, the trust terms are for individuals absolutely with an overriding power of appointment among a class including (this is the second new feature) the settlor's wife. There is a subsequent loan to the trustees, who buy policies and make 5% tax-free withdrawals to repay part of the loan. So the two new features are the segregated original settled cash and the settlor's wife among the discretionary beneficiaries rather than the settlor, both to avoid reservation of interest.

Moreover, since it appears to be generally agreed that the grant of a loan interest free and repayable on demand does not constitute a gift for IHT, there is no reason to think that this scheme, as well as the first new style one above, will not be taken up by those seeking to benefit their families. Both these schemes serve to emphasise that PETs are outright gifts and one must seek at all costs to avoid gifts with reservation.

There is a final series of schemes involving a 'carve-out' of benefits retained by the donor and 'discounted' gifts to the donee(s) claimed to be PETs. The first arrangement involves a lump sum investment into an offshore capital redemption policy (not a life policy and therefore claimed to be outside FA 1986, Sch 20, para 7). The donor specifies at the outset the level of income he requires from the bond (the retained portion) and he gives away (under trust) the balance to his beneficiaries. The second arrangement involves a series of single premium endowment policies planned to mature at yearly intervals or earlier death. If the donor is alive when each policy matures he takes the benefit himself. If he dies, the proceeds of the remaining policies go to the beneficiaries. The final 'discounted' arrangement utilises pure endowment together with term assurance policies (shades of the old PETA plans). The pure endowment provides income benefits for the donor himself and the term policy provides benefits on the donor's death under trust for his beneficiaries. The death benefit which is given away is a fixed amount while the income benefits payable to the donor vary according to the performance of the fund. This last group of arrangements is particularly complicated and open to argument. No one should take up such a scheme or indeed any scheme without careful legal advice and without remembering that success cannot be guaranteed because it may well depend on the law and practice at some future time, say the death of the donor/settlor.

Threat of changes in policy taxation

One irritant which could have affected the smooth running of inheritance trust schemes was caused by the announcement from the then Chancellor at the time of the November 1994 budget of radical proposals to shake up the taxation of long-term policy contracts (see budget press release of 29 November 1994: Taxation of life assurance policy holders). Draft clauses were eventually announced with a consultation document in a budget press release of 29 November 1996: Payments under life insurance policies and reform of policy holder taxation. This draft legislation did not disturb the tax exemption of the capital proceeds of normal regular premium life policies and minimum ten-year plus endowments. However, with regard to single premium policies (such as are utilised in the inheritance trust above) the long established and very useful 5% tax free annual withdrawals would be replaced by complicated provisions for the taxation of all sums withdrawn, on a part disposal sort of basis. Fortunately, these proposals were overtaken by the change of government. In an Inland Revenue press release of 8 October 1997 it was announced that the new government did not intend to proceed with these proposals, so that the 5% tax free withdrawals are now safe. Nevertheless, the announcement added that loopholes would be looked at (there are, for instance, gaps in taxation where the settlor of a single premium policy linked to two or more lives dies before the policy matures); and further consultation with the insurance industry would take place in the light of the review of other areas including capital gains tax.

Personal portfolio bonds

These are single premium policies where the purchaser retains the ability in conjunction with his investment adviser to choose, switch, and manage the investments in the fund to which each individual bond is linked. In *IRC v Willoughby* [1997] STC 995, HL, a case concerned with the anti-avoidance provisions of TA 1988, s 739, on transfer of assets abroad, the Revenue contended that the underlying reality was that the holder of such a personal portfolio bond continued to benefit from his own portfolio of investments but was saved from tax by the insertion of the bond structure. (The case was concerned with offshore life company bonds.) Lord Nolan, with whom his four colleagues agreed, rejected that argument. He concluded that the bondholder had a contractual right to the benefits promised by the policy alone. Whether this case will herald a resurgence of the personal portfolio policy is perhaps doubtful, given changes to taxation of such bonds introduced for tax years 1999–2000 onwards.

8.4   TRAPS FOR THE UNWARY

8.4:1   Own life own benefit policies

An estate owner should be discouraged from taking out whole life policies which upon his death accrue to his estate unless bequeathed to his spouse. Clearly this merely swells the IHT payable on his death. It is far better to effect the policies in trust for children or grandchildren (perhaps on accumulation and maintenance trusts). On the other hand, in the case of an endowment policy, an own benefit policy may be desirable, for example, to cater for retirement; and in the case of a whole life policy in own estate, this avoids new policies being taken out in the event of remarriage. Indeed, if a policy is to provide the surviving wife with an income-producing fund (as opposed to paying for IHT, not required if passing to her) an own life, own benefit policy may well be the policy that is required. However, it might be even better, to avoid full IHT on her death, to effect the policy on discretionary trusts including the widow among the beneficiaries. She might well be given the bulk of any income, but on the ten-year anniversary date or if the capital were distributed by the trustees following her death, any IHT would be on the favourable 30% of lifetime rate basis.

8.4:2   Flexibility

As a general rule the advantages of deferring a decision on actual beneficiaries which may be gained by having a flexible policy, for example, discretionary or with a power of appointment, may give rise to a higher IHT charge than cases where policies are either written in trust for a beneficiary absolutely or on an appropriate harmless trust, particularly the children's accumulation and main-tenance trust, or with a fixed interest in possession. In particular, discretionary trust provisions do not contain a reverter to settlor or settlor's spouse exemp-tion, such as is available for trusts with an interest in possession.

8.4:3   The £250 per annum to any donee exemption (s 20)

As a general rule this exemption should not be used for insurance planning for two reasons: first, because as the exemption must be by way of an 'outright' gift, it cannot be used by way of a gift *into* settlement, and secondly, so that an estate owner can keep this exemption in reserve for casual gifts, for example, entertainment and day-to-day presents (particularly since it is not available to exempt part of a larger gift to the donee, nor where other gifts are made to the donee so that together they total more than £250).

8.4:4   Life assurance relief

Life assurance premium relief has been abolished in respect of policies taken out after 13 March 1984, but relief continues to be available for premiums on policies taken out beforehand, and those policies should be kept up in order to continue to get the benefit of the relief. Currently the relief is given by way of a $12\frac{1}{2}$% deduction from gross premiums (TA 1988, s 266, as amended), so that the payer merely pays over the net premium to the life company (and the life company is then compensated by a refund from the Revenue), so that any gift element relates to the net amount handed over only; with the result that the annual £3,000 exemption and other exemptions apply to the extent that they cover the *net* premium. In the case of policies effected after 13 March 1984, the transfer is of the gross premium and it is the gross amount paid which is the measure for IHT. See Inland Revenue Press Release, 17 January 1979.

In this chapter we have highlighted some of the possible advantages of estate planning through insurance. As the proposals are in the main designed to take advantage of the existing exemptions and reliefs and do not concern themselves with the artificial marketed schemes (apart from explaining them) they are unlikely to be attacked by the anti-avoidance operations or be subject to future retrospective or nullifying legislation.

Chapter 9

Estate Planning—Special Classes of Assets with particular reference to Business and Agricultural Property and Woodlands

9.0 BUSINESS AND AGRICULTURAL ASSETS: INTRODUCTION (ss 103–114, 115–124)

Business property relief and agricultural property relief operate by reducing the value transferred by a transfer of value. The rate of reduction is 100% or 50%.

Business property relief is only available on certain types of assets, described as 'relevant business property'. These include a business or an interest in a business; land, buildings, machinery and plant used for the purposes of a business; and shares in an unquoted trading company. The relief is available wherever the business is carried on, but is not available if the business consists wholly or mainly of dealing in securities, stocks or shares, land or buildings, or making or holdings investments, see **9.2** below.

Before 6 April 1996, unquoted shares were only eligible for 100% relief if the transferor held more than 25% of the ordinary shares. For transfers on or after 6 April 1996, the 100% relief is available whatever the size of the transferor's holding. The relief is not available to reduce any part of the transfer of value which is attributable to 'excepted assets'. In general terms, an asset will be an excepted asset if it was *neither* used for the purposes of a business during the preceding two years (or period of ownership, if less) *nor* required at the time of the transfer for future use for those purposes.

Agricultural property relief is available on 'agricultural property' as defined. This means primarily agricultural land or pasture. It also includes woodland and buildings used for the intensive rearing of livestock or fish, but only if the occupation of that woodland or those buildings is ancillary to the occupation of the agricultural land or pasture. It also includes cottages, farm buildings and farmhouses and the land occupied with them, but only if of a character appropriate to the property.

Broadly, the relief is 100% for vacant property, or property subject to a lease created or succeeded to on or after 1 September 1995; and 50% for other tenanted property. The value to which the reduction applies is the value which the property would have if subject to a perpetual covenant prohibiting its use otherwise than as agricultural property. This will typically be less than the open market value, particularly where there is development potential. Thus even 100% agricultural property relief will not often eliminate the entire transfer of value attributable to the agricultural property in question.

9.1 LIFETIME TRANSFERS AND CLAWBACK

If a donor has made a lifetime gift of business or agricultural property and dies within seven years, there is a risk that the business or agricultural property relief will be clawed back. This will only *not* be the case if the transferee retained the original property from the date of the transfer until the date of death or, if he disposed of it during that period and reinvested the net proceeds of sale in replacement business or agricultural property. In the second case, the reinvestment must take place within three years of the sale of the original property. In contrast to the position for capital gains tax rollover relief, reinvestment during the 12 months before the disposal of the original property is not permitted.

The Capital Taxes Office is understood to accept that professional costs and capital gains tax may be deducted in computing the net proceeds of sale.

It appears from the Inland Revenue *Tax Bulletin* No 14 that reinvestment into business property when the original property was agricultural property or vice versa is acceptable.

A transfer by the donee into an interest in possession trust for himself (but not for his spouse) involves no clawback.

In practical terms, the donee of a potentially exempt transfer of business or agricultural property can safely dispose of it four years after the gift. Then, if the donor dies within the next three years, the donee can smartly reinvest the net proceeds. There is no requirement to retain the reinvested assets for a minimum period. On the other hand, if the *donee* dies within the seven year period, the opportunity to reinvest and thereby prevent clawback is lost. Reinvestment by the donee's personal representatives will not prevent clawback.

Where the original business property consisted of shares or securities, they need not still qualify as relevant business property at the time of donor's death, or the donee's death if earlier (IHTA 1984, s 113A(3)(b), (3A), inserted by FA 1996, s 184).

If death within seven years is likely, a chargeable transfer may be preferable to a PET: for a failed PET there is full clawback; for a chargeable transfer there is clawback only on the death rate uplift.

A chargeable transfer does not affect cumulation. It is important to be aware of the risk of clawback if the donee makes a gift into a discretionary or accumulation and maintenance trust. It may be better to wait until the seven-year period has elapsed. Alternatively, in the case of a principal beneficiary over the age of 18, consider an interest in possession trust.

9.2 INVESTMENTS

Property will not be relevant business property if the business consists wholly or mainly of making investments. This is so whether the gifted asset is a direct interest in the business concerned, or shares in or securities of a company (IHTA 1984, s 105(3)). In *Brown's Executors v IRC* [1997] STC (SCD) 277, the Inland Revenue refused business property relief on shares on the grounds that, at the date of death, the business consisted wholly or mainly of making investments. The company had been in the night club business but had sold this before the shareholder's death. The proceeds were held on a short-term bank deposit pending acquisition of a new business. The executors appealed success-fully to the Special Commissioners.

The Capital Taxes Office now appears to accept that if a company is wholly or mainly trading, the fact that it owns some investments does not prevent the shares from being relevant business property. To determine whether the 'wholly or mainly' test is satisfied it is legitimate to consider turnover, profitability and underlying asset values. The CTO normally interprets 'mainly' as over 50%.

In *Farmer and another (executors of Farmer deceased) v IRC* [1999] STC (SCD) 321, the deceased was a shareholder in a company that carried on the business of letting properties as well as the business of farming. The profits of the letting business were greater than the farming profits, but the farming assets were (at death) more valuable than the properties used for letting. The Revenue refused business property relief, arguing that because the profits of the letting business were greater than those of the farming the business was wholly or mainly one of making investments. The executors appealed to the Special Commissioners and won. It was held that the nature of the business had to be considered in the round and that no single factor—such as profitability— should be determinative. On the facts, although the lettings were more profitable than the farm, the overall context of the business, the capital employed, the time spent by the employees and consultants and the levels of turnover supported the conclusion that the business consisted mainly of farming.

9.2:1   Letting property

The Special Commissioners' decisions in *Martin v IRC* [1995] STC (SCD) 5 and *Burkinyoung v IRC* [1995] STC (SCD) 29 should be noted. In these cases the taxpayers' claims for business property relief failed. In *Martin*, the business consisted of owning and letting industrial units on three year leases at fixed rents. The activities included finding tenants, granting and renewing leases, complying with the landlord's covenants under those leases and managing the premises. To the extent that these activities went beyond straightforward investment activities, they were nevertheless held to be incidents of the business of making or holding investments. Thus business property relief was denied.

A similar decision was reached in *Burkinyoung*, where the deceased had divided a house into four flats and let them, furnished, on assured shorthold tenancies. Although she was actively involved in the control and management of the let properties, these activities were incidents of the landlord-tenant relationship and accordingly part and parcel of making and holding investments.

Two points clearly emerge from these two cases. First, no distinction is to be drawn between investments that are actively managed and those that are passively held. Secondly, in the case of property investment, one must distinguish between activities carried on *qua* landlord and activities which are independent of the landlord-tenant relationship. Activities undertaken by the landlord to ensure compliance with his own obligations under the lease; to enforce compliance by the tenant; or to preserve his investment in the property (eg repairs) are in the first category. The second category consists of activities which are independent of the lease and which are charged for separately. Examples might include heating, cleaning and catering. Even if these services are provided separately, the charges are likely to be insignificant compared to the rental income and thus it will be rare for business property relief to be available.

9.2:2 Caravan parks

In *Hall (deceased) v IRC* [1997] STC (SCD) 126, the business consisted of a caravan park of 18 acres for 100 caravans and 11 wooden chalets. These were let and various services and facilities were made available to the tenants, eg water, electricity, telephone, refuse disposal and lavatories. Nevertheless, the Special Commissioners denied business property relief on the grounds that the business was substantially one of investment, ie the receipt of rents. A similar approach was adopted in another caravan park case, *Powell v IRC* [1997] STC (SCD) 181.

In contrast, in *Furness v IRC* [1999] STC (SPC) 232, the business of running a caravan park was held not to consist wholly or mainly of making or holding investments. However, the business was unusual because over 50% of the profits came from caravan sales and charges for caravan rallies, neither of which were investment activities. The amount of work carried out on the park by the deceased and his employees was also considered.

In *Weston (executor of Weston deceased) v IRC* [2000] STC 1064, a decision of the Special Commissioners, that shares in a company that ran a caravan site were not relevant business property, was upheld by the High Court. The business included buying and selling caravans; buying and selling caravans for commission on behalf of the owners; and granting the right to pitch caravans in return for pitch fees. The question was ultimately one of fact and the Special Commissioner had applied the right test in considering the overall context of the business, the capital employed, the time spent by the employees, the turnover and the profit and had then stood back and looked at the business in the round to determine whether it consisted wholly or mainly of making or holding investments.

9.2:3 Groups of companies

Groups of companies raise special issues which require the provisions dealing with investments businesses to be adapted. Without special provision, there would be no possibility of business property relief for a shareholder in a holding company that held the entire share capital of a trading subsidiary but carried on no business itself.

This result is initially avoided by IHTA 1984, s 105(4)(b). This applies to a company whose business consists wholly or mainly in being a holding company, provided that at least one of its subsidiaries carries on a permitted trade. Permitted trade in this context is shorthand for a business which is not excluded from relief by section 105(3) because of consisting wholly or mainly of dealing in securities, stocks or shares, land or buildings or making or holding investments.

Section 105(4)(b) disapplies section 105(3) in the case of such a holding company. However, section 111 lays down further conditions that are designed to ensure that one or more investment subsidiaries do not effectively benefit from relief purely because a single sister company carries on a permitted trade. On the other hand, the section seeks to preserve relief where the investment subsidiary holds property which is let to its trading sister in circumstances where, had both the property and the trade been held in a single company, relief would have been available. Where relief is not preserved for an investment subsidiary, its value is excluded from the value available for relief.

There is no definition of a group for these purposes but it has recently been held by a Special Commissioner that companies do not form a group merely on account of having some or all of their shareholders in common: *Grimwood-Taylor and another (executors of Mallender deceased) v IRC* [2000] STC (SCD) 39.

These provisions mean that group structures and the way in which property is held within those groups require careful consideration. Assume that a holding company owns various trading subsidiaries which trade in valuable buildings. It is desired to insulate these buildings from trade creditors by holding them outside the trading companies. Assume that the group also owns various buildings which it lets to third parties not in the group. The value of the buildings let to the third parties exceeds the value of the buildings used by the companies.

(1) A single property-holding subsidiary

If all the buildings are placed in one property-holding subsidiary, no relief at all will be available on the value of the properties. The property-holdings subsidiary's business does not satisfy section 111(b). It does not consist wholly or mainly of holding land or buildings wholly or mainly occupied by members of the group for permitted trades because the value of the buildings let to third parties exceeds the value of the buildings used by the group members. Thus the whole value of the property-holding subsidiary is excluded from relief.

(2) Two separate property-holding subsidiaries

If the properties used by other group members are held in one subsidiary and those let to third parties in a second subsidiary, the first subsidiary will qualify for relief and the second subsidiary will not.

(3) Properties held by parent company

It may be that relief for all the properties can be obtained if they are held by the parent company. This depends on whether, despite its property interests, its business consists wholly or mainly in being a holding company. This will depend on whether its interest in its trading subsidiaries significantly exceeds its interest in the properties. Before this strategy is even considered, this test should be satisfied whether the measure used is turnover, profitability or underlying asset values. Even then, there is a risk that the trading activities will diminish or the property values increase so that the wholly or mainly test applied to the holding company ceases to be met. This is a high-risk strategy because it could result in loss of relief on the value of the entire group.

(4) Scattering the properties

This suggestion is a combination of *(1)*, *(2)* and *(3)* above. The holding company has three subsidiaries. The first is the trading company. The second owns the properties used by the trading company. The third owns some of the properties let to third parties. The remaining properties let to third parties are distributed between the holding company and the second subsidiary. They can be distributed in this way as long as:

(a) the properties held by the holding company do not prevent its business from consisting wholly or mainly in being a holding company. This is the most important requirement because if it is breached there is a risk that relief on the value of the whole group will be lost (see *(3)* above). A very large margin of error should be allowed for;

(b) the properties owned by the second subsidiary should consist wholly or mainly of properties occupied by the trading subsidiary for the purpose of its business. A slightly smaller margin of error is required here for two reasons. First, the value of the permitted properties is unlikely to fluctuate dramatically as against the value of the properties let to third parties, unless there are special circumstances. This contrasts with the potential for relative changes in the values of trading subsidiaries and properties, which is a risk in case *(3)* above, particularly because in *(3)* the value of the permitted properties is aggregated with the value of the properties let to third parties in applying the wholly or mainly test. Here, that is not so. The second reason why there is a reduced risk in this case is that the worst case scenario is losing relief on the whole of the second subsidiary. That would have been the case in any event had option *(1)*—a single property-holding subsidiary—been adopted. It should not affect relief for the trading subsidiary.

The third subsidiary holds those properties let to third parties that cannot safely be held by the holding company or the second subsidiary. It is accepted that relief will not be available on the value of the third subsidiary on account of section 111. In that sense, this strategy is equivalent to option *(2)*. However, the value of the third subsidiary on which relief is lost will be diminished by those properties that have been scattered into the holding company and second subsidiary.

9.3 EXCEPTED ASSETS

If the assets are essentially relevant business property, the amount of relief may still be restricted if the value of that property is partly attributable to *excepted assets*. These are assets which had *neither* been used wholly or mainly for the purposes of the business during the two years preceding the transfer *nor* were required at the time of the transfer for future use for those purposes.
If the asset was used wholly or mainly for the personal benefit of the transferor or a person connected with him, it is deemed by IHTA 1984, s 112(6) not to have been used wholly or mainly for the purposes of the business concerned.
The second condition was the subject of a decision by the Special Commissioners in *Barclays Bank Trust Co Ltd v IRC* [1998] STC (SCD) 125. At the date of the deceased's death, the company held £450,000 in cash. The Revenue accepted that £150,000 of cash was required by the company at that time, but maintained that the remaining £300,000 was an excepted asset. The Special Commissioner upheld the Revenue's view, rejecting the argument that the cash was required for the future purposes of the business. The possibility of using the money in two, three or seven years, should a suitable opportunity arise, was not sufficient. To be required for future use, there must be some imperative that the money will be required for a given project or for some palpable business purpose. For example, money will be required for the future purposes of the business where a company had negotiated the purchase of a business asset and there was a realistic possibility at the time of the transfer that it would buy the business asset with the money.

Contrast the case of *Brown's Executors v IRC* [1997] STC (SCD) 277, discussed at **9.2** above, where the cash proceeds of the sale of a night-club were held on short term deposit with a bank pending acquisition of a new business. It was held that the company's business consisted wholly or mainly of making investments and accordingly business property relief was denied under IHTA 1984, s 105(3). Although the issue in that case was a different one, there is clearly no point ensuring that an asset is not an excepted asset if it is not relevant business property in the first place.

9.4 RETIREMENT OF A BUSINESS PARTNER

A partner's share in a partnership is relevant business property. On retirement, the partner's capital account is converted into a debt owed to him by the partnership. Neither the debt—nor any cash ultimately paid in satisfaction of it—is relevant business property. To preserve business property relief, it may be wise to delay retirement, possibly taking on a partner to perform the bulk of the work and retaining only a small share.

Any land, building, machinery or plant which is used for the purposes of the partnership's business will lose the 50% relief on the partner's retirement. In some circumstances, this problem could be avoided by giving away the capital account *before* the partner retires.

This was illustrated in *Beckman v IRC* [2000] STC (SCD) 59. The deceased (H) and her daughter (B) had been business partners until H's retirement in 1993. H's financial interest in the business immediately before her retirement, represented by her capital account, remained the same after her retirement. However, it was held by a Special Commissioner that her legal interest was radically changed on her retirement. Prior to that, she had all the rights of management conferred by the Partnership Act 1890 and all the liabilities of a partner. After retirement, in the absence of any agreement to the contrary, she became simply a creditor of B. Accordingly, on H's death four years later, business property relief on the sum due to her was denied. For the purposes of IHTA 1984, s 105, H's interest in the business ceased when she retired from the partnership that carried on that business. This unsatisfactory outcome could have been avoided if H had made a gift of the capital prior to retiring; or had remained a partner with a reduced share.

9.5 FREEHOLD REVERSION OF BUSINESS LEASE

If a business lease is owned for at least two years and the freehold reversion is bought in, the latter does not need to be owned for the two-year period.

9.6 OWNERSHIP ISSUES

9.6:1 Minimum period of ownership (s 106)

Property is not relevant business property unless it was owned by the transferor for two years before the transfer. This is the basic requirement imposed by IHTA 1984, s 106. It is subject to the provisions of sections 107 to 109, which deal with replacement property, acquisitions on death and successive transfers respectively.

9.6:2 Spouses

An exception to the minimum period of ownership requirement applies to a transferor who acquired the property on the death of his spouse. Section 108(b) deems the transferor to have owned the property for the period of his spouse's ownership in addition to his own period of ownership. If the aggregate is equal to or greater than two years then the test is satisfied. This aggregation only applies to periods of ownership falling either side of a transfer on the death of the first spouse. It does not apply if the first spouse made a lifetime gift.

Example

Wife ('W') acquired the entire issued share capital of Widgets Ltd on 1 January 1999. On 1 January 2000, W made a lifetime gift to her husband ('H') of 40% of her shareholding in Widgets Ltd. On 1 July 2000, W died, leaving her remaining 60% shareholding in Widgets Ltd to H.

On 1 July 2001, H wished to transfer his shares in Widgets Ltd into a discretionary trust with the benefit of business property relief.

H will satisfy the minimum period of ownership in relation to the 60% shareholding that he inherited on W's death. In relation to those shares, section 108(b) permits him to aggregate his period of ownership (one year) with W's period of ownership (one and a half years), giving a total of two and a half years.

H will not satisfy the minimum period of ownership in relation to the 40% shareholding which was given to him by W during her life. Because the transfer was not on death, H may not aggregate his period of ownership with W's. His period of ownership alone is only a year and a half. He should retain these shares until at least 1 January 2002.

9.6:3 Successions (s 108)

A legatee is deemed to have owned the assets from the date of death. Where the legacy was from his spouse, the spouse's period of ownership is also deemed to be his.

If the legatee acquired business property from a person—whether his spouse or not—who satisfied the minimum period of ownership requirement, then that requirement is effectively waived on a subsequent transfer by the legatee as will be seen in the next paragraph.

9.6:4 Successive transfers (s 109)

Where there are two successive transfers, and the earlier transferor satisfied the ownership requirements, these requirements are waived for the transferee subject to certain conditions. The most significant condition is that at least one of the transfers was on death. It does not matter whether this was the earlier transfer or the subsequent one.

If A—qualifying for BPR in all respects including minimum period of ownership—leaves his shares to B on death, then B can qualify for BPR on a transfer even if it occurs less than two years after A's death. Because the transfer by A to B ('the earlier transfer') was on A's death, the transfer by B ('the subsequent transfer') can be either a lifetime or a death transfer and still benefit from section 109.

If C—again, qualifying in all respects—makes a lifetime gift of his shares to

D, D will qualify for BPR on a transfer on his death even if that is within two years of the gift. Because the transfer by C to D ('the earlier transfer') was a lifetime transfer, the transfer by D ('the subsequent transfer') will only benefit from section 109 if it is on D's death. If D wishes to make a lifetime transfer which qualifies for BPR he will need to build up his own period of ownership.

In both of the examples just given, it is irrelevant whether A and B or C and D are spouses because A and C had each owned the shares for the required period. The special treatment given to spouses would only be relevant if (i) the earlier transferor had not satisfied the minimum period, and (ii) the earlier transfer was on death.

Revisiting the example of A and B, and supposing this time that A had owned the shares for one year only, B could benefit from BPR on a subsequent transfer by holding the shares until a year after A's death. This is by virtue of section 108. Section 108 would have no application if C and D were spouses and C had only held the shares for one year before the gift. This is because the gift by C to D was a lifetime gift and section 108 has no application to these.

9.6:5 Replacements (s 107)

The minimum period of ownership requirement will be satisfied if the business property, together with other business property that it directly or indirectly replaced, had been owned by the transferor for a total of two of the five years preceding the transfer. If this section is used to satisfy the period of ownership, then there is a limit on the relief. It is limited to the relief that would have been available if the replacement had not been made. In other words, it is limited to the value of the earliest property relied on. This limit does not apply to changes resulting from the formation, alteration or dissolution of a partnership, nor from the acquisition of a business by a company controlled by the former owner of the business.

Under TCGA 1992, ss 126 to 136, an original shareholding and a new holding arising from a reorganisation of share capital, a reconstruction or an amalgamation, may be treated as a single asset for capital gains tax purposes. Where those provisions applied for capital gains tax, and where the new holding consists of unquoted shares, the period of ownership of the new holding for IHT business property relief is extended to include the period of ownership of the original holding.

9.6:6 Residuary estates

A legatee or transferee whose minimum period of ownership has been waived or reduced by sections 108 or 109 must nevertheless hold the property as business or agricultural property if he is to get either relief. It has been suggested that this might be hindered if the legatee dies or makes a gift before the administration of the estate is complete. This argument is probably unsustainable in view of IHTA 1984, s 91. Nevertheless, to err on the side of caution, it might be worth vesting the business or agricultural assets in the surviving spouse as soon as possible after the first spouse's death. Alternatively, a deed of variation could specifically vest the assets in the surviving spouse. Such steps must of course only be taken after careful consideration of the solvency of the estate, the potential inheritance tax payable and the assets available for other legatees.

9.7 MINORITY SHAREHOLDER—NO RELIEF

Where a controlling shareholder owns land or buildings, machinery or plant used by the company to which the 50% business property relief accrues under section 105(1)(d) as amended, that shareholder should consider making a gift of the asset in question before losing control. As a minority shareholder, the 50% relief on those other assets will not apply. Consider the IHT advantage of the company owning the assets, thereby bringing them within the net of the 100% relief. This is particularly important since the extension of relief on shares since 6 April 1996.

9.8 RELEVANT BUSINESS PROPERTY

To be 'relevant business property', assets must fall within one of the six categories listed in IHTA 1984, s 105(1). Those within the first three categories, section 105(1)(a), (b) and (bb), potentially qualify for 100% relief. Those within the next three categories, section 105(1)(cc), (d) and (e) can only qualify for 50% relief.

9.8:1   The current position: assets qualifying for 100% relief

(1)   A business or interest in a business (section 105(1)(a))

The term 'interest' is not defined, but is likely to mean to a proprietary share. Thus a share in a partnership could potentially qualify for relief under this heading, as could a business run by a sole proprietor. There is no limit on the size of the interest or the degree of control held by its owner. The 100% relief will apply to most Lloyd's Special Reserves.

(2)   Unquoted securities giving the transferor control (section 105(1)(b))

The securities must be unquoted and must give the transferor control of the company, either alone or together with other unquoted securities and any unquoted shares. Although the transferor must have control of the company immediately before the transfer, the gift need not be of a controlling interest.

(3)   Unquoted shares (section 105(1)(c))

For transfers on or after 6 April 1996, transfers of unquoted shares can obtain 100% relief whatever the size of the transferor's holding. Note that:

(a) the shareholding can be entirely passive. There is no requirement that the shareholder be actively engaged in the business of the company in contrast to the position for capital gains tax retirement relief. However, the business of the company itself must not be wholly or mainly an investment business. See **9.2**;

(b) from 6 April 1996, the shareholders no longer need to have voting powers on all questions affecting the company as a whole in order to be eligible for BPR;

(c) the Alternative Investment Market ('AIM') was substituted for the Unlisted Securities Market ('USM') from June 1995. The Treasury has decided that AIM issues will qualify for all unquoted security tax reliefs including business property relief.

Other such reliefs include income tax relief on losses on shares subscribed for (TA 1988, ss 573–576); capital gains tax holdover relief for gifts of business assets (TCGA 1992, ss 165–169—although note the amendments to holdover relief introduced by FA 2000); Enterprise Investment Scheme for capital gains tax—but beware, the shares must be *'new* ordinary shares' in order to qualify for the relief—see TCGA 1992, Sch 5B para 19 and TA 1988, s 289(7); business asset taper relief (TCGA 1992, Schedule A1); and Venture Capital Trusts (TCGA 1992, s 151A). See the Inland Revenue Press Release of 20 February 1995.

9.8:2   The current position: assets qualifying for 50% relief

(1)   Quoted shares or securities giving the transferor control (section 105(1)(cc))

Controlling holdings in fully quoted trading companies or groups qualify for 50% relief, but note that there is no relief for a minority holding in a quoted company. Control is defined by IHTA 1984, s 269. A shareholder with a 50% shareholding and a casting vote has control for these purposes. *CIR v BW Noble* 12 TC 911 is authority for this proposition and it has recently been confirmed by a Special Commissioner's decision in *Walker's Executors v IRC*, decided on 14 April 2001 and so far reported in Issue 18 (3 May 2001) of Simon's Tax Intelligence at page 13.

(2)   Assets owned by a partner and used in the partnership or owned by a controlling shareholder and used in the company (section 105(1)(d))

First, the assets must be land, buildings, machinery or plant. Otherwise there is no prospect of relief. Secondly, the relief is only available for as long as the transferor remains a partner in the partnership, or retains control of the company. Thirdly, the assets must be used for the purposes of a business carried on by the company or partnership. Fourthly, the transferor's shareholding or other interest in the business must itself be relevant business property in order for the assets to qualify. This means that the business must amount to a permitted trade. In other words, it must not consist wholly or mainly of dealing in securities, stocks or shares, land or buildings, or making or holding investments.

If the assets are used for the business of a company which is wholly owned by the transferor, there is a clear inheritance tax advantage in arranging for the company itself to own the assets. Their value reflected in the shares can then qualify for 100% rather than 50% relief.

Similarly, there will be often be inheritance tax advantages in the partnership rather than the individual partner owning the assets, although this will only be a sensible option where the particular partner's share is a significant one.

Transferring assets to the company or partnership is complicated by a number of things. One is the potential dilution of ownership and the risk of an inheritance tax charge on the transfer. The transfer into a company is not a PET and may be charged under IHTA 1984, s 98 unless it can be shown that the estate of the transferor has not been diminished or that the transferor had no gratuitous intent and the transaction was one that might have been entered into by parties at arm's length. Other difficulties concern the capital gains tax consequences of a transfer into a company, particularly the re-starting of the period of ownership for taper relief purposes.

(3)   Settled property in which the transferor had an interest in possession and which was used for the purposes of the transferor's business (section 105(1)(e))

This provision will rarely apply. If the transferor has an interest in possession in the assets used for his business, those assets will normally be treated as part of his business and will be entitled to 100% relief (see *Fetherstonaugh v IRC* [1984] STC 261).

9.9   VALUE OF BUSINESS

The value of a business for the purposes of business property relief is determined by IHTA 1984, s 110. It is the value of the assets used in the business less the aggregate of the liabilities incurred for the purposes of the business.

In *Hardcastle and another (executors of Vernede deceased) v IRC* [2000] STC (SCD) 532, a Special Commissioner had to decide whether an unprofitable insurance contract of a member of Lloyd's fell to be taken into account in valuing the business. The Revenue argued that it should be taken into account thereby reducing the amount of the relief. The Special Commissioner rejected this and allowed the executors' appeal. The deceased was a member of eleven syndicates and thus entered into a number of such contracts. The distinction applied for income tax purposes, between an ordinary commercial contract and one amounting to an asset of the business, was applied by analogy and this contract was found to be an ordinary commercial contract. It was not a capital asset and liability in section 110(b) was to be construed on an equivalent basis, and thus it was not a liability. The valuation of business property under section 110 is different from the valuation of a person's estate as a whole under section 5. The contract inevitably reduced the value of the deceased's estate but not—following this decision—the amount on which relief was available.

It follows that trading profits will not increase the value of a business for business property relief purposes, nor will trading losses decrease that value.

9.10   AGRICULTURAL PROPERTY

It must be born in mind that agricultural property relief is only available against so much of the value transferred as is attributable to the agricultural value of the property. The agricultural value of the property is the value that it would have if it were subject to a perpetual covenant prohibiting its use otherwise than as agricultural property (IHTA 1984, s 115(3)). This may be less than its value in the open market without such a restriction. If so, then even if 100% agricultural property relief is available, a transfer will generate a transfer of value equal to the difference between those two values.

The Capital Taxes Office is thought to be making more of this point than it has in the past. It is important to be aware of it if the agricultural property consists of a farmhouse, which may have a greater value as a second home or straightforward residence than it would have if tied to agricultural use. Similarly, part of the value of agricultural land may represent its development potential and the CTO may seek to deny relief on that part of its value.

9.10:1 Assets qualifying for 100% relief

The circumstances in which 100% relief is available are set out in IHTA 1984, s 116(2)(a) to (c).

(1)   Transferor has vacant possession or the right to obtain it within twelve months (section 116(2)(a))

This provision covers owner-occupied farms and farms where the transferor's interest entitles him to vacant possession or will do within the next twelve months. The Revenue have, by concession, extended this to 24 months. See **9.10:3** below.

(2)   Transferor has held his interest since before 10 March 1981 (section 116(2)(b))

Relief is available under this heading if the transferor has held his interest beneficially since before 10 March 1981 and, had he given away that interest before then and made an appropriate claim, paragraph 2 of Schedule 8 to FA 1975 would have applied in computing the value transferred without limitation by paragraph 5. The main elements of these pre-1981 rules are a limit of £250,000 in value and 1,000 acres in area; and the requirement that the transferor was wholly or mainly engaged in farming during five out of the previous seven years. The latter test is deemed to be satisfied if not less than 75% of his income was derived from agriculture.

Relief will be denied if at any time between 10 March 1981 and the transfer of value in question the transferor acquired the right to vacant possession, acquired the right to obtain vacant possession within twelve months, or failed to acquire either such right by reason of an act or deliberate omission.

100% relief will be applied to an appropriate *part* of the value transferred if paragraph 5 of Schedule 8 to FA 1975 would have limited the relief available on a transfer before 10 March 1981, but otherwise the conditions for relief under this heading are satisfied. The remaining part will be entitled to 50% relief. See section 116(4).

(3)   The property is let on a tenancy beginning on or after 1 September 1995 (section 116(2)(c))

This heading applies where the only reason relief is unavailable under **9.10:1**(1) above is that the property is let on a tenancy that began on or after 1 September 1995. This relief coincides with the introduction of the Agricultural Tenancies Act 1995 which deregulated the market for let farmland. The policy was to encourage the granting of new agricultural tenancies.

If a tenant dies on or after 1 September 1995 and his tenancy vests under his will or intestacy in another person, that other person's tenancy is deemed to have commenced at the date of death under IHTA 1984, s 116(5A) for the purposes of determining whether 100% relief is available. Similar provision is made—although this is not applicable to property in Scotland—where, on the death of the surviving tenant on or after 1 September 1995, another person obtains a tenancy under a legislative right.

If a tenant has given notice to retire in favour of a new tenant, but before such retirement takes place the landlord dies, then the new tenant is deemed to have commenced his tenancy immediately before the transfer of value that the transferor is deemed to make immediately before death (IHTA 1984, section 116(5D)). The effect of this is to allow the landlord to benefit from 100% relief under this head if he would have benefited had the new tenancy already commenced. This extension of the relief is subject to the condition that the tenant does indeed retire in favour of the new tenant after the landlord's death and within 30 months of the giving of notice.

There are a number of possible traps to be aware of. First, a surrender of an existing lease followed by a re-grant on a non-arm's length basis in order to obtain 100% relief in the future risks amounting to a PET. Secondly, for capital gains tax the arrangements could constitute dispositions under the value shifting provisions in TCGA 1992, s 29. This might be avoided if a new lease is granted in an arm's length transaction on the same property at a different rent but otherwise on the same terms.

9.10:2   Assets qualifying for 50% relief

50% relief is available on agricultural property which qualifies in all other respects but does not fall within any of the three heads of 100% relief identified at **9.10:1** above. This will mainly comprise property which has been let since before 1 September 1995 and will not become vacant within the next twelve (or 24) months.

9.10:3   Inland Revenue Concessions

In a Press Release dated 13 February 1995, the Inland Revenue published two further extra-statutory concessions relating to inheritance tax.

The first (ESC F17) confirms the Inland Revenue's practice of regarding the condition in s 116(2)(a) as satisfied where the transferor's interest in the property immediately before the transfer carried the right to vacant possession within 24 months of the date of the transfer. It also treats the conditions as satisfied where, notwithstanding the terms of the tenancy, the transferor's interest is valued at an amount broadly equivalent to the vacant possession value. See *IRC v Gray (Executor of Lady Fox)* [1994] STC 360, CA.

The second concession (ESC F16) also gives 100% agricultural relief in respect of transfers of agricultural property which include a cottage occupied by a retired farm employee or spouse. This is subject to the occupier being a protected tenant or having a lease for life as part of his contract of employment.

9.11   WHAT ARE THE MAIN ESTATE PLANNING LESSONS?

Business and agricultural property reliefs are currently very generous. They will probably not survive indefinitely. Because they are available on lifetime gifts as well as transfers on death, those who currently qualify for relief might consider making lifetime gifts to insulate themselves as far as possible against future changes in the law. On the other hand, there are some advantages in delaying making gifts and these need to be considered too.

9.11:1 Shareholdings and partnerships

Those with shares or interests in partnerships that could qualify for relief should consider the following points:

(a) Selling the shares or retiring from the partnership could cause significant loss of relief. Not only will the possibility of 100% relief on the shares or partnership interest themselves be lost, but so will the 50% relief on assets belonging to the individual and used in the business of the company or partnership.

(b) If it is likely that shares which qualify for business property relief now will cease to do so, or will do so at a less favourable rate, consider making a lifetime gift now. It may be possible to hold over capital gains tax under TCGA 1992, section 165. The downsides to this are the possibility of clawback (see **9.1** above); the lack of capital gains tax exemption on death; and that the holdover will stop the period of ownership for CGT taper relief purposes from running.

(c) The gifts with reservation provisions must not be ignored where a lifetime gift of business or agricultural property is made. Paragraph 8 of Schedule 20 to FA 1986 adapts the gifts with reservation provisions. In general terms, if the donor reserves a benefit, then the conditions for relief must continue to be met until the donor's death in order to preserve the relief and reduce the charge on death.

9.11:2 Use of discretionary trusts

Business and agricultural property reliefs are both expressly made available to the special inheritance tax regime applicable to discretionary trusts. In determining whether certain conditions, such as the minimum period of ownership, are met, references to the transferor are treated as references to the trustees (IHTA 1984, ss 103(1)(b) and 115(1)(b)).

A discretionary trust consisting exclusively of business property that qualifies for the 100% relief can be run in a way that avoids any ten-yearly or exit charges. Although the business property relief does not necessarily reduce the *rate* at which tax is charged under the discretionary trust regime, this is not a problem so long as the value transferred is reduced to zero. Note that anything multiplied by zero equals zero.

The position is not so simple when dealing with the 50% relief—or the 100% agricultural property relief if IHTA 1984, section 115(3) has prevented the transfer of value from being reduced to zero. In these cases it is important to remember that, on the ten-yearly charge and on exit charges *after* the first ten-yearly charges, the relief can reduce both the rate of tax and the value transferred. However, before the first ten-yearly anniversary, the relief will only reduce the value transferred. It will not reduce rate of tax. Accordingly, to obtain maximum benefit from the relief, distributions during the first ten years should be avoided where possible.

(1) Discretionary trusts

The transfer of business assets into a discretionary trust by lifetime gift or by will is often one of the best estate planning methods available. In particular, certain business and agricultural assets can be held in such trusts indefinitely with 100% relief, with no ten-yearly charges nor exit charges after first ten-year anniversary. At the ten-year anniversary, the trustees will need to satisfy the relevant business or agricultural property conditions. Assuming that the 100% relief applies—and that any other assets in the trust are within the nil rate band—the ten-year anniversary charge rate will be zero. That zero rate will apply until immediately prior to the next ten-year anniversary, even though the assets are no longer business or agricultural assets, for example, because the trust fund consists of the proceeds of sale.

If the trust fund continues to consist of business or agricultural assets, one possibility is to vary the discretionary trust to create an interest in possession. The variation will not be a disposal for capital gains tax purposes if the interest in possession is part of the same umbrella settlement as the discretionary trust and not, for example, an appointment on to a new or separate settlement. On the death of the life tenant, a capital gains tax free uplift of the base cost to market value should apply (TCGA 1992, s 73 and IHTA 1984, ss 46 and 49(1)). If, on the death of the life tenant, the assets still consist of business or agricultural property and the interest in possession has subsisted for at least two years, relief should be available.

Example

A discretionary trust was subject to a ten-yearly charge on 31 October 2000. On that date, the trust fund comprised £150,000 in cash, a 20% holding in the ordinary share capital of Trading Co Ltd (an unquoted company) and a farm owned and managed by the trustees. The trust was created on 31 October 1990.

There was in fact no charge on 31 October 2000. The rate of tax is computed on the basis of a hypothetical chargeable transfer described in IHTA 1984, section 66(3). The value transferred on that hypothetical transfer is essentially the value of the property at the date of the ten-yearly anniversary, but that value is reduced by the available business and agricultural property reliefs. Accordingly, the hypothetical transfer of value is of an amount less than the applicable nil rate band which produces a rate of tax of zero.

Any distribution of the trust fund in whole or part at any time before the next ten-yearly anniversary will therefore be effectively free of inheritance tax. The zero rate of tax applies to any property leaving the settlement within the following ten years.

If the property leaving the settlement was the business or agricultural property, this zero tax rate is not strictly necessary because as long as the relief is available the transfer of value is reducible to zero, making the tax rate irrelevant. However, the zero rate also extends to cash leaving the settlement and continues to apply even if the business or agricultural property is sold or otherwise disposed of. The clawback provisions of sections 113A, 113B, 124A and 124B are inapplicable unless the settlor died within seven years of creating the trust—which would be known one way or the other by the time the first ten-yearly anniversary had passed.

In the above example, the trustees might usefully vary the trust so that a beneficiary receives a life interest in the trust fund. This is for the reason discussed above: on the beneficiary's death, a capital gains tax free uplift to market value should be available as well as business or agricultural property relief if still available. However, care should be taken not to forfeit the relief by a gift to a beneficiary who will not continue to qualify. The beneficiary must satisfy the minimum period of ownership requirements, but in the case of business property relief he might be saved by section 109: see **9.6:4** above. This will only apply if the trustees satisfied the minimum period of ownership requirements prior to the variation and if the transfer by the beneficiary is on his death. If he makes a lifetime transfer without holding the property for the minimum period, then relief will be lost.

(2) Double relief

Business or agricultural property relief can effectively be obtained twice on the same property in certain circumstances. Suppose that the first spouse to die leaves business property on discretionary trusts in favour of the surviving spouse and issue. Business property relief, as well as a capital gains tax free uplift of the base cost to market value, should be obtained on that first spouse's death. This could be done pursuant to an option. The surviving spouse then purchases the business property from the trustees at market value. Subject to surviving the requisite two-year period, he may then obtain business property relief a second time—either on his death or on a lifetime transfer. The capital gains tax free uplift should also be available a second time.

Life assurance is worth considering where, as here, the effectiveness of a plan to minimise inheritance tax depends on a particular individual surviving for a particular period. One option would be to purchase term cover for the surviving spouse for at least two years. This would be appropriate if the matter is being considered at or after the date of the first spouse's death.

Alternatively, even before the death of the first (business owning) spouse, life assurance could be taken out to cover the risk of the second spouse dying first. Obviously, if that risk materialised, it would prevent the plan for double relief from working. In this case, one would want to cover (i) the risk of the second (non-business owning) spouse dying first *and* (ii) the risk of that second spouse dying within two years of the first spouse. It should be possible to obtain suitable cover on the second spouse's life for these eventualities. It would be a form of term assurance, but that term would be dependent on the date of death of the first spouse, ie the life of $X + 2$ years.

Example

Mrs Chambers owns the following assets:

		Value
1.	Stock Exchange securities, Building Society and bank deposits	£1,242,000
2.	A 30% holding in Eve Chambers Ltd which manufactures widgets	£400,000
3.	Chambers Farm which Mrs Chambers has owned and farmed for many years	£600,000

In her Will, Mrs Chambers leaves assets numbered 2 and 3 to a discretionary trust in favour of her widower, children and grandchildren. She also leaves so much of the assets in number 1 as are equal in value to the current nil rate band into the trust. The remaining (investment) assets she leaves to her widower coupled with an option to buy the business and agricultural assets from the trust at market value.

On Mrs Chambers' death

Supposing that Mrs Chambers dies in September 2001, there will be no inheritance tax. There will also be a capital gains tax free uplift to market value of the base cost of all the assets. The nil rate band for 2001–02 is £242,000 so that amount would go into the trust. The remaining £1 million would go to Mr Chambers absolutely. He also, of course, acquires the option to buy the business and agricultural assets from the trust at market value.

On Mr Chambers' death

If Mr Chambers exercised the option to buy the business and agricultural assets from the trust—using the £1 million that he inherited absolutely and which, in this example, equates to the market value of those assets—and survived a further two years from the exercise of the option, there would be no inheritance tax on his death either. The only assets in his estate would be the business and agricultural property. The number 1 assets (now all in the trust, the majority having been used as purchase money) would no longer be part of his estate. Nevertheless, he could have benefited from the income of those assets during his life as a beneficiary of the trust created by his wife. The business and agricultural property will benefit from a second capital gains tax free uplift of their base costs to market value on Mr Chambers' death.

Note that when dealing with lifetime discretionary trusts the capital gains tax position is different from when they are created on death. There was some uncertainty about the availability of holdover relief under TCGA 1992, section 260 on non-business assets. The concern was that, if 100% relief applied, there was no chargeable transfer. The CTO have now confirmed that, in their view, a gift qualifying for 100% business or agricultural property relief is a chargeable transfer for the purposes of section 260 (see [1994] PPCB 6).

(3)   Multiple discretionary trusts: protection against future changes in the reliefs

The following arrangement uses a number of discretionary trusts to maximise the nil rate band. It can be adapted where 100% business or agricultural property relief applies.

Example

Assume that Mr X has business or agricultural assets worth £1,452,000. He creates six discretionary trusts over the course of 2001–02 at staggered intervals. Each trust contains assets worth £242,000. There should be no inheritance tax liability on the transfers into the trusts on the assumption that the 100% relief applies. Capital gains tax should be held over.

Each trust should be protected by the nil rate band rule even if the business property or agricultural property relief rules are altered in the future and even if the assets cease to be relevant business property or agricultural property.

There is a risk that a scheme of this sort would be attacked on account of its artificiality. There is also a serious risk that the associated operations provision may apply. This risk can be reduced by ensuring the there are genuine differences between the trusts—eg different trustees and beneficiaries—and that the staggered intervals are as far apart as practicable and not pre-ordained.

Other points to be aware of are:
– possible loss of capital gains tax rollover relief under TCGA 1992, s 152;
– possible loss of retirement relief under TCGA 1992, s 163 and Schedule 6.

Retirement relief is in any event being phased out by April 2003. Relief is available by reference to the circumstances of a beneficiary with an interest in possession but not a beneficiary of a discretionary trust;

– the capital gains tax clock for taper relief will commence for the trustees on the date of the gift.

9.11:3 Use of life interest trusts

If the estate owner has business or agricultural assets eligible for 100% relief and such assets are retained in the trust, consider the following estate planning steps:

(a) the estate owner transfers the assets into a flexible interest in possession trust (ie with wide powers of appointment);

(b) inheritance tax is nil because of the 100% business or agricultural property relief;

(c) capital gains tax can be held over (TCGA 1992, s 165) but consider not electing—see (e) below;

(d) termination of the life interest during the life tenant's lifetime will be free of inheritance tax (without the normal seven-year survival requirement for PETs) because of the 100% business or agricultural property relief. Capital gains tax will be payable only if someone becomes absolutely entitled, subject to holdover relief;

(e) termination of the life interest on death will likewise be free of inheritance tax. The capital gains tax exemption and uplift of base cost to market value will apply (TCGA 1992, s 73), except that capital gains tax will be payable on the lower of any held over gain (see (c)) and the actual gain (TCGA 1992, s 74) if holdover relief has been claimed;

(f) in *Fetherstonaugh v IRC* [1984] STC 261, the Court of Appeal held by a majority that the value of land, of which the deceased was tenant for life under a strict settlement, which was used in the deceased's business, was capable of being taken into account in determining the amount of business property relief available.

9.11:4 Other ways of using business and agricultural property relief

(1) Using an accumulation and maintenance trust under IHTA 1984, s 71

A similar result to that outlined in **9.11:2** and **9.11:3** above could be achieved by a trust which begins as an accumulation and maintenance trust but which, when the beneficiaries attain the specified age, converts into an interest in possession trust. This prevents a disposal for capital gains tax purposes from occurring at that time because the beneficiaries do not become absolutely entitled as against the trustees (TCGA 1992, s 60).

If the interest in possession still subsists at the death of the life tenant, the assets still comply with the requirements for 100% business or agricultural property relief, and if the law has not changed, the position will be as in **9.12:2** and **9.12:3**. In other words, a capital gains tax free uplift will be available.

(2) Gifts to elderly relatives

Where valuable assets are eligible for 100% business or agricultural property relief, the main disadvantage to a lifetime gift is the capital gains tax position. Whilst holdover relief may be available under TCGA 1992, s 165, the tax free uplift to market value on the death of the owners is clearly the much better alternative.

In appropriate cases, one should now consider whether the asset could be given to an elderly relative, for example a grandparent. The gift to the elderly person would be free of inheritance tax and normally capital gains tax holdover relief will be available. On the elderly person's death, 100% business or agricultural relief should be available and the normal minimum period of ownership may also be relaxed under IHTA 1984, s 109 or s 121. On the death of the elderly relative, the property may then pass under the relative's will to the intended beneficiaries with the benefit of the capital gains tax uplift to market value.

Alternatively, the elderly person's will could provide for the business or agricultural property to pass into a non-resident trust. The settlor charge would not apply to the trust, he or she being deceased, and the assets would have a base cost equal to market value at death. On the other hand, a non-resident trust with a deceased settlor accumulates its realised gains as 'trust gains'. These are later attributed to beneficiaries who receive benefits from the trust with a surcharge if there is a delay between the realisation of the gain and the benefit. The surcharge can increase the effective tax rate to 64% after a 6-year delay, so a charge on the settlor at the time of the gain may be thought preferable.

If the transfer into the offshore trust is done by way of deed of variation, rather than under the elderly relative's will, then the beneficiary effecting the variation would be the settlor for capital gains tax purposes (*Marshall v Kerr* [1994] STC 638). This would mean that any gains realised by the trustees would be attributable to and taxable on the beneficiary concerned under TCGA 1992, s 86. Although the legislation (paragraph 6 of Schedule 5 to TCGA 1992) gives the beneficiary a right of recovery against the trustees, there is considerable doubt over whether that right is enforceable. With the possible exception of trusts resident in a Brussels Convention country, the better view is that such rights of reimbursement will be unenforceable. Voluntary reimbursement by the trustees is not necessarily a solution, but these complex issues are outside the scope of this book.

Example

Anne owns 80% of Widget Manufacturing Co Ltd and currently qualifies for business property relief. She wants to give 30% of the shares to her daughter Emma. Assume that a 30% holding of these shares is currently worth £600,000 and that there is an inherent gain on such a holding of £300,000 (ie potential capital gains tax of £120,000).

Anne's father George is still alive but in his 80s. Anne gives the shares—ie the intended gift to Emma—to George free of inheritance tax as business property. Capital gains tax is held over. It is then hoped (there must be no prior agreement or arrangement) that George will leave these shares to his granddaughter Emma under his will.

On George's death, there will be no inheritance tax on account of the business property relief. That part of the plan could have been achieved by a straight gift by

Anne to Emma. However, significantly, there is a capital gains tax free base cost uplift to market value at the date of George's death. Capital gains tax of £120,000 has been avoided.

Supplementary Points

There are four additional points to make concerning this example:

(1) It is not essential for George to survive two years from the date of the gift. As long as Anne's period of ownership qualified, and the transfer by George to Emma occurs on George's death, IHTA 1984, s 109 should ensure that business property relief remains available.

(2) If George did not leave the property to Emma by his will, the beneficiary under the will could execute a deed of variation to achieve the same result. This course depends on the co-operation of the beneficiary. Not much can be done if George's will leaves everything to the wicked step-mother or to charity and fails to change it in time.

(3) It may be possible to achieve the result described in the example without the risk of George's will benefiting the wrong person—or indeed the risk of George's estate becoming insolvent and the property being required to pay his debts. Anne settles the business property on George for life with remainder to Emma.

(4) If this plan is adopted instead of an immediate gift to Emma, it means gambling on the continuation of business property relief in its current form for George's life. Those involved should be made aware of this risk.

(5) The risk just identified could be minimised by using the life interest trust described at (3) above combined with overriding powers to advance the whole trust property to Emma. These should not be exercised within the first two years of the trust, because section 109 will not save what is effectively a lifetime gift by George. After that, however, the power will give the trustees flexibility to make an advancement if they think that the relief is likely to be abolished.

9.11:5 Will planning

Leaving business or agricultural property to a spouse means that the relief is wasted. A gift to a spouse is exempt anyway. Business or agricultural property that may qualify for 100% relief should be given to the lower generations (children and grandchildren) or to appropriate trusts. This overcomes the problem that such assets, if left to the surviving spouse, may become investment rather than trading assets; or that on that spouse's death the law may have changed for the worse. Frequently, a surviving spouse does not need the business assets, such as shares in the family company, which may be illiquid. He will need the liquid assets.

If, on the other hand, he does need the business or agricultural assets, those assets can be placed into a discretionary trust and distributed to the surviving spouse more than three months after the first spouse's death but not later than two years after that date. See IHTA 1984, s 144.

If the testator wants to give business and agricultural assets to chargeable beneficiaries to supplement a nil rate band gift, and leave the residue to the surviving spouse, he must ensure that specific property, eg the shares or the farm, is given to the non-exempt beneficiaries to avoid an apportionment of the relief between them and the exempt surviving spouse under IHTA 1984, s 39A.

Beware of unfairness between more than one chargeable beneficiary. For example, a gift of shares subject to 100% business property relief to the testator's daughter and a gift of an equivalent cash sum to the testator's son would result in an effectively exempt gift to the daughter while the son's gift would be subject to inheritance tax.

9.11:6 Other advantages of delaying such gifts until death

If an estate owner is reasonably confident that 100% business or agricultural property relief will be available on his death, there is little incentive to relinquish control or reduce a substantial minority holding by making lifetime gifts. Advantages of delaying gifts until death include the following:

– There is no question of clawback of business or agricultural property relief. This only applies to lifetime gifts: see IHTA 1984, sections 113A and 113B (acquisition of replacement property within three years with whole of consideration of original property) and sections 124A and 124B on business and agricultural property respectively.

– There will be full capital gains tax death exemption and tax free uplift. Contrast this with capital gains tax holdover relief which is usually only a deferral, but note that for a lifetime gift there may be no capital gains tax after taking into account retirement relief, rebasing to 31 March 1982, indexation and taper relief where applicable.

– The estate owner can retain control of his shareholding.

An alternative would be for the estate owner to create a settlement in which he retains a lifetime interest in the shares. If he wants his children to have voting control in the meantime, they could be appointed trustees. On his death, a capital gains tax free uplift will normally apply and the 100% inheritance tax relief will be available (TCGA 1992, s 62 and IHTA 1984, s 49(1)). In some cases, it may be better not to claim the holdover relief into trust—particularly if the transferor could benefit from a substantial amount of taper relief.

9.11:7 Deeds of variation (IHTA 1984, s 142)

For death within the two-year period, consider varying the gifts of business or agricultural property subject to 100% relief away from spouses and in favour of non-spouses, such as children, grandchildren or discretionary trusts.

9.11:8 Mortgaging or charging agricultural or business assets

(1) Avoid mortgaging or charging a farm

There are three basic alternatives. First, the farm itself is charged without other security. This should be avoided where possible because, on a transfer of value, the agricultural property relief will be restricted to the net value of the farm, ie the value of the farm less the mortgage.

Secondly, the loan could be secured against some other asset, such as a life policy, and not the agricultural property itself. In that case it appears that the indebtedness is set first against the collateral security, leaving the farm and agricultural relief unabated by the charge to the extent that the collateral security is sufficient to redeem the charge. This is preferable to the first scenario, even if it means that some relief may be lost.

In *IRC v Mallender and others (executors of Drury-Lowe deceased)* [2001] STC 514, the deceased had given security to a bank over some land in return for the bank providing a guarantee to Lloyd's which was lodged as part of the deceased's underwriting business. Initially, the Special Commissioners had held that the land itself was business property, albeit that its value was several times the value of the guarantee. This decision was overturned by the High Court.

Thirdly, the loan may not be secured on any particular asset. This is less favourable than the second method because the loan may reduce the agricultural value of the farm on a pro rata basis. It may also be unacceptable commercially to the lender.

(2)   Avoid mortgaging or charging a business asset

The same principles apply to business assets as to agricultural assets. Any security charged on the assets eligible for relief will reduce the amount of relief and increase the tax on the assets not so eligible. Wherever practicable, loans should be secured on collateral assets. It has been suggested that for business and payment by instalments, reliefs such as charging of collateral assets may not work. The theory is that these reliefs are only available in respect of the net value of the business (sections 110(1) and 227(7)) and therefore, if the proceeds of the borrowing are used for the purposes of the business, they reduce the reliefs for that reason. Note the words in section 110: '*reduced by the aggregate amount of any liabilities incurred for the purposes of the business*'. The solution could be to interpose a partnership so that the borrowings are used to provide the partnership capital. The problem does not apply to agricultural relief.

9.11:9   Tax planning for agricultural property

(1)   Agricultural cottages and the farmhouse

Whether or not the conditions for agricultural relief are satisfied, where cottages are occupied by persons employed in agriculture, their valuation will be on the basis that they are only suitable for that purpose. They can therefore be transferred at a low value (section 169).

The reference in section 115(2) to 'agricultural land or pasture' should be given the narrow meaning of the bare land, not the wider meaning under the Interpretation Act 1978 as automatically including buildings on the land (*Starke (Brown's Executors) v IRC* [1995] STC 689, CA). Therefore, for inheritance tax purposes, a farmhouse or building will only qualify for agricultural property relief if its occupation is ancillary to that of agricultural land. On the facts in *Brown's Executors*, a six-bedroom farm house on 2.5 acres did not qualify for agricultural property relief.

Consider an estate owner who gives 85% of his farm to his daughter and retaining, say, 15% together with the farmhouse. If the estate owner continues to be involved in the farming business (eg through a partnership), the farmhouse may be eligible for 100% relief. It is a question of degree. One can have a 100% interest in the farmhouse and, say, a 15% interest in the partnership.

In *Harrold v IRC* [1996] STC (SCD) 195, agricultural property relief was claimed under the seven-year occupation test but, because the farm was unoccupied as dilapidated at the donor's death, no agricultural property relief was available.

For a farmhouse to be agricultural property, it is largely a question of the purpose of occupation rather than the actual use put to it by the owner or occupier. In an extract of a letter from Peter Twiddy (*CTO Taxation 15 June 2000*), he described the test adopted by the CTO as follows: 'The CTO asks the District Valuer to consider the appropriate test through the eyes of the rural equivalent of the reasonable man on the Clapham omnibus . . .'. The CTO now appears to apply the following tests in relation to farmhouses:

– is the unit primarily a dwelling with some land? Or is it an agricultural unit incorporating such a dwelling as is appropriate?

– Is it normal local practice for land of this quality, use and area to have with it a dwelling of this type and size?

– Is the size and character of the dwelling appropriate to the land and the scale of agricultural operations?

Having considered those questions, a balanced view is taken 'in the round'. This appears to be another example of the notorious elephant test: something which is difficult to describe but you know one when you see one. However, whereas there may be a consensus as to what is an elephant and what is not, an equivalent measure of certainty will not be present when dealing with a question of fact and degree, such as the present one. Is an animal an elephant if it is half elephant and half lion—supposing such a thing to be possible? Or if it is 3/4 elephant? Or if it is a dead or deformed elephant? Once the test is adapted to one which involves drawing a line somewhere, it is likely to emerge that we do not all agree on what is an elephant and a more specific test is needed if there is to be some certainty.

Say Mr and Mrs X retire and give the farm to their daughter who takes over the farming, but Mr and Mrs X stay in the farmhouse. The daughter lives elsewhere. In those circumstances, the farmhouse plainly will not be agricultural property. The solution may be for the Xs to retain some partnership interest in the overall farm.

Whether pasture land was 'occupied for the purposes of agriculture' was considered by the Special Commissioner in *The Executors of Walter Wheatley Deceased* (SpC 00149). He held that grazing by horses such as draught animals could qualify because the horses would have a 'connection with agriculture'. Grazing by horses used for leisure pursuits did not so qualify.

To avoid the house being an excepted asset within IHTA 1984, s 112(2), because used wholly or mainly for the personal benefit of the transferor (section 112(6)), an arm's length contract of employment should be considered.

(2) Fallow land

Fallow land (eg under an EC set-aside scheme) is allowed as agricultural property so long as it is not used for another business purpose.

(3) Holiday lettings

Holiday lettings are not agricultural property and may well not qualify for business property relief either unless the landlord contributed active management and services. In other words, it is necessary to show that the activity in question constitutes 'trading' and not 'a mere investment'. The matter was illustrated by Brian Friedman in *Taxation*, 3 May 1990, p 126. Mr Friedman outlined an appeal before the Special Commissioners in which the appellant successfully maintained that the letting of a property (a substantial four-storey building in the medical area of London used for medical, dental and residential purposes) constituted a business for inheritance tax purposes. The daily activities of Mr S, one of the co-lessors, involved conferring with his tenants and staff and he was obliged to provide both a receptionist and a housekeeper /cleaner. Those and his other obligations far exceeded those normally placed upon the holder of an investment. He was therefore held to be carrying on a business for inheritance tax purposes. The interest of his wife, Mrs S, did not constitute carrying on a business because she did not supply those personal services and was not in partnership with Mr S. See, however, the two Special Commissioners decisions referred to in **9.2:1** above.

(4) Milk quotas etc

Milk and other quotas will normally qualify for business property relief, but following the *Cottle* case (see below) not agricultural property relief. See Capital Taxes Office Advanced Investigation Manual paragraph 232.1 and Nigel Popplewell's article 'Milk Quota Taxation' in *Taxation*, 3 June 1999, p 244.

For capital gains tax there is at present a conflict. The decision in *Faulkes v Faulkes* [1992] 15 EG 15, where Chadwick J expressed the view that the quota interest was part of and indistinguishable from the land, contrasts with the Revenue's view that milk quota exists separately from the land for capital gains tax purposes, normally with no base cost (see the Tax Bulletin, issue 6, page 49).

The Revenue view was supported in the Special Commissioner's decision in *Cottle v Caldicott* SpC40 in September 1995. It was held that the taxpayer was not entitled to deduct any part of the cost of the holding of land from the consideration for the milk quota. The milk quota was a personal asset separate from the incorporeal property: TCGA 1992, s 21(1)(a) and (b). The *Cottle* decision is nowadays generally applied and accepted.

(5) Diversification

Diversification to non-agricultural use (eg golf courses) will lose the agricultural relief but may qualify as a business asset. There is no need to own for two years as business property to qualify for business property relief if it was previously owned as agricultural property and the aggregate is at least two years.

(6) Grant of tenancies etc

In the 1970s and to a lesser degree in the 80s, granting tenancies produced substantial tax savings because of the double discount, ie the capital transfer tax agricultural property discount plus the reduction in value from open market vacant possession value. With the 100% discount on vacant possession and let land since 1 September 1995, there is little point in effecting a reorganisation to achieve the double discount and the plan should be to keep matters simple. This, however, does depend on whether one expects any changes in government policy. If the agricultural relief discount is going to be reduced, the double discount plan may revive.

In an era where vacant possession gives full exemption, the grant of a tenancy is not generally advisable for inheritance tax purposes. Instead of family-type tenancies, consider a partnership with vacant possession (or at least vacant possession within 24 months). Licensing arrangements that do not constitute leases or tenancies are fine, for example for grazing. Note the case of *Lubbock Fine & Co v Customs and Excise Commissioners* at the European Court of Justice Case 6-63/92: [1994] STC 101, indicating that surrenders of leases are exempt from VAT but bear in mind that tenants who currently have security of tenure may be reluctant to agree to a surrender.

The income and capital gains tax implications of retaining a tenancy should be taken into account.

For the position on or after 1 September 1995 for new leases and successions, see **9.10:1**(3) above.

In *IRC v Gray (Executor of Lady Fox)* [1994] STC 360, the Court of Appeal decided that, for valuation on death purposes, a freehold reversion in land must be aggregated with a partnership interest which holds a tenancy of that land (following the principle of realising the maximum practicable price without undue expenditure of time and effort: *Duke of Buccleuch v IRC* [1967] 1 506, HL). In other words, it was a single 'natural unit'. The existence of a tenancy can therefore bring about the worst of both worlds. The valuation will be initially on vacant possession principles notwithstanding the tenancy, but, by virtue of section 116(2)(a), only a 50% agricultural property discount will be available rather than 100%. Note that in this case the testatrix was the freeholder and had a 92.5% interest in the partnership which held the tenancy of that freehold estate.

Walton v IRC [1996] STC 68, CA, concerned the valuation of an agricultural tenancy for capital transfer tax purposes. The W family were the freeholders. They let the farm to a partnership of Mr W and son. On Mr W's death, the Revenue claimed that the capital transfer tax value of the lease was the difference between the value of the freehold with vacant possession and its value subject to the lease. Its reasoning was that, on Mr W's death, there was a hypothetical sale of the tenancy valued at £70,000.

The taxpayer's claim—accepted by the Land Tribunal and the Court of Appeal—was that there was no hypothetical sale, as the son did not wish to sell but to continue the farming. Therefore the value of the tenancy was based on a potential profit rental basis (£8,000), ie a real-world situation. This was typically a small value in the absence of any special purchaser, who did not exist in this case.

9.11:10   Partnership land

The Partnership Act 1890, section 22 (which converts partnership property into personal and moveable property) has been repealed by the Trusts of Land and Trustees Act 1996. For land held outside a partnership—or company controlled by the taxpayer—and made available as agricultural property, there is 100% relief (section 116). If held as an other business asset, 50% relief is available (section 105(1)(d)). Therefore section 22 need not be specifically excluded from the partnership agreement.

9.11:11   Tenant farmer

A tenant farmer should consider purchasing the freehold title in order to acquire exempt IHT assets, in contrast with his other assets, reducing his liquid estate not eligible for reliefs. See also **9.10:1**(3) above.

If the tenant has been in occupation as tenant for a minimum of two years, then on a purchase by him the 100% discount becomes immediately available.

9.11:12 Farming companies

Farming companies (section 122) are at a disadvantage: the 100% relief is only available if the transferor controls the company, ie has an interest of more than 50%. Contrast this with business property relief, where a 100% discount is currently available whatever the size of the holding. A holding of 50% or less in a farming company attracts no agricultural property relief. On the basis that the farm is a business, it may be possible to obtain 100% business property relief if the relevant conditions apply.

The shares or securities of a company qualify for agricultural property relief where the company's assets include agricultural property and the value of the shares or securities can in whole or part be attributed to such property, but only if the transferor of the shares has control of the company within section 269(1)—see sections 122 and 123. Note that this control is only required to exist immediately before the transfer, ie the transferor need not have had control for the full two or seven-year period. Accordingly, for companies control is required; and there is no agricultural relief for lesser holdings as with business relief, but a minority interest may well qualify for business property relief.

In order for the shares to obtain agricultural relief, the company must fulfil the same requirements and minimum periods as an individual; and the shareholder transferor must have owned the shares for whichever of the two or seven-year minimum periods is appropriate to the company (section 123(1)). There are provisions which preserve the relief where the shares replace other eligible property during the relevant period (section 123(3)).

Example

On 10 October 2000, Alice gave her farm to her niece by way of a PET. The farm consisted of 400 acres worth £2,500 per acre, thus having a total value of £1 million. Alice had made no gifts in the previous seven years and had occupied the farm and farmed it herself for 20 years. The value is reduced by 50% for inheritance tax to £500,000. The niece farmed the land until Alice's death on 10 February 2001, whereupon the PET became a chargeable transfer with no tapering relief. The niece can pay the inheritance tax of £140,000 over ten years by interest-free instalments (sections 227 and 234(1)), ie annual instalments of £14,000.

If Alice had rolled over her farming business (including the land) into a company, A Ltd, a year before the transfer in return for 90% of the shares (the other 10% being separately subscribed) the transfer of her 90% shareholding to her niece (together with her niece's retention of the shares and A Ltd's ownership of the farm property up to Alice's death) would obtain relief. One could add together the separate occupation of both Alice and A Ltd. Inheritance tax would similarly be payable by interest-free instalments.

9.11:13 Habitat schemes

Since 26 November 1995 certain habitat schemes have been eligible for agricultural property relief. Such schemes are for the protection of the environment and preservation of the countryside and take land out of farming for 20 years.

9.11:14 Special types of farming

(1) Farm sharing

The system of farm sharing is likely to become popular in the 100% relief era. Its features are:

– it is a joint contractual venture between the owner of the farmland and the operator who farms the land;

– the owner provides land, fixed equipment, machinery and an agreed share of inputs;

– the operator provides working machinery, labour and inputs;

– the gross outputs are shared under the agreements.

The results may be summarised as follows:

– there is no partnership;

– there are separate businesses;

– there is no landlord-tenant relationship;

– IHT 100% relief should be available. Both parties should have vacant possession rights. In particular, the owner should be involved in policy-making decisions and exercise rights of inspection.

The Revenue now appear to agree that farm sharing qualifies for capital gains tax reliefs such as rollover, retirement and reinvestment reliefs; and constitutes trading as farmers for income tax purposes (TA 1988, ss 53 and 837(1)). Further details can be found in *Farm Sharing*, a booklet available from the Country Landowners Association (tel: 020 7235 0511).

(2) Contract farming

Consider also contract farming, where the estate owner owns the farm and the actual farming is carried on by sub-contracting, usually to someone who is self-employed. Again the 100% relief should normally be available.

9.11:15 'Buy and sell' agreements/arrangements

Agricultural and business property reliefs can be unavailable where the partners or company directors or shareholders have entered into a 'buy and sell' agreement whereby, on retirement or the death of one of them before retirement, his personal representatives are obliged to sell and the others are obliged to buy his interest or his shares. Typically, in these arrangements, the funds will be provided through a life assurance policy. The Revenue take the view that such an agreement, entailing an obligatory sale and purchase (not merely conferring an option) constitutes a binding contract for sale within section 124 so that agricultural relief is forfeited. The same argument applies to business property relief (section 104). See the Revenue Statement of Practice 12/80 of 13 October 1980.

The solution is to use the option method. This can achieve the same result if appropriate put and call options are granted. See also the memorandum reproduced in *Simon's Tax Intelligence*, 28 September 1984, page 651, which reviews correspondence between the accountancy bodies and the Revenue on buy and sell agreements. Faced with the strict Revenue attitude, the sensible attitude has to be to avoid buy and sell agreements. It should be noted that automatic accrual arrangements between members of a partnership may possibly be looked upon by the Revenue as binding sale contracts. This difficulty does not arise with options and thus options should be favoured. Cross options—ie a put and a call—are arguably equivalent in substance to a binding contract for sale on the grounds that the terms will be beneficial to one party or the other and thus a sale is inevitable. However, the merits of this argument may be exaggerated. The legal effect of cross options is conditional on the exercise of one or other of them. Until any such exercise takes place, the vendor (or his estate) still has full rights of beneficial ownership in the asset itself (see *J Sainsbury plc v O'Connor* [1991] STC 318, CA). The Revenue appear to accept the option method (see *Law Society Gazette*, September 1996). Cross options should be made successive in time. A partnership agreement which does not included this precaution may be cured after its term has expired and it has become a partnership at will, or by variation.

9.12   WOODLANDS—THE RELIEF

The acquisition of interests in forestry became very popular because of the favourable income tax treatment. Taxation of the occupation of commercial woodlands used to be assessed to income tax under Schedule B. This regime was abolished with transitional relief provisions by FA 1988, s 64 and Schedule 6. Commercial woodlands have been taken out of income tax. Losses on planting are not allowable against other income and the proceeds of sale of the mature timber are free from income tax.

So far as inheritance tax relief is concerned, a measure of relief for woodlands is contained in IHTA 1984, ss 125 to 130. The relief applies only to trees and underwood. Although the underlying land is excluded, its value will usually be relatively low and will be eligible for agricultural relief if occupied with, and ancillary to, agricultural land or pasture.

In a Schedule D case the High Court held that the terms 'woodlands' and 'forestry' were not words of art but were in common usage and to be treated as synonymous. Although woodlands connoted a wood of sizeable area and to a significant extent covered by growing trees, it could not be assumed that any land covered with any trees constituted woodland. The rule of thumb was whether the wood was capable of being used as timber. Accordingly, a plantation of Christmas trees which had neither the maturity, the height nor the size to be useful as timber, and which resembled bushes rather than trees, did not constitute woodland. See *Jaggers v Ellis* [1997] STC 1417. The analysis in the judgment provides useful guidance on the meaning of woodland in the inheritance tax legislation.

9.12:1   Nature of relief

Inheritance tax relief, on death only, is available if claimed by notice in writing within two years of death or such longer period as the Board will allow. The relief is not available for lifetime transfers of woodlands. It applies to woodlands other than agricultural property. The value of the trees or underwood is left out of account at death but inheritance tax may be payable on disposal (section 126). Growing timber is in fact the only commercial asset in the UK in respect of which inheritance tax can be deferred on death.

Inheritance tax is payable on a disposal in relation to the last death on which the timber passes. The person entitled to the sale proceeds or who would be entitled if the disposal were a sale is liable to the tax. An inter-spouse disposal is ignored. Inheritance tax is only charged on the first disposal of the trees or underwood following the death (section 126(3)).

Inheritance tax is calculated on the net sale proceeds on a sale for full consideration and on the net value at the date of disposal in other cases. The inheritance tax rate scale is the one which would have applied if the chargeable value as above had been included in the estate in relation to the latest death on which it passes and represented the highest part of that estate (section 128). If the inheritance tax charge crystallises after a reduction in the rates, the reduced rates apply (Schedule 2, paragraph 4). Where the woodlands were being managed commercially (ie would have qualified as relevant business property for business relief under sections 103–114) the amount on which inheritance tax is charged under section 126 is reduced by 50%.

The inheritance tax relief is not available on lifetime transfers of woodlands—these will be potentially exempt transfers or lifetime chargeable transfers in the normal way. Where woodlands relief has been given on death, and the later disposal is also subject to inheritance tax as a chargeable transfer, there will be two computations of inheritance tax. The first will relate to the earlier death and the second to the later chargeable transfer. The inheritance tax relating to the death may be deducted from the value of the chargeable transfer to arrive at the inheritance tax liability on the latter (section 129). Since, by section 3A(4), a potentially exempt transfer made within seven years of death is a chargeable transfer, presumably the inheritance tax on the earlier death may be deducted not only against lifetime chargeable transfers but also against those potentially exempt transfers that ultimately become chargeable.

9.12:2   Conditions of relief

Relief is only available if the deceased held the land beneficially for the five years preceding his death or acquired it otherwise than for money or money's worth. The relief therefore is of no use in deathbed schemes, ie purchasing woodlands shortly before death. The land must be situated in the UK.

Net values are after selling expenses and expenses of replanting within three years or such longer period as the Board may allow (section 130(2)) except to the extent that these expenses are allowable for income tax (section 130(1)(b)).

Where the woodlands are being managed commercially and would qualify as relevant business property for business relief under sections 103 to 114, the amount on which inheritance tax is charged is reduced by 100%. However, if there is an election under sections 125 to 127 to leave the value of the woodlands out of account in determining the value of the estate on death, only 50% business property relief will be available under section 127(2) on an eventual sale. Obviously, if at all possible, it is sensible for the owners of woodland to endeavour to manage the woodlands in a commercial and active manner in order to obtain 100% business property relief. Separate accounts should be kept in relation to the woodlands and these accounts should not be included in the overall farming accounts.

Example

Hawker died on 30 September 1982 and left the following estate, there having been no lifetime transfers:

	£
Sundry assets	215,000
Value of timber	80,000
	295,000
CTT was payable on death on £215,000	60,000
On 1 May 2001, the timber was sold for the sum of £305,000 (on which 50% business relief is due) after allowing for selling and replanting expenses so that CTT is payable on	152,500
Other assets at death	215,000
	357,500

		£
IHT payable (at current rates)		
First	£242,000 @ 0%	nil
Next	£125,500 @ 40%	50,200
	£367,50	

Less: Payable (current rates) on estate of £215,000 on death	nil
Payable on sale of timber	50,200

If no claim had been made, then CTT on death in 1982 would have been:	
First £250,000	87,500
Next £45,000 @ 60%	27,000
	114,500

9.12:3 Transfers of woodlands subject to a deferred ED charge

Under the estate duty regime, duty on a death on woodlands could be deferred until the heir felled or sold the timber. If the heir died before the timber was sold, estate duty on his death replaced the earlier deferred charge and could itself again be deferred. Under paragraph 46 of Schedule 19 to FA 1986, any transfer which includes woodlands subject to a deferred estate duty charge is denied PET treatment so that there is an immediate lifetime chargeable transfer and the deferred estate duty is treated as discharged. As it stands, any single large transfer which includes some small part of woodlands subject to deferred estate duty is refused PET treatment. An extra-statutory concession (announced by the Revenue in a Press Release dated 5 December 1990 and now designated F15) restricts the denial of PET treatment only to such part of the transfer as consists of the woodlands subject to the deferred estate duty. Thus there is an immediate inheritance tax charge on the woodlands subject to the deferred estate duty but the remaining part of the transfer constitutes a PET.

9.13 WOODLANDS—PLANNING

9.13:1 The decision to elect or not

In many cases it will not be advisable to make a section 125 election because— as illustrated in the example above—the eventual inheritance tax liability will be fully aggregable with the deceased's estate and liable to any inflationary increase in value. By contrast, if an election is not made, the value of the timber will be crystallised at the value at the date of death and the inheritance tax will be payable by instalments. As a general rule, one should not elect in the case of a young softwood (because of the large growth expectation) whereas election for a mature forest may prove advantageous subject to the business property relief point referred to earlier. In the case of the former, the ideal situation could be to pay inheritance tax on a death or lifetime gift (if no election is made, there is a low value and the disposition is made in favour of a younger generation who could fell and dispose with no further charge). Note, moreover, that a section 125 election does not have to extend to all woodlands in the same estate. It may be appropriate to elect in relation to certain parts only of a deceased's timber estate. Where two or more persons are jointly liable for inheritance tax on woodlands of a deceased, one or more of the co-owners may wish to elect while the others decide not to. Where the conditions are satisfied for 100% business property relief (see **9.8:1** above), there will be no need to consider any sort of election.

Inheritance tax is payable on a disposal in relation to the *last* death on which the timber passes. As already mentioned, the inheritance tax liability relates to the last relevant death. Accordingly, where the original estate owner had a substantial estate including the timber, it is sometimes possible to save inheritance tax by granting a life interest to an elderly impecunious individual by will and then making an election. When that life tenant dies, the inheritance tax liability may fall wholly or partly within the nil rate band. There will be no capital gains tax.

However, the best approach is to aim for business property relief where possible.

9.13:2 Use of exemptions

Instead of using the very restricted relief in section 125, an estate owner should consider transferring his interest in timber by using his available exemptions, particularly the annual exemption, and possibly the mortgage charging proposals.

9.13:3 Own use

It appears that timber felled for use on the owner's property is not a disposal, for example, where used for estate maintenance and repairs. This could be particularly relevant where the estate owner also had agricultural property. There is, however, no specific inheritance tax exclusion as there was for estate duty.

9.14   WORKS OF ART, HISTORIC BUILDINGS ETC (ss 25–27, 30–35 and 77–79 and Schedules)

9.14:1   Summary

The exemption covers death and lifetime gifts and property held in discretionary trusts or transfers. The relief is given by way of conditionally exempt transfers. No claim for conditional exemption in respect of a potentially exempt transfer can be made unless and until the donor dies within seven years. Gifts to spouses and charities—both categories exempt from inheritance tax anyway—are outside these conditional exemption rules.

9.14:2   Requirements and conditions

These are that the property in question is appropriately designated by the Board of Inland Revenue; that requisite undertakings are given to the Board; and that—for lifetime transfers—the transferor or spouse has held the property for at least six years or inherited it on a death to which conditional exemption (or the estate duty equivalent) applied. Details of conditional exemption are given in Revenue booklet IR 67 'Capital Taxation and the National Heritage' obtainable from Somerset House.

For tax charges arising after 16 March 1998, claims for exemption usually have to be made within two years of the relevant chargeable event.

9.14:3   Designation and scope

The exemption can apply to pictures, prints, books, manuscripts, works of art and scientific collections where the objects appear to the Board to be pre-eminent for their national, scientific, historic or artistic interest. The exemption may also apply to land and buildings if, in the opinion of the Treasury, they are of outstanding scenic or historic or scientific interest (section 31 as amended by Schedule 25 to FA 1998). The undertaking that has to be given to the Board is to the effect that the property will be kept permanently in the UK with such provisions as to preservation and maintenance and reasonable access to the public as are agreed between the Treasury and the person giving the undertaking. Slightly different undertakings are given if the property is land or buildings. The owner of a work of art has to complete application form 700A.

Fundamental changes have been made to the undertakings required by the Revenue with respect to public access to works of art. The changes were introduced by the FA 1998 and can be found in section 33(4A) to (4G) and section 35A of the IHTA 1984.

Prior to March 1998, public access to exempt assets usually involved making a prior appointment with the owners of the assets or their agents. Under the new rules, owners may no longer elect for public access by prior appointment only. Both future and existing undertakings are open to amendment and owners may be required to publicise their undertakings and disclose relevant information. Owners will have six months from the Inland Revenue's proposal to vary an existing undertaking to agree to the variations. If no agreement can be reached and the Special Commissioner considers the proposed variations to be just and reasonable the Special Commissioner may make a direction accordingly. Not surprisingly, these changes were greeted with horror by many owners of valuable assets who had expected to be able to rely upon agreements reached with the Revenue. The matter is highly contentious and plans are afoot to challenge the provisions or their exercise in the light of the Human Rights Act 1998 which came into force in England and Wales on 2nd October 2000. It is argued that variations of existing agreements can only be insisted upon by the Revenue against the wishes of the taxpayer if the Special Commissioner is satisfied that it is just and reasonable in all the circumstances to direct that the proposed variation be made. The Special Commissioner ought not to be satisfied that a forced variation of an inherently non-variable agreement (at the time it was entered into, before the FA 1998) is just and reasonable. See *Country Life*, 8 April 1999, page 108 for a letter by Stephen Allcock QC. A possible solution is for owners of such works of art to exhibit them in specially arranged public exhibitions.

9.14:4 Chargeable events

A conditionally exempt transfer becomes liable to inheritance tax on the happening of a chargeable event. This can be breach of an undertaking, death, sale, gift, or other disposition unless the disposition is a sale to an approved institution or the asset is transferred to the Board of Inland Revenue in satisfaction of inheritance tax. A death or gift is not a chargeable event if the transfer itself is a conditionally exempt transfer and similar undertakings are given by the legatee or donee. Inheritance tax will be payable on a chargeable event on an amount equal to the value of the property at the time of the chargeable event and at the appropriate cumulative lifetime rates, if the transferor is alive and at the death rate if he is dead, as if it were the highest part of his estate. A sale at an arm's length value not intended to confer any gratuitous benefit is deemed to take place at the sale price. If there have been two or more conditionally exempt transfers within 30 years of the chargeable event, the Board need not take the *latest* transfer, but may take any of the previous transfers—a measure designed to prevent a wealthy property owner passing assets to an impecunious individual by a conditionally exempt transfer, who then sells the assets; or to prevent the property passing on the death of an elderly impecunious individual who has had a life interest in the property.

A chargeable event is treated as part of the transferor's cumulative total. Where conditionally exempt property is comprised in a discretionary settlement it is exempt from the ten-yearly charge until after a chargeable event has taken place. When a chargeable event occurs, inheritance tax is payable at the special rates specified in section 79(6).

No inheritance tax liability arises on a disposal to the Revenue in satisfaction of tax liability, nor in the case of a private treaty sale to a specified national heritage body. In the latter case, one normally negotiates a price which shares the benefit of the freedom from tax between the vendor and the acquiring institution, an arrangement known as the 'douceur'. The national heritage body pays less than the full market price on the one hand, but the vendor receives more than he would have done on a net basis if inheritance tax were payable. The government have advised museums and galleries in general to offer the seller an amount equal to 25% of the benefit of the tax exemption subject to negotiations above or below where flexibility is required. This practice is explained more fully in chapters 10 and 11 of the Revenue booklet IR 67.

Both a disposal in satisfaction of tax and a private treaty sale are exempt from VAT (VATA 1994, Schedule 9, Pt II, Group 11).

Example

	£
Hawker died on 1 May 2001 leaving sundry assets of	262,000
and a painting valued at	85,000

Exemption is claimed on the picture which is subsequently sold by the legatee for £200,000. This sale is a chargeable event and inheritance tax is payable under section 33(1) on the value of the property at the time of the chargeable event. The rate is that which would have applied if the value of the property had been added to the value transferred on death and had formed the highest part of that value.

		£
Inheritance tax on death (no lifetime transfers)		
£242,000 @ 0%		0
£20,000 @ 40%		8,000
		———
		8,000
		══════
IHT on sale (chargeable event)		
£200,000 @ 40%		80,000
		══════

9.14:5 Discretionary trusts

Conditional exemption is given to approved works of art etc held in a discretionary trust when transferred out of the settlement provided that the property has been in the settlement for the whole of the six years ending with the transfer out (sections 78(2) and 79). There is also an exemption from the ten-yearly charge.

9.14:6 Planning

It may be appropriate for an estate owner to charge other assets in his estate and invest the proceeds in such works of art, etc.

The relief applies similarly for capital gains tax purposes under TCGA 1992, s 258. Following the FA 1998, consequential changes to the capital gains tax relief have been made.

9.14:7 Maintenance funds for historic buildings (s 27, Sch 4)

A transfer of value for the maintenance, repair or preservation of historic buildings and assets of outstanding scenic, historic or scientific interest etc is, subject to certain conditions, an exempt transfer to the extent that the value transferred by it is attributable to property which becomes comprised in settlement for a minimum of six years and the Board of Inland Revenue (formerly the Treasury) so direct (whether before or after the time of the transfer).

Moreover, not only is the transfer into the trust exempt, but so long as the conditions are complied with there is no inheritance tax charge on payment out of the trust for approved purposes of or on the ten-yearly anniversary (Schedule 4).

Schedule 4 imposes conditions with particular reference to the official directions including that the property is of a character and amount appropriate for the purposes of the settlement, the appointment of a custodian trustee, the application of the capital and income of the trust, and the character of the building and land in relation to the national interest and national heritage.

In relation to transfers of value made after 16 March 1998, the tax exemption for transfers to approved heritage maintenance trusts must be claimed within two years after the date of the transfer concerned or within such longer period as the Revenue may allow.

9.15   LLOYD'S MEMBERSHIP

Insurance business at Lloyd's is conducted by Lloyd's underwriting members known as 'Names'. As has recently become more widely known, they are personally liable as individuals for all claims made on them to the extent of their assets on the basis of unlimited liability (although stop-loss insurance can be effected). Underwriting members are formed into syndicates and each syndicate is managed on a day-to-day basis by managing agents. The acceptance of insurance risk is the basis of Lloyd's activities; and the interest of an underwriting member qualifies both for business relief and for payment of inheritance tax by instalments.

The interest of the typical Lloyd's name will consist, first, of his Lloyd's deposit. This comprises investments lodged with Lloyd's as security for the underwriting activities of the syndicate. The name may also have contributed to a Special Reserve Fund to which an individual can transfer a proportion of his underwriting profits. Income tax relief is available on payments into the fund but income tax is payable on any withdrawals. New regulations came into force on 31 December 1999—the Lloyd's Underwriters (Special Reserve Funds) Regulations SI 1999/3308—designed to clarify the charges that arise on his share of a Special Reserve Fund when a name ceases underwriting.

There is also a Personal Reserve Fund, which is a fund designed as a practical measure to cater for losses in the current difficult insurance climate. There is no income tax relief on this fund. Alongside these funds, the name will normally seek a stop-loss policy offering protection against losses over and above an agreed specified amount, although recently the cost of such cover has been very high. There may also be an estate protection plan, limiting the liability of his estate in the event of his death and thus easing administration.

Increasingly, instead of lodging investments as their Lloyd's deposit, names have put up bank guarantees in lieu. The bank will normally demand security for the issue of the guarantee and, provided that the assets forming the bank's collateral security are held subject to restrictions on use, business relief should be available on those assets. Where, however, the individual has put forward his private residence as collateral security, the Revenue appear to reject business property relief on the grounds that the residence cannot satisfy the 'wholly or mainly for the purposes of a business' test in section 105(1).

Subject to the usual conditions, business property relief at 100% will normally be available at least in part on an individual's Lloyd's interest. Therefore, it is important to maximise the effect of that relief by giving assets representing the Lloyd's interest—whether during life or on death—to persons other than the exempt spouse, eg children.

From 1 January 1994, Lloyd's has for the first time allowed corporate members alongside the existing individual members. Also, Scottish Limited Partnerships now provide a limited liability option of a partnership registered in Scotland which is a separate legal entity. Corporate members are companies in which investors can take up shares without the risks associated with unlimited liability. Corporate names are to be taxed by reference to the time when profits are declared—traditionally three years in arrears. The profits of the 1994 account will be taxed in 1997 when they are declared (FA 1994, section 220). At the same time, the year of assessment for individual Lloyd's names is also being linked to the year of declaration of profits rather than to the Lloyd's account year. Thus the profits of account year 1994 will be declared in 1997 and will form the basis of assessment for the individual for the year 1997–98. Under the present rules the profits for the account year 1993 are assessed for 1993–94 but three years late after they have been declared. As a transitional measure, individual names will have no assessments for the years 1994–95, 1995–96 or 1996–97 (FA 1994, section 228 and Schedule 21). In those three missing years the individual names will be dealing with their pre-1994 years three years in arrears under the old rules.

On the death of an individual Lloyd's member under the pre-1994 income tax rules the position has been that, because the current year's account will not be closed for another three years, the estate could not normally pay out until then. Accordingly, the normal practice under these rules has been to pay annual instalments of inheritance tax until the final payment out whereupon the unpaid portion of the inheritance tax is immediately payable. The three-year delay will rectify itself as the new 1994 rules take effect.

In the context of Lloyd's, see the two recent cases concerning business property relief on underwriting businesses: *Hardcastle*, discussed at **9.9** above; and *Mallender*, discussed at **9.18**(11:) above.

Chapter 10

Foreign Domicile

10.0 INTRODUCTION

Inheritance tax is subject to territorial limits. The UK does not seek to tax a transfer where neither the transferor nor the property transferred has a sufficient connection with the UK. The factors used to determine whether a sufficient connection exists are the domicile of the transferor and the place where the property is situated. If both of these are outside the UK, then the property is excluded from the transferor's estate for inheritance tax purposes. A different test is applied to settled property. Whether or not an interest in possession exists in the property, it is the settlor's domicile, together with the place where the property is situated, which determines whether or not it is excluded property. Property which is not taxed on account of its location and the domicile of the owner or settlor is described as *excluded property* and is discussed at **10.3** below.

Under UK law, every individual has a domicile, but only one domicile. For inheritance tax purposes, a person is domiciled in the state in which he is domiciled under the general law, but with two exceptions. First, a person who is domiciled outside the UK under general law will nevertheless be deemed to be domiciled in the UK for inheritance tax purposes in specific circumstances (see **10.2:1** below). Secondly, a person may be treated as domiciled elsewhere under the provisions of a double taxation treaty and taxed on the basis of that treaty domicile. A third quasi-exception is that the inheritance tax legislation describes a person as domiciled in the UK or not domiciled in the UK. In reality, a person will be domiciled in, say, England, or Scotland, but cannot be domiciled in the UK as such because the UK does not have a unified system of law.

Acquiring a non-UK domicile could be described as the most effective form of inheritance tax planning. On the other hand, it is difficult to acquire a domicile of choice which will displace a UK domicile of origin, difficult to know if this has indeed been achieved, and it requires fairly drastic lifestyle changes which will normally make it undesirable. However, those who do have a non-UK domicile can use this to minimise the impact of inheritance tax on their estates.

10.1 DOMICILE UNDER THE GENERAL LAW

There are three different types of domicile: domicile of origin, domicile of dependence and domicile of choice. They are described as different *types* of domicile because they can be acquired and lost in different ways. The country in which a person is domiciled is sometimes described as his permanent home (see *Winans v Attorney General* [1904] AC 287). This can be a useful description, and it is certainly true that domicile requires a degree of permanence which residence, by contrast, does not. On the other hand, it should be born in mind that both a domicile of origin and a domicile of dependence are acquired by operation of law rather than by choice and that it is possible for a person to be domiciled in a place where he has never been, let alone had a home or lived permanently.

For inheritance tax purposes, a person can be deemed to be domiciled in the UK even though he is domiciled elsewhere under the general law. First, he will be deemed domiciled when he has been resident for 17 out of the 20 years of assessment ending with the present one. This rule is the most relevant to someone coming to the UK. Secondly, he will be deemed domiciled if he was domiciled here within the previous three years.

10.1:1 Domicile of origin

Everyone acquires a domicile of origin at birth and this remains his domicile until it is replaced by a domicile of dependence or a domicile or choice. It is important to identify a person's domicile of origin because it can revive when a domicile of choice is lost. A person's domicile of origin is his father's domicile at the time of his birth unless he was illegitimate or his father died before he was born. In those cases, his domicile of origin will be his mother's domicile. Although as a matter of fact it will often be the country in which he was born, this need not be so. A child might be born in California to parents who have lived there for twenty years. But suppose that the father had an English domicile of origin and that this had not been displaced by a domicile of choice. In that case, the child would acquire an English domicile of origin at birth despite the fact that it might never come to England.

A domicile of origin is the most clinging tenacious form, and will only be displaced if a person acquires a domicile of choice or a domicile of dependence.

10.1:2 Domicile of dependence

Domiciles of dependence now only affect children under 16 and persons of unsound mind. Prior to 1 January 1974, this category included married women. Before that date, a woman acquired her husband's domicile on marriage and her domicile changed when his did.

This rule has now been abolished by the Domicile and Matrimonial Proceedings Act 1973 but has some relevance to women who were married before 1 January 1974. On that date, their existing domiciles of dependence were not abandoned, but became domiciles of choice. Thus a woman may have a domicile of choice on that basis—if it has not been abandoned in the interim—which she would never have acquired on an independent basis. The rule has no relevance to women married on or after 1 January 1974.

10.1:3 Domicile of choice

A domicile of choice is acquired by both physical presence in another country *and* the intention of settling there permanently. It will not be acquired if, for example, that intention is conditional. It will also not be acquired by going to a country for work, even for a an extended period, unless there is a definite intention to stay there permanently once the employment has ceased.

A domicile of choice can be lost by leaving the country without any definite intention of returning. A person will acquire a new domicile of choice if he goes to another country with the intention of settling there permanently. If no new domicile of choice is acquired, his domicile of origin will revive.

A person seeking to establish that a domicile of origin has been lost and a domicile of choice acquired has to discharge a heavy burden of proof. This is equally so whether it is the taxpayer whose domicile of origin is in the UK and who is arguing that it has been superseded by the acquisition of a domicile of choice; or the Revenue arguing that a taxpayer whose domicile of origin is outside the UK has lost that domicile and acquired a domicile of choice in the UK. An example of the latter type of case came before the Special Commissioners recently in *F and another (personal representatives of F deceased) v IRC* [2000] STC (SCD) 1. The Revenue failed to prove that the deceased had lost his Iranian domicile of origin and acquired a UK domicile of choice.

In *IRC v Bullock* [1976] STC 409, the taxpayer had been brought up in Canada but had come to live in England in 1932. He married here and lived here virtually constantly thereafter but was held to have retained his Canadian domicile of origin because his intention, in the event of surviving his wife, was to return to Canada permanently. This meant that he could not be described as having a settled intention of remaining in England permanently.

In *Re Furse, Furse v IRC* [1980] STC 596, on the other hand, the taxpayer had been born in Rhode Island in 1883 and was a US Citizen but had a close connection with England throughout his life. He and his wife had a family house in New York and visited it regularly but they also had a farm in Sussex. It had been bought by the wife in 1924 and the taxpayer lived there until his death in 1963. Unlike the taxpayer in *Bullock*, there was evidence that this taxpayer was happy and contented in the Sussex farm. The only suggestion that he might ever leave England was if and when he was no longer fit enough to lead an active life on the farm. He did not really wish to leave England and was quite settled here. The court accordingly found that he died domiciled in England.

The case of *Re Clore (No 2)* [1984] STC 609 shows how important it is, if there is a settled intention of acquiring a domicile of choice in another jurisdiction, that there is plenty of clear written evidence of that intention and that matters are not just left to the recollections of friends and acquaintances after the death of the individual.

A case highlighted in the Tax Faculty's *Taxline* journal concerned the effect on domicile of the acquisition of British citizenship. *Mr Mohammed Bheekhun* had a domicile of origin in Mauritius. He came to the UK to find work in 1960 at the age of 29. When Mauritius became independent he had to choose whether to take British citizenship or Mauritian citizenship. He chose British citizenship, although he retained business links with Mauritius, acquired properties there and later acquired a Mauritian passport. At all times, he continued to live and work in the UK. When he renewed his UK passport, it described him as resident in the UK.

After his death, his separated spouse claimed under the Inheritance (Provision for Family and Dependants) Act 1975 and her claim depended upon establishing that he died domiciled in the UK. The Court of Appeal upheld the decision that he had acquired a domicile of choice in the UK by the time of his death.

It would be wrong to conclude from this decision that citizenship is a determinant of domicile. It is well settled that it is not. While the case remains unreported, one has to assume that Mr Bheekhun's choice of a UK passport was simply one fact taken into account as evidence of his intention to settle permanently in the UK; but that the question ultimately remains one of fact and that the weight attached to any particular fact will depend on all the circumstances.

10.2 DOMICILE FOR INHERITANCE TAX PURPOSES

A person who is domiciled outside the UK may nevertheless be treated as domiciled in the UK and taxed accordingly if he falls within the scope of IHTA 1984, s 267. Conversely, although domiciled (or deemed domiciled) here, it may be that he is treated as a non-domiciliary under an applicable double tax treaty and his liability for inheritance tax purposes determined accordingly.

In the inheritance tax context, the legislation refers to a person being domiciled in the UK rather than one of its constituent legal systems, such as England and Scotland. There are cases where, under the general law, a person could be domiciled in, say, Germany, but as a result of the wording of the inheritance tax legislation may be domiciled in the UK for tax purposes. This depends on the proper construction of the words used in the legislation and is discussed at **10.2:3** below.

10.2:1 Deemed domicile under IHTA 1984, section 267

A person will be deemed domiciled in the UK if:

(1) he was so domiciled within the last three years; or

(2) he was resident in the UK for 17 out of the last 20 years of assessment *ending with the year of assessment in which the relevant time falls*.

An individual emigrating to the Channel Islands or the Isle of Man is in the same position as someone making a permanent home elsewhere abroad.

In relation to (1), two points should be noted. First, under the general law, the acquisition of an overseas domicile of choice does not depend on any particular time period. Secondly, the three-year period only starts from the actual change of domicile under the general law. This may of course be later than the date of departure from the UK.

In relation to (2), the question of whether a person was resident in the UK in any year of assessment is to be determined as for income tax except that the available accommodation rule does not apply for this purpose. For 1993–94 and later years, that rule does not apply for income tax purposes either, but obviously the question of deemed domicile may turn on a person's residence in earlier years. Thus the former distinction between residence for income tax purposes and residence for inheritance tax purposes (deemed domicile)—ie that the latter excluded the available accommodation rule—remains relevant. For the Revenue's views on residence and ordinary residence, see the Inland Revenue booklet IR20.

Example

Mr Anglophile arrives in the UK on 1 October 1985 and stays. In the tax year 1985–86, the Inland Revenue consider him to be resident because he is in the UK for more than 6 months. He remains resident in the tax year 1986–87 and all later years up to and including 2000–01. On 6 April 2001, at the start of 2001–02—the seventeenth year—he transfers his foreign assets. Unless he went abroad immediately, so as to be non-resident in 2001–02, and stayed abroad until at least 6 April 2002, the gift would be caught for inheritance tax (although it might only be a PET). To be safer still, he should have left the UK in March 2001 before the start of 2001–02 and stayed out the whole tax year, making all the dispositions of his foreign assets during his absence.

In order to avoid breaching either of the above rules (namely the three-year and the 17 out of 20 years rules), a person leaving the UK with a view to acquiring a domicile elsewhere needs to be aware of the different ways in which the two rules work. Then he can ensure that he does not take any action based on his newly acquired non-domiciled status until he is clear of both rules.

Example

Mr Knowall is aged 50 with an English domicile of origin and has been resident in England all his life. He decides to acquire a domicile of choice in Monaco. He leaves England permanently on 31 December 1994.

If he successfully acquired a Monacan domicile of choice on arrival under the general law, he will cease to be deemed domiciled for inheritance tax purposes under rule 1 on 1 January 1998. However, he will not lose his deemed domicile under rule 2 until he has 3 clear years of non-residence behind him and the fourth year has begun. In this case, Mr Knowall was resident in 1994–95 because he spent six months in England during that year. His three years of non-residence would be 1995–96, 1996–97 and 1997–98. Not until 6 April 1998—the first day of the fourth clear year, ie 1998–99—will he have lost his deemed domicile.

The deemed domicile rules do not apply for all purposes (see IHTA 1984, s 267(2)). They do not apply to:

(1) the exemption for specified government securities in the beneficial ownership of persons neither domiciled nor ordinarily resident in the UK (section 6(2));

(2) certain types of national savings by persons domiciled in the Channel Islands or the Isle of Man (section 6(3));

(3) the interpretation of pre-CTT double taxation agreements still in force by section 158(6)—such agreements entered into in the CTT/IHT era contain their own rules for domicile and for resolving the question where both countries claim domicile.

In the three instances above, the general law of domicile applies. In circumstances where the assets are located abroad and the actual residence of the parties liable to inheritance tax is abroad, albeit strictly domiciled in the UK for inheritance tax purposes, the Revenue may have difficulties enforcing the liability: see *Government of India v Taylor* [1955] AC 491. The Revenue are unlikely to be able to enforce inheritance tax or indeed other tax liabilities abroad although they may be able to recover from UK-resident beneficiaries. Arguably, in the case of states that are parties to the Brussels and Lugano Conventions, these difficulties of enforcement are reduced: see the article on this subject by Alastair Ladkin [2000] PTPR, volume 7, issue 3, at 215.

10.2:2   Treaty domicile

If a person is domiciled or deemed domiciled here under UK law, but is also domiciled in another state under that state's domestic law, then the terms of any applicable double tax treaty should be consulted in order to determine whether or not he will in fact be taxed as a domiciliary. Typically, a treaty will have a tie-breaker provision which contains a list of factors which determine which country the person will be treated as domiciled in for the purposes of the treaty.

A taxpayer who is neither domiciled nor deemed domiciled need not be concerned with treaty tie-breaker provisions. These may cause a domiciliary to be taxed as a non-domiciliary but they do not work the other way around. However, treaties may still help a non-domiciliary who has some UK situs property. This will depend on the terms of the particular treaty.

Currently, we have capital taxes treaties with France, India, the Irish Republic, Italy, the Netherlands, Pakistan, South Africa, Sweden, Switzerland and the US. Using the US treaty as an example, fiscal domicile for treaty purposes is determined by article 4, set out below:

(1)   For the purposes of this Convention an individual was domiciled—

   (a)   in the United States: if he was a resident (domiciliary) thereof or if he was a national thereof and had been a resident (domiciliary) thereof at any time during the preceding three years; and

   (b)   in the United Kingdom: if he was domiciled in the United Kingdom in accordance with the law of the United Kingdom or is treated as so domiciled for the purposes of a tax which is the subject of this Convention.

(2)   Where by reason of the provisions of paragraph (1) an individual was at any time domiciled in both Contracting States, and

   (a)   was a national of the United Kingdom but not of the United States, and

   (b)   had not been resident in the United States for Federal income tax purposes in seven or more of the ten taxable years ending with the year in which that time falls,

he shall be deemed to be domiciled in the United Kingdom at that time.

(3)   Where by reason of the provisions of paragraph (1) an individual was at any time domiciled in both Contracting States, and

   (a)   was a national of the United States but not of the United Kingdom, and

   (b)   had not been resident in the United Kingdom in seven or more of the ten income tax years of assessment ending with the year in which that time falls,

he shall be deemed to be domiciled in the United States at that time. For the purposes of this paragraph, the question of whether a person was so resident shall be determined as for income tax purposes but without regard to any dwelling-house available to him in the United Kingdom for his use.

(4)   Where by reason of the provisions of paragraph (1) an individual was domiciled in both Contracting States, then, subject to the provisions of paragraphs (2) and (3), his status shall be determined as follows—

(a) the individual shall be deemed to be domiciled in the Contracting State in which he had a permanent home available to him. If he had a permanent home available to him in both Contracting States, or in neither Contracting State, he shall be deemed to be domiciled in the Contracting State with which his personal and economic relations were closest (centre of vital interests);

(b) if the Contracting State in which the individual's centre of vital interests was located cannot be determined, he shall be deemed to be domiciled in the Contracting State in which he had an habitual abode;

(c) if the individual had an habitual abode in both Contracting States or in neither of them he shall be deemed to be domiciled in the Contracting State of which he was a national; and

(d) if the individual was a national of both Contracting States or of neither of them, the competent authorities of the Contracting States shall settle the question by mutual agreement.

(5) An individual who was a resident (domiciliary) of a possession of the United States and who became a citizen of the United States solely by reason of his—

(a) being a citizen of such possession, or

(b) birth or residence within such possession,

shall be considered as neither domiciled in nor a national of the United States for the purposes of this Convention.

Where a person is domiciled in both states as a matter of their respective domestic laws (article 4(1)), the succeeding sub-paragraphs operate as tie-breakers, to determine in which state he will be treated as domiciled for the purposes of the treaty.

10.2:3 Domicile within the UK

Property which is not settled property can only be excluded property if the person beneficially entitled to it is an individual *domiciled outside the United Kingdom* (section 6(1)). Settled property can only be excluded property if the settlor was not *domiciled in the United Kingdom* at the time the settlement was made (section 48(3)(a)). The property must also be situated outside the UK in order to be excluded property. This is discussed at 10.4 below.

On the domicile point, it is slightly surprising that the legislation refers to domicile in or outside the UK. This is because, under the general law, a person is not domiciled in the UK as such. The UK is not a unified legal system. He will be domiciled in England or, say, Scotland. This is more than a difference of form. Consider the following examples.

First Example

Beatrice's domicile of origin is in France. She comes to England and takes up residence in Sussex. She is quite certain that she will never return to France and she intends to settle permanently in Scotland.

Beatrice has not lost her domicile of origin in France.

Second Example

Bertrand's domicile of origin is in France. He comes to England and takes up residence in Sussex. He is quite certain that he will never return to France and he intends to settle permanently in Cumbria.

Bertrand has acquired a domicile of choice in England.

It has been argued that the wording of the excluded property provisions means that Beatrice would be domiciled in the UK for inheritance tax purposes, albeit that she remains domiciled in France under the general law. This argument assumes that the inheritance tax legislation is introducing a new concept of UK domicile, which involves treating the UK as a single jurisdiction and applying the law of domicile to that deemed jurisdiction.

This is probably wrong. The wording of the legislation is not sufficient to create this new concept and the Revenue are not believed to have taken the point. It is more likely that a person is domiciled in the UK for the purposes of section 48(3)(a) if she is domiciled (in the real sense) in one of the parts of the UK. She is domiciled outside the UK if she is not domiciled in any of those parts. Beatrice falls into the latter category.

10.3 NON-UK DOMICILIARIES—EXCLUDED PROPERTY

Note that reference is made to the place where a property is situated. This is discussed under **10.4** below.

10.3:1 Non-settled property

Property situated outside the UK is excluded property if the person beneficially entitled to it is an individual domiciled outside the UK (section 6(1)). This rule does not apply if the property is settled. This is so even if there is a person with an interest in possession who is treated as beneficially entitled to the property in which the interest subsists: section 49(1). This is because of a specific provision (section 48(3)(b)) preventing section 6(1) from applying to settled property and, notwithstanding section 49(1), property subject to, say, a life interest remains settled property.

10.3:2 Settled property

Property comprised in a settlement and situated outside the UK will be excluded property if the settlor was domiciled outside the UK at the time the settlement was made. The domicile of the beneficiary is irrelevant even if he has an interest in possession. Note that reversionary interests are dealt with separately at **10.3:3** below.

Suppose that a settlor was domiciled in Switzerland and, at that time, settled assets in France on his UK-domiciled son. If that son transfers his interest in the settlement or dies, there will be no transfer of value and accordingly no chargeable transfer. This is because excluded property is simply left out in valuing a person's estate. This means that a person's estate, as defined, is not diminished by a transfer of such property.

Conversely, a settlement made by a UK domiciled settlor is not excluded property even if all the beneficiaries are domiciled abroad, all the property is situated abroad and the trustees are non-resident. In such circumstances, a distribution to a non-domiciled beneficiary in the hope that he will re-settle will often be advisable. However, care should be taken not to trigger an inheritance tax charge by doing so. If the trust is discretionary, an exit charge may be triggered. If there is an interest in possession, the distribution is likely to be a PET.

Although a settlement made by a non-domiciliary is clearly in an advantageous position from the point of view of inheritance tax, there are a number of points which should be born in mind when planning for these settlements.

- **First**, if the settlor or spouse has an initial interest in possession which is followed by discretionary trusts, IHTA 1984, s 80, will treat the settlement as made by the person with the interest in possession at the time of the termination of that interest. The property in which that interest subsisted is treated as becoming comprised in a new settlement at the date of that termination. To be excluded property, the person beneficially entitled to the interest in possession must have been non-domiciled at the date of termination of his interest (IHTA 1984, s 82). This condition must be met in addition to those in section 48(3)(a). This rule means that one needs to be wary of these initial interests in possession lest, for example, a deemed domicile is acquired from the spouse who is entitled to the interest before that interest terminates.

- **Secondly**, one should not normally mix UK situated assets and non-UK situated assets in the same discretionary trust. This is because the overseas assets will be taken into account in computing the effective rate of tax applicable to the UK property.

- **Thirdly**, one should avoid having a UK-domiciled individual as a joint settlor of an otherwise excluded property settlement. In most cases, such settlements will be treated as two separate settlements by IHTA 1984, s 44(2). One will consist of excluded property and the other will not. However, section 44(2) is qualified. The settlements will only be treated as two separate settlements *where the circumstances so require*. Although the Revenue accept that the determination of the extent to which overseas assets in a settlement are excluded property by reason of the settlor's domicile will normally be a relevant 'required circumstance' (RI 166), this will not invariably be so. In particular, if an attribution of the settled property between the contributions made by each settlor is not feasible, this treatment will not be adopted. To ensure that such attribution is feasible, the trustees need to keep very careful records. This can become very complicated and time-consuming. The creation of two separate settlements in the first place will normally be a more practicable solution. For similar reasons, a settlor who subsequently becomes UK domiciled should avoid adding assets to the settlement.

- **Fourthly**, the excluded property character of the settlement overrides the gift with reservation rules: see *Law Society Gazette* 10 December 1986—exchange of letters between Touche Ross and the CTO. There are, however, indications that the Revenue may change their views. Therefore there is no current objection to the settlor being an object of the discretionary trust, but note the warning of a future change in practice: see **10.5**(2) below. The settlor beneficiary should not, however, be excluded subsequently by the trustees from benefiting in his or her lifetime as that will then constitute a deemed potentially exempt transfer under FA 1986, s 102(4).

- **Fifthly**, the creation of this settlement could have income tax disadvantages as a transfer of assets under TA 1988, ss 739–740.

10.3:3 Reversionary interests

The circumstances in which a reversionary interest will be excluded property are different from other assets. The general rule is that a reversionary interest is excluded property by definition irrespective of anyone's domicile (IHTA 1984, s 48(1)). This is the counterbalance to the treatment of a person entitled to an interest in possession as beneficially entitled to the whole property in which that interest subsists (s 49(1)). If the reversion were not excluded property, then the same property would be treated as comprised in more than one person's estate. There are, however, three exceptions to this general rule:

(1) if the reversionary interest has been acquired at any time for a considera-tion in money or money's worth (section 48(1)(a));

(2) if the settlor or his spouse has been beneficially entitled to the reversionary interest (section 48(1)(b));

(3) if the reversionary interest is expectant on the determination of a lease treated as a settlement by s 43(3) (section 48(1)(c)).

In relation to (1), it applies even if the person currently entitled to the interest did not acquire it for a consideration. It is sufficient to prevent the reversion from being excluded property that a person previously entitled acquired it for money or money's worth.

There are two notable qualifications to (2). First, if the interest is under a settlement created before 16 April 1976, then (2) does not apply. Secondly, if the person entitled to the reversion acquired it before 10 March 1981, then it will not be within the exception if the settlor or spouse was beneficially entitled to it only before that date.

A lease of property is treated as a settlement if the term of the lease is for life or lives or for a period ascertainable only by reference to a death and it is not granted for full consideration in money or money's worth. Exception (3) provides that a reversionary interest in property treated as settled under that definition is not—or not automatically—excluded property.

Probably most reversionary interests will be excluded property under the general rule because they do not fall within one of the three exceptions just discussed. However, even if they do fall within one of those exceptions, they may nevertheless be excluded property under one of the normal rules.

(1) If the reversion has itself been settled, then it will be excluded property if the settlor was non-domiciled when it was settled and it is situated outside the UK (section 48(3)(a)). Note that this rule only applies where the reversion has been settled on other trusts and it is the domicile of the settlor of those other trusts that matters. The rule expressly does not apply to a reversion arising under trusts created by a non-domiciliary if it has not been re-settled.

(2) If the reversion has not been settled, it will be excluded property if the

person beneficially entitled to it is non-domiciled and—again—the reversion is situated outside the UK (section 6(1) and 48(3)(b)).

Example

A, who is non-UK domiciled and non-resident, settles some US-registered shares on trustees resident in the Cayman Islands for B for life and thereafter for C. B and C are both domiciled in the UK and the proper law of the settlement is the law of the Cayman Islands.

At this stage, both the shares themselves and the reversionary interest are excluded property. The shares (to which B is treated as beneficially entitled under section 49(1)) are excluded property under section 48(3)(a): they are situated in the US and the settlor (A) was non-domiciled when the settlement was made. The reversionary interest is excluded property under the general rule in section 48(1). It does not fall within any of the three exceptions.

Suppose that C then sells his reversion to a non-domiciliary, D, for a cash sum. In D's hands, the reversion is no longer excluded property under the general rule because it falls within the first exception. It has been acquired for a consideration in money or money's worth. However, it will remain excluded property if, but only if, it is situated outside the UK. In that case, its situs combined with D's domicile will make it excluded property under section 6(1).

The law on the situs of a reversionary interest is not entirely clear but, unless the property in which the interest subsists is land, the reversion is treated as a chose in action and is situated where it is enforceable. In this case, that is probably the Cayman Islands.

10.4   SITUS

The following is a very brief summary of the situs of some assets under the common law. However, this is a complex subject and if there is any doubt over the situs of an asset reference should be made to a more detailed work on the subject such as *Dicey & Morris*.

10.4:1   Immovables

Land, buildings on the land and interests in the land are immovable property and are situated where the land itself is situated. However, the characterisation of property as an interest in land is probably a question for the law of the country where the land itself is situated.

10.4:2   Tangible movables

These are situated in the place where they are physically located at any particular time. Tangible movables include chattels and cash.

10.4:3   Shares and securities

A share or security whose mode of transfer is an entry in the company's register is situated in the place where that register is kept or where the transfer would normally be effected.

A bearer share or security—ie one transferable by mere delivery—is situated in the place where it is physically present.

10.4:4 Debts and choses in action

These are normally situated in the place where they are enforceable, ie generally where the debtor resides.

10.4:5 Equitable interests

These must be divided into proprietary interests and rights against the trustees. The former are situated where the underlying property is situated and the latter (as choses in action) where the trustees are resident or, possibly, in the place of the proper law of the trust.

In very general terms, one would expect absolute interests, interests under bare trusts and interests in possession to be treated as proprietary interests and thus situated where the underlying assets are situated; and discretionary interests, interests in unadministered estates and reversionary interests to be choses in action.

10.5 IHT PLANNING—NON-UK ASSETS OF NON-UK DOMICILIARY

A non-domiciliary who has assets abroad would generally be well advised to settle these if there is any risk of becoming UK-domiciled or deemed domiciled. The assets can be settled on discretionary trusts with the settlor as a possible beneficiary and still benefit from excluded property status.
Note that in these circumstances:

(1) the domicile of the beneficiaries is immaterial; and

(2) the gift with reservation rules (FA 1986, s 102) should not apply because the excluded property rules prevail. The Revenue accept this. See the exchange of letters between Touche Ross and the Capital Taxes Office, *Law Society Gazette*, 10 December 1986 and CTO Advanced Instruction Manual at D8. However, there are rumours that this Revenue practice may change.

In the case of an individual who has been resident for 17 or more of the last 20 years, the solution may be for that individual to become non-resident for the period necessary to lose this deemed domicile before making the settlement.

In the example below, the shaded area shows the last 20 years of assessment including the current one, 2001–02.

Clients B and C have been resident for at least 17 out of the last 20 years of assessment ending with the current year. This will be so whether or not either is resident for 2001–02. In the case of client B, he will have been resident for 20 out of the last 20 years if he remains resident this year; 19 out of the last 20 years if he does not. In either case, he will be deemed domiciled. Client C will have been resident for 18 out of the last 20 years if he remains resident this year and 17 out of the last 20 years if he does not. If client C is non-resident in 2001–02 and remains so in 2002–03 he will lose his deemed domicile under rule (2) in the latter year.

Clients A and D, on the other hand, will only be deemed domiciled under rule (2) if they remain resident for 2001–02. If either becomes non-resident this year, he will not be deemed domiciled under rule (2). In the case of client A, if he remains resident in 2001–02, then he will not be able to lose his deemed domicile under this rule until 2005–06.

	Client A	Client B	Client C	Client D
2005–06				
2004–05				
2003–04				
2002–03				
2001–02	*******	*******	*******	*******
2000–01	16	19	17	16
1999–2000	15	18	16	15
1998–99	14	17	15	14
1997–98	13	16	14	13
1996–97	12	15	13	12
1995–96	11	14	12	11
1994–95	10	13	11	10
1993–94	9	12	10	9
1992–93	8	11	9	8
1991–92	7	10	8	7
1990–91	6	9	7	6
1989–90	5	8	6	5
1988–89	4	7	5	4
1987–88	3	6	4	3
1986–87	2	5	3	
1985–86	1	4	2	
1984–85		3	1	
1983–84		2		2
1982–83		1		1
1981–82				
1980–81				

An individual who is neither domiciled nor deemed domiciled, but is likely to become so, should aim to set up an excluded property settlement. If he is not yet clear about who he wishes to benefit he can simply create a discretionary settlement with a wide class of beneficiaries (including himself) and with power to add further beneficiaries nominated by him. The trust assets need to remain abroad to ensure that they are excluded property.

Having done this, the trust property will remain excluded property so long as it remains settled and outside the UK. The trustees can appoint life interests to domiciled and resident beneficiaries without incurring any inheritance tax charge at that time or on the later disposal by the beneficiaries of their interests on death or otherwise—again, so long as the property remains settled and outside the UK.

This is subject to one important caveat. If the settlor retains an interest in the property, for example as a discretionary beneficiary, he is treated as making a gift with reservation. This does not matter if he retains his interest in the property until his death. The charge that would arise in relation to that property on his death under FA 1986, s 102(3), is currently accepted by the Revenue as inapplicable to excluded property. However, if his interest comes to an end during his lifetime, he is deemed by FA 1986, s 102(4), to make a potentially exempt transfer. Technically, this will become chargeable if he dies within seven years, despite the property being excluded property. The risk of this charge can be avoided by ensuring that if the settlor has an initial interest in the property he retains that interest until his death.

There is no need for an excluded property settlement to have non-resident trustees. If there is no real prospect of any of the beneficiaries being non-resident or non-domiciled then it might be simpler to choose resident trustees. On the other hand, non-resident trustees can roll up income from foreign property tax-free provided that it is not remitted to the UK (TA 1988, s 739) or paid to ordinarily resident beneficiaries (TA 1988, s 740). Capital gains tax can similarly be deferred until a beneficiary receives a capital payment (TCGA 1992, s 87) but the advantage of doing so tends to be outweighed by the surcharge which can lead to an effective tax rate of up to 64%. On the other hand, if there is some chance that the beneficiaries may be resident or domiciled outside the UK, then using non-resident trustees preserves flexibility for the future.

10.6 POSSIBLE IHT PLANNING—UK ASSETS OF NON-UK DOMICILIARY

10.6:1 Government securities free of tax while in foreign ownership (ss 6(2) and 48(4))

Certain government securities which are not settled property and are in the beneficial ownership of persons neither domiciled nor ordinarily resident in the UK are exempt from taxation under the provisions of F(No 2)A 1931, s 22(1), or F(No 2)A 1915, s 47. Such securities are excluded property and will therefore give rise to no inheritance tax charge. These exempt gilts can be found quite easily by a distinguishing mark in the *Financial Times*. They are, however, a dwindling species because no new exempt issues have been made since 18 March 1977 to discourage inflows of capital into sterling. Nevertheless, earlier issues of this kind remain protected.

In the same way, if the exempt gilts are settled property and such a non-domiciled and non-ordinarily resident person is beneficially entitled to an interest in possession in them they will likewise be excluded property.

In the case of a discretionary trust (ie a trust in which no interest in possession subsists), the securities will be excluded property provided that all known persons for whose benefit the settled property or income from it has been or might be applied or who might become beneficially entitled to an interest in possession in it are persons neither domiciled nor ordinarily resident in the UK.

A charity is not 'a known person for whose benefit the settled property might be applied' because it does not itself benefit and therefore the presence of a UK charity amongst non-domiciled beneficiaries does not mean that the exemption will be lost (*Von Ernst & Cie SA v IRC* [1980] STC 111, CA). *Von Ernst* was a case on the wording of paragraph 3(2) of Schedule 7 to FA 1975. Sections 6(2) and 48(4) now refer to a 'person of a description specified in the condition in question' (FA 1996), ie a person who is neither ordinarily resident nor domiciled in the UK. The case remains relevant in marginally reducing the otherwise wide list of likely beneficiaries.

As an anti-avoidance measure, where property leaves one settlement for another, the conditions have to be satisfied in respect of both. Similarly, pursuant to sections 6(2) and 267(2), certain savings certificates and similar deposits held by persons beneficially entitled to them and domiciled in the Channel Islands or the Isle of Man are excluded property. In the case of government securities and these savings the deemed domiciled rules in section 267(1) do not apply. The exemption could be particularly useful if exchange control were to be re-imposed and the individual in question was prevented from investing these sterling funds abroad. Similarly, where for future exchange control or other reasons assets have to remain in the UK for a period of time it might then be appropriate for such an individual to charge these assets in the UK and use the proceeds to purchase such exempt government securities or savings as appropriate.

10.6:2   Selling UK assets

In other circumstances, where a non-domiciled individual wishes to make a gift and has chargeable UK assets, he might consider selling those assets and remitting the proceeds of sale abroad. The sale of the assets will not generate an inheritance tax liability, although the capital gains tax consequences should be born in mind. There should not be any CGT if the individual is neither resident nor ordinarily resident at the time of the sale. Once the proceeds have been remitted abroad, a gift of the cash—or the foreign assets in which it has been reinvested—can be made: and see *Carter v Sharon* 20 TC 229.

10.6:3   Interposing overseas investment company

Owning assets through a company whose shares are situated abroad is a common strategy for non-domiciliaries. The shares in the non-UK company will be excluded property. If a UK-situated asset, such as house—which is obviously not excluded property—is transferred into such a company, its value is taken outside the scope of inheritance tax. The shares in the non-UK company might be put into a non-resident trust, thereby preserving their excluded property status in the event of the settlor acquiring a UK domicile or deemed domicile in the future.

This strategy will usually be sound for inheritance tax purposes but there are a number of risks associated with it, particularly where the property is occupied by a person who exercises *de facto* control over the company and the trustees. This has recently been dramatically illustrated by the Court of Appeal in *R v Dimsey; R v Allen* [1999] STC 846, although the case is due to be heard in the House of Lords shortly and so the following comments must be reconsidered in the light of that decision.

There are two principal risks. The first is that the individual is a shadow director whose rent-free occupation of the property is an emolument taxable under Schedule E. The second is that the company is resident in the UK—which may happen even while the shares remain situated outside the UK for inheritance tax purposes. The first risk follows from the Court of Appeal's finding that a shadow director within TA 1988, section 168(8) is an office holder for the purposes of sections 145 and 146. A shadow director is someone in accordance with whose instructions the directors are accustomed to act. The value of his rent-free occupation is treated as an emolument taxable under Schedule E.

At the outset, the individual needs to decide whether to make absolutely certain that he is not a shadow director, or whether to accept that he is a director and mitigate the tax liability. To avoid being a shadow director, he needs to ensure that there is an independent board of directors who do not take instructions from him. These directors must not simply ratify suggestions made by him or, where the shares are held in trust, by the trustees at his direction. The directors must take decisions independently. Unless they disagree with the individual and reject his ideas from time to time, this will be difficult to prove. From the adviser's point of view, you must ensure that the client is genuinely prepared to cede control of the company to independent directors without interfering and that he will stick to this throughout the lifetime of the arrangement.

If he is not prepared to do this, he could take the second option of accepting that he is a director but mitigating the income tax liability in one of two main ways. First, if he is also non-resident, he could try to ensure that most of his emoluments (the value of the rent-free occupation) are attributable to duties performed outside the UK. As a non-resident, he will not be taxable on these foreign emoluments. This can be achieved by performing substantial duties outside the UK, such as attending board meetings etc. Whilst it may not be possible to avoid performing *any* duties within the UK—decorating or repairs may be considered duties—it should be possible to keep these to a minimum. There is a risk that the Revenue will argue that the emoluments are exclusively referable to the UK duties, but this risk can be minimised by suitably drafted contracts between the individual and the company.

The second mitigation strategy is to pay a market rent for the period of occupation. In the case of a non-resident, the periods of occupation will be relatively short, but perhaps longer if the individual is UK resident. If the property cost £75,000 or less, then the true cost of paying the market rent would only be the basic rate income tax payable by the company. However, for properties costing more than £75,000, TA 1988, s 146 treats the occupier as receiving emoluments equal to the appropriate percentage of so much of the cost as exceeds £75,000. The appropriate percentage is the official rate of interest—currently 6.25 per cent. This can lead to a significant charge: on a property worth £1,000,000 a 40% taxpayer would have an annual tax charge of £23,125 under this provision. It is possible to avoid this charge using two separate trusts.

The second risk of an offshore company is that it becomes UK resident. If this risk materialises, there are very serious income and corporation tax consequences. The company will be subject to corporation tax on its Schedule A profits and on any chargeable gains it realises. This is particularly unfortunate for a non-resident individual who would himself have been outside the scope of capital gains tax. There will also be a Schedule F charge on dividends or distributions that are not specifically excluded from income tax. In contrast, if the company is non-resident, there is no UK tax charge on dividends or distributions to a non-resident shareholder. Additionally, even if the individual has avoided being a shadow director, he will become taxable on the value of his rent-free occupation under TA 1988 section 418 if the company is resident, assuming that it is a close company.

To avoid this scenario, first, of course, the shares must be registered outside the UK. Secondly, there must be absolutely no possibility of the company's central management or control being in the UK. Board meetings must take place outside the UK. Major decisions should be taken at these meetings and they should be properly minuted. The individual must not take any remotely significant decisions or actions in relation to the company whilst in the UK. He may be on the board—although see the discussion above in relation to sections 145 and 146—but he must only perform his duties as director whilst outside the UK.

It may be possible to reduce both of the above risks if the shares are held by non-resident trustees instead of by the individual but this is by no means automatic. Whether central management and control is exercised in the UK and whether the individual is a shadow director are both questions of fact. The interposition of trustees will not itself affect the answer to either question. If the individual takes management decisions, which are effectively conveyed to the board by the trustees, the results will be just as disastrous as if the individual had given instructions to the directors himself. In theory, the trustees may hear suggestions from the individual, then make an independent decision as to whether or not to instruct the directors accordingly. In practice, if the individual's suggestions are invariably adopted, it will be difficult to demonstrate that the trustees' decision is truly independent. The best advice is always to ensure that the individual only makes suggestions outside the UK and—if he does not want to be a shadow director—that he does not make them at all.

10.6:4 Utilising the inter-spouse exemption

Note that the exemption for inter-spouse transfers is limited to £55,000 where the transferor spouse is UK domiciled and the transferee spouse is not.

10.6:5 Non-sterling bank accounts in foreign ownership (s 157)

A foreign currency account with the Post Office or a recognised bank in the UK is left out of account for inheritance tax purposes on the death of a person who is neither domiciled, resident nor ordinarily resident in the UK immediately before he dies. This exclusion does not apply to a sterling bank account in the UK. It does, however, apply to a foreign currency account in the UK held on the terms of a settlement in which the non-domiciled, non-resident and non-ordinarily resident person had an interest in possession as long as the settlor was non-domiciled when the settlement was made *and* the trustees were neither domiciled, resident nor ordinarily resident in the UK immediately before the beneficiary's death.

10.7 PRACTICAL POINTS

10.7:1 Wills

On acquiring a new residence, the individual should either make a new will complying with the relevant foreign law (possibly with a view to a change of domicile)—as well as English law if assets remain situate here—or at least check that his UK will is valid under the foreign law in question. An alternative is to have more than one will, dealing separately with the assets situated in each jurisdiction on death. This has the advantage that those ultimately applying for probate in the UK will only be concerned with UK assets under the UK will. If there is any likely doubt over whether a person has acquired a new domicile of choice, his relevant intentions should be recited in the will and in any deeds effecting lifetime gifts.

10.7:2 Statutory declaration

Immediately after taking up foreign residence and domicile, the individual could swear a statutory declaration outlining the facts relevant to this change. Alternatively, a declaration could be sworn immediately before leaving the UK. Some advisers do not favour this course on the basis that it might raise doubt in the mind of the Revenue as to the change of domicile, but the case of *Re Clore (No 2)* [1984] STC 609 (see **10.1:3** above) illustrates the need for clear evidence of the individual's own state of mind and intentions.

10.7:3 Deeds of variation

A beneficiary under the will of a non-domiciled testator could enter into a deed of variation settling his interest under the will. This will create an excluded property settlement if the assets consist of (or later become) non-UK situated, whatever the domicile of the varying beneficiary or the other beneficiaries under the settlement. For inheritance tax purposes, the variation—subject to complying with all the conditions of IHTA 1984, s 142—is treated as made by the testator for all the purposes of IHTA 1984. The interests under the varied settlement could include a life interest for the varying beneficiary or a discretionary settlement for a class of beneficiaries including him. The only possibility of an inheritance tax charge during the lifetime of the settlement is if trust property becomes situated in the UK and a transfer of value occurs whilst it remains situated in the UK or if the law changes. The gifts with reservation rules do not apply because FA 1986 is construed as one with IHTA 1984 and thus the variation is treated as made by the testator not the varying beneficiary.

However, the capital gains tax and income tax legislation are not so generous. The capital gains tax legislation deems the variation to have been made by the testator for limited purposes. First, TCGA 1992, s 62(6)(a) prevents the variation itself from being a disposal. Secondly, it provides for section 62 itself to apply as if the variation had been effected by the testator (s 62(6)(b)). This means that those benefiting from the variation will be deemed to have acquired the assets on the testator's death at their market value at that date.

Beyond those two specific provisions, the variation has its normal consequences for capital gains tax purposes. In particular, the varying beneficiary will be the settlor for the purposes of TCGA 1992, ss 77 and 86 and chargeable on gains accruing to the trustees. See the House of Lords decision in *Marshall v Kerr* [1994] STC 638.

For income tax purposes, there are no special rules applicable to variations and so, again, the varying beneficiary will be the settlor.

Being the settlor for income and capital gains tax purposes is unlikely to put the beneficiary in a worse position than he would have been in had he retained the assets absolutely, so it should not deter him from varying a will to create an excluded property settlement. The last statement should be qualified in the case of a non-resident settlement. Whilst the provisions deeming income and gains to be those of the settlor generally include rights of reimbursement against the trustees, the enforceability of these rights against non-resident trustees is somewhat doubtful. See *Government of India v Taylor* [1955] AC

491. If the settlor is not a beneficiary, the trustees may be unable to reimburse him without committing a breach of trust. This problem can be averted by ensuring that the settlor is a beneficiary.

10.7:4   Application to HM Inspector of Taxes as to acquisition of new residence

As soon as a dramatic break with the UK is made, the individual's advisers should write to his inspector of taxes explaining the change of residence and domicile as the case may be, with reasons. This is clearly primarily concerned with obtaining the income and capital gains tax advantages. The inspector will normally give provisional agreement that there has been a change of residence but final confirmation is unlikely before the expiry of at least three years. The Revenue have in recent years shown a marked reluctance to give this final confirmation unless the emigrant needs to continue completing UK tax returns because of UK source income. This uncertainty has increased with self-assessment.

10.7:5   Transfer of assets abroad

The income tax consequences of transferring assets abroad under TA 1988, ss 739 and 740 must be carefully considered. These provisions apply to persons ordinarily resident in the UK. Section 739 applies to transferors and section 740 to other persons. The Revenue originally considered that section 739 applied to both transferors and non-transferors but this view was rejected by the House of Lords in *Vestey v IRC (Nos 1 and 2)* [1980] STC 10. The consequence was the introduction of what is now TA 1988, s 740. There are similar provisions for capital gains tax purposes: TCGA 1992, s 86, which taxes settlors, and TCGA 1992, s 87, which taxes those who receive capital payments from the trustees.

10.7:6   Reporting requirements

Under IHTA 1984, s 218, any professional person other than a barrister who is concerned with making a settlement with a UK-domiciled settlor and non-resident trustees must make a return to the Board within three months, giving the names and addresses of the settlor and trustees. A person is absolved from this requirement if someone else has already reported the settlement or if the settlement is made by will.

Section 219 gives the Revenue wide powers to obtain information from any person, although barristers and solicitors are not obliged to disclose privileged information without the client's consent. A solicitor may nevertheless be required to give the name and address of the client. In the case of non-resident clients whose businesses include creating or managing offshore companies or trusts, the solicitor may also be required to disclose the names and addresses of persons for whom such services have been provided.

10.7:7   Testing domicile

The concept of domicile can be a grey area for a number of reasons and it will often be desirable to test the position with the Revenue. There are two main methods for testing domicile.

For further details, see the article by Giles Clarke in *Capital Taxes and Estate Planning Quarterly* 1991 No 2 p 21:

> 'First, in the case of an individual claiming to have a foreign domicile (eg of origin) but who is UK resident and where it is feared that a UK domicile of choice may have arisen. In respect of foreign source income, the test involves claiming assessment on the remittance basis (ie available to a non-domiciled though UK resident individual) and not on the world-wide arising basis. An appropriate amount should be so remitted and a tax return suitable for a non-domiciled person completed.
>
> Secondly, and with more difficulty, is the situation of a person who has had a UK domicile, eg of origin, but considers he should have acquired a domicile of choice outside the UK and who is non-resident. As he will be non-UK resident, the first method will not help. Instead, a pilot settlement can be set up of discretionary type with non-UK situs assets and somewhat exceeding the IHT nil rate band plus the available annual exemptions. Confirmation would be sought of the CTO that no IHT is payable. If he is non-UK domiciled, the gift into settlement is excluded property; if he is UK domiciled, it is a chargeable lifetime transfer. If only very little IHT is involved in the use of the pilot settlement, the CTO might defer a definitive judgment, therefore a substantial amount of IHT may have to be put at risk.'

Finally, on the subject of domicile, an adviser should remember that it will not always be beneficial to a client to establish a non-UK domicile. An example might be a US citizen with established roots in the UK, whose assets consist mainly of business and agricultural property. It may be—and this must of course be checked by reference to the advice of his US lawyers—that he would pay less tax if taxed as a UK domiciliary than if taxed as a US domiciliary. In that case, the advice should be aimed towards losing his US domicile, or at least ensuring that he acquires a UK domicile which would override the US domicile under the treaty tie-breaker provisions.

Appendix 1

IHT rate scale

The following scale applies for transfers made on or after 6 April 1999.

Band Up to £	Rate %	Cumulative tax £
242,000	Nil	Nil
Over 242,000	40%	

Note The mechanism in s 8 provides for annual upgrading of tax bands by reference to the retail price index, unless in any year Parliament should decide otherwise. Parliament did in fact decide otherwise in FA 1997, and the Finance Bill 1997 published by the new Labour government has left it intact. With just the one positive rate of 40%, it is only the ceiling of the nil rate band that may be indexed. For lifetime chargeable transfers the normal rate of 40% is halved to 20% under s 7(2). If, however, the transferor dies within seven years, the tax is recalculated under s 7(4) using the normal 40% rate, subject to any taper relief due (see **1.2:1**).

Grossing up For lifetime chargeable gifts the transferor can either leave the donees (say the trustees of a discretionary trust) to pay the immediate IHT out of the gift itself, or he can pay the tax himself so that the donees keep the amount given. In this latter case the gift has to be grossed up.

Example

Mr A has already made lifetime chargeable gifts totalling £242,000 gross on 6 April 2001. On 10 May 2001 he makes another lifetime chargeable gift by transferring £100,000 on discretionary trusts. He wants to pay the IHT of 20% himself so that the trustees are left with a net £100,000. The gift of £100,000 is therefore grossed up by a factor of 100/80 = £125,000. The IHT at 20% is £25,000, which Mr A pays. The gift for the cumulative ladder is the gross £125,000: see **1.2:5**.

Tapered rates

The rates below apply to gifts made within seven years of death. The taper relief is given by charging the percentage below of the normal death rate, ie, in the fourth year before death the rate is 80% × 40% = 32% on the gift (s 7(4)).

Years before death	Percentage of death rate
0–3	100%
3–4	80%
4–5	60%
5–6	40%
6–7	20%

Examples
Note In these examples it is assumed:
(i)   No annual exemptions
(ii) No change in *rates of IHT*.

Example 1 (All property passes on death or treated as so passing)
Estate of £576,000

	£		£
IHT payable on	242,000	=	Nil
on next	334,000 @ 40%	=	133,600
Total IHT		=	133,600

Example 2 (showing PET and taper)
Estate of £576,000
Assume gift (eg outright to individual) of £276,000 made
in the 7th year before death.
IHT payable at 20% of death rate on first £276,000.

	£		£
first	242,000	=	Nil
next	34,000 @ 20% of 40%	=	2,720
IHT payable on remaining estate at death:			
	300,000 @ 40%	=	120,000
Total IHT			120,000

Expectation of life

Life Expectancy Tables

Age	Males	Females
20	64.0	67.8
21	63.0	66.8
22	62.0	65.8
23	61.0	64.8
24	60.0	63.8
25	59.0	62.8
26	58.0	61.8
27	57.1	60.8
28	56.1	59.9
29	55.1	58.9
30	54.1	57.9
31	53.1	56.9
32	52.1	55.9
33	51.1	54.9
34	50.1	53.9
35	49.2	52.9
36	48.2	51.9
37	47.2	50.9
38	46.2	49.9
39	45.2	49.0
40	44.2	48.0
41	43.2	47.0
42	42.3	46.0
43	41.3	45.0
44	40.3	44.0
45	39.3	43.0
46	38.3	42.0
47	37.4	41.0
48	36.4	40.0
49	35.4	39.0
50	34.5	38.1
51	33.5	37.1
52	32.5	36.1

Age	Males	Females
53	31.6	35.1
54	30.6	34.1
55	29.7	33.1
56	28.7	32.1
57	27.8	32.1
58	26.8	30.2
59	25.9	29.2
60	25.0	28.2
61	24.0	27.2
62	23.1	26.3
63	22.2	25.3
64	21.3	24.3
65	20.5	23.4
66	19.6	22.4
67	18.7	21.5
68	17.9	20.6
69	17.1	19.7
70	16.3	18.7
71	15.5	17.9
72	14.7	17.0
73	14.0	16.1
74	13.3	15.3
75	12.6	14.5
76	11.9	13.6
77	11.2	12.9
78	10.6	12.1
79	10.0	11.4
80	9.4	10.7
81	8.8	10.0
82	8.3	9.3
83	7.8	8.7
84	7.3	8.1
85	6.8	7.6
86	6.4	7.0
87	5.9	6.5
88	5.5	6.0
89	5.2	5.6
90	4.8	5.2
91	4.5	4.8
92	4.2	4.4
93	3.9	4.1
94	3.6	3.8

95	3.4	3.5
96	3.1	3.2
97	2.9	3.0
98	2.7	2.8
99	2.5	2.5

These life expectancy tables were produced from a standard program issued by the Institute of Actuaries and the Faculty of Actuaries using IMA92 and IFA92 projected forward to the year 2020. They were derived from a study of the mortality of males and females respectively, purchasing annuities on their own lives.

(Reproduced by kind permission of Milliman UK Consultants and Actuaries)

Appendix 4

Instructions/agenda for IHT estate planning[1]

CONFIDENTIAL

CLIENT [*Name*]   [*Tel no*]   [*Date*]

A   BACKGROUND & ASSETS

(1) *Composition of family*

Member/relationship	*Address*	*Date of birth*	*State of health, occupation and other remarks[2]*

Client:
Family:
Any other dependants:

	Husband[3]	Wife[3]
(2) *Present assets and approximate value*	£	£
Principal residence (? jointly owned; ?subject to Mortgage £. ....)		
Shares in family company(ies) (% holding)[4]		
Shares in any partnership (% holding)[4]		
Other properties		
Agricultural property and assets		
Stock Exchange securities[5]		
Other investments including reinvestment relief, enterprise investment scheme and personal equity plans[5]		
National savings products[5]		
Insurance policies[5]		
Interests under settlements		
Cash, bank accounts, building societies, TESSA accounts, ISA, etc		
Cars, furniture, jewellery, miscellaneous[5]		
Other assets[5]		
TOTAL approx GROSS ESTATE	£	£

	£	£

LESS liabilities
    Mortgages
    Other loans/debts
   		

TOTAL approx NET ESTATE

	£	£
CUMULATIVE IHT RECORD (see B below)		

IHT on NET ESTATE
Estate Rate   %   %

                                               £   £

(3) *Details of income*
      earned:
      unearned:
      future alterations, pensions, etc
      ? surplus for saving, normal
          expenditure exemption
      please provide copy of latest
          income tax returns for. . . .

(4) *Expectations*
      approx. details/valuations re:
          inheritance(s)
          interests under trusts[5]
      (NB Reversions are excluded
      property)

---

[1] Cross references to relevant parts of book are given in brackets.

[2] Give details, as relevant for example whether married, single, engaged, names and ages of any children of the family member. If any individual not domiciled or resident in UK note as ND and/or NR in column.

[3] NB s 161 on related property.

[4] Please indicate rate of likely IHT business property relief and provide latest accounts and, as relevant, memorandum and articles of association.

[5] Give details/separate inventories/copies.

PT

B

INHERITANCE TAX CUMULATIVE RECORD[1]

CLIENT   FILE NO

Transaction	Date	A Value transferred	B Exempt/ potentially exempt	C Taxable transfer A-B	D Cumulative net transfers (CNT)	E Tax on CNT or CGT	F Tax previously paid	G Tax due E-F	H Cumulative gross transfer (CGT) D + E	Return sent	Assessment received	Date due (d) and paid (p)

[1] This is based on a Record form prepared by Mr N. Eastaway, FCA

Note As to column B, distinguish between 'exempt' (eg, a gift within the annual £3,000 exemption or a gift to charity) and potentially exempt (a PET, where IHT will be payable only on death of client within seven years). It is very important for personal representatives to be aware of all gifts and especially former PETs, since a certificate of discharge under s 239 does not protect them if a further gift comes to light as 'failure to disclose material facts' in s 239 (4) would appear to include an innocent failure.

C WILLS

(1) Is *inter-spouse exemption* to apply (**2:1** and **3.2**)? If so:

   (*a*) deferring IHT subject to 'bunching'; **or** skipping generation; or compromise, but with particular reference only to nil rate band;

   (*b*) as to principal residence and contents;

   (*c*) as to other specific gifts in particular consider gifting business/agricultural assets to chargeable parties, eg into a discretionary trust;

   (*d*) as to legacy of £ ... ...;

   (*e*) as to ... % of *residue*;

   (*f*) are the *commorientes* provisions to apply? (**2.5:1**)

   (*g*) is the nil rate band being wasted? (consider use of mini-discretionary trust (**2.5:3**));

   (*h*) consider whether free of tax legacies are advisable (ss 36–42) especially where part of residue to a non-exempt party = complications (**2.4**);

   (*i*) application of s 142—deed of variation etc?—but because of possible introduction of anti-avoidance legislation consider use of disclaimers as less likely to be attacked. NB also the flexibility of life interest wills (**2.1:2**).

(2) *Will of the other spouse*

(3) *Instructions for will*
      Complete separate instruction sheet (see **Appendix 5**).

(4) Any *existing wills* for individual/spouse
      Location of originals; their terms; proposals for destruction.

D TOWARDS USE OF THE NIL RATE BANDS OF BOTH HUSBAND AND WIFE

(1) *Valuation* = related property (s 161); but otherwise treated as separate individuals (**1.3:4**).

(2) Use the nil rate band (? discretionary trust including surviving spouse as a beneficiary) but utilise the cash flow advantage of inter-spouse exemption (**3.2**) for survivor especially if younger to make PETs (with new CGT base value—see (4)).

(3) Consider *assets* to be transferred (for example, **E** (3) below), the principal residence and method of ownership (see also **H** below).

(4) CGT—no taxable disposal involved under TCGA 1992, s 62 on death. Contrast the restricted lifetime holdover under TCGA 1992, s 165 and 260—merely a *deferment* and stops taper relief.

E GIFT PROPOSALS—The art of giving (**Chapter 7**)

(1) *Attitude and practicality* motives; availability of assets and funds.

(2) *Identity of donee(s), order of gifts* (**7.1:4**).

(3) *Identity of assets*. Business/agricultural property at 100%/50% discount. Likelihood of *appreciation*. Any part to be retained or carved out, for example lease (**7.3**).

(4) *PETs or lifetime chargeable transfers?* watch 14-year cumulation (**1.2:2**) payment of lifetime IHT by *donor* (gross up), or *donee*? Cover liability of personal representatives by indemnity.

(5) Utilising available *exemptions and reliefs* (**7.0**). For example

Seven-year cumulation available instalments (ten years)		Wedding gifts
Business/agricultural property		
Inter-spouse		Excluded property
£3,000 pa[1]		Charities/political parties
£250 pa per donee		Works of art, etc
Normal income expenditure		
nil rate band		

(and see K below)

(6) Substituting *sales* for gifts (**7.7**).

(7) *Channelling* through the poorer spouse (**3.3**).

(8) Consider applying the various exemptions and reliefs—see **Chapter 7**.

(9) Possible use of *loans*: NB make repayable on *demand* (**7.7**).

(10) Exchanging assets between donor (or spouse) and donee (**7.6:4**).

(11) CGT implications; restricted holdover relief in lifetime, and stops taper relief—new base value on death.

(12) Political climate: re-elected Labour Government: likelihood of a change in the generous IHT regime eg PETs; BPR; APR; variations.

---

[1] NB Only one year carry forward, ie £3,000 may drop out after 5 April in a particular year. Action?

F   SETTLEMENTS. I: CREATION

(1)   *Fiscal motives: basic trust planning*

    (*a*)   *Settlor's intentions*
IHT life vs death rates
Contrast CGT—death exemption TCGA 1992, ss 62 and 63 with
contingent CGT retained on holdover relief for gifts if still available
or CGT if relief not available. Consider respective CGT rates—
34% for all trusts unless settlor/spouse retain interest: then settlor's
rate.
?A trust at all.

    (*b*)   *Timing*
IHT at low cumulative amount;
Channelling husband to wife or vice versa.
IHT and CGT appreciating assets eg insurances, new business,
troughs.

    (*c*)   *Choosing/marshalling assets*
Business/agricultural property CGT creation TCGA 1992, s 19
connected: restricted losses.
Sterile assets IHT and CGT.
Splintering IHT and CGT valuations.
Creation.
CGT holdover: beware loss of taper relief—should become less of
a problem from 6 April 2002.

    (*d*)   *Family company* TA 1988, s 677—beware in particular sub-s
(9)—loans.
Waivers.
Different classes of shares.

    (*e*)   *Retirement relief CGT Taper Relief* or even EIS relief.

    (*f*)   *Stamp duty*: voluntary dispositions exempt; but beware taking over
liabilities—Stamp Act 1891 s 57, and also gift with reservation for
IHT.

    (*g*)   *Settlor's will inter-relation with: Will trusts*

    (*h*)   *UK trustees remaining liable.*
Overseas trusts: postponement of CGT on beneficiaries, TCGA
1992, s 87. BUT having regard to TCGA 1992, ss 80–98 it is unlikely
to be beneficial for a UK resident *and* domiciled individual to set up
a non resident trust unless no substantial gains then exist eg on
death.

    (*i*)   *A nasty trap*! If settlor arranges for the trustees to pay his CGT the
Revenue may bring in aid the anti-avoidance income tax provisions
of TA 1988, Part XV ie trusts may be ineffective for income tax
purposes. Particularly if the arrangement is covered by express
terms. Otherwise there may be an income tax liability as a capital
payment under TA 1988 Part XV. But see SP1/82: Revenue attitude reasonable.

(2)   *Choice of appropriate 'harmless' type* **(4.4–4.7)**, for example:

Children's and grandchildren's
accumulation and maintenance
(s 71)

Interest in possession (ss 49, 50)	Revertor to settlor (s 54)
Inter-spouse (s 18)	Superannuation (s 151)
Discretionary trusts (ss 58–85)	Employee trusts (ss 13, 72, 75, 86)
Life assurance MWP and other trust	Protective trusts (s 88)
New style inheritance trust (see **8.3:11**)	Charitable trusts (ss 23, 70)[1]
Disposition for maintenance of family (s 11)	Overseas trusts (ss 48(3), 267(3))
	Reversionary interests (ss 48(1)–(3); 55)

(3) *Details for preparing deed:*

    (*a*) Settlor: names [   ] occupation [   ]
                         address [   ]

    (*b*) Type of trust
          eg, interest in possession;
          accumulation and maintenance;
          discretionary trust.

    (*c*) Trustees: names [   ] occupation [   ]
                     addresses [   ]
          For IHT normally no basic objection in settlor or spouse being trustees but consider having at least one independent eg professional trustee—possibly as the first named.

NB—in context of IHT business relief—ie *control* (*IRC v Barclays Bank Ltd* [1961] AC 509, HL) eg for quoted shares; and the 50% discount for assets used by company and see *Walker v IRC* [2001] STC (SCD) 86—a casting vote can give control.

---

[1] But beware of the related property rule in s 161(2)(b)(i).

Separate trustees for separate assets.

Power of appointment of new trustees, and investment decisions: such powers can be vested in settlor and if wished on death in surviving spouse and/or legal personal representatives.
Voting: *unanimous*/or by *majority* (suggest latter)

(*d*) Protector
to be appointed   YES/NO

(*e*) Beneficiaries:
names [   ] addresses [   ]
class
relationship to settlor
date of birth
power to add *additional* beneficiaries YES/NO
settlor's widow OK for IT but NB IHT
ultimate default beneficiary (unconditional)

(*f*) vesting provisions

entitlement to: Income Capital	at age	irrevocable or revocable	gift over in default	other provisions

NB s 58 et seq if applicable

(*g*) Trust fund to consist of:

assets	approx value £

Specify form of assets (eg, shares, land) and approximate worth
memo of addition
future proposals
bank accounts

(*h*) Full investment powers

(*i*) Trustees' indemnity

(*j*) Trustees' charging clause

(*k*) Exclusion of settlor and spouse. Unconditional gift over in default with particular reference to TA 1988, s 673

(*l*) Irrevocability

(*m*) Trustees' additional powers—and see: Trustee Act 2000, STEP standard provisions (see below)

eg	Vary instruments	☐	Insure, eg gift protection, education etc ☐
	Maintenance/ advancement	☐	
			Improve/repair ☐
	Accumulation	☐	
			Wide powers of delegation ☐
	Borrow	☐	
	Lend money to anyone	☐	Act by majority ☐
	Appropriation in specie	☐	
			Trade/carry on business ☐
	Permit beneficiaries to reside in/use trust assets	☐	Appoint protector (esp. if overseas trust) ☐
	Administer abroad and appoint foreign trustees	☐	Exclude settlor and settlor's spouse ☐
			Other powers: eg consider application of *Trustee Act 2000* ☐

NOTE   Consider adopting the *STEP standard* provisions, see Appendix 5 Part IV para 33.

> *Caution*—an unrestricted use of certain powers may breach the conditions of a s 71 accumulation and maintenance trust, eg a power to allow another beneficiary to occupy a house: need for 'self-denying ordinance' (see **4.4:1**).

(*n*)   *Trusts of Land and Appointment of Trustees Act 1996*. Consider excluding or limiting certain provisions, eg consultation with beneficiaries (s 11(11)); appointment and retirement of trustees at instance of beneficiaries (ss 19 and 20 apply to any trusts).

(*o*)   As to administrative provisions consider including a clause 'The standard provisions of the Society of Trusts and Estate Practitioners (1st edn) shall apply' (see James Kessler, *Drafting Trusts and Will Trusts*, 5th edn, Sweet & Maxwell).

(*p*)   Special factors/requirements.

(*q*)   Transfer document eg share transfer. Consider pre-emption provisions in Company's Articles of Association. Are waivers necessary?

(*r*)   CGT holdover election. Query eligible? Query desirable?: taper relief.

(*s*)   Exporting requirements?

(*t*)   Timing.

(*u*)   Notices? s 218 (**10.7:6**)

      (*v*)   Review dates

      (*w*)   Letters of wishes or (preferably) trustees' memorandum of wishes. consider whether or not to inform beneficiaries

(4)   *Check points and traps*

      (*a*)   Gift protection *insurance* by trustees/beneficiaries against settlor's death within seven years of disposition; or taken out by settlor on *trust* (**8.3:5**).

      (*b*)   *Family company* share settled; beware capital sums received by settlor or spouse directly or indirectly from settlement TA 1988, s 677.

      (*c*)   *Creation of* settlement may be able to hold over the gain for CGT (NB restrictions TCGA 1992, s 165 and 260) ditto on termination; death is exempt.

           Notes: (i) advantage of a cash settlement no gain on 'cash' disposal;

                  (ii) settlor and trustees are 'connected persons' therefore a loss accruing on such disposal will only be allowed against a gain on a further disposal by the settlor to the trustees TCGA 1992, s 18(3).

      (*d*)   *Stamp duty* exempt on voluntary dispositions and see F (1)(*f*) above.

      (*e*)   *Perpetuity period* (choose period of years, say 80 years—may be longer abroad).
           Accumulation periods: Law of Property Act 1925, ss 164 and 165 and Perpetuity and Accumulations Act 1964.
           For overseas settlements check on local rules (eg, perpetuity period in Jersey is 100 years; Gibraltar 100 years; Isle of Man 80 years).

      (*f*)   Are settlor and spouse fully *excluded* from benefiting?—income tax, CGT; exclusion of settlor for IHT but not necessarily spouse.

      (*g*)   Informal *letter of wishes* by settlor to discretionary or other trustees or memorandum by trustees.

      (*h*)   *Administration* and keeping of records: trustees to hold regular, eg quarterly, meetings; keep minute book; arrangements for termination or variation of any settlement including:

      (*i*)   *Settlor* can remain *liable* for IHT where foreign resident trustees are appointed (s 201(1)(d)).

      (*j*)   *Accumulation and maintenance* trust—keep duration to *under* 25 years or one generation (s 71). Beware IHT taper charge s 70(6)

      (*k*)   Consider effect on *settlor's will*.

G   SETTLEMENTS. II: TERMINATION/VARIATION
        including

(1)   *Variation with consent* (**4.9**) including:

Division, partition		Enlargement by purchase	
Release or surrender by life tenant to remainderman		Release or surrender by remainderman	
Enlargement by gift: Remainderman to life tenant		Disclaimer of life interest	
		Advancement by way of settlement upon new trusts if for benefit of beneficiary(ies)—see *Pilkington v IRC* [1962] 3 All ER 622, HL and Trustee Act 1925 s 32 extended to 100%	

NB (i)   Use of IHT life rates.

(ii)   Remainderman should take *appreciating* assets.

(iii)   Note that termination of life interest is a PET; but? CGT in view of restrictions on holdover under TCGA 1992, s 165.

(2)   *Variation by application to court* (**4.10**), for example under Variation of Trusts Act 1958.

H   PRINCIPAL RESIDENCE (**3:4**)

(1)   *Consider* a joint holding between husband and wife.
        NB—advantage of 'tenancy in common' over 'joint tenancy' (eg joint tenancy cannot be disclaimed but can be varied), especially where surviving spouse has a mere *licence* to occupy: avoid right to occupy = interest in possession.

(2)   Is severance of a joint tenancy appropriate?

(3)   *Details* of any mortgages—obtain their consent if transfer will be subject to mortgage.

(4)   Consider a flexible life interest eg 2nd etc marriages.

I   BUSINESS INTERESTS (s 103–114)

NB *Business relief:* 100% for interest in a business or partnership; 100% for unquoted shares; 50% for property used in company controlled by transferor or a partnership in which he is a partner.

(1)   *Shares in* [main/family company] Ltd and any other companies (**5:1**).

(*a*) Consider *re-allocation* between members of the family etc; but bear in mind CGT rules counteracting division of assets on disposals to connected persons (TCGA 1992, s 19);

(*b*) *Method:* for example, gift or sale, subscription, transfer or renunciation bonus issue;

(*c*) *Gift or sale* method (see **E.6** above); but beware of clawback of business relief (**9.1**);

(*d*) *Waivers* of dividends remuneration (ss 14, 15) (**5.1:7** and **5.1:8**):

(*e*) *Hiving-off* to new business (**5.1:3**);

(*f*) *Freezing operations*—bonus issue of deferred ordinary shares; re-organising share capital (**5.1:4**); keep preference shares with income, give away ordinary shares with high capital value;

(*g*) *Splitting* = separating trading functions (**5.1:5**);

(*h*) *Watering down* operations, for example commercial rights issues (**5.1:6**);

(*i*) *Takeover:* amalgamation, merger; using a financial institution; flotation (**5.2:7–5.2:9**);

(*j*) *Protection* by:
service/consultancy agreement on commercial terms as step one before gift of shares to avoid reservation of interest pensions—funded, or self administered, or personal pension plan **5.3:3–5.3:5** pre-emption provisions in Articles of Association (**5.3:6**).

(*k*) Company purchasing own shares Companies Act 1985, ss 162 et seq and TA 1988, s 219.

(2) *Partnership* interests (**6.1–6.3**)
NB availability of the business relief.

(*a*) Test of *reciprocity*;

(*b*) *Transfer of shares*—A-G v Boden [1912] 1 KB 539;

(*c*) Treatment of *goodwill*—writing it out;

(*d*) Gifts especially of land—carve out: do not re-acquire interest. Contrast *Munro v Stamp Duties Comr* [1934] AC 61 with *Chick v Stamp Duties Comr* [1958] 2 All ER 623.

(*e*) *Re-allocation* 'juggling': capital v income rights—watch reservation;

(*f*) *Incorporating* a partnership;

(*g*) Using a *limited partnership*; or a *limited liability partnership* under the Limited Liability Partnerships Act 2000 as from 6 April 2001;

(*h*) Reverting to *employee* status;

(*i*) Adapting 1 (*c*), (*e*) and (*g*) above;

(j)   *Protection* by:
      consultancy
      pension payments by continuing partners (TA 1988, s 683) retire-
      ment annuity or personal pensions (TA 1988, Pt XIV, chs III and
      IV)
      life assurance arrangements.

J.   INSURANCE (**8.0**)

(1) *MWPA and trust policies*, for example as part of normal income expendi-
     ture, £3,000 per annum, marriage, etc exemption—use where skipping a
     generation.

(2) *Joint survivor life policies*. Likewise using the relevant exemptions—use
     where deferring IHT till survivor's death.

(3) *Life of another policies*. Check existence of insurable interest.

(4) *Term insurance*, for example to cover the seven-year gift period for
     PETs; seven-year cumulation cut-off problems; and acquisition of for-
     eign domicile s 267.

(5) *Education* policies, for example by parents under s 11.

(6) New style *inheritance trusts*, to alleviate the IHT problem while retaining
     an income.

(7) *Pensions*, etc for directors and partners (see I (1)(*j*) above).

(8) *Quotations* to be obtained:

     from: ....

     by: ....

K.   OTHER IHT PLANNING ASPECTS

(1) Disposition for *maintenance of family* (s 11) (**7.12**).

(2) Relief for *business agricultural property* (ss 103–114; 115–124) (**9.0**).

(3) Relief for *woodlands* but aim for 100% business and agricultural prop-
     erty relief (ss 125–130) (**9.12**).

(4) Works of art, etc (ss 125–130) (**9.14**).

(5) Gifts for national purposes (s 25) (**7.17**).

(6) (Gifts for public benefit) (s 26) (**7.18**).

(7) Instalment payment basis (ss 227–229) (**1.5**).

(8) Quoted securities, etc sold within 12 months of death (ss 178–189)
     (**1.6:3**).

(9) Transfers within seven years before death (ss 131–140) (**1.6:2**).

(10) Falls in value of *land* four years after death (ss 190–198) (**1.6:4**).

(11) Sales of related property within three years of a death (s 176) (**1.6:5**).

(12) Exempt government securities (ss 6(2), 48(4)) (**10.6:1**).

(13) Foreign domicile (ss 6(1) and 267) (**10.1–10.6**):

(*a*)   procedure for acquiring, including *intention*, choice of country

(*b*)   re-allocation of assets abroad

(*c*)   no exchange control but other procedural matters

(14) Other matters:

L.   FURTHER ACTION

ACTION   BY:

STEPS

TIMETABLE

COMPLETE RECORD FORM AT **B** above and ensure that all PETs are regularly reviewed and recorded there.

Appendix 5

Instructions for will or codicil Client/s

Interview/Telephone call

Date:

Time:

Persons present:

Client Questionnaires—? attached ? (refer below)

Degree of Urgency: [scale of 10–1]

NB: are you taking instructions from the **right** person?

Part I—General

GENERAL DETAILS   (H = Husband   W = Wife where applicable)

1. First names	Surname	Date of birth

H:

W:

2.   Occupation and/or Description

H:

W: Mrs/Ms
                                       Widow

3.   Address

4. Domiciled in UK	Yes/No
Resident in UK	Yes/No

5.   Any previous Will/s?   Yes/No
          Codicil/s?   H   Yes/No   W   Yes/No
       Location of original(s)

Arrangements for destruction:

6. Is there now/will be any **foreign property**?
    Concurrent Wills? (beware **revocation** trap)
    Consider: **community of goods** application

7. State of health/marriage:

8. Any other relevant factors:

FAMILY DETAILS

Are any: Adopted   —   Step   —   Illegitimate

     Is this to make a difference: Yes/No If so, HOW

     Previous marriages?
     ask for family tree

A. CHILDREN:

First Names   Surname   Address   DoB

_____

B. GRANDCHILDREN:

First Names   Surname   Address   DoB

Are grandchildren born after testator's death to be included as beneficiaries or not?

_____

TECHNICAL DETAILS
(Clauses to be included)
(tick where applicable)

1. REVOCATION OF ALL FORMER WILLS AND CODICILS

2. BURIAL/CREMATION/ANATOMICAL USE

3.   EXECUTORS AND TRUSTEES

First Names	Surname	Qualification/ Relationship	Details of Gift (if any) ?conditional on taking up the **office?**

3.   GUARDIANS OF MINOR CHILDREN IF SPOUSE
      PREDECEASED

First Names	Surname	Qualification/ Relationship	Details of Gift (if any) ?conditional on taking up the **office?**

Children Act 1989 and 'parental responsibility' aspects

---

4.   SPECIFIC GIFTS eg jewellery: all/residue personal chattels (consider
      distribution in accordance with a list compiled on, and, or after date of
      Will in a **letter of wishes** to surviving spouse/executors)

First Names	Surname	Qualification/fot Relationship stt	Details of Gift (if any)

---

5.   SPECIFIC DEVISE/BEQUESTS of freehold/leasehold eg Matrimo-
      nial Home

First Names	Surname	Qualification/fot Relationship stt	Details of Gift (if any)

Business/agricultural property—leave *specifically not* as part of residue:
IHTA 1984 s 39A

---

6.   PECUNIARY LEGACIES, GIFT OF NIL RATE BAND (NRB)—
     see also 8

First Names	Surname	Qualification/fot Relationship stt	Details of Gift (if any)

NB: **Charities**—specify with regn no:

---

7.   SHARES IN COMPANIES

Name of Company	Type of Share or umbrella definition	Number of Shares	Beneficiary fot/stt

Consider **pre-emption** provisions eg in Articles of Association

8.   MINI-DISCRETIONARY TRUST OF NIL RATE BAND
     THE BENEFICIARIES:
     POSITION OF WIDOW(ER)
     LETTER OF WISHES
     (eg as to income, loans
     [capital], absolutely):

     ? need for lifetime steps **towards** equalisation/consider severing joint
     tenancies

     OR OTHER USE OF THE NIL RATE BAND—eg charging the
     home
     (NB: the nil rate band available to each spouse)

9.   RESIDUE, ABSOLUTE AND/OR LIFE INTEREST (delete appro-
     priately)

First Names	Surname	Address	Relationship/ Qualification	Age to Vest/Bare	Per Stirpes at age..... Accruer	Per cent or Share

INSTRUCTIONS   —gross division = *Re Ratcliffe*
                —net division = *Re Benham*

10. SURVIVORSHIP CONDITION eg 1 or 3 months (NB: **excluded** as
     between spouses in Will of **elder** spouse in **commorientes** circumstances!)

TECHNICAL CLAUSES TO BE INCLUDED: ?incorporate the
SOCIETY OF TRUST AND ESTATE PRACTITIONERS Standard
provisions 1st Edition (copy for client)

DETAILS OF CLAUSE   YES   NO   ANY MODIFICATION

FULL INVESTMENT

APPROPRIATION

TRUSTEES DELEGATION

ARE TRUSTEES POWERS TO BE EXTENDED?
             TRUSTEE ACT 1925

             SECTION 31 INCOME
             SECTION 32 CAPITAL

PARENT OR GUARDIAN OF MINOR TO HAVE
POWER TO GIVE RECEIPTS TO TRUSTEES

CHARGING CLAUSE FOR PROFESSIONAL
TRUSTEES

INDEMNITY

TRUSTEES POWERS TO: CARRY ON BUSINESS
                         TRANSFER BUSINESS
                         INTO A COMPANY
                         INSURE
                         NEGATIVE EQUITABLE
                         RULE
                         Re: Apportionment of income
                         NB: LIFE INTEREST

HOTCHPOT and/or IHT INDEMNITIES eg in favour of donees of PETS

TRUSTEES TO CONSIDER–DEED OF ARRANGEMENT or
VARIATION/DISCLAIMER IHTA 1984 s 142

MISCELLANEOUS
ORIGINAL TO BE RETAINED BY/SENT TO:

COPIES TO BE SENT TO:

Arrangements for **execution** (beware *Esterhuizen v Allied Dunbar* [1998] 2
FLR 668).

● ?exclude responsibilities in the **original** letter accepting instructions?

● Arrangements as to checking **original**/photostat as to correct execution

---

DECLARATION TO BE MADE UNDER THE INHERITANCE (PROVISION FOR FAMILY AND DEPENDANTS) ACT 1975 eg ex-spouse

[Firm] TO ACT IN THE ESTATE? (eg non-binding request) (but don't be pushy!)

OTHER PROFESSIONAL ADVISORS = contacts

ENDURING POWER OF ATTORNEY

H — DoB appoints

W — DoB appoints

LIVING WILLS (eg use the Terence Higgins Trust Form— NB: the limits!)

LIFETIME ESTATE PLANNING measures

— use separate sheets

— ?separate appointment

---

fot–free of tax   **stt**–subject to tax   **foc**–free of charge

Part II—Value of estate

Assets of estate for IHT purposes—approximate value

(see **Appendix 4** section A)

Part III—Type of will

(1) Absolute interest will:
Gift of estate (whole or part) to one beneficiary or beneficiaries with gift(s) over in case of beneficiary(ies) predeceasing testator/rix.

NB: Consider possible waste of nil rate band by giving all estate to surviving spouse. Important to *avoid* this waste (2001–02 = £96,800 IHT wasted).

(2) Disaster will: (where period of survival 30 days or up to six months) thereby negating rule in *Commorientes* (where younger deemed to survive older).

(3)   Life interest: whole/part
      Notes:
      (i) If spouse life interest, consider including flexible powers for trust-
      ees to appoint capital or income and/or make loans in favour of
      surviving spouse etc.
      (ii) Where surviving spouse has a lease/licence in the matrimonial
      home, query provide that this spouse is liable for all outgoings,
      eg insurance.

(4)   Hybrid: life interest/discretionary plus trustees powers to advance capital
      and/or make loans.

(5)   Discretionary: including:
      two-year span s 144
      using a nil rate band fund

      But NB: CGT and IHT trap (two-year and three-months periods
      respectively—see **2.5:3** above)

(6)   Any power(s) of appointment exercisable by will or deed in favour of
      testator/rix:
      General power   YES/NO
      Special power   YES/NO
      Details of will or settlement and (if necessary) inspect same.

Part IV—Clauses to be included

(1)   Revocation of all former wills and codicils.

(2)   Guardian of infant children
      (a)   If spouse survives
      (b)   If spouse predeceases

(3)   Executors and trustees:
      (a)   *Relations*: Relationship to testator/rix
      (b)   *Professional*: eg solicitors, accountants.
            NB: Charging clause (see No (24) below). Inform testator.
      (c)   *Bank or trustee company*: Follow its form of appointment
            Consider submitting draft to them for approval
            Is the bank nominated joint or sole executor and trustee?
            Obtain charging rates/scales

(4)   Appointment of specific firm of solicitors.

      NB: Not legally binding

(5)   Specific gifts:
      (a)   Are they to be free of all tax/subject to tax?
            Household, furniture and effects
            Jewellery, clothes, furs and other personal effects
            Motor car (?business car).
            Shares in family or other companies (cover amalgamations/
            reconstructions)

(b) Is spouse to receive all/residue of 'personal chattels': s 55(1)(*x*) of the Administration of Estates Act 1925?

(c) Consider covering by letter of wishes utilising s 143 (see also (25) below).

(6) Specific devise(s) of freehold property:

$$\frac{\text{Is it}}{\text{Are they}}$$ to be free of all tax/subject to tax?

$$\frac{\text{Is it}}{\text{Are they}}$$ to be free of mortgage? Are trustees to discharge mortgage out of residuary estate?

If matrimonial home is specifically mentioned: add 'or other principal residence at the date of my death'.

NB: Burden of IHT (see s 211). Need to specify whether subject to, or free of IHT.

(7) Specific bequest(s) of leasehold property:

$$\frac{\text{Is it}}{\text{Are they}}$$ to be be free of all tax/subject to tax?

$$\frac{\text{Is it}}{\text{Are they}}$$ to be free of mortgage? are trustees to discharge mortgage of residuary estate?

NB: (i) Banks and other professional trustees may be reticent to be appointed because of liability under repairing covenants in lease or underlease.

(ii) Does not bear own IHT unless so provided, ditto freeholds.

(iii) Consider grant of mere *licence*.

(8) Pecuniary legacy(ies) (are they to be free of all tax/subject to tax?) and whether or not in forgiveness of debt(s).

NB: If to executors and trustees, whether to them 'for their own absolute use and benefit' or for them only if they act as executor and trustee.

(9) Annuity(ies) to be provided? Generally: don't.

(10) Charities, political parties, etc: legacies of whatever size free of IHT (ss 23 and 24).

(11) Residue:
Is division into specified shares (%) to be subject to a life interest/ protective trust?

(12) Full investment clause.

(13) Appropriation clause gives flexibility.

(14) Power to appoint capital and/or income
 whether a limited or an unlimited power
 beware conditions of accumulation and maintenance trust, s 71.

(15) Power for trustees to make loans (at whatever rate of interest/interest free in their discretion).

(16) Power to appoint foreign trustees and administer trust abroad— possibility of saving future CGT and consider in context for excluded property for IHT.

(17) Negative equitable rule re apportionment of income
 Howe v Earl of Dartmouth (1802) 7 Ves 137
 Allhusen v Whittell (1867) LR 4 Eq 295
 General clause to negative all equitable apportionments.

(18) Are the trustees' powers to be extended beyond the provisions of the Trustee Act 1925, ss 31 and 32 as amended, ie appointment of capital and income to infant children or grandchildren?

(19) Power to transfer a business into a company.

(20) Power for trustees to carry on business, for example become directors, receive remuneration (NB: trustees to be free of any liability.)

(21) Accruer clause.

(22) Lifetime chargeable gifts and PETs made within seven years of death: provisions for (additional IHT). Query insure or indemnify donee.

(23) Parent or guardian of infant beneficiaries to give receipt to trustees so that trustees are fully released.

(24) Charging clause for professional trustees.

(25) Any special non-legally binding direction to trustees. (Query: by separate letter). NB: use of precatory implied trusts within two years of death (s 143).

(26) Trustees' power to insure property, for example, where surviving spouse takes lease/licence in matrimonial home.

(27) General clause that all gifts to be free of all tax or subject to tax.

(28) Hotchpot, for example adjust IHT liability in respect of earlier gift(s) at lower IHT rate(s).

(29) Grant options.

(30) Direction to executors to consider application of deed of variation.

(31) Authorising partial disclaimers. (Also consider staggered legacies and gifts of residue.)

(32) Any other provisions.

(33) Consider adopting *the standard provisions of the Society of Trust and Estate Practitioners* as prepared by James Kessler and included in his book 'Drafting Trusts and Will Trusts' 5th edn Sweet & Maxwell. These cover in the main the common, detailed administrative powers needed in a will *and* lifetime trust.

These provisions could be adopted by the following wording 'The Standard provisions of the Society of Trust and Estate Practitioners (1st Edition) shall apply to this will [trust] with the deletion of paragraph 5—Trusts for sale.'

Note a 2nd edition is planned for the near future following enactment of the Trustee Act 2000.

Part V—Miscellaneous

(1) *Subsequent marriage* automatically revokes will unless made in contemplation of that particular marriage which is later solemnised.

(2) Revocation of gifts by *termination of marriage*. Administration of Justice Act 1982, s 18(2), eg divorce or nullity—applies in respect of deaths, on or after 1 January 1983; namely that on the termination of the marriage:

(i) An ex-spouse ceases automatically to be executor/trustee of the former spouse's will.

(ii) Gifts to an ex-spouse lapse subject to clearly expressed contrary intention and subject to rights under the Inheritance (Provision for Family and Dependants) Act 1975. For example, if an ex-spouse had been given a life interest in a will, once divorced the ex-spouse's life interest would lapse and the remainder would be accelerated.

(iii) Other provisions of a will remain valid.

Having regard to (ii) above, it has been good practice in a will that all gifts to a spouse, whenever made, would provide for a gift over not only in the event of that spouse predeceasing the testator, but also 'if the gift shall fail for any reason'. This would remedy the defect highlighted in the case of *Re Sinclair* [1985] 1 All ER 1066, where a testator gave his estate to his wife contingent on her surviving him for one month and, in default, to charity. The Court of Appeal held that because the marriage had been *dissolved*, both the gift to the former wife (overruling *Re Cherrington* [1984] 2 All ER 285) *and* the gift to charity failed, ie lapsed, and the estate devolved as on *intestacy*. Although the testator had provided for the contingency of the wife not surviving, he had not provided for the alternative contingency of the dissolution of the marriage. This defect has been remedied by Law Reform (Succession) Act 1995, s 3 under which such former spouse is deemed to have died as at the date of dissolution etc of marriage for succession purposes. Therefore in the above circumstances the gift in default to the charity would not have failed. Section 3 takes effect in respect of a will where the testator(rix) dies on or after 1 January 1996.

(3) If the testator has *nominated* any asset (eg, national savings or certain friendly society benefits) or made recommendations over any asset

(eg, death in service pension benefits) give details, as will cannot operate on such asset.

(4)   If the testator has any asset on *hire or hire-purchase*, such asset cannot be given as it is not the testator's to give.

(5)   (a)   If the testator owns *shares* etc in a private limited company consider the articles of association to determine any restriction on disposal thereof (ie pre-emption provisions).

(b)   If the testator is a *partner* in a business, consider the partnership agreement and ascertain the effect thereof on disposal of his interest.

(6)   Arrangements as to *execution*. Do not *pin* or attach anything to will. Can necessitate affidavit of plight.

Beware of negligence claims if the will has not been properly executed—see *Esterhuizen v Allied Dunbar* [1998] 2 FLR 668. Consider an initial letter of disclaimer.

(7)   Copy of original will to be sent to:
Original will to be retained by:
Original will to be sent to:

(8)   Account, to be sent to:

(9)   Wishes as to burial/cremation.
Eyes and other organs to be left for therapeutic purposes or transplants (not legally binding on executors and trustees).

(10)   Address of beneficiaries:
Note:
(i)   The relationship to the testator/rix if any of the beneficiary(ies) should be inserted in the will.
(ii)   Where no relationship inserted the address of the beneficiary(ies) should be given.

It is not necessary to insert both (i) and (ii) above as either is sufficient for identification purposes: a record should be taken for the file.

(11)   Declaration by spouse under the Inheritance (Provision for Family and Dependants) Act 1975 (this can be included in will or codicil but preferably by an entirely separate document).

(12)   Special form of testimonium and attestation where applicable, for example testator/rix blind.

(13)   Future scope for deed of variation/disclaimer including the authorisation of partial disclaimers (s 142).

(14)   Need to review—when? Diarise.

Appendix 6

Deed of variation election alternatives; precedent and notes

INTRODUCTION

(1) The precedent in (5) below covers a situation where a wealthy father has left the bulk of his estate to his daughter. She does not wish to take all the estate and has set up an appropriate family settlement for her children (eg an accumulation and maintenance trust under s 71). She decides to vary her entitlement under her father's will so that a part of the residue (say £242,000 being the 2001–2002 nil rate band) goes to the trustees of the said settlement instead of her.

Note that for income tax purposes, in view of TA 1988, s 660B, any income should generally be accumulated during the children's minority (or until earlier marriage).

(2) For further precedents of deeds of variation and disclaimers etc, the reader is referred to the following—

Butterworths Wills, Probate and Administration Service

Practical Will Precedents published by Longmans

Butterworths Encyclopaedia of Forms and Precedents, 5th edition, volume 42(1) (reprint)

Butterworths Wills Precedents on Disk

Post-Death Rearrangements—Practice and Precedents
Matthew Hutton, 5th edition (FT Law & Tax)

Drafting Trusts and Will Trusts
5th edition James Kessler, (Sweet & Maxwell)

Brighouse's Precedents of Wills
12th edition David Endicott (Sweet & Maxwell)

(3) For the purpose of satisfying s 142 and TCGA 1992, s 62 the document need not be a deed although it often is: the requirement is merely 'an instrument in writing'. (Can be formal correspondence, or an order under Variation of Trusts Act 1958: probably *Re Holt's Settlement, Wilson* v *Holt* [1969] 1 Ch 100).

(4) *Whether to elect or not.* However, the section is no panacea. In particular there are circumstances when it is better not to elect (under s 142(2)) and for the beneficiary under the will or intestacy, to make his/her own, lifetime gifts.

The table below summarises the main circumstances.

Variations: s 142: elect or not

		Elect	Not Elect	Comment
1.	Deceased's gift chargeable[1]	√	—	Generally the beneficiary should elect, because the alternative of receiving the gift from the deceased and the beneficiary then making a lifetime gift, could involve a double IHT liability—once on the estate and again on the lifetime gift subject to the PET rules.
2.	Deceased's gift EXEMPT	—(but see 3–6 below) = general rule only	√	eg deceased's exempt gift to widow. Assuming widow's cumulative IHT lower (and bearing in mind it will be at her life rates or as one or more PETs—subject to seven-year survival). Moreover after seven years widow's gift ceases to cumulate.
3.	Deceased's gift EXEMPT but of (or up to) the NIL RATE BAND[2]	√	—	A gift of the nil rate band to an exempt person wastes the nil rate band, hence the need to elect for variation. Even if the estate was well in excess of the nil rate band and the surviving spouse did not need it all, it would normally still only be worth electing for the nil rate band. Any exempt estate over the nil rate band ceiling could, assuming good health, be disposed of if desired by way of PETs, with a new CGT base at death.
4.	Deceased's gift EXEMPT—but value of estate has risen sharply in the two-year period	√	—	It should be possible to pass on free of IHT the benefit of certain posthumous increases in the value of an estate. The appropriate technique should be along the lines of the example at **2.6:3**. Income tax problems would remain in that income arising before the deed was entered into and actually appropriated to the widow, would be treated as the widow's for income tax purposes.
5.	Variations by personal representatives of a deceased beneficiary		—	To achieve steps towards posthumous equalisation, using the nil rate bands and mitigating the bunching effect of assets of two estates being assessed in one estate. For example, Adam who dies on 30 June 2000, leaves his estate of £200,000 to his wife Eve who has an estate of £300,000 and dies on 6 April 2001 leaving estate to son, John (neither having made lifetime chargeable transfers). Without a variation (or disclaimer) on Eve's death the IHT on £500,000 is

---

[1] A chargeable gift indicates it is not made to an exempt person such as a spouse or charity.

[2] Even if the deceased's gift and the gift the beneficiary would make if there is no election, is within the nil rate band, the election procedure is correct—the election enables the deceased's nil rate band (if any) to be directed to the desired person without using up any part of the beneficiary's nil rate band.

£103,200. Eve's personal representatives vary Adam's will whereby Adam and Eve's son John inherits Adam's £200,000 direct from him and the £300,000 direct from Eve's estate, giving rise to IHT liabilities of nil and £23,200 respectively, ie total of £23,200—representing a saving in IHT of £80,000 (£103,200 less £23,200).

With a nil rate band of £242,000 from 6 April 2001 and a single death rate of 40%, £96,800 is the maximum saving on the use of an additional nil rate band in this way.

6. Variations for, ie in favour of the estate of a deceased beneficiary

A beneficiary, eg a son, who inherits from his parents who have both died within the past two years with **unequal** estates (having made no chargeable lifetime transfers), can equalise those estates thereby reducing the IHT payable. For example assume parent A left £400,000 to the son, and parent B left £60,000 to the son. The son varies the gift from parent A by redirecting £170,000 to parent B who survived A. Accordingly no IHT is payable on A or B's estate as to £230,000 each; instead of inheriting from **one** estate £400,000 (IHT £63,200) and the other estate £60,000 (IHT nil). A saving is thereby achieved in IHT of £63,200.

Note, however, that one **cannot increase** the estate of someone who has **pre-deceased**: *Re Corbishley's Trust* [1880] 14 Ch 3 846. This decision does not therefore apply if that person (ie whose estate is **increased**) has **survived** the other but also dies in the two year period, ie **in succession**.

The CTO **may** try to argue that the variation is invalid in that the son has not varied the amount of the aggregate inheritances–except by way of attempt to pay less IHT.

7. Variations to apply the 100% business/ agricultural asset plan

See **9.11:7**

(5) The **precedent** referred to in (1) above
THIS DEED OF VARIATION is made **(1)**
the   day of   200   BETWEEN ABC of
(hereinafter called 'the Legatee') of the first part   DEF   of
and
GHI of   (hereinafter called 'the Trustees') of the second part
and   JKL of   MNO of   and PQR of
(hereinafter called 'the personal representatives') of the third part.

WHEREAS:

A   The Trustees are the present Trustees of a Settlement dated
    200   (hereinafter called 'the Settlement') and made between the Lega-
    tee of the one part and the Trustees of the other part principally for the
    benefit of the Legatee's children.

B   By his last Will dated   (as varied by [two] Codicils dated
    respectively   , and   ) STU (hereinafter called
    'the deceased') who was the father of the Legatee left his residuary estate
    to the Legatee (the deceased's wife having predeceased him).

C   The deceased died on the   **(2)** without having varied or
    revoked his said Will as so varied by the said Codicils and was survived by
    the Legatee but not by his wife.

D   The said Will with the [two] Codicils were proved in the [Principal]
    Probate Registry Family Division of the High Court of Justice on
          day of   by the personal representatives.

E   [The Legatee has received no benefit directly or indirectly from the
    deceased residuary estate **(3)** and] the parties hereto are now desirous of
    varying **(4)** the terms of the said Will and Codicils by way of family
    arrangement so that [£242,000] out of the Legatee's share in the deceased's
    residuary estate (hereinafter called 'the fund') is given to the Trustees to
    be held by them on the trusts of the settlement insofar as the same are now
    subsisting.

NOW THIS DEED WITNESSETH **(5)** as follows:

1 (a) **(6)** The said will of the deceased shall be read and construed and be
       deemed to have taken effect from the death of the deceased as if in
       the said will [and in priority to any other gift in the said will as hereby
       varied] he had made a gift in the terms and the wording set out in sub-
       clause (b) hereof and as if the Settlement was then in existence.

   (b) The wording and terms of the gift deemed to have been contained in
        the said will of the deceased are as follows:

        'I give [subject to tax] the fund and all income therefrom (but only as from
        the date of this variation) to the Trustees of the Settlement TO BE HELD by
        them upon the trusts of the Settlement and as an accretion for all purposes to
        the existing sums held on the trusts thereof.'

2   The fund shall comprise the assets set out in the Schedule hereto. **(7)**

3   In furtherance of the foregoing (but without prejudice to the generality
    thereof) each of the parties agrees and confirms that this deed is entered
    into and shall apply as if the variation of the deceased's bequests as herein
    referred to had been effected by the deceased and for the purpose in
    particular (but without prejudice to the generality of the foregoing) in
    pursuance of the provisions of the Inheritance Tax Act 1984, s 142 and
    TCGA, s 62 and any statutory modifications or re-enactment thereof.
        [In furtherance also of the foregoing **(1)** the parties to this Deed hereby
    GIVE NOTICE to the Board of Inland Revenue under the Inheritance

Tax Act 1984, s 142(2) and the Taxation of Chargeable Gains Tax 1992, s 62(6) respectively as to the entering into of this Deed]

4   Accordingly the Legatee and the Trustees hereby irrevocably request the personal representatives to give effect to the provisions of this deed in lieu of the relevant provisions contained in the said Will and Codicils and hereby indemnify the personal representatives and each of them and their respective estates and effects from and against all claims, demands and expenses arising at any time by reason of their so doing. The personal representatives agree to implement the foregoing requests.

5   It is hereby certified **(8)** that this instrument falls within category 'L' in the Schedule to the Stamp Duty (Exempt Instruments) Regulations 1987.

THE SCHEDULE above referred to:

(the £242,000 fund)

IN WITNESS etc.

FOOTNOTES on the precedent

(1) **General Aspects**

- Wherever practical the will should **itself** be drafted as flexibly as possible eg revocable life interests, thereby making variations less relevant/applicable, for two main reasons.

    First, whichever government is in power, it is highly likely that anti-avoidance legislation will be introduced curtailing the use and scope of variations, (remember, Norman Lamont's attempt in the Finance Bill 1989!)

    Secondly, the beneficiary in question, eg the widow, may not agree to execute a variation eg because of the nursing home fear syndrome.

- **The parties** to the deed:

    The **original beneficiary** making the variation or disclaimer—an essential party. This would include anyone even **contingently affected** by the deed.

    Personal representatives—not essential but advisable. However, if as a result of the deed **more IHT** is payable, they must join in the **election** notice (s 142(27)(b)) which may, or not be included in the deed—see footnote (2).

    Donees—not essential—but may well be desirable.

- **Position of minors**—their interests cannot be adversely affected without a Court Order. Contrast the position if a minor's position is unaffected or improved.

- Note it is **not** a requirement that the settlement referred to in recital A need have been in existence on the testator's death, nor that beneficiaries benefiting under the variation were alive on the testator's death.

- To make a variation the beneficiary must be of age.
- Where a will benefits several beneficiaries, a variation can be made by any one beneficiary of his entitlement without the concurrence of the others.

(2) **Time Limits**

(a) Up to two years from the date of STU's death: s 142(1)

(b) As this case involves a variation, an election notice has to be given within six months from the date of the deed to the Board of Inland Revenue (ie the Capital Taxes Office and usually also the Inspector of Taxes) or such longer times as the Board may allow: s 142(2)—

Such notice could be in the following form:

To Board of Inland Revenue

(Capital Taxes Office)

Re STU deceased—Deed of Variation

dated   200...

Election IHTA 1984 s 142

We the undersigned being the parties to the above deed (a certified true copy of which is attached) HEREBY GIVE YOU NOTICE that in pursuance of the Inheritance Tax Act 1984, s 142(2) we ELECT that sub s 1 of that s 142 shall apply to the variation effected by the said deed. Please return the attached copy of this notice duly acknowledged

Dated   200...

Signed

ABC	JKL
DEF	MNO
GHI	PQR

(ON COPY)

We acknowledge receipt of the above notice under IHTA 1984, s 142(2)

Dated   200...

Signed

for and on behalf of the Board of Inland Revenue.

NOTES: The notice is signed by all relevant parties including the personal representatives (see s 142(2)(b)) but see note (1).

See also note (4) below.

A separate election for CGT should be sent addressed to the Inspector of Taxes and pursuant to TCGA s 62(7). Although a notice to the CTO should cover both elections provided both statutory provisions are specified.

A **separate election** is often preferable to including it in the deed itself as it gives up to six months' leeway to consider whether to elect or not. However, a form of election notice incorporated in the deed itself, is provided as an alternative in clause 3 of the precedent which should be deleted, if a **separate** notice is to be issued within the six months' period. The CTO prefer to be sent a **certified true copy** of the variation deed rather than the original. The CTO point out that if the election notice is not contained in the variation **itself**, problems can arise in that the six months' period may elapse inadvertently before a separate election notice is sent. It is understood that Nottingham Trust District do not want to see the actual deed/variation at all, but prefer an explanatory letter of its contents. This does not fully correspond with the CTO's preferences.

(3) The receipt of any such benefit no longer prevents relief under s 142 for a variation—see Inland Revenue Press Release of 11 April 1978. Contrast the position for **disclaimers**.

(4) (a) As there is here clearly a 'variation' (contrast a disclaimer), the election notice procedure applies. In some cases it can be appropriate not to elect—see above in the Introduction to this appendix.

    (b) As to CGT, normally elect because of CGT death exemption. BUT consider not electing to get the higher base value at time of beneficiary's disposal especially if the gain can be mopped up by the beneficiaries' small gain exemption, currently (2001–2002) £7,500; or available losses.

(5) (a) There must be **no consideration** in money or money's worth (other than consideration consisting of a qualifying variation or disclaimer): s 142 (3) and s 49(8). NB s 10. Payment of legal costs, interest free loans, or indemnities in favour of the donor of the variation, taking over liabilities, can constitute consideration.

    (b) In *Russell v IRC* [1988] STC 195 it was decided that there cannot be two bites of the cherry of the same asset. Once a deed of variation has been entered into, a further purported redirection deemed to have been made by the deceased in respect of the relevant assets was not valid. See also the reference to *Lake v Lake* [1989] STC 865.

(6) Following the announcement in the *Law Society's Gazette*, 7 November 1984, p 3058, it is advisable to use this wording, ie indicating that the deceased's property comprised in the estate immediately prior to his death is being varied. This is so even though the Revenue's strict view has apparently changed–see the *Law Society's Gazette*, 22 May 1984 p 1454.

(7) It is presumed that the personal representatives have the appropriate power of appropriation eg under the Administration of Estates Act 1925, s 41.

(8) Variations are now exempt from stamp duty and the need for adjudication provided an appropriate certificate is given under the Stamp Duty (Exempt Instruments) Regulations 1987 (SI 1987/516). (Disclaimers are also exempt from stamp duty.)

Personal Data Sheet

This appendix suggests appropriate arrangements for leaving one's affairs in good order.
One does not have to be wealthy or elderly to appreciate that financial affairs have become increasingly complex in our 21st century society: nothing is simple. As that is true of the lifetime situation, the problem becomes more acute on a death when the next-of-kin are faced with that traumatic experience. The difficulties can, however, be considerably eased if one's affairs are left in a tidy order.

To assist in this aim a pro forma is set out below whereby an individual can provide the main, basic information of his/her financial affairs in an easily understandable form.

It is suggested that the pro forma be completed as soon as an individual has any assets of substance, eg a home and particularly if family responsibilities are involved. The details should be updated regularly as circumstances change—preferably annually—for example, when one is completing the tax return. Allied to this suggestion is the planning of one's will (see **Chapter 2** and **Appendix 5**). It is clearly of great importance to keep the pro forma regularly updated.

A pro forma such as is set out below clearly cannot cover every circumstance and variant of the individual concerned; and the form should be adapted accordingly. In particular, detailed and numbered schedules/inventories can be attached. The form should not become cluttered; only the more important information, the main assets and liabilities need be noted. Where the relevant details are considered too numerous to be included on or attached to the form it may be appropriate merely to refer to the source of the information, eg solicitor, accountant, stockbroker or others mentioned in section 2 of the form. Section 9 'Miscellaneous items', can then be used to indicate where further details can be obtained with appropriate cross-references to section 2.

The completed pro forma should be kept with the individual's private papers and the next-of-kin (eg wife or husband) informed of its contents and whereabouts.

Information re estate and assets of:

Name:
Address:
Former addresses in the last 10 years:
Date of birth, marriage; [divorce]:
National insurance/social security number:

1. *Immediate, essential information*
    1.1 Location of will

    1.2 Funeral wishes (cremation, burial, no flowers, etc)

    1.3 Other wishes eg anatomical use (NB Human Tissue Act 1961)

    1.4 Details of any living will

2. *Relevant personal information*
    2.1 Executors

    2.2 Solicitor

    2.3 Accountant

    2.4 Stockbroker

    2.5 Bankers (see also 3.6)

    2.6 HM Inspector of Taxes
    Address:
    Reference No.
    Location of copy tax returns (copy attached):

    2.7 Doctor

    2.8 Others, eg local authority; public utilities

    2.9 Location of personal documents, eg birth/ marriage certificates, credit cards (details of safe deposit box)

3. *Assets and liabilities*
    3.1 Main residence
    Address:
    Sole name or jointly: Does it pass by survivorship?
    YES/NO
    Subject to/free of mortgage: £
    Mortgagee lender:
    Address:
    Reference no:
    Estimated value (net of mortgage):
    Council tax band:

    3.2 Other properties
    Sole name or jointly: Does it pass by survivorship?

YES/NO
Subject to/free of mortgage: £
Mortgage lender:
Address:
Reference no:
Estimated value (net of mortage):
Council tax band:
Location of deeds re 3.1 and 3.2

3.3 Stock Exchange/government securities (state if held jointly); PEPs.

3.4 Family company/unquoted shares

3.5 Other investments, eg Premium Bonds, National Savings, TESSAs, ISAs.

3.6 Bank accounts/building society accounts
Bank/Society:
Type of account:
Account no:
Mandate/signing powers/? joint:

3.7 Other business, agricultural assets

3.8 Miscellaneous assets

3.9 Liabilities eg bank overdraft arrangements, loans

4. *Pension/insurance arrangements*

4.1 Retirement annuity pensions (self-employed), personal pensions, stakeholder pensions, etc.

Insurance Company	Policy Number	Type	Location of Policy

Details of any assignments of rights

4.2 Employee's occupational (or life) scheme. Brief details. NB what rearrangements have been made for nominating death benefit (eg letter of wishes to the trustees)?

5. Cancellation/notification/alteration

5.1 Membership or subscriptions to:
Professional/trade associations
Clubs
Other organisations, eg AA

5.2 Offices held (eg Company Secretary, Treasurer, Chairman, Trusteeships, Executorships, Guardianships, etc)

5.3 Credit cards/bank, retail store/cash dispenser cards,
Type   Number

5.4 Direct debits/standing orders (see also 3.6)

5.5 Registration documents for vehicles

5.6 Deeds of covenant ceasing on death

5.7 Agreements/licences, etc (eg hire purchase, car, TV and other contents of home)

5.8 Gift Aid arrangements

Type	Other Party(ies)	Date	Location of Document	Renewal Date (if applicable)

6. *Family settlements*

   6.1 Set up by the individual

Date of Trust	Type	Trustees' Names & Addresses	*(Main)* Beneficiaries Names & Addresses	Location Original Deed

   6.2 Details of any settlements where the individual is a
        beneficiary
        Type: (eg life interest, discretionary)
        Approx value of trust fund
        Date of trust deed and whereabouts of the deed (or
        copy)

7. *IHT history*

Transaction	Date	*(approx)* Value Transferred	Name & Address of Donee

8. *If you are non-UK domiciled*

   Are there assets situated in UK (=IHT chargeable)?
   Consider remedial steps (ie for the assets to be
   abroad), eg

   – sale and remitting proceeds abroad—but beware
     CGT

   – transfer abroad, eg chattels, bank accounts, bearer
     shares

   – exploiting the spouse exemption

   – gifting fixed assets, eg land/buildings to a foreign
     company (but beware CGT and income tax)

   – borrowing cash secured on UK assets and
     depositing the cash abroad

9. *Miscellaneous items*

   Signed ....

   Dated ....200....

Temporary assurance—gift inter vivos policies

Provided that the donor is in relatively good health and insurable it is worth considering whether in the case of PETs' insurance should be effected to cover the death of the donor within seven years. Below are very broad single premium quotations for illustration only to give a general idea of the possible cost of an assured sum of £10,000 (being 40% on a cash PET of £25,000) for three years and then reducing in line with taper relief. Annual premium quotations might be obtained as an alternative. The policy should be written for the benefit of the donee.

Age	Male	Female
50	£160	£104
60	£370	£252
70	£935	£552

Note

The rates shown are for non-smokers.

(Acknowledgement—Ian Mereweather)

Index